TURQUOISE DAYS:
THE WEIRD WORLD OF
ECHO & THE BUNNYMEN

CHRIS ADAMS

SOFT SKULL PRESS
2002

TURQUOISE DAYS:
THE WEIRD WORLD OF ECHO & THE BUNNYMEN

ISBN: 1-887128-89-1
©2002 Chris Adams

First Edition

Editorial: Daniel Nester
Design: David Janik
Production: Tom Hopkins
Cover photo: Gary Lornie

Soft Skull Press
1140 Broadway, Suite 704
New York, NY 10001
www.softskull.com

Printed in the United
States of America

10 9 8 7 6 5 4 3 2

ACKNOWLEDGEMENTS

My sincerest thanks to the following for their help, input, patience, and encouragement:

Mary and Joseph Adams, Carl Arnheiter, Dave Battersby, Mike Bellwood, Henry Bidenkamp, Jake Brockman, Pete Burnand, Pete Byrne, David Caristi, Carmen @ Da Capo, Frank Coleman, Rob Collins, Lucy Dillon, Stephen Dodd, Steve and Shelagh Doughty, Birgit Gunnarsson, Harlan and Dania Heidelmeier, Heinz, Sander Hicks, Mick Houghton, Adam Kray, Jim Kutler, Gazz Lornie, Ian and Lorraine McCulloch, Dan Nester, JR Nolf, Peasy, Will Sergeant, the Sevenseas listserv, Paul Simpson, Ivan Smith, Beth Sweet, Talbot @ Ochre, Paul Toogood, Lisa Tripodi, Ted Turner, Barry Whiting and Helen, David Whiting, Johan Winegard, Andy Zax, and all those who took the time and energy to send in photographs and press clippings. I'm also indebted to the many journalists, publications, and authors whose editorials and opinions were essential in contextualizing and illustrating this story.

CHAPTER THUMBNAIL PHOTO CREDITS

TABLE OF CONTENTS

The author wishes to thank all the photographers, artists, and image copyright owners whose work is contained herein for their kind permission to reprint their work in this book. Every effort has been made to acknowledge authorship; but if you have any more information or corrections for later editions of this book, please contact the author, care of Soft Skull Press.

Starman: photo 2001 by Tom Sheehan, courtesy of Cooking Vinyl; Eric's: photo courtesy of *Liverpool Explodes*, Neil Taylor; Geoffs / Love Pastels: Jim Kutler; Industrial Domestic: Gary Lornie; Weird as Fish: Euphoria Records; Bunnymen are Born: Scott Miller/Bunnygod Productions; Monkeys: Unknown; Zoo Records: Zoo Records; Pictures on My Wall: Zoo Records; Going Up: David Whiting; Korova: Korova Records; Enter Trippo: Johan Winegard; Rescue: Idle Time; Let It Croc: WEA/Korova ad; Crocodiles: WEA LP cover; Camo: Gary Lornie; Shine So Hard: Gary Lornie; The Long Days: David Whiting; Pounding the Road: Jim Kutler; Heaven Up Here: WEA/Korova LP cover; 1982: On the Chopping Block: Ochre/Spiffing; WOMAD: Jim Kutler; Sefton Park: Gary

Lornie; The Cutter: David Whiting; Porcupine: WEA LP cover; Never Stop: Jim Kutler; Outer Hebrides: Gary Lornie; Lay Down Thy Raincoat and Groove: Promo ad; Gods Will Be Gods: Henry Biedenkamp/Ivan Smith; Hippy Hippy Shakespeare: Gary Lornie; Play at Home: Lucy Dillon; The Killing Moon: WEA ad; Mac the Mouth: Adam Peters; Ocean Rain: WEA LP cover; Crystal Day: Gary Lornie; Seven Seas: WEA ad; Pictures on My Wall: WEA ad; September Song: WEA ad; The Year Off: Jim Kutler/Mike Bellwood; We Can Be Heroes: Birgit Gunnarsson; Glastonbury: Promo ad; Bring on the Dancing Horses: WEA promo; Songs to Learn and Sing: WEA promo; Sex God: Gary Lornie; Shades of Grey: WEA promo; Echo & the Bunnymen: WEA LP cover; Death of Pete de Freitas: Jim Kutler; Off and Running: Unknown; Candleland: WEA LP cover; Bunnymen Mark II: Stephen Dodd; Mysterio: WEA LP cover; Mac & Marr: JR Nolf; Electrafixion: Electrafixion/Spacejunk; Burned: Elektra LP cover; Revenge of Voodoo Billy: Voodoo Billy; Evergreen: London Records LP cover; What Are You Going to Do With Your Life?: London Records LP cover; Flowers: Cooking Vinyl LP cover.

For Lisa, Patrick, and El

In memory of Pete de Freitas and Roger Eagle, without whom ...

FOREWORD

I spent the month before my trip out to Western Canada for my first Bunnymen show totally consumed with the countdown that lay before me. How could it be that in only a coupla weeks the mighty silhouettes that covered my walls were gonna be real and performing in front of me? How could it be that easy? Was this right? Had I somehow skipped a step? See, I had constructed quite an in-depth Bunny cosmology for myself. Thank God I had a few weeks to prepare. But no amount of tree-watching or hair-spiking could have readied me for the Raw Existential Groove and Impossible Pop Truths that the Bunnymen laid down that night in Vancouver. As they played, it seemed like remote corners of my psyche connected and renewed themselves, and I felt a fullness and warmth in my soul. Surely, with this music on my side, I was now destined for ... *something*. I would walk around and stare at trees, or the sky, and it seemed that the music was "in there" somehow, like the Bunnymen's magic had somehow slipped itself in between the grooves of nature. My hair looked perfect and I had a direct line into some kind of total metaphysical sex-trip at age 17! What a gift! Thank you Echo & the Bunnymen!

I'm sure that many, many others got equally screwed up by the awesome beauty of this band, but the only other confirmed case that I know of is that of Chris Adams. He had a similar Bunny-youth, but then went on to give so much back through his Bunnymen zine & as hip-priest (a rank he's never asked for) of the Sevenseas listserv. Now Chris has given us the updated and complete record of this band as only he could. As the Laureate and general shit-worker of good Bunnyvibes, this was his book to write, and he has done so with wit, joy, and a sense of wonder that leaves you feeling warm and permanent about this unlikely story. Chris has given us triumphant portions of esoteric untold Bunnylore within a story that should be compelling to anyone curious about the transcendent power of a great rock & roll band. Chris writes in the spirit of the Bunnymen, with equal parts swoon and swagger. His pen is dry & edgy & he uses his bullshit detector like a saint. But these pages make their ultimate statement as a celebration of the impossibly dedicated vision of four shy kids from Liverpool and their polite insistence on becoming the greatest rock & roll band in the world.

I went for a late night walk the other night, Walkman in hand, with an old cassette copy of *Heaven Up Here*. I am happy to report that the trees still have their magic. God bless Chris Adams and God bless Echo & the Bunnymen.

—Theodore Turner, CKUW, 95.9 FM
Winnipeg, Canada
November 2001

The purpose of the Bunnymen was a guiding light ... at one time I believed everyone in the world knew what the Bunnymen were about. They might not even have heard of us but they kind of knew—in the wind, on the wind—what it was all about.

—Ian McCulloch, 1989

It was a rainy gray Sunday afternoon in November 1982. I was at the home of my (still) best friend, Patrick, on Bullard Road, a cozy little side street tucked alongside the county jail in our hometown of Dedham, just south of Boston. As we would often do on weekends, Patrick and I had whiled away the afternoon hanging out in his bedroom, idly leafing through music magazines, cracking adolescent jokes, and listening to his records. Still barely into my teens, I hadn't allowed my tastes to venture too far beyond tried-and-true classic artists—The Beatles, The Stones, Presley, and some of the more obvious Doors stuff—although I also dug Adam and The Ants, Bow Wow Wow, and the few Clash and Sex Pistols tracks I'd heard. But Patrick was investigative and obsessive enough to amass an eclectic collection of a few hundred records, many of them Jem imports by groups I'd never heard of; bands with strange and vaguely unsettling names like Throbbing Gristle, Joy Division, The Virgin Prunes, and Eyeless in Gaza.

I remember it was about 4:30 in the afternoon—the autumn darkness was making its descent, and I knew pretty soon I'd have to take the 40-minute walk home to be in time for dinner. Patrick and I had just finished playing a selection of dub cuts off the Clash's excellent (and still misunderstood) *Sandinista!* LP, and a terrifying roar of a song by what I then considered to be some appallingly talentless monsters ("Dead Joe" by the Birthday Party). I was putting on my puffy ski parka, preparing to depart (not "split"—I was too young and awkward to "split" anything except the arse of my beige corduroys), when I noticed the sleeve of a single, precariously balanced on top of a stack of imported 7-inches, the kind that didn't need an adapter for the turntable.

Something about the cover attracted me—it was an evocative, atmospheric photograph, a wide-angle shot of a beach on a rainy day, with a few seagulls dotting the skyline. It reminded me of inclement days on Cape Cod, where my Mom and Dad took me, my brothers, and sister every summer. At my request, Patrick put the single on the turntable.

Over the course of the next four-plus minutes, my world was inextricably altered. This was the kind of music that I thought existed only in my head. It churned and slashed and soared Heavenward, created unheard-of stratospheres, only to burst through them and go even farther; it was overflowing, cascading with a sumptuous, shattering emotionalism that sent silver mercury talons skidding down my spine. This music transcended the beer and blood and sweat of simple "rock & roll" showbiz—this was something mystical, something *magic*. The idea that mere humans had created something so glorious and majestic was unthinkable.

I stood there in that little room, transfixed, slack-jawed, watching the tone arm of the turntable as it progressed towards the inner edge of the lacquered black vinyl. As the final chorus faded out, Patrick looked at me, a precocious, knowing smirk smeared across his countenance.

"Whadidja think?" he asked, his eyes glinting with a conspiratorial glow.

"That's the greatest record I've ever heard in my life." And it was.

The name of the song was "A Promise."

The name of the group was Echo & the Bunnymen.

Eighteen years have passed since that day, when I was first bitten by the Bunnygod. Eighteen years, during which I've completed high school and college, fallen in and out of love a few times, bounced around a couple of continents, purchased over a thousand records, seen countless gigs, and written God-knows-how-many words about rock & roll. In retrospect, if someone were to ask me what the most pivotal moment of my life was, I'd have to refer to those four minutes and five seconds in 1982. After that, *everything* changed.

As I searched for new records that could simulate that transcendental experience, rock & roll began to assume an increasing significance in my life. I began to see that it could be more than just a blast of sheer mindless entertainment. The parameters of self-expression as I had known them seemed blown wide open. Suddenly, it occurred to me that there was a lot more to life than struggling through the drudgery of school and worrying about whether you'd make the cut on the baseball team. There were new, weird worlds out there just begging to be explored, vast untapped vats of potential and possibility waiting for me. Punk and post-punk records widened my vision, told me that I had other options, that I didn't have to swallow the bitter, small-minded, small-town suburban crap I'd grown up with. My records became more than music; they were ideas about life and how to live it, captured on slick black vinyl and neatly shrink-wrapped—philosophy with the volume turned up to 10. These records inspired me to stop desperately trying to look, think, and act like my contemporaries. I started to swagger with my own vibe, my own persona, given the courage and the strength to express myself assertively and follow my own lead, a message I heard repeated over and over again in the art and actions of the Bunnymen, the Clash, the Pistols, and a host of others. These records became a forum through which my hidden rages, desires, frustrations and dreams were funneled—"hey! there are others out there who feel just like me!"—and through which a fledgling sense of the spiritual was given room to blossom. I've found more religion emanating from the speakers of a second-hand stereo than I've ever discovered in a cathedral. I think that the Bunnymen's *Heaven Up Here* and *Porcupine* alone led to what has become a consuming interest in theology and metaphysics.

My ongoing quest for imports—remember, this was in the days when "alternative" meant that you couldn't find the fuckin' records anywhere—led me out of the cozy couched familiarity of the suburbs and into the excitement and mystery of nocturnal, subterranean Boston culture. *Melody Maker* and *New Musical Express* interviews with bands like the Bunnymen turned me onto scores of artists that affected me profoundly, hallowed names like The Velvet Underground, Leonard Cohen, Television, and Iggy and the Stooges, to name just a few. Inspired by photographs within these periodicals, I replaced the corduroys, Keds, and parka with pegged black Levis, Beatle boots, and a leather car coat. My hair began to suffer all manner of blow dryer and hairspray–induced tortures. Freed from sartorial constraints, and subsequently dismissed by many of my peers as a freak, I became more inquisitive about the world and my place in it, assimilating and discarding ideas and philosophies until I arrived at something that could accommodate my own rapidly increasing confidence, and belief in the dignity and sanctity of existence. In short, the concentric reverberations of those few minutes in November 1982 shook my life to its very foundations, and created who I am today. Eighteen years on, I have no regrets.

Except, perhaps, one or two of those hairstyles. A small price.

But this book is not intended as a valentine to the Bunnymen. What I've attempted to do here is capture the real story of the band with a collage of perspectives from the mouths and pens of the people who were there as it happened; to document the dramatic and fascinating history of the group with as much objectivity as possible, and by doing so, produce what will be considered the definitive work on the subject. Have I succeeded? I leave you to determine that for yourself.

Hope you dig it.

—Chris Adams, July 2001

1972: STARMAN

I don't remember much. I was in a daze until I was 18.

—Ian McCulloch, 1987

It was on the thin green-eyed boy's thirteenth birthday, May 5, 1972. Wandering into his mother's sitting room at 86 Parthenon Drive, Norris Green, Liverpool, he idly switched on the television to a rebroadcast of "Top of the Pops" and flopped down on the settee. After a few minutes of yawning through your standard early 70's AOR pop boredom, the lanky lad was preparing to muster up the energy to extract himself from his adolescent slouch and turn off the TV.

Then it happened. David Bowie, resplendent and glittering as his otherworldly Ziggy Stardust alter-image, appeared on the screen, singing a spiraling, dizzy swoon of a song called "Starman." The boy was stunned with awe and wonder, with a sense of mystery, of Heaven, of *night*, to the point where he not only experienced shivers down his spine, but what he would later refer to as a form of astral projection. It was better than the best birthday present he could have hoped for. Never again would Ian McCulloch be the same.

It just changed my life completely. I'd never really liked music up 'til then except for the odd thing like 'The Wonder of You' by Elvis Presley. But now it became an obsession. I used to stare at pictures of Bowie and wonder how anyone could look so good. I used to listen to the *Ziggy Stardust* LP every night. 'Five Years' was my favorite track, and I also liked 'Lady Stardust' ... I never wanted to share it with anyone. I wanted to be the only Bowie fan in the world. When I was 13 I tried to be him, in spirit.   —Ian McCulloch, 1983

I loved all the ethereal lifestyle thing. It wasn't even glam, it was something I couldn't grasp at all at that age. When I used to see pictures of Bowie or on TV, I thought, 'Where's he from? He definitely can't live in Beckenham.' I used to think Bowie had so much charisma and mystique at the time, '72, and he did, to a 13-year-old me. It was the high point, in that way, of me life. I'd never felt that way at all. Every day I'd shiver. He took me somewhere that I'll never go again. I miss all that. I miss being overawed a lot. But, you know, that's life. Part of growing up.   —Ian McCulloch, 1984

Bowie separated me from me parents, me brother and sister, and me friends at school. I was in a different world. It was the most incredible feeling that I've ever felt in me life. I'd be just walking down the street and I'd have these split-second things, almost like astral projection, like 'seeing the light,' where I'd want to hold the moment. I've been in love—and its not the same as that. I know I'll never feel like that again.

—Ian McCulloch, 1995

[It was] the best thing that ever happened in my life.
                                        —Ian McCulloch, 1994

What I loved about Bowie ... was that outer space thing, not because he sang about outer space, but that general feeling of the music and the sound of his voice being from another planet. Even if he was singing about quicksand it sounded like outer space. I got that atmospheric feel from Bowie.   —Ian McCulloch, 1994

Born in 1959, Ian "Mac" McCulloch had a fairly standard Liverpudlian working-class upbringing. He was the middle child of Robert McCulloch, a machine shop steward, and his wife Evelyn. Mac had an elder half-brother, Steven, and a sister, Julie, who came along in 1961. Mac's childhood wasn't particularly difficult, but it was slightly weird. He was always a very shy and sensitive boy, and, in his first half-decade, easily prone to tears. (Mac still falls victim to what he calls "the ol' waterworks" fairly frequently.) Although he made friends easily enough, he wasn't overtly social. Instead, he was content to play the loner and live within the realms of his imagination. He'd spend entire evenings sitting in a chair by the sitting room windows, gazing dreamily at the elm trees across the road and singing quietly to himself. Even at a young age, Mac felt a little set apart, somehow different from his peers. From his early childhood on through his adolescence, he was, by his own admission, a little tense, nervous, and ... well ... *spacey*.

I was worried about everything: the way I walked, the way I looked ... all manner of shit. Being blind, pretty much. Going to an all-boys school. I felt like I came from outer space.
                —Ian McCulloch, 1999

I was always a loner.
                —Ian McCulloch, 1994

Ian McCulloch has always been a weird bastard who didn't fit in.   —*Melody Maker*, 1998

I was a ghost. When I think about my early life, I was never in it, never in my body. I was so immobile in expression, I withdrew.
                —Ian McCulloch, 1997

I used to get really claustrophobic when I was a kid, the walls used to move in. Now *that* was my first psychedelic experience! I used to watch telly and it would start going 'round me ... it would be behind me head and me still watching the screen. I couldn't get out of it and then, all of a sudden, it would all shrink again, and things on the wall would just come out here. Weird. I just couldn't move. That doesn't happen so much now, which is a pity, really. Probably just bad eyesight.   —Ian McCulloch, 1984

I've had [compulsive disorder syndrome] since age 10, or whenever. I once went to the doctors as a kid ... not knowing how to explain it ... just kind of a nervous thing. Maybe that's why I wanted to be cool and loose and laid-back and stuff, 'cos underneath the skin there's all manner of 'nervosity.' going on.   —Ian McCulloch, 1998

It's touching things a lot of the time, just moving them for no real reason. It started when I was about 10 and my mum noticed it. I'd be fiddling with the door and she'd be saying, 'What the bloody hell's up with you?'
                                        —Ian McCulloch, 1997

Despite his oddities, Mac was similar to other Liverpool lads in one respect: his love of Liverpool's football club (Liverpool FC). Bob McCulloch regularly brought his son to Anfield Stadium to see "The Reds" in action, and the exploits of the club quickly became an all-consuming passion. Before Ziggy Stardust catapulted Mac into a moonage daydream, his future goals were rooted firmly on the pitch of Anfield. To this day, Mac retains season passes to the hallowed football ground, and he still entertains fantasies about playing for his beloved team.

Football was everything. It was the focus of the whole city. If Liverpool lost, then my weekend was truly ruined. I still believe in football. I'm still more in awe of footballers than any rock star. It's just so powerful.
                                        —Ian McCulloch, 1998

My biggest failure in life is not becoming centre forward for Liverpool.
                                        —Ian McCulloch, 1994

[Footballers] scare me. I get tongue-tied speaking to them, because they're doing something that I wanted to as a lad. With players, some humility kicks in, which is kind of strange for me.
                    —Ian McCulloch, 1998

When I heard David Bowie singing ... I thought, 'This is what it's all about. Sod football!' From then on I knew I wanted to be a singer.
                    —Ian McCulloch, 1983

But any hopes Liverpool FC might have fostered for a slightly odd star striker named Mac were dashed on May 5th, 1972. After his Ziggy epiphany, the boy knew exactly what he wanted to be, and there was no turning back.

1976-1978: ERIC'S

It's literally impossible to overestimate the impact the Sex Pistols had on Britain's musical landscape. In their wake, hundreds of bands sprung up around Britain, fired by the flash of imagination and possibilities that the Pistols provided. Kids who once believed they lacked the talent to reach the proficiency demanded by a virtuoso-oriented music scene shrugged their shoulders and declared 'to hell with it, let's just do it.'
                                        —Goldmine, 1998

Fast-forward four years and four miles from the strains of "Starman" rising from Evelyn McCulloch's sitting room, to Mathew Street, near the center of Liverpool. Here, just 15 years earlier, Beatlemania was born at the Cavern Club, where the Four Lads Who Shook the World gave their first lunchtime performances. Just a couple of doors down from the site of that infamous cellar stood Eric's. This club, previously called Gatsby's, then Eric's at the Revolution, was founded by Roger Eagle, a giant teddy bear of a man who lived and breathed music ever since he'd heard Ray Charles's 1958 live

Roger Eagle could do no wrong.
                    —Julian Cope, Head-On

album *At Newport* as a teenager. Eagle was a man who made a huge impression on virtually all the Eric's regulars.

Towering and glowering. The man who invented the concept of Northern
Soul. The Third Greatest Visionary in rock & roll. Anyone from my generation out of Liverpool who ever made a record is eternally in his
debt—or can blame him for the mess we have made of our lives.
    —Bill Drummond, *From the Shores of Lake Placid and Other Stories*

Eagle's timing was perfect, if not visionary. He'd opened the club just as the concentric tremors of London punk had reverberated northwards to Liverpool, and Eric's subsequently became the epicenter of Liverpudlian punk. On its opening night in September, 1976, a young Pete Wylie, later of the many incarnations of Wah!, and Bunnyman-to-be Ian McCulloch were the 49th and 50th people past the door.

It was the first club I'd ever been to. It was the Stranglers, the
Pistols, and Runaways … just great. There was a queue down Mathew
Street. To get in, it was sixty pence, I think, and you became a
member. Me and Wylie were both underage, and it was like, 'Will we
get in?' And when we got in, and were members, it was like…mega!
                                            —Ian McCulloch, 1994

If you wanted to feel like you were part of some happening, subterranean vibe, you couldn't do much better than Eric's. First of all, it really *was* subterranean—once past the front doors, you had to descend a steep flight of stairs to enter the cavernous grotto of the club. And it was filthy—a total dive. There were frequent flooding problems, and it wasn't uncommon to see the occasional rat scurry across the bar. The toilets were simply undiscussable. As the ladies room was slightly less malodorous than the men's, males among the Eric's elite would occasionally duck furtively in there to relieve themselves. Or something.

I was only in there to put my make-up on and talk about philosophy.
                                            —Ian McCulloch, 1994

Although these squalid conditions might not sound like much of a night out nowadays, at the time they just contributed to punk's vibe of breached innocence and underground insurrection. Revolutions, after all, don't start in overlit pastel-painted fern bars. The club had two main rooms: the bar area, which contained what has been referred to as "the coolest jukebox in the world"; and the painted-red-and-black main hall, where bands would play, and where, when the stage was vacant, Eagle would blast a diverse selection of sounds through the booming PA system. Eric's was where Mac would first encounter future Bunnymen Will Sergeant and Les Pattinson, and where a host of other stars-to-be like Julian Cope, Pete Burns, Pete Wylie, Holly Johnson, Bill Drummond, and Jayne Casey congregated. In those days, Eric's was, by all accounts, a very special, unique place.

It was as if everyone in the audience was not just in one group, but two or three groups—and you'd know they couldn't play, but it was fun to do, and then the fun became serious. And it was just so exciting … a total adrenaline rush.   —Ian McCulloch, 1987

Going to Eric's got me … into the guitar. The Pistols, Television, Suicide, Iggy Pop, The Slits, they all played there. It was just a small, shitty in-the-basement kinda vibe. It was actually below the new Cavern. When the original Cavern got knocked down, they moved it over there. It's all very weird, 'cos that street, Mathew Street, has always been a part of what's going on in Liverpool. And now it's just 'orrible down there. All the dickheads got hold of it and made it all touristy.   —Will Sergeant, 1997

Eric's had this great big feeling that was mutual. Everyone was just part of something that was a lot bigger than anyone realized at the time, but you knew you were onto something all the same.
                                    —Pete Wylie, 1987

But if young Liverpudlian punks saw themselves as inheritors to The Beatles' rock & roll throne, they certainly didn't advertise it.

We hate anything to do with Merseybeat … that just ruins everything. I hate The Beatles.   —Will Sergeant, 1979

Although years later Will would cite George Harrison as one of his favorite guitarists (and the Bunnymen would cover "Twist and Shout," "All You Need is Love," and "Ticket to Ride"), Sergeant's rejection of The Beatles fit perfectly with the DIY punk ethos of "no more heroes." In fact, it wasn't long before Liverpudlian punks began drifting from the ideals of the London scene that had initially inspired them.

Even at punk's apex, it would have been difficult to mistake Mathew Street for King's Road. Eric's was never really a spiked and safety-pinned *Rocky Horror Show*, like London's Roxy or 100 Club. In Liverpool, the punk

The thing about Eric's was everyone in Liverpool was always there and you could do whatever you liked in it. The people who ran it were always open to suggestions.
                —Les Pattinson, 1986

It was filthy, it was disgusting—but it did have a great atmosphere. —Pete Burns, 1994

I started going down there on my own. I met everyone there. It was a great place then. There'll probably never be anywhere the same. —Will Sergeant,
                Liverpool Explodes

One night it would be The Police, the next the Sex Pistols, and so on. That kind of pedigree was bound to rub off.   —Julian Cope, 1987

It was always my intention to sing, but I didn't know how you went about getting a band or anything. By going to Eric's, week in, week out, people were forming bands around me, like The Spitfire Boys and Big In Japan, and I thought, 'If they can do it … ' It was important for the first time in your life to be like, 'Yeah, I can do this.' All that dreaming of doing stuff, and then people wanted me to be in a group with them … it was a good confidence boost. Especially for me, because I was so shy.

                —Ian McCulloch, 1994

Q: "What was it like growing up in the shadow of The Beatles?" Will Sergeant: "Shady."

—MTV Online Interview, 1995

I remember being on a bus going to the Pierhead, that's where all the boats come in, and somebody had a transistor radio on the top deck playing 'I Want To Hold Your Hand,' and that was my only memory of Beatlemania. I wasn't even aware there was Beatlemania going on. It was just a song and I knew the group were from Liverpool. At my school when I was young we were more interested in Liverpool Football Club than The Beatles.

—Ian McCulloch, 1981

phenomenon served more as a catalyst than as an end unto itself. For a couple of months after punk vommed its vitriol onto Mathew Street, you couldn't kick a football without striking a facsimile of Johnny Rotten. Then the Eric's crowd got bored with simple imitation, stopped reading about the filth and the fury of Southern punks in *The Daily Mirror*, and got on with developing their own unique musical, philosophical, sartorial, and tonsorial visions. While much of London punk was bent on sociopolitics and serious manifestoes, the Liverpudlian version was steeped in demented Scouse silliness. For example, while the Pistols and The Clash were spitting slogans like "Anarchy in the UK" and "White Riot," Liverpool punks were coming up with song titles like "Kowalski of the Seaview Has Got the Best Hairstyle I've Ever Seen" and "You Don't Notice Time on The Bury New Road." As far as clothing went, it was more common to see Pete Wylie using a toilet seat as neckwear, or Holly "Frankie Goes to Hollywood" Johnson sporting a Cadbury's chocolate box for a cap than it was to spot a cartoon rent-a-punk with hedgehog hair and PVC pants. Similar to New York's Factory crowd of the late 60's, or the 70's CBGB's scene, punk in Liverpool celebrated diversity, oddity, and individual style.

[We were] all well into Warhol and Lou Reed, and we'd sort of got into the New York alternative subculture, and modeled our little scene on that.
—Jayne Casey, 1993

The punk thing was great, going down to Eric's and all that, but the good punk stuff you can count on one hand, and we regarded bands like Chelsea as just a joke. The American punk was far more interesting. They brought in all the things that I liked, Bowie, Lou Reed, and Iggy. Eric's played a real mishmash of material, Television, reggae, dub, Bowie, really cool bands with a wide appeal. It was a music club, first and foremost.
—Ian McCulloch, 1994

Eric's wasn't just a punk club. The Roxy [London] was people in dog collars. The Electric Circus [Manchester] was the same but dour, whereas in Liverpool there was an underground from '75. Strong Bowie and Roxy following. There was this big clothes thing in Liverpool; even now, people buy clobber, they don't get their cars fixed. But it was just this very flamboyant scene, very New York, Andy Warhol, streets steeped in mystery, underage drinking, that had nothing to do with 'Gabba Gabba Hey.'
—Ian McCulloch, 1999

Mac recalls disliking the limiting aspect of the punk uniform—although he reckons he "would have made a good punk rocker—bondage trousers, the lot." Which isn't to say he was devil-may-care about his appearance—far from it. He was, and admittedly still is, achingly appearance-conscious, to the point of vanity.

Mac used to go 'round with a gray anorak, his trousers tucked into his socks, and ... hair like Bowie.   —Les Pattinson, 1984

Make-up's a great invention. I wish I'd been born with eyeliner and eyeshadow. I *was* born with lip gloss on.   —Ian McCulloch, 1985

Without being big-headed, I think the way I looked was one of the big factors in whatever success we had as a band. It was like all the fellas wanted to be me and all the girls wanted to ... be friends with me. Echo & the Bunnymen would never have worked if I'd ... been ˉ bastard at 23 ... the band would never have worked and the ˉ never have worked. Not that I was ever likely to becomˉ

If I had this voice and I looked like Van Morrison,
          —Iaɳ

Q: "How many times a day do you look in the mirror?"
Ian McCulloch: "How many seconds are there in a day? In ϲ hundred times. Easy."   —*The Right To Imaginatioɾ.*

Mac spent ages getting his hairstyle together. It was a comˌ dure, which involved a towel, blow dryer, comb, and hairspray (oˏ ˍrt of that, orange juice and/or Coca-Cola). The end result was a Keith Richard circa '66 teased bird's nest tangle. Dyed orange. Pete Wylie recalls having to wait over an hour for Mac to get out of bed and arrange his barnet into its studied disarray. Mac would complement what the music press has called the "hairstyle of the gods" with a long green kaftan or an oversized polka dot shirt, and a pair of blue tinted *Easy Rider* shades with one arm missing. He adamantly refused to wear prescription glasses, although his myopia was so severe it approached blindness. When forced to take an eye exam at school, he slyly memorized the letter chart and recited it to the optometrist, thus avoiding the humiliating and Bauhausian gracelessness of National Health Care glasses, which he dismissed as "Buddy Holly Specs."

If they'd let me look at the blackboard through a sheet of glass I wouldn't have minded, but you have to be at least 20 to wear glasses properly.   —Ian McCulloch, 1984

I spent a lot of time staring into mirrors back then. Still do, for that matter ... [but] I looked a bit odd ... I'd sit on the bus and imagine that all the girls were drooling over me ... but I was probably fooling myself.—Ian McCulloch, 1997

Masturbating to my own photos? Nah. I draw the line well before that. Mind you, I wouldn't mind if someone else fancied having a go at it while looking at my photos. Hand down the knickers and all that.
          —Ian McCulloch, 1997

an adolescent I was always scared of looking like a By being scared it makes in, it makes you worry. ˌn I decided I looked ˍ best pop star in the ˌd, I would always worry that something wasn't quite right ... like me hair.
          —Ian McCulloch, 1990

Although Mac loved the electricity of Eric's and the punk scene, Bowie was still his musical priority, to the point where, rumor has it, he wouldn't answer to anything but "Duke," after Bowie's "Thin White Duke" character from the *Station to Station* album. Mac denies this.

That was Pete Wylie telling … not a lie, but a fib. It was him who used to introduce me as 'Duke' because he knew I liked Bowie a lot, and I used to say, 'Don't do that, Pete,' but it got twisted and everyone fell for it.   —Ian McCulloch, 1983

Even if Mac objected to the "Duke" label, he wasn't about to fuss desperately to ensure that everyone at Eric's knew his proper name. At this point in time, he was extremely introverted and quiet, exuding a diffident demeanor that bordered on verbal catatonia—a sharp contrast to the acid-tongued "Mac the Mouth" character that emerged a few years later.

Whatever contribution I made to the conversation would always be the one-liner. I wasn't brought up to act the fool like a lot of people did at Eric's. I was glad of my shyness 'cos everybody seemed to be making prats of themselves.
—Ian McCulloch, *Liverpool Explodes*

People would wonder if Mac ever spoke ... the only time you'd hear Mac speak was when he didn't like something. He'd say 'scummy turd' or somesuch and you could hear the boredom and contempt in his voice.
—Pete Wylie, *Liverpool Explodes*

Some assumed that Mac's taciturn nature implied some unhealthy habits.

It's really funny. I dunno why, but people always think I'm really *strung out* or something.   —Ian McCulloch, 1985

No, it wasn't drugs. I'd always [been] like that. At school people used to ask my mates, 'What's he on?' just 'cos I wasn't particularly into being excited by boring things … like staying awake.
—Ian McCulloch, 1983

One can imagine that Mac's vocal reticence acted as an almost comic foil to the excitable 90-mile-a-minute psychobabble of his constant companion Wylie, with whom you couldn't, and still can't, get a word in edgewise.

He's got the loudest voice I've ever heard. If you were in the toilets at Eric's you could hear him barking away as he entered the club.
—Ian McCulloch, 1983

Perhaps no one personified the distinctly Eric's attitude of "anyone can be a star if you're cheeky and/or unique enough" than the young Pete Wylie.

At the height of punk, Wylie was hanging around Eric's with a full beard, a "Rebel Without a Degree" badge, and "Cliff God" chalked onto the back of his leather jacket; chalked, instead of painted, because by next week he might become a new character, and he didn't want to have to go to the trouble of painting over the old lettering.

I used to go to Eric's with Pete because we went to school together. He was a year older. He was a mate and he was really loud and nothing ever fazed him. The minute we went down there he became one of the main people. Initially, it was people like Pete Burns and Holly because they looked so weird. But Wylie pretty much ran that place. He knew everyone. He shagged everyone! Girls, that is. He was great, and still is.
—Ian McCulloch, 1995

THE CRUCIAL THREE

Never were three egos less destined to co-exist on a permanent basis.
—*Mojo*, 1997

On May 5, 1977, Mac's 18th birthday, The Clash brought their infuriated call-to-arms to Eric's, and the Liverpudlian underground flooded the place. Mac traipsed down to the gig with Wylie, who had a confrontation with a blonde spikey-haired teacher-in-training named Julian Cope, while Strummer seethed onstage.

I'd been waiting to see The Clash, and I'd fought me way to the front, and next to me was this dickhead in a boiler suit dancing really badly, just rocking back and forth, and he kept rocking back into me. In his book, he says he turned around and gave me a 'manic punk stare' and I backed off, and I say I said, 'If yer don't stop doin' that, I'm gonna chin yer.' And he says, 'Oh, don't do that, why don't we form a band, pour our anger into guitars.'   —Pete Wylie, 1994

And so Wylie, Cope, and Mac became The Crucial Three. Initially, the name was "Arthur Hostile and the Crucial Three" but Mac decided that the "Arthur Hostile" sounded "crap," and it was promptly dropped.

The group lasted four rehearsals. Sort of. Rehearsals consisted, basically, of Wylie pretending to be Bruce Springsteen by way of Joe Strummer, blasting his guitar through a tinny practice amp, as Cope fumbled through the bass line of Pink Floyd's "Money." Wylie's friend Steve "Spenner" Spence clattered away on "drums" (one of Mrs. McCulloch's kitchen chairs) and Mac, slumped on a couch, refused to sing "sod all if it's gonna sound crap." Everyone wanted to be the star of the show, but it was determined that Mac had to be the frontman, because he couldn't play anything, and, besides, with his bee-stung lips, he looked the most like Mick Jagger.

Once or twice, Mac's embarrassment faded just enough for him to pick up his mom's teakettle (to amplify his voice, in the absence of a microphone) and *hum* the vocal line from The Velvet Underground's "Waiting for the Man." Ideas and titles for songs emerged, but were never developed. These included early McCulloch compositions like "Nazi Stomp," "Spacehopper," "Bloody Sure You're on Dope" (Mac's mother's favorite expression), and "Salomine Shuffle." The latter boasted the lyrics "When I get hives I use Calomine/When I wanna dance I do the salomine/Shuffle." Wylie still insists that it was a "pop classic." Mac flatly disagrees.

It was really crap. I used to suffer from heat bumps at that time, and I used to whack on some calamine lotion. The first line had 'calamine' in it, so I rhymed it with 'salomine' ... it was a crap song. The reason it was crap from the off was that it stemmed from a Julian Cope bass line. It was 'Money' by Pink Floyd. Punk was at its peak and we were doing this Pink Floyd rip-off. —Ian McCulloch, 1995

Before Phil Spector had a chance to visit Liverpool and record The Crucial Three's potential top tens, Spence packed up and split for college, and the project was promptly aborted. And thus endeth the overblown legend of The Crucial Three—not so much with a bang or a whimper, but an indifferent shrug.

But even without a Spenner in the works, The Crucial Three would likely have been doomed to quick failure. Mac, Cope, and Wylie all had massive egos, and each of them yearned to be the leader of whatever group they were in. Even if that weren't the case, the tried-and-true musical differences would have eventually pulled them apart.

Copey turned up with 'Life Is A Factory' sprayed on his bass, and he'd changed his name to 'Juven Ile'—and these were the dodgy fag-ends of London punk ideas, like D. Generate and Eater—it was never cool, y'know? The final straw was, Julian brought in this song he'd written, and it was a rent-a-punk kinda thrash anthem. And there's only one line that I can remember, which went '…and the apathy that's spreading through our country for the shores!!!' And when he did it,

McCulloch and I both knew that *this* was over.　　　—Pete Wylie, 1994

That reminds me of a Wylie lyric, which would have told me 'this was over' just as quickly: 'What are they doing to the inner city/tearing it up with no remorse or pity.'　　　—Ian McCulloch, 2001

However ill-advised these forays into sociopolitical punk may have been, the actual musical rifts were deeper. Mac's love of the melody and lyricism of The Velvet Underground's third album and Leonard Cohen clashed with Cope's perverse passion for avant garde groups Can and Captain Beefheart. Wylie the populist, meanwhile, was interested in pursing a more anthemic avenue.

These days, Mac barely acknowledges that the band, such as it was, even existed. It's not difficult to believe him, as the majority of groups in Liverpool at the time were entirely imaginary—and extremely bitchy to boot. The running joke was as follows:

"Have you heard that so-and-so has a new group?"
"Am I in it?"
"No."
"They're crap."

You could see they were all trying to put their oar in. You'd have three different styles. One person would bring something in and the other two would attack it and try to switch it to suit one person or the other. And in the end it was [clenches teeth] 'It's *my* idea—we're doing it *this* way.'　　　—Steve Spence, 1981

THE GEOFFS AND THE LOVE PASTELS

One individual who had a real proclivity for excellent imaginary groups was a boatbuilder named Les Pattinson. By the time The Crucial Three began stumbling through their attempted rehearsals, Les had already been the leader of not one but *two* fictional pop sensations. One was called The Geoffs, a group whose primary concept was that all the members were named Geoff, after Pattinson's alter ego, Geoff Lovestone. It was this character who began visiting Eric's on a regular basis.

In about June 1977 he came into Eric's with a blue fitted polo neck in nylon with a red and black stripe down the side, tapered trousers, Chelsea boots, and his hair dyed blond like Heinz ... like one of those clean-cut American acid gurus, he always had a big chain with a pendant around his neck.　　　—Julian Cope, *Liverpool Explodes*

According to Julian Cope's *Head On,* The Geoffs would play "slow and Doors-y." Geoff Lovestone would preach his songs, like Elvis Presley doing

It was more or less a race for bands in the city to come up with the weirdest and funniest name.   —Les Pattinson, 1979

I used to have white hair—a sort of Joe Punk with 60's overtones.
                    —Les Pattinson, 1984

'The Battle Hymn of the Republic.'" Geoffs classics included "You Me and the Sea," "Outer Town/Outer Space," and "I Can Face the World Now":

I can face the world now
Now that you're with me
Everything's alright now
Switch on the TV

After The Geoffs disbanded—not a drawn-out legal process, one would imagine, as Pattinson was the only flesh-and-blood member of the group— Les went on to form the Love Pastels. Pattinson was the lead singer of this a capella quartet, with backing vocals provided by nonexistent girls named Arlene Smith, Shirley Alston, and Rosie Hamlin. Les recalls the Pastels concept as "really psychedelic, funnily enough, though I envisioned it more like sort of cartoon fantasy psychedelic—Bowie 'Images' sort of stuff." Love Pastels songs sported such titles as "Apples From France," "Underneath the Upper Atmosphere," and "The Balloon Man Will Know." These songs remain unheard and, quite probably, unwritten. Suffering a fate similar to The Geoffs, The Love Pastels disbanded before they could fight their way out of the steely confines of Pattinson's imagination.

When he wasn't conjuring up new fictitious groups or working at the Douglas Boatyard near Preston, Les packed his time with as many pursuits as possible. A bright, amiable, enthusiastic character, he sated his boyish thirst for speed by racing motorcycles, bicycles, and boats. His artistic side was expressed through experiments in amateur photography. The latter skill would later prove useful in documenting candid moments of Echo & the Bunnymen's travels. But of course, in the summer of '77, Echo & the Bunnymen wasn't even a concept, and Les, despite his experience as the leader of two bands, had never actually played an instrument in his life.

INDUSTRIAL DOMESTIC

While Mac fell asleep during Crucial Three rehearsals, and Les perfected his 60's hipster image, Pattinson's old schoolmate from Deyes Lane elementary, Will Sergeant—known in those preadolescent days as "The Greaseball Kid"—was experimenting with his own project, Industrial Domestic, with friend Paul Simpson.

Paul had this organ, and we had guitars and an echo unit, and you could sing into the amp. I've got tapes of Julian playing with us and others with this lad who used to work … with me

—Will Sergeant, *Liverpool Explodes*

Armed with little more than a drum machine and a few vague concepts, the duo churned out a sound that was, fittingly, industrial.

Although Will has since stated that Industrial Domestic consisted of little more than marketing devices in the form of "a badge and a paper bag," in truth, the group recorded an array of tapes, which were then distributed to friends and acquaintances around Liverpool.

When not exploring Industrial Domestic's complete lack of commercial potential, Will worked days as a short-order cook at a local café called Binn's. He spent his free time listening to records, collecting *Star Trek* memorabilia, and riding a motorbike around the sand dunes of Southport, Merseyside.

From the age of 12, Will had toyed with guitars. His first was a gift from his father, a plastic Hofner that he immediately cut into a coffin shape, which goes a long way in illustrating Will's arid, morbid sense of humor. In his early teens, he was interested in Led Zeppelin and heavy metal bands, and eventually his tastes widened to the sounds of The Velvet Underground, The Residents, and mid-late 60's garage punk bands, the kind of three-chord wonders that grace Lenny Kaye's massively influential *Nuggets* compilation.

Extremely introverted and shy, Will wasn't exactly a social dynamo when he started visiting Eric's, but like most of the other genuine characters on the scene, he made his own distinct impression.

I used to go to Eric's on me own 'cos I didn't know anyone. I had me motorbike boots on with my black shiny plastic keks. I went there once with these yellow skintight keks and everyone thought I had no keks on.

—Will Sergeant, 1984

What a legend! Industrial Domestic was going to rule the world! Actually, it was just something to do on the dole.

—Will Sergeant, 1981

It made Throbbing Gristle sound like Dollar.

—Will Sergeant, 1984

Unmoved by the punk fashion of viciously cropped coifs, Will had "dead long hair," which he'd colored red, yellow, and black, like a psychedelic

Richard III. He did, however, resemble many of his Eric's contemporaries in one respect.

I was dead depressed—you have to be when you're a punk, don't you?
—Will Sergeant, 1984

A tape of Industrial Domestic and Julian Cope performing a transcendentally awful version of the Stones' "Satisfaction" has recently emerged on Julian Cope's *Floored Genius 3* collection.

We split up after that one gig because Pete Wylie wanted to wear a toilet seat on his head.
—Pete Burns, 1994

THE MYSTERY GIRLS

Roger Eagle just decided I should be in a group because I dressed up freaky.
—Pete Burns, 1994

In the second half of 1977, after the demise of The Crucial Three, Wylie and Cope went on to form The Mystery Girls with Pete Burns, later of Dead or Alive. Burns was a flamboyantly gay Eric's regular whose mouth was the only thing more colorful than the hairstyles and outfits he strutted at Eric's, a place he regarded as his own personal catwalk/gossip column. It's hard to believe that The Mystery Girls ever managed to pull anything together.

Julian Cope would say, 'Oh, I know, I've got a really good idea. You stand at the back with a blanket over your head, and I'll stand at the front.' They didn't want people to look at me. They just couldn't stand the fact that I was so fucking glamorous. —Pete Burns, 1994

Ironically, by Eric's standards, The Mystery Girls became virtual rock dinosaurs, in that they actually played one gig, supporting Sham 69. Their ragtag set was notable only for shredded approximations of the Who's "I Can See for Miles" and the Troggs' "Wild Thing." Although this collaboration didn't sound particularly promising, the band made an undeniable visual impression.

Burns was Burns, with his make-up and his hair. Cope was in an overcoat, probably, playing his bass. I had me mum's white mac with gold buttons, white nylon blouse with blue flowers, red satin keks, and a toilet seat that I used to wear.   —Pete Wylie, 1994

Conceptually, they were a pretty hot group.

—Bill Drummond, 1987

In early 1978, Cope and Wylie went on to form The Nova Mob, named as such because they perversely enjoyed the unimaginative bohemian cliché of alluding to a William Burroughs novel, á la The Soft Machine and Steely Dan. The Mob's primary purpose was to annoy people—a task that they achieved with minimal effort. During their first and only gig, they played a mind-numbingly monotonous riff, over which Cope intoned the mantra, "We're in love with beauty/We're in love with wealth/We're in love with mental health" until all audience members simply left the room. Never one to let a lyric go to waste—self-penned or otherwise—Cope exhumed the mantra for "Going Crazy" on The Teardrop Explodes's debut LP *Kilimanjaro*.

The Nova Mob's secondary *r'aison d'être* was to break up Big In Japan, a virtually unlistenable theatrical punk band fronted by the sexy, striking Jayne Casey, and featuring a slightly older, gawky, and only semi-sane Scottish lad named Bill Drummond on guitar. Other members included future Lightning Seed Ian Broudie; Budgie, who eventually played drums for Siouxie and the Banshees; and a young Holly Johnson, later of the hugely successful Frankie Goes to Hollywood.

The Nova Mob went so far as to post a petition at the hipper-than-thou Probe Records, demanding the immediate dissolution of Big In Japan. At this pursuit, they were not quite so successful; they only received seven signatures—one from each member of Big In Japan.

Perhaps The Nova Mob's most significant accomplishment was a T-shirt which, in a display of self-conscious irony, sported an image of the aforementioned Jayne Casey. Nova Mob fans were few to the point of mythical, but, as the comparatively popular Big in Japan didn't have a T-shirt, these concessions generated a slight profit.

Big In Japan did eventually split, splintered in a fit of inter-band bitchery, due in no part whatsoever to the petty machinations of the Nova Mob.

We were so purist then I don't
know how we got anything done
      —Julian Cope, *Head-On*

In June 1978, after The Nova Mob disbanded, Mac and Cope reunited to form Uh? with a mutual friend named Dave Pickett. The group acquired its name from Pickett's favorite expression, which he used to make people repeat things twice for his own amusement. Although the trio ostensibly intended to work off the template of the classic third Velvet Underground LP, Mac recalls that the group's most pressing concern was to create a T-shirt with Uh? printed in the smallest possible lettering in the center.

This task accomplished, the band played not one, but—*gasp*—two gigs. During the first, supporting Pete Wylie's Crash Course at Kirklands wine bar, vocalist Mac refused to sing a note, and opted instead to preserve his dignity—and hide a mean case of nerves—behind a set of melodicas. He walked out on the second show—which finished with the ubiquitous thrash through "Louie, Louie"—insisting that the band had "sold out" by playing more than once.

One amusing Uh? composition, "Robert Mitchum," can be heard on Cope's obscure *Droolian* LP, and Mac's been known to sing a line or two upon request. (Sample lyric: "Robert, Robert Mitchum ... don't you cry don't you weep/You're such a dude/You're such a guy/You know you're so half asleep.") "Jefferson Davis," a heroic McCulloch epic, remains forgotten.

A SHALLOW MADNESS

In early July 1978, shortly after the demise of Uh?, The Cope/McCulloch/Pickett trio conspired on one more project. According to Cope, a Svengali character named Arrow dubbed the group "A Shallow Madness," after a poem he had written. Other members were Paul Simpson, who had recently abandoned Will Sergeant's Industrial Domestic, and a guitarist named Mick Finkler. They rehearsed in a shared flat on Penny Lane. Although A Shallow Madness primarily concentrated on writing and rehearsing originals, their claim to notoriety was a version of the Stones' "Satisfaction" that began in Scottish and ended in German.

But Mac's ego and love of rock traditionalism didn't tally with such self-conscious gestures of obscure weirdness, and he eventually made a habit of not turning up for rehearsals on time, if at all.

Mac was ... bloody late all the time. And he stopped coming up with stuff. We'd write music while we waited for Mac, then Mac would hate it ... I wanted the group *now*. I told everyone. I said I would sing if McCull didn't get his shit together. I loved Mac. It did my head in to do it. It was my first guilt trip. I could tell Mac wasn't happy. He wanted a rock group, and we were too stumbling. I didn't want it to end our friendship and I thought it wouldn't. July 1978 was the end of A Shallow Madness. I asked Mac to leave and he kind of took the name with him.   —Julian Cope, *Head-On*

I felt like a failure when I was kicked out. I didn't really have any self-confidence. But all these bands were like build-ups because we all wanted to be singers, and everyone was striving for the spotlight. It was just too much. The time wasn't really right for the band I wanted to be in.   —Ian McCulloch, 1998

WEIRD AS FISH

In July, 1978, after Paul Simpson had departed the cinder gray of Industrial Domestic for the brighter palette of A Shallow Madness, Will Sergeant continued on his own, creating the experimental bedsit psychedelia of the semi-legendary "weird as fish" tapes.

There are only seven copies of this made, The Magnificent Seven. They're all slightly different and they've all got different covers. These were just done on two tracks ... they're all instrumental except for a bit of grunting. I didn't give the songs titles because they aren't about anything, so it would be pretentious. I suppose it's pretentious not to as well.   —Will Sergeant, 1981

I was into this total concept that an LP should just be one copy really. You do it yourself: you print it, you make everything yourself. Selling the record was like getting prints of it; like the Mona Lisa—there's only one of it, but you can buy prints of it, can't you? It was that sort of idea. So, on 'Weird As Fish' I did everything: I made the covers—they were all slightly different, all individual. It sounded kind of like industrial weirdness. I was just experimenting with sounds, and I didn't have that much equipment, so I had to be inventive.   —Will Sergeant, 1998

There's a distinct possibility that the "Weird As Fish" tapes will be re-released as a CD on Ochre Records as a sort of collector's item, despite Will's raised eyebrow regarding their musical value.

They're crap, really.   —Will Sergeant, 1995

THE GIFT OF VISION

One evening in August 1978, Mac sauntered into the ladies' toilets of Eric's to ensure that his hair was retaining its spikey loftiness. There, he stumbled across a short lad in ripped jeans with a Ramones hairstyle and a black leather motorcycle jacket with 'The Velvet Underground' scrawled on the back. Alongside him was a platinum-coiffed boy who Mac recognized, albeit short-sightedly, from previous visits to the club. The two were singing an impromptu version of "Love You 'Til Tuesday" from the rare *World of David Bowie* LP, recorded when Bowie was still marketed as David Jones. Ian McCulloch had just met Will Sergeant and Les Pattinson.

The first thing Will said to me was, 'You've got a good voice,' and apparently I answered with, 'I'm waiting for the gift of vision.' Don't ask me why.   —Ian McCulloch, 1984

Although Mac immediately liked Will's weird, almost mole-like manner and his cretin haircut, he had reservations about Les.

I can't remember saying it, but it's the sort of thing we would say. It could've been any Bowie line. It could've been, 'we could be heroes' or, 'we've got five years.' It was probably one of the better ones, but it could have been 'The Little Bombadier.'

—Ian McCulloch, 1995

I used to hate him, 'cos he looked great and he was dead handsome. I used to see him on the dancefloor surrounded by all these girls. I was very shy at the time. Les used to have this catalogue shirt on with scissor cuts in it. Not too big, so that his mum could sew them back up again.   —Ian McCulloch, 1994

Mac was suitably impressed by Will and Les's obscure choice of songs, but nothing of note emerged from this meeting. But it wouldn't be long before Mac and Will ran into each other again at a birthday party for a mutual friend.

It all started on an August night in Kirklands. I'd just been kicked out of this jazz-funk group that later became The Teardrop Explodes and ... Will and I were both sitting there, with no one to talk to, so we talked to each other.   —Ian McCulloch, 1984

Fueled by pints, they discussed their mutual love of Bowie, Television, and The Velvet Underground, and discovered they had both employed their passion for the Velvets for homework assignments. Will had once cribbed the sleeve notes of a Velvets compilation for an essay, and turned it in to his professor with a tape of "The Black Angel's Death Song," the manic noisefest near the end of the first Velvets LP; Mac had done much the same, except he'd chosen to tape the slightly more conventional "Waiting For the Man." Bonding in similar tastes, Will suggested they start a group, and Mac agreed. They felt a natural kinship—Will was still bitter about Paul Simpson having left Industrial Domestic to join A Shallow Madness, and Mac was equally unhappy at having been kicked out of that group. Such was their resentment that the two almost chose to call their group "The Outsiders."

So this odd duo, which Julian Cope has described as "the two most emotionally autistic people I've ever met" started hanging out at Will's and picking out riffs to the monotone of Will's Minipops drum machine. By this time, Mac had learned some rudimentary rhythm guitar chords from Wylie.

His house smelled of dope, had carpet tiles. He only spoke about three sentences, about the drum machine. 'Shall we have Rock 1 or Rock 2?' I thought he was genuinely weird.   —Ian McCulloch, 1998

This marked the beginning of a bizarre relationship that has since been both blessing and curse.

McCulloch and Sergeant are an odd couple, make no mistake. Two sides of two different coins, a benign collision of unstoppable force and immovable object. Individually, these two men seem poles apart, yet theirs is a chemistry—an unspoken bond from the same compound as Lennon and McCartney or Morrissey and Marr—that's not to be messed with.   —Uncut, 2001

I felt awkward around him, as he does around me. Despite what we say about each other, there's a real bond there, and it's only ego, pride, and stubbornness that fucks it up. It's a weird chemistry, because sometimes socially, it's an anti-chemistry. Other nights, we're laughing so much we're both in tears. I've got this respect for him, but he infuriates me, as probably I do him.   —Ian McCulloch, 1999

There's always been a bit of weirdness between the two of us and that's never gonna go away, but it's useful, creative. —Will Sergeant, 1994

I would go over to his house where he had this crappy guitar his Dad had made him and he would plug it into the radio amp. I would bring my guitar and we'd sit around this crappy drum machine. Back then we would always start off with a drum beat, even though this machine only had about six different beats on it! That was good because it helped us play with a steady groove. Will would often come up with a real naive guitar line and I would lob something in and work out how to play that as a song.
                    —Ian McCulloch, 1994

Mac's two completely different people. Sometimes he's totally brilliant, another day you just know he's going to be a turd.
                    —Will Sergeant, 1997

Will's not perfect at all, but he has a way of looking at me that makes me think I'll keep meself in check. I'm sure if I'm about to lose perspective … he would tell me ... I'm the man for Will and he's the man for me.   —Ian McCulloch, 1995

We've always been instinctive, naive songwriters, and that helps you learn new things while avoiding formulas and traps. We're both driven by what we do, and it's truly a great partnership. I don't know how or why, but as long as it works, I don't really want to, mate.   —Ian McCulloch, 1995

His opinions are those of a caveman; they're written in stone and haven't been altered in the last 15 years. He's bound to annoy me the second he opens his mouth ... that said, he's still the best guitarist walking the planet. I trust him, and he trusts me, which is a good basis to work from. I think we really value each other's [musical] opinions.   —Ian McCulloch, 1995

By early November 1978, A Shallow Madness had changed its name to The Teardrop Explodes. Cope had found the phrase exclaimed, for no apparent reason, in a Marvel *Daredevil* comic. It was a fantastic name for a group—weird, psychedelic, bright, and catchy. Roger Eagle liked the sound of it, and, without having heard the band, offered Cope a gig at Eric's. Eagle was magnanimous about this kind of thing, permitting the regulars to show off their talents—or lack thereof—just because he liked a band's name, or their wacky conceptual angle. One of the more legendary of these was The Table, who refused to advertise their performances. They would merely place a particular table outside the venue, and you were supposed to catch on.

Cope agreed to do the gig, and, perhaps feeling guilty for edging Mac out of A Shallow Madness, mentioned Mac and Will's new partnership to Eagle, suggesting they open the show. Eagle good-naturedly complied, and Julian presented the taciturn two with the opportunity. They immediately accepted—despite the fact that they still had no real songs written.

By this point, Les had been turning up regularly to watch Mac and Will play, and act as their biggest and only fan. Despite initial reservations, Mac found that he had come to genuinely enjoy Les's upbeat demeanor. On November 11, 1978, just four days before the gig at Eric's, Les bought a cheap bass. On the strength of this purchase alone, he became a member of Mac and Will's group. That he had never played a note before simply didn't enter into the equation.

He just turned up with his bass. I thought, 'A boat builder with a bass? Steve McQueen meets Scott Tracy from The Thunderbirds? Fantastic!'   —Ian McCulloch, 1999

Les was perfect. He'd never played anything before; he got this bass for like 40 pounds, and he just had this natural knack. He had big hands with thick fingers, which were perfect for a bass player. And his vibe was good; he was a dead nice bloke, a kind of balance between me and Will, maybe.   —Ian McCulloch, 1998

THE BUNNYMEN ARE BORN

The new trio—or four-piece, if you counted the drum machine—still needed a title. Mac had a roommate at the Penny Lane flat named Paul Ellerbeck, known as "Smelly Elly" for his lax hygienic habits, who specialized in inventing far-out band names. Among those suggested were Mona Lisa and the Grease Guns, Glisserol and the Fan Extractors, and The Daz Men. Although these had a certain no-wave, CBGB's appeal, the names didn't quite fit. Smelly Elly's final suggestion was Echo & the Bunnymen.

The name worked. "Echo" had connotations with the Liverpool evening newspaper, and "the Bunnymen" seemed somewhat alien. And everyone agreed that, overall, it just sounded good. Almost everyone, anyway.

I thought it was just as stupid as the rest.   —Will Sergeant, 1984

It is one of the all-time great band names; meaningless, but hip, sharp, and evocative.   —*Uncut*, 1999

[It] just happened, and it was never intended to have any meaning. Our name has a round feel to it, it's got sort of round vowels.
                                              —Ian McCulloch, 1980

Someone came up to me ... and said they heard that 'Echo & the Bunnymen' came from the Castro years. There used to be these guerrillas trained by the CIA, and to disguise themselves, they used to have burrows to go under Echo Valley in Cuba. They were termed as the Bunnymen. They were known as these people who'd come out and kill people at night ... it might warrant some research. —Les Pattinson, 1997

We're very serious. But that's why we have a funny name. It's just that we didn't want to sound pretentious and over the top. If something like a name puts people off 'cos it sounds a bit funny, then maybe those people weren't worth bothering with anyway.

                    —Ian McCulloch, 1979

We were the first ones to use a drum machine like a human being, because we weren't weird about it, making it go blip blopp, but having a proper rhythm. It's the best beat ever. Every song we've ever written could have had that beat on it.—Ian McCulloch, 1985

Everyone loved us, so we were dead chuffed. There was me playing the guitar, the drum machine pounding, and Mac screaming over the top of it all.   —Will Sergeant, 1985

Echo & the Bunnymen made their debut at Eric's on November 15, 1978. Silently and self-consciously, they ambled onstage in front of a crowd of 43 people. Will then switched on the drum machine. Naturally, it didn't work.

After Will fiddled nervously with the instrument for a few long minutes—during which all three members were no doubt shitting themselves—the Minipops reluctantly kicked in, hissing a primitive, monotonous, Suicide-like beat. Les throbbed in with a simple, repetitive bass line, which Will countered with waves of feedback and an equally amateur spindly guitar line. Mac, looking "like Bowie if he'd gone to see the cricket" in a red polo neck, assumed centerstage, pushed his multicolored hair out of his eyes, and pulled a crumpled sheet of lyrics from his pocket. He squinted myopically at it for a few seconds, took a deep breath, and began to sing. Really *sing*. The voice was mannered and arch, but deep, rich, sonorous, and distinct. The song's title was "I Bagsy Yours," an early version of "Monkeys." As the Bunnymen had only managed to assemble one composition over the previous four days, this would have to do. They churned "Monkeys" out for 20 minutes—it was perhaps as much of an homage to the Velvets' virtually endless "Sister Ray" as testament to their own shortage of material—after which Will and Les faded out, Mac wandered off, and the drum machine was left pulsing by itself on a chair.

For twenty seconds, there was a stunned silence.

Then someone started clapping.

Then a few others joined in.

Then, a roar of applause.

Wylie catapulted up from the audience and grabbed Mac, shouting, "That was soddin' mad—yer great!" Julian Cope was equally impressed.

Mac, Will, and Les all breathed sighs of relief. They were really in a group. A legendary group. A legendary weirdo group. They were The Bunnymen.

As soon as it was finished it was like, 'Oh shit, I wish we had more songs, other than just one.' To me, it just made an impression on a lot of people … word went 'round Liverpool that there was this group that were weird, like nothing else. I think that made us feel from day one that we were different, and that you could get away, not so much with murder, but by being fairly unique. So that, to me, was a key moment, because we began, and we wanted more as soon as we did it. God, it was fantastic!   —Ian McCulloch, 1998

It was stunning. Suddenly, it wasn't just your mate on the stage—it was a guy who was born to be a star.　　　　　　　—Pete Wylie, 1994

It was the best thing I'd ever seen. You know I did think they were brilliant.　　　　　　　—Jayne Casey, 1993

In the beginning they were like a little clockwork band. Just three young Liverpudlians and a drum machine called Echo. The Bunnymen played their frail, tick-tock tune in a little room, and looked as if they might split up on the spot if you asked them to. But there was a definite magic being born.　　　　　　　—*Mojo*, 1997

I had no idea what I was doing.　　　　　　　—Les Pattinson, 1984

Mac just became incredible ... this real quiet bloke, and all of a sudden he was a cross between Iggy Pop and Mark E. Smith ... like, real serious attitude coming across, y'know? Everyone was gobsmacked.　　　　　　　—Will Sergeant, 1994

The band couldn't play a note and they had nothing going for them, but they decided they were going to be the best band on the planet. And that belief came first.　　　　　　　—Bill Drummond, 1997

ZOO RECORDS

Encouraged by the positive response, the Bunnymen wrote a handful of simple songs, played a few more gigs at Eric's, then recorded a demo at a run-down studio above a cheap Chinese café. The three songs were primitive, stark, haunted versions of "Monkeys," "Happy Death Men," and "The Pictures On My Wall."

One person who apparently never heard this tape was former Big In Japan guitarist Bill Drummond. Drummond was a man who lived for rock & roll, to the point that, when Elvis died in 1977, it was as if the universe had imploded.

I was camping on this beach, dozing away in a sleeping bag, in Brittany. I got up and saw this French bloke reading a newspaper. I saw the world 'Elvis' but couldn't read the other one. Then I thought the other word must be 'dead.' I rushed around trying to find an English paper, and, when I did, I just couldn't believe it. It was like The End, the collapse of everything for me. I felt there was no one there to take over. When I got back from holiday, I had to try to cope with what I was doing, thinking, 'How can I carry on?' Elvis was everything to me, in that he was the first for me, the first thing that made me go, 'fucking 'ell!'　　　　　　　—Bill Drummond, 1987

Somehow Drummond had managed to keep breathing and, after Big In Japan dissolved, he and David Balfe, the ex-bassist from Dalek I Love You

(another seminal Liverpool band), had created a small independent label named Zoo Records. Zoo occupied a tiny office on Button Street in downtown Liverpool. The office consisted of a telephone, desk, and tape recorder sitting on a chair. Drummond's goal for the label was to release a string of classic pop—as opposed to punk—singles; records with mass appeal that actually made the charts, that were financially as well as artistically successful. At the time, this attitude was extremely unfashionable, as it directly opposed the harsh political stance of bands like The Fall, whose aesthetic was to snub the music industry by releasing deliberately trashy-sounding, lo-fi, DIY singles.

Drummond had signed The Teardrop Explodes to Zoo solely on the dazzle of their name. In his book *From the Shores of Lake Placid and Other Stories*, he recalls a conversation Cope initiated shortly thereafter:

'You should make a record with McCull's band.' 'What are they called?' 'Echo & the Bunnymen.'

It didn't have the instant 'I'm already into this band and I haven't heard or read anything about them' that 'The Teardrop Explodes' had, but it was in the right area ... it sounded strange, psychedelic, enticing.

A couple of weeks later, I was sitting in a kitchen with McCull. (It was only later that the McCull got shortened to Mac.) 'The thing is, we're doing these badges for The Teardrop Explodes and the Zoo and if you agree to do a record with Zoo we will do an Echo & the Bunnymen badge as well. I need to know by tomorrow.'

Next day I got a call from Mac. Will and Les agreed; the badge would be made, a record recorded. As for Echo & the Bunnymen's music, I still hadn't heard it.

In addition to pressing their badges and records—in Liverpool, at this point, it's possible that the former were considered more important—Drummond offered to manage the Bunnymen and the Teardrops. Both bands accepted, and agreed that Zoo also handle their publishing contract.

Despite his business savvy, Drummond was not going to be your standard cigar-chomping rock & roll manager, eyes aimed unwaveringly at the bottom line. Never Mr. Practical, Drummond had a huge, mystically inclined imagination, and indulged lofty ambitions for Zoo Records/Management. Operating on a deliberately amateurish and idealistic philosophy, Drummond recognized a spark in the Bunnymen that he intended to fan into an inferno.

No one is more responsible for the initial success of the Bunnymen than Bill Drummond. It was Drummond who cracked the whip and forced his extremely lazy investment to rehearse regularly. Rehearsals occurred at the

---

My aim is to have my own label, to put out music I like by people I like. It wasn't a punk thing or a political thing that inspired me. I don't want to be identified with the idealistic, ideological elements in small labels.   —Bill Drummond, 1979

Zoo had a good name, it felt hip; obviously, it became hipper when we joined! It was a good independent, even though I didn't trust anyone involved with it, though Bill was one of the crowd. The best thing about Zoo was that they took risks. Nobody believed Zoo was the start of anything big, it was just a good vibe. Drummond was the fan, he was just as flaky as anybody else. Balfe was the serious management type. But they started making mistakes when they signed the Expelaires. They should've been signed to a soddin' pig fanciers label.

—Ian McCulloch, 1991

home of a woman named Gladys Palmer, who for the price of one pound fifty a week, allowed local bands to set up shop in her basement—free toast and tea provided. (A photograph of the basement appears on the inner sleeve of the Bunnymen's debut LP, *Crocodiles*.) In this setting, Drummond acted as the Bunnymen's primary critic, constantly urging them to craft actual *songs*, rather than merely recycle run-of-the-mill buzzsaw punk and Velvet Underground riffs. (Apparently, this hit machine mentality was a little unsettling for Will, who in those days considered changing chords a sell-out.)

Drummond also took advantage of the industry connections he'd made in his Big in Japan days to score out-of-town gigs for the Bunnymen, thus preventing them from becoming just another minor provincial success. In addition, Drummond fronted the capital for a Zoo PA system that the Bunnymen had to share with the Teardrops. (This situation contributed to the growing rift between Mac and Cope; as the two bands had to tour together to use the PA, arguments about who would open and who would headline erupted regularly.) Finally, it was Drummond who insisted on the moral stipulation that the Bunnymen break up after five years.

My job was to trick Echo & the Bunnymen into being the greatest band in the world ... as a band they could be a band that people would die for. A band to follow to the ends of the earth.

—Bill Drummond, *From the Shores of Lake Placid and Other Stories*

No band worth any sort of respect hung around for more than five years.

—Bill Drummond, *From the Shores of Lake Placid and Other Stories*

THE PICTURES ON MY WALL

The Bunnymen's debut single was recorded over the course of one day in March 1979 at August Studios in Liverpool. It was produced by Dave Balfe and Drummond, operating under the collective title "The Chameleons," as the duo was moonlighting in Lori and the Chameleons, another Zoo band. Zoo initially pressed an optimistic 4,000 singles. "The Pictures on My Wall" was released on May 5, Mac's 20th birthday. The B-side, "Read It In Books," was credited to Julian Cope and Ian McCulloch, and appeared, in radically different forms, on both the Teardrops' and the Bunnymen's debut albums—although, to this day, Mac insists that Cope didn't contribute whatsoever to the writing of the song.

It annoys me when people rip off other people's songs with the same tune and call it their own. It's called theft, y'know? ... especially when [the song] is by someone who's put his heart and soul into it. Y'know, hubcaps, fine, but songs ... people ripping off things thinking they can get away with it 'cos they're on 'Top of the Pops' ... it's disgusting, I think.   —Ian McCulloch, 1995

Regardless of the B-side's authorship, the 45 received unanimous critical praise in the music press, and won "Single of the Week" accolades in both the

New Musical Express (*NME*) and *Sounds*, two of England's most influential and time-honored rock publications.

Whoever Echo & the Bunnymen are, they sound so experienced and assured. 'The Pictures on My Wall' is chunky and acoustic, determined and haunting, and puts me in the mind of Love at their most treacherous, with the same kind of penetrating flexibility. Despite/because of its refreshing lack of obvious discordance, distortion, or anything angular, it is compellingly contemporary. Echo & the Bunnymen are a rich, new, and welcome sound. Go to them.   —*NME*, 1979

The opening to 'Pictures…' still sends a shiver up the spine.   —*Record Hunter*, 1991

A beguiling, ambiguous blend of the semi-acoustic, electric, a drum machine, heartache, and fragile youngian [sic] vocals. An attractive and intriguing debut.   —*NME*, 1979

Over a spooky, hooky, apocalyptic New Seekers acoustic wall of strumming, piercing Syd Barrett-style synths wail eerily as terribly urgent, threatening vocals breathlessly tell of a terrible horror. The great thing is that (unlike nearly all 'different' records these gloomy days) everything is suggested and nothing rests pathetically on the characterlessness of pretension. The B-side is quite brilliant, too.   —*Sounds*, 1979

Ironically, two of the few people who questioned the quality of the single were Mac and Will themselves, who thought it would just be ignored by the press and public alike.

It's nothing like it should have been … it should have been really powerful.   —Ian McCulloch, 1979

It wasn't that great, was it? I suppose it was just different to everything that was about; an acoustic guitar, a drum machine, and an organ. It was just, like, weird.   —Will Sergeant, 1999

Despite Mac and Will's reservations about the single, the hype was such that Zoo had to press another 3,000 copies just a few short weeks after the initial print run. Clearly, the record had an appeal—an appeal that was magnified by a certain playful obscurity. If you investigated the run-out groove of the 7-inch (and, in the days of vinyl, you invariably did), you'd find the words "The Revenge of Voodoo Billy" cryptically inscribed.

Can't listen to it. My voice is horrible. It doesn't ring true. But at the time it was, 'We're making a record! With a weird cover!' Although they credited Copey with 'Read It In Books,' which was a real bone of contention.   —Ian McCulloch, 1999

Voodoo Billy was this weirdo doll which moved around on its own accord. Gary Dwyer of the Teardrops said one night he woke up after a rough night out on the piss, getting drunk, and this doll was floating around in mid-air, and it spat at him.
                —Pete de Freitas (Bunnymen drummer), 1981

It used to appear all over the house we used to live in and it spat
milk.   —Les Pattinson, 1981

In addition to this opaque reference, the single marked the first appearance of what would become the Bunnymen's strange insignia, generally referred to as the Bunnygod or Bunnymonster. The image provided the Bunnymen with an aura of mysterious, otherworldly exotica.

The weirdness of something half-human, half rabbit ... is eerie: an
outline of a strung-out, muscle-bound hero with the pointed, floppy
ears of a bunny, it's decidedly inhuman.   —*The Independent,* 1997

The cover art affected the fanciful Drummond profoundly, and it was the primary catalyst for the aura of mysticism and myth that has since been associated with the Drummond-era Bunnymen—

Balfe and his friend Kevin Ward did the artwork for the sleeve. They
delivered a silhouette illustration of a ghostly rabbit figure with
devil's horns rising arrogantly from the ashes ... this devil-like
rabbit took a vice-like grip on my imagination.

It was about this time that I started to slope off and disappear
into the library. I was on the hunt for real or even imagined information on who this weird Echo character was. I assumed the name 'the
Bunnymen' referred to his followers ... I found this:

The concept of the Trickster is related to that of the twin heroes,
either or both of whom embody some of his aspects. A protean figure,
Trickster is a creator, but also cunningly devious and sometimes
spiteful, sometimes 'too clever by half.' He appears in both myth and
folk tale, forming first the world, recreating the earth after the
flood, obtaining fire, creating man, causing his death and loss of
immortality, defeating monsters. Where the creative role is assigned
to some other figure, Trickster's role as an adventurer is predomi-
nant, but even where he is the creative demiurge, he is also a joker.
He is usually conceived of in the woodlands as the Great White Hare
or Rabbit.

It was over a period of time that various strands of myth and folk-
lore started to emerge and grow in my imagination to form a, still
vague, entity that I knew to be Echo.

—Bill Drummond, *From the Shores of Lake Placid and Other Stories*

During the summer of 1979, the three-piece Bunnymen gigged sporadically, first at Eric's, then eventually at a few dates in Manchester, York, Leeds, and Middlesborough. Perpetually on the verge of bankruptcy, Zoo didn't have the capital to provide the Bunnymen with a crew, so Les doubled as the band's driver. He purchased a 1968 Minibus Transit with a diesel engine, to which he added the luxury of an interior carpet and a stereo. These out-of-town dates provided Les with a fairly grueling schedule: he'd leave his job at the boatyard, drive the band to a gig, sound check, and perform the show. Afterward, he'd help load up the gear, drive back to Liverpool, drop the others off, and head directly back to the boatyard on no sleep. Amiable to the end, he handled all this without complaint.

Although these junkets took their toll on Les, they helped keep the Bunnymen name hip. Their cult mystique afforded the band their first and only television appearance as a three-piece: they performed "The Pictures On My Wall" on "What Goes On," a program produced by Factory Records owner Tony Wilson. A snippet of this performance can be seen on 2001's "Meet the Bunnymen" Granada Television special.

But the Bunnymen were not content with mere provincial recognition. On August 15, 1979, they went to London and played their first Peel Session for the BBC, with David Balfe adding texture and depth to the sound on keyboards. The four tracks recorded were spectral, assured versions of "Villiers Terrace," "Ashes to Ashes" (an early version of "Stars are Stars"), "Monkeys," and "Read It in Books."

The absolute classic. This is one of those gems where the group surpassed their reputation even before they had a record out. So new were the Bunnymen that they'd not even got a drummer. Four classic renditions of naive temperamental guitar pop. Five stars. —*Offbeat*, 1988

With Echo chugging away in the background, the Bunnymen deliver four jagged, nervy slices of Merseybeat 1979 style, culminating in the decadent 'Villiers Terrace': a classic Peel Session.
—*Record Collector*, 1988

Zoo intended to follow up the Peel Session by releasing the ominous rumble of "Happy Death Men" as the band's sophomore single. The 7-inch was initially slated for a summer release, and was then pushed back to November. For whatever reasons, it never happened, so the second and final appearance of the three-piece Bunnymen on vinyl was a version of

"Monkeys," the last track on a Liverpool compilation LP called *Street To Street,* on Open Eye Records. Released in September 1979, this version (misspelled "Monkies" on the album's sleeve) was markedly different from the one that eventually emerged on the Bunnymen's debut LP. Minimal, tinny, and monotonous, it was virtually identical to the group's debut performance—albeit about sixteen minutes shorter. And the lyrics would undergo some dramatic rewriting before the definitive version was heard.

It had the line in it 'talking to you about evolution/all you want to do is swing like a monkey,' which I thought was quite good at the time.

　　　　　　　—Ian McCulloch, 1985

KOROVA

In the Fall, the Bunnymen once again traveled to London to play what was only their 10th show. Despite their obvious inexperience, their quirky panache was becoming notorious.

There's something undeniably classy about a band which can absorb so many mentorial influences (Velvets, Doors, Love) and yet regurgitate them in a valid, idiosyncratic way. Echo & the Bunnymen, further enhancing the Liverpudlian legend, do the New Wave proud. They worked through their modest repertoire with systematic self-assurance, McCulloch spitting with laid-back Jim Morrison angst while Will Sergeant and Les Pattinson belt out a rhythm in the best Velvets tradition … [the music] has a stark, haunting quality. Echo gave plenty of credence to the theory that the new Mersey suss is very much the one that is going places.　　　　　—*Sounds*, 1979

The singer looked so charismatic. He was beautiful. His voice had that Jim Morrison ring to it. The songs weren't well-formulated, but you saw 'Star' in neon above his head.　　　—Rob Dickens, WEA, 1997

The star, however, was still a bit suspicious, almost embarrassed about all the attention the fledgling three-piece was attracting.

In the early days, if you played well it was just sheer luck. We won people with charm more than anything else. We were three naive, innocent-looking chumps from Liverpool with a drum machine, and people felt sorry for us.　　　　　—Ian McCulloch, 1981

Despite Mac's doubts about the band, his innate charisma was beginning to work politically in the Bunnymen's favor. Seymour Stein, who ran the hip and influential Sire Records, was particularly impressed with the singer.

Rumour has it he thought I looked great and wanted to shag me, and didn't mind the songs. After that we were signed to Sire/Korova.
                                                                    —Ian McCulloch, 1999

We were supposed to sign to Sire, but they used all their money up on the Undertones, so we got transferred over to Warner Brothers, and they invented this label for us, Korova.   —Will Sergeant, 1998

Stein, and the young managing director of Warner Brothers Music, Rob Dickens, named the new Sire subsidiary Korova after the milk bar Alex and his Droogs frequented in Stanley Kubrick's film *A Clockwork Orange*. Perhaps aware of the Bunnymen's love of the Velvets and the New York Factory scene, Stein made sure that the Korova insignia was an image of one of Warhol's famed silk-screens.

Although a few purist voices grumbled that the Bunnymen were selling out by signing to a major label, it was in fact the correct thing to do. Bill Drummond would stay on as manager, but all involved recognized that Zoo Records didn't have the financial means to help Drummond achieve his goal of turning the Bunnymen into the greatest group in the world.

For a start, Zoo wanted us to [sign with Korova]. If we hadn't signed, we wouldn't be doing this tour and have all these lights and things. Would you criticise a bloke who works for Ford for not making his own car?   —Ian McCulloch, 1980

The Bunnymen were excited about signing to Sire because it made them label-mates with one of their favorite bands, Talking Heads. Plus, their advance checks provided them with the capital to buy some new equipment. Never gearheads, the Bunnymen invested in Fender amplifiers with grilles, not on the basis of their technical strengths, but because they *looked* cool, and were on the inner sleeve of Television's legendary *Marquee Moon* LP.

Will defined the whole Bunnymen ethos. Everything he played was loosely based on [Television's] Tom Verlaine's guitar sound. Everything that approached a rock 'n' roll song, he'd say, 'I hate that. It's corny.' He'd come out with the next 'Satisfaction' riff, and we'd go, 'It's fantastic,' and he'd go, 'It's too catchy. I'm never playing it again.' We'd say, 'Come on, Will, please. It's probably a massive hit.' And he'd go, 'No. I hate it. It's embar-rassing.' He's still a bit like that.   —Ian McCulloch, 2001

Pete Wylie and I used to go to Eric's and he was really into this. I was more into Iggy and the Pistols and I thought *Marquee Moon* was all guitary and solo-y. But a couple of years later I met up with Will Sergeant and it was his favourite album. He played it all the time going to gigs and I finally realised how powerful the sound of guitars could be.   —Ian McCulloch, 1994

The Bunnymen's advance also gave Will the luxury of quitting his day job as a chef—a development that must have relieved discerning Liverpudlian palates.

I tried to cook liver with soap once.   —Will Sergeant, 1984

As the Korova contracts were being drawn up, the national music press had its first taste of interviewing the Bunnymen. Journalists quickly discovered that confronting the band was not going to be a particularly easy task. The trio was extremely insular and verbally economic. Will and Les generally chose not to speak at all, and Mac would often answer questions with monosyllabic, deadpan quips dripping with sarcasm and irony. Sometimes he'd just preen his hairstyle and stare blankly at the interviewer—especially when the journalist addressed him improperly.

A lot of [people] would think I was 'Echo' at the beginning, and we'd say 'no, it's the drum machine,' just to divert the stupid assumption that because I was the singer I must be Echo.   —Ian McCulloch, 1981

Echo or not, the drum machine was on its way out. Both Bill Drummond and Sire insisted that the Minipops be replaced with a live drummer. Although affronted by their first taste of artistic compromise, the Bunnymen reluctantly agreed.

Our manager was saying, 'I really think you should get a drummer, it will bring everything to life.' We were very insular, we always were, and we were saying, 'Can't we just get a more expensive drum machine that does a few more things?'   —Ian McCulloch, 1998

We couldn't find anybody in Liverpool because drummers here are always too old and thick and drunks in the bargain. Will had spent this 80 pounds on a drum machine and we thought we should get the full value out of· that. And it made us really hip for awhile, having a drum machine. People thought it was really DIY. I was still a bit worried

Tom Verlaine was brilliant. I just love the way he sort of wobbled his fingers. That's what I used to try and do. Just dead atmospheric, the whole thing, for rock. None of it's corny. *Marquee Moon* is a definite must for anyone.
—Will Sergeant, 1997

I think a lot of your memories are linked to a particular time ... like *Marquee Moon*, the time it came out was back when we were just starting to get into … music and things.
—Will Sergeant, 1985

I used to play *Marquee Moon* every time before going down to Eric's in the summer. It was just great.
—Les Pattinson, 1985

We were a bit scared of getting someone who might be a real musician when we obviously weren't.   —Ian McCulloch, 1981

Learning with the drum machine gave the three of us a triangular tightness. But Seymour wanted us to get a drummer, and Bill was very aware that all the classic rock groups had drummers.   —Ian McCulloch, 1999

about changing, frightened of what we would gain, that it might make us just another dumb rock & roll band. We were safe with the drum machine, but it was time for a change, we'd got too comfortable.

—Ian McCulloch, *Liverpool Explodes*

ENTER TRIPPO

Pete de Freitas was not a Liverpudlian. He was born in Port of Spain, Trinidad, in 1962, and raised in Goring-on-Thames, a borough in southern England. As the Bunnymen came to terms with the idea of having a human drummer, Pete was attending school with David Balfe's brother. Balfe discovered that Pete had played drums with a short-lived London group.

I had been in a punk band called Rigor Mortis and the Gravediggers. We were as bad as that sounds, believe me.   —Pete de Freitas, 1984

I first came across him when he was sharing a flat with my brother, waiting to go to Oxford University. Bill and I would crash at their flat when we came down to distribute our records to the London shops, and I can remember he had his drum kit set up there and he played an impromptu gig one night for us with some of the other guys in the flat. He impressed me as a drummer right away.   —David Balfe, 1989

Balfe and Bill invited Pete to a Bunnymen gig, so the Bunnymen could check him out, and vice versa. He watched the trio co-headline in London with Joy Division at the Prince of Wales Conference Centre.

I saw them play and thought they were great.   —Pete de Freitas, 1984

He came up and he was very shy and southern. He looked pretty good, but he grew to look great. He just had this natural feeling, and it was kind of different than playing with a drum machine, because at the time he was all over the place. That was because he hadn't played drums for very long. But there was something there, and we decided to go with it, and we never looked back. And I think he was the best drummer easily of those jives, of all time.   —Ian McCulloch, 1998

We didn't know anything about drummers; he was just the first one we saw. We really didn't want to have to go through seeing others.

—Will Sergeant, 1998

Although the other Bunnymen were as impressed with Pete as he was with them—they particularly appreciated his comparison of their sound to The Velvet Underground's—it was obvious to all that they didn't share much in common.

He was definitely the odd man out in the group. They were all working class Liverpool and he was middle class from the South. But he was usually the first person in the band to talk to anyone who came to see them, while the others were taciturn and only spoke when they had something sarcastic to say.

—David Balfe, 1989

He used to be the brunt of the piss-take, but it was an affectionate piss-take. He was called 'Trippo' for a long time, because he'd always trip up. He'd come in, suited up, glass of wine, trip over the first thing, wine all over the suit: Trippo! And Will and Les decided to call him 'Taff' from day one, I can't remember why. I think they thought 'de Freitas' was Welsh. He was kind of an outsider, but Will and Les worshipped him.

—Ian McCulloch, 1999

Despite this slightly awkward match, the Minipops was laid to rest in October, and Pete became a fully fledged Bunnyman. By November the band had officially signed to Korova.

I wanted to be in a band at school and everyone I knew played guitar, and I could play guitar, so I thought 'Well, I'll have to do something else then' so I learned how to play drums. There was no particular drummer that made me think 'Wow! I've got to play drums' or anything, it was just a matter of wanting to be in a band playing something ... so when the Bunnymen decided they wanted a drummer [Balfe and Bill] said 'Well we know someone down in London' and they called me up. I came down and it seemed to work out.

—Pete de Freitas, 1985

The machine had a better sense of humour, and it didn't smoke as much dope either.

—Ian McCulloch, 1981

In early 1980, after a few months of gigs and rehearsals with Pete, the Bunnymen recorded their second Peel Session, which featured "The Pictures on My Wall," a razor-sharp, explosive rocker called "All That Jazz," and the dreamy, atmospheric "Over the Wall." The foursome then entered Rockfield Studios in Wales to record their debut major label single and LP.

"Rescue" was the first song the band wrote as a four-piece. It was recorded live in studio, with just a few overdubs added. The single was produced by Bill Drummond and David Balfe, with the help of former Big In Japan guitarist/future Lightning Seed Ian "Kingbird" Broudie. "Rescue," b/w "Simple Stuff" was released by Korova/Sire on May 5, 1980, Mac's twenty-first birthday, exactly a year after the release of the Bunnymen's only Zoo single.

One of my all-time favourite Bunnysongs. A turning point—possibly our purest pop song. The lyrics were written in bed at my mother's house and I can still connect with them.
—Ian McCulloch, 1992

It's the most personal thing I've written. I was really pleased when I wrote those words because they mean something to me, and they can mean something to anybody. I think they're some of my best lyrics, really. —Ian McCulloch, 1980

It was the first song where I dealt with what was going on in my head, as against what I thought people wanted to hear. It was kind of a cry for help early on: no big drama, but I was feeling fairly sad.
—Ian McCulloch, 1994

RESCUE

If I said I'd lost my way
Would you sympathize?
Could you sympathize?
I'm jumbled up
Maybe I'm losing my touch
I'm jumbled up
Maybe I'm losing my touch
But you know I didn't have it
    anyway

Won't you come on down to my
Won't you come on down to my
Rescue

Things are wrong
Things are going wrong
Can you tell that in a song?
I don't know what I want anymore
First I want a kiss and then I
    want it all

Won't you come on down to my
Won't you come on down to my
Rescue

Things are wrong
Things are going wrong

Can you tell that in a song?
Losing sense of those harder
    things

Is this the blues I'm singing?

Clearly, it was going to be impossible to resist anybody who sang lines like 'I'm jumbled up, maybe I'm losing my touch, but you know I didn't have it anyway.' Dismissive and self-destructive, perhaps, but anybody who could sum up so much doubt in so short a space obviously had their head screwed on. —*Melody Maker*, 1984

Even with simple songs like 'Rescue,' we just have this edge—which is kind of an overused description—but it's got something that is so unique it's threatening. It does surprise people when they see a band like the Bunnymen. It's different, y'know? It's not just 'rock & roll.' —Ian McCulloch, 1997

'Rescue' is sheerly magnificent, a monumental edifice, scaled and conquered with enormous vigour, Will's berserk guitar ravishing the simultaneous grandeur and stateliness of Mac's vocal. —*Melody Maker*, 1984

One girl wrote saying that 'Rescue' was the sexiest song she's ever heard ... [but] the line 'first I wanna kiss and then I want it all' was more metaphorical than 'let's go gung-ho in the hay'; it was more like 'give me an inch and I'll take a soddin' mile.' —Ian McCulloch, 1989

SIMPLE STUFF

We sat all night around a table
Trying to string three words together
Time has come
And by the way, mine's a double
By the way, mine's a double

Lucky for some
We don't understand
Everything we hear
We just pick out the simple stuff

Simple stuff
We don't need all those complications
We're tough stuff
And we've got no intentions

I really hate intellectuals. I like intelligence, just ... common sense thinking. I am fairly intelligent but I never wanna be an intellectual because I think they just waffle on about complicated crap. —Ian McCulloch, 1983

I think that's the most important thing—what [the lyrics] sound like. I like to use simple words in a subtle way ... Sometimes you don't know what it means or what I want it to mean. And I think that's, like, the crucial thing in the words you write and the way you sing them. It takes a lot to sing, or even to say a line convincingly, and I think it is that ability to sound convincing that's important in music. —Ian McCulloch, 1985

The Bunnymen's debut LP, *Crocodiles*, was recorded over the course of three hectic weeks at Rockfield. Will wrote most of the music on the album, while Mac penned the majority of the words—although Will contributed somewhat to the lyrics on the album's epic closer, "Happy Death Men." Like "Rescue," *Crocodiles* was produced by The Chameleons and Ian Broudie—although at one point there was talk of getting Del "Runaway" Shannon in!

The completed album was short—only 35 minutes—partially because of an error on Rob Dickens's part. He had decided that "Read It In Books" and "Do It Clean" should be left on the cutting room floor, due to Mac's alleged cursing on the songs. Mac in fact did not swear on these recordings, although live he'd been known to open "Do It Clean" with "I've got a handful of shit" as opposed to "a handful of this." On "Read It In Books," instead of singing "who wants love without the looks" he'd occasionally smirk "who wants love without the fucks?"

Eventually, Dickens became aware of his error, and the songs were included on the American release of the LP. In the UK, the two tracks were issued as a free single. Nevertheless, this set the precedent for what would prove to be an unremitting struggle between the Bunnymen and record company bureaucracy.

In June, after receiving positive critical response to "Rescue," the Bunnymen embarked on their first national tour, a 12-date sweep of small clubs and colleges that culminated with a sold-out show at London's YMCA.

It was quickly becoming evident that the Bunnymen were not going to be just a minor flash in the pan, so Drummond expanded the Zoo Management Team to accommodate what he hoped was immanent world domination. Harry de Mac was hired as the Bunnymen's soundman, and Bill Butt, an old art school friend of Drummond's, was taken on as lighting engineer, with Kit Edwards as his assistant. Butt was acquainted with an out-of-work actor named Jake Brockman, who became the band's roadie. At the Zoo offices, Pam Young was hired to answer the phones and provide administrative assistance. Echo & the Bunnymen now meant business.

For the sleeve art of *Crocodiles*, the Bunnymen traveled to the Rickmansworth Woods with photographer Brian Griffin. He snapped a series of photos of the band in poses that reflected the themes of introspection, despair, and confusion that seeped from the album. To accentuate a sense of drama, the Bunnymen wanted to set fire to some stakes in the ground, but, after deciding that this would be 'a bit too Ku Klux Klan,' they settled for some atmospheric lighting for the moodily evocative sessions.

At forefront, Mac is slumped against a tree wearing a hound's-tooth overcoat that he had borrowed and never returned to Mark E. Smith, the leader of The Fall, one of Mac and Will's favorite groups. This image would eventually spawn a cult Bunnymen army of spikey-haired youths burrowed morosely in long Oxfam outerwear. Mac recalls his initial reason for adopting the famed overcoat look.

I used to look at myself in shop windows, and I had this 'orrible spazzy walk—more of a lope, really. I got this two-tone coat from me dad's wardrobe. I found that in a long coat I could cover up the walk and, well, swing better. I remember seeing *The Man Who Fell to Earth*. Bowie had this great oversized coat—one of the best looks in film. I even tried to get my hair cut like that for a while.
—Ian McCulloch, 1996

In addition to whatever fashion trends it might have inadvertently created among the UK's disenfranchised youth, the album cover deeply impressed both the Bunnymen and Bill Drummond.

I was sitting on the battered sofa in the Zoo office ... a copy of the *Crocodiles* sleeve on the floor, front side up. From where I was sitting, the photograph on the front was foreshortened. I imagined I could see something in the picture that I hadn't noticed before. The picture depicted the four members of the band all looking aimlessly in different directions. Les, the most central figure, was leaning against the trunk of an ash tree. The tree must have been coppiced at some time, because it had two primary trunks that had grown to twist gently around each other. I went out into the street with the sleeve of the record and asked a passer-by if she would look at this album sleeve from a certain angle. What did the ash tree in the middle look like? 'The head of a spooky rabbit.' She confirmed my suspicions ... I spent most of the day looking at this weird apparition, kinda hoping it was a mistake but knowing this was the real Echo making his presence known on the sleeve.
—Bill Drummond, *From the Shores of Lake Placid and Other Stories*

To me, the cover of *Crocodiles* is better to look at than the Mona Lisa. —Ian McCulloch, 1984

★★★

The album was released on July 18th 1980, and was greeted with almost ridiculously ecstatic reviews. To this day, it's still spoken of with awestruck reverence.

Compulsive listening for anyone who ever found the dark at all fascinating, who ever felt unexpressed energy in their soul, or whoever can accept and enjoy the power of mystery without feeling obliged to analyse it. This is a very good album and a great start.

—*The Face,* 1980

A moody, mysterious, fascinating record. The cover art suggests four boys dazed and confused in a drugged dream, a surreal where-are-we landscape. The Bunnymen's images are of loneliness, disconnection, a world gone awry. But *Crocodiles* isn't doom and gloom music. The best songs are spirited, catchy, and rock hard. The Bunnymen have things to say about the rather gray world they live in, and though their tone is often pessimistic, it's also very soulful.

—*Creem,* 1980

Crocodiles was a gorgeous post-punk blast of star-flung angst which was as perfect for its time as *Sergeant Peppers* ... or *Nevermind.*

—*Stylus,* 1999

The transformation of Echo & the Bunnymen from the appealing but erratic beatniks of a year ago to the dynamic modern rock group of today has been little short of remarkable. If 'Rescue' hinted broadly at the shift that had taken place, then *Crocodiles* ... confirms it in the most gratifying manner. There truly is a different kind of tension at work now. Together, [the Bunnymen] have a great sense of rock dynamics ... [they] betray a host of influences throughout the album. There are shades of both Jim Morrison and Iggy Pop in McCulloch's voice, shreds of Wilko Johnson in the vicious crosscut riffing of Sergeant on the title track (or is that you, Andy Gill?), and definite aspects of Talking Heads in 'Rescue.' But this crocodile is no imitation skin, and the whole is far greater than the sum of the various inputs. McCulloch's lyrical landscape is scattered with themes of sorrow, horror, and despair, themes that are reinforced by stormy animal/sexual imagery. But the message filtering through the darkness is primarily one of hope ... *Crocodiles* is destined to be one of the contemporary rock records of the year.   —*NME,* 1980

All of the trademarks of Bunnyism were present and accounted for. Mac and Will's guitars scrubbed and chimed like the Velvets or Television, Les and Pete had already developed a persuasive line in tension and release, and overhead, Mac's mordant, nagging vocals and itchily cryptic words sealed the entire package with a frission of terror and a sly grin. The album's apparent preoccupations—death, doubt, drug-addled dementia and a fixation with non-domestic animals—rapidly hoisted the Bunnymen into a position of some preeminence in a landscape littered with Two-Tone and prosaic power pop. The Bunnymen credited listeners with imagination and the capacity for awe, and what's more they wore long macs. This was the stuff of myth.

—*Melody Maker,* 1984

Where were the Bunnymen at? (We know where they came from.) Heads in the clouds, feet on the ground, brain in their pockets? They certainly didn't flog their quirky Liverpudlian sense of humour in clearly marked cans. The word 'Bunnymen' hardly conjures up dark, brooding imagery, but the band did. *Crocodiles* was the debut LP of a band who might've been the first post-punk hippies—a rather shocking amalgam of velvet undergroundness, bedroom politics, drug density and Mersey fun; a band with a silly name and animal crackers in their soup; acid highs and hangover lows, and that all pervasive PROMISE. I have revisited 'Villiers Terrace' (and the rest) and if I once thought no one got out of there alive, I was very much mistaken. I can still feel, in my aging bones, the urgency and agitation inherent in *Crocodiles*. Okay, so the Bunnymen are sons of Morrison and Reed, but NOT in the same way that The Mighty Lemon Drops are now a byproduct of The Bunnymen. We're talking about a tightened-up, refined homage, rather than a sloppy pastiche. *Crocodiles* [is] a taut, frightening expulsion of frenetic energy and cathartic juices; a discipline and cumulative end-product of frustrated wit and wisdom and defused hero-worship. (10 out of 10). —*NME*, 1990

Still, to this day, one of the most classic debut LP's of our time. —*International Music Publications*, 1997

Crocodiles benefits from a terse simplicity ... 10 spikey whirls of mangled, spectral pop. Dominated by Mac's youthfully dazed despair and Will's chilly guitar lines, it's more like the freshly risen ghost of Ian Curtis twisting with The Fall…almost every track is a dark little jewel. Monstrously confident happy death pop, to be played at night. —*Record Mirror*, 1987

CROCODILES

GOING UP

Ain't thou watching my film
Analyzing me
Rusty chalk-dust walker
Checking up to see
If we should pull the plugs out
On all history
And all the mystery, yeah
Of things that shouldn't be
Things that couldn't be, no
Things that had to be
Don't you see?
Don't you see?
It's going up, up, up
It's going up
It's going up, up, up
It's going up

Let's get the hell out of here
Let's get the hell out of here
Going up
Going down

D'ya wanna know what's wrong with
    the world?
Everywhere there's people with no
    flowers in their hair

'Going Up' is the band's uncontrollable, pounding heartbeat; its dreamily ecstatic opening, building and shuddering forward to a glowing declaration of magnificence, flooding ... with glorious, matchless sound … who dares quarrel with this? —*Sounds*, 1983

'Going Up' epitomises Bunnymen music, full of space, atmospherics and echo. —*Musicians Only*, 1980

In the first song of the first album, I sang 'Do you wanna know what's wrong with the world?' Brilliant! And I still know what's wrong with the world—too many dickheads.

—Ian McCulloch, 1989

The first line in 'Going Up': 'Ain't thou watching my film?' I had this feeling everyone was soddin' filming me, way before the Truman thing (*The Truman Show*). So I'm walking 'round town checking out me walk. Get the coat ... all of a sudden it is a film and I'm in it.

—Ian McCulloch, 1999

I like it when [Mac] gets a bit spacey. Like 'rusty chalk-dust walker' on 'Going Up.' I don't know what the hell it means, but I like the sound of it.

—Will Sergeant, 1995

It's about having and keeping your integrity; 'do it honestly' —Ian McCulloch, 1995

You shouldn't be afraid of being what you are. To see things for what they are.

—Ian McCulloch, 1983

The band's attitude, which their overseers have found both enchanting and infuriating, is that failure and success are not what matters, it's your dignity that counts. Your panache. —*Mojo,* 1997

'Going Up,' the first track, seeps into the world like a disease. Something wicked this way comes ... [it] is as representative a Bunnymen bash as any other, built, as it is, around a stabbing drum idea and nodding bass that's peppered with the unmistakable guitar stitching of Will Sergeant. Meanwhile, in the margin, are scrawled the somewhat idle thoughts of Ian 'Mac' McCulloch. If stars are, indeed, stars, then Mac was conceived with shades on. —*NME,* 1990

I do have answers, but they're always vague and obscure. 'Do you wanna know what's wrong with this world? Everywhere there's people with no flowers in their hair.' That is what's wrong with the world—there's not enough people who...not that aren't hippies, but that haven't got an attitude that will allow themselves to communicate, because they think all that communication in the sixties was false. I think the idea of true communication is what's missing—y'know, stripping all the crap down, all the waffle. So there is an answer, but it's a fairly intangible thing, and that's why a lot of my lyrics are fairly intangible. I think the more you go on about precise things or events, it gets in the way of what is behind it all, which, in the end, you can't talk about in a specific way. —Ian McCulloch, 1983

DO IT CLEAN

I've got a handful of this
What do I do with it?
I've got a barrel of this
What do I do with it?
I do it clean
I do it clean

Hey, do it clean
Do it clean, know what I mean
Do it clean
Do it clean, I know what I mean
I mean ...

Where am I going?
Where have I been?
Where are you going?
Where have you been?
I've been here

I've been there
I've been here, there, everywhere
Here, there, nowhere
Itzy bitzy witzy witzy everywhere
I've been here and I've been there
I've been ...

I had a handful of this
What did I do with it?
I had a barrel of this
What did I do with it?
I did it clean
I did it clean

Hey do it clean
Do it clean, know what I mean
Do it clean
Do it clean, I know what I mean

In America, 'Do it Clean' was *the* song. It was great live. I remember Will came up with that opening riff, and he played it down the phone to me. It was the song that took me down a certain road as a performer. I learned to be a frontman on that song. It's where I started to become Jimbo or Iggy. It's the song that proved where all else failed that we knew how to rock. It aligned us with that great ancestry of bands like the Stones and The Who.   —Ian McCulloch, 2001

I have a pride in honesty, simply because I always believe that I'm doing this for the right reasons and with all the right motives. There has always been that morality in the Bunnymen, recognizing the difference between 'right' and 'wrong.'   —Ian McCulloch, 1983

I think it's important, the stuff we do in music, and I'd like to do it with dignity instead of just throwing the stuff out there.
—Ian McCulloch, 1999

The Bunnymen defined themselves almost as much by their actions as their music ... they always had a wit and sense of honor that stopped them pursing the crass or the simply obvious.
—Q, 2001

STARS ARE STARS

The sky seems full when you're in
    the cradle
The rain will fall and wash
    your dreams
Stars are stars and they shine
    so hard

Now you spit out the sky because
    it's empty and hollow
All your dreams are hanging out
    to dry
Stars are stars and they shine
    so cold

I saw you climb
Shadows on the trees
We lost some time
After things that never matter

I caught that falling star
It cut my hands to pieces
Where did I put that box?
It had my name in it

I saw you climb
Shadows on the trees
We lost some time
After things that never matter

The cogs have clicked and
The clocks will have their say
In the making of a day
You came here late
Go home early
Who'll remember?
Now you've gone away
Gone away
Gone away

'Stars Are Stars' was great. Fantastic words. Nobody was doing anything like that at the time. Anywhere.
—Ian McCulloch, 2001

A pivotal encapsulation of doom, youth, and melancholia
—Uncut, 1999

An obscure dirge salvaged only by a few crisp minor chords
—NME, 1980

I don't believe that sad songs have to naturally be 'depressive' or 'depressing.' Sadness can be treated in a song and the song can still be uplifting.
—Ian McCulloch, 1983

'Pride' is a disposable collection of parental hopes and fears.   —*NME*, 1980

There's real life, real emotion ... the interfamily trouble that Mac's talking about on 'Pride' is almost too close to the bone for comfort.
        —*Sounds*, 1980

[My parents] thought I should get an ordinary job; and the laughing got louder as I got older. I know they never laughed out loud, but to themselves.   —Ian McCulloch, 1980

Like Lou Reed said, 'Things are never good/things go from bad to weird.' I used to get annoyed with the human race—like a tribe of monkeys. There are only five things you ever really think about ... and now I can only remember three of them! Sex, religion, security. That's what the apes think about. I used to worry about that, but now I think there must be a reason why these things are so dominating. It's just getting an equation that makes it all make sense. Having a baby has done that for me.
        —Ian McCulloch, 1987

PRIDE

Mother says
Sister says
D'ya mind if I laugh at you?
D'ya mind if I sing with you?
Daddy says
Brother says
Make us proud of you
Do something we can't do
Do it

John waits
Barry hates
They think I'm headed for a fall
They hope I'm headed for a fall
Peter says
Julie says

I think it's time you
    stop stalling
We think it's time you
    start falling
Fall

MONKEYS

I bagsy yours
If you bagsy mine
I'll take a chance
If you'll take the blame
Forget it
Forget it

Keymon-keymon

Boys are the same
Brains in their pocket
Girls are the same
Knock it and rock it
Remember
Remember

Keymon-keymon

I'm not a holy man
I'm too lowly for that
I'm not a praying man
I'm not ready for that

Keymon-keymon

I don't know why the term 'human race' was invented so soon. There really aren't that many 'human beings' knocking around. That's why I wrote 'Monkeys,' which is about the limitations of people who don't begin to see, yet are still arrogant enough to believe that they're well-formed humans. So many people seem underdeveloped to me, not yet human and never likely to be. You should be contributing to the progress of the human race, rather than staying the same as it's been for the last 5,000 years. Yet it seems that nothing's changed, we don't seem to develop. If this is the way the world's meant to be, it's disappointing. With all this potential … we all settle for routines that don't make sense, like sitting in pubs, or riding around in buses, or going to school. People accept these routines as the obvious way to live, but to me they're disappointing, they don't really make sense. If this is how the world's meant to be, it's probably the simplest thing in the world to understand, but the fact is, I don't.

—Ian McCulloch, *Liverpool Explodes*

'Monkeys' is about when Les told me about some monkey that he used to have. It's about the relationship between Les and his monkey. They were very close.

—Ian McCulloch, 1980

CROCODILES

I read it in a magazine
I don't wanna see it again
I threw away the magazine
And looked for someone to explain

I don't wanna look back
I can't look 'round
I don't wanna see it
    coming 'round

Listen to the ups and downs
Listen to the sound they make
Don't be scared when it gets loud
When your skin begins to shake

'Cos you don't wanna look back
You gotta look tall
Gotta see us creeps crawl

I know you know
I know you know

Well I can see you've got
    the blues
In your alligator shoes
Me I'm all smiles
I've got my crocodiles

I don't wanna look back
I can't turn 'round
I don't wanna see it coming down

Met someone just the other day
He said wait until tomorrow
I said hey, whatcha doing today?
He said I'm gonna do it tomorrow

In Liverpool, as elsewhere, it's easier to dream than to do. You can sit around in the tea rooms with your friends and spend your days gossiping and dreaming. If you try to put your dreams into action, chances are you'll be slagged off for trying, so why bother? Bands come and go, and most of them never leave Liverpool. A good idea gets you through the day, it's not meant to take you anywhere, and outside Liverpool there's always the possibility of failure.

—Mark Cooper, *Liverpool Explodes*

Although I wanted to be in a serious group, at the time it was all punk and everything had to be serious social comment. I just wrote one-liner jokes.

—Ian McCulloch, *Liverpool Explodes*

Originally, it wasn't about drugs or parties, except maybe a party of people. There are other kinds of parties. It was political at first. It's about a group of individuals being into depravity and not knowing, or not appreciating, the consequences. In that way, it can apply to loads of things—bevvy, Moroccan, acid—all kinds of things. And politics as well. Villiers Terrace isn't a place, it's a state of mind. And it's one some of us have been in.

—Ian McCulloch, 1980

I was 19 when I wrote that, a kid…it was about Adolf Hitler. That was an idea I got from my brother, as many were on *Crocodiles*. He actually coined the term 'Villiers Terrace.' 'I've been up to Villiers Terrace/I've been in a daze for days/I drank some of the medicine/And I didn't like the taste.' I had nicked it slightly from Dylan, but it was actually about Hitler throwing a wobbler and chewing the carpet, although the song obviously hinted at drugs. Hitler had this meeting with all these Heads of State and he'd had to make a compromise on his position, which he wasn't happy about. He was so cheesed off that he had a fit and started biting the carpet. That's what my brother told me, and I built it around that, although I think I prefer the interpretation that it is about being off your cake on drugs.

—Ian McCulloch, 1994

VILLIERS TERRACE

I've been up to Villiers Terrace
To see what's-a-happenin'
There's people rolling 'round on the carpet
Mixing up the medicine
I've been up to Villiers Terrace
I saw what's-a-happenin'
People rolling 'round on the carpet
Biting wool and pulling string
You said people rolled on carpet
But I never thought they'd do those things

I've been up to Villiers Terrace
I've been in a daze for days
I drank some of the medicine
And I didn't like the taste
I've been up to Villiers Terrace
I've been in a daze for days
People rolling 'round on your carpet
Biting wool and pulling string
You said people rolled on carpet
But I never thought they'd do those things

Been up to Villiers Terrace
To see what's-a-happenin'
There's people rolling 'round on the carpet
Passing 'round the medicine
Been up to Villiers Terrace
I saw what's-a-happenin'
People rolling 'round on my carpet
Biting wool and pulling string
You said people rolled on carpet, boys
But I never thought they'd do those things

Bop-showaddywaddy shake your money
(Been down to Villiers Terrace)
Bop-showaddywaddy Sheik Yamani
(Been down to Villiers Terrace)
Bop-showaddywaddy Hailie Sellasie
(Been down to Villiers Terrace)
Hailie Sellasie
Who the hell's he?
He's the one, two, three, four
Absolute absolution

A wired descent into a bad-acid basement. *—Melody Maker*, 1997

I can't think of anything less interesting than someone rattling on about a trip. 'Villiers Terrace' wasn't an anti-drug song because I'm not necessarily anti-drugs. But I'm against the abuse of drugs, and the scummy people making money off it. *—Ian McCulloch*, 1984

The stand-out. Lyrically, a typical Kafkaesque nightmare come real, it has transcendent pace and flow, could be a hit single, and, if it is, should be the most bizarre and wonderful lyric that the charts have seen in a very long time. *—Sounds*, 1980

The McCulloch style of wordplay seems to operate more like a transcendental Simon Le Bon approach: 'if it sounds good, use it.' 'A Kafka?' said Mac once, 'Isn't that something you wear?' *—Record Mirror*, 1987

'Villiers Terrace' use to go on for about ten minutes just 'cos we liked playing the riff. *—Ian McCulloch*, 1983

A lot of the ad-libs that I'd done at the end of 'Villiers Terrace' became other songs. It's good to ad-lib even if you come up with a pile of crap 99 percent of the time, because you might get a song out of the other one percent. *—Ian McCulloch*, 1981

And no, there isn't a Villiers Terrace in Liverpool. *—Liverpool Hoopla*, 1999

READ IT IN BOOKS

You said you couldn't find anyone
    to love ya
I said there's more to life than
    a broken heart
Did it console ya?

I've seen it in your eyes
And I've read it in books
Who wants love
Without the looks?

You know the word is please
You say it from your knees
Show some respect
Hey baby, genuflect

Once I like crying, twice I like
    laughter
Come on tell me what I'm after

I said you gotta stop chasing
    rainbows
You said I'm just staying up

And anyway I like it when the
    rain goes

I've seen it in your eyes
I've read it in books
Who wants love
Without the looks?

Once I like crying, twice I like
    laughter
Come on tell me what I'm after

There's not that much to us
I hide the little with the lot
You still expect a loving fuss
After showing all you've got

I've seen it in your eyes
I've read it in books
Who wants love
Without the looks?

That's all

I don't read books or anything. Y'know 'I've seen it in your eyes and I've read it in books, who want love without the looks?'—that was like a key to how I write lyrics. *—Ian McCulloch*, 1983

'Read It In Books'—it's half a cliché. A well-known line. 'I've seen it in your eyes'—that's another cliché. It's the way you stick them together. I'm the best putter-together in rock music. Just now. I don't know about ever. Nah, Dylan was sometimes good. *—Ian McCulloch*, 1981

You point out the bad in order to realize the good. If you see the shit and you point out that it's there, the logical step then is to get rid of it. I know I keep sounding like I'm God's gift to humanity when I know I'm exactly the same as everyone, the only difference is I *know* I am, whereas a lot of other people don't.
—Ian McCulloch, *Liverpool Explodes*

It's obvious what's crap and what's good. Some people choose to focus on the good, but we've focused on a lot of the impurities.   —Ian McCulloch, 1984

'All That Jazz' was aimed at potential fascists and left-wingers—that flock of sheep out there that are led through their lives. 'See you at the barricades, babe' was a bit of a rip-off of 'slip out the back, Jack.' It was a fanciful way of saying something slightly heavy.   —Ian McCulloch, 1987

… employs to devastating effect the same relentless rhythmic thrash that drove PIL's 'Annalisa' and Magazine's 'The Light Pours Out of Me.'
—*NME,* 1980

… a nuclear war soundtracked by Television. *—Melody Maker,* 1997

THE PICTURES ON MY WALL

Can you hear it?
The sound of something burning
Something changing
On the merry-go-round tonight

The pictures on my wall
Are about to swing and fall
Love it all
Love it all

Ooh, we should have
Should have got it right
Ooh, we should have
Should have got it right tonight

People come, I count everyone
Faces burning
Hearts beating
Nowhere left for us to run

The pictures on my wall
Are about to swing and fall
Love it all
Love it all

Ooh, we should have
Should have got it right
Ooh, we should have
Should have got it right tonight

Can you hear it?
The sound of someone thinking
Someone thinking
On the merry-go-round tonight

The pictures on my wall
Are about to swing and fall
Love it all
Don't you just love it
All

ALL THAT JAZZ

Where the hell have you been?
We've been waiting with our best
   suits on
Hair slicked back and all
   that jazz
Rolling down the Union Jack

See you at the barricades, babe
See you when the lights go low,
   Joe
Hear you when the wheels turn
   'round
Someday when the sky turns black

It appeals because it's what
   I feel
I know I don't understand
If you ask you know I don't mind
   kneeling

But when my knees hurt I like
   to stand
Instinct is the common law, y'all
A million years won't erase
Strike that chord I'm searching for
Call it a committed race

No matter how I shake my fist
I know I can't resist it
No matter how you shake your fist
You know you can't resist it

See you at the barricades, babe
See you when the lights go low,
   Joe
Hear you when the wheels turn
   'round
Someday when the sky turns black

Happy death men stand in lines
Happy death men
Happy death men polish and shine
Happy death men

Happy death men
The last breath men
Happy death men
Take 'em to your heart
Happy death men
No regret men
Happy death men
Like to keep things dark

Happy death men stand in lines
Happy death men
Happy death men polish and shine
Happy death men

Happy death men
The last breath men
Happy death men
Take 'em to your heart
Happy death men
No regret men
Happy death men
Like to keep things dark
Okay
Here we go ...

★★★

Although *Crocodiles* rose as high as #17 in the UK charts, the Bunnymen were still very much a cult band, one that was discussed and dissected with a rare intensity. One focus of debate was Mac's lyrics, which were both lauded for their ability to evoke emotion and atmosphere, and criticized for being doomy and obscure. Although Mac has recognized a few lyrical faults on *Crocodiles*, he has steadfastly defended the dark silhouettes that his words cast on 1980's flamboyant pop circus.

I'd scrutinize every line. And I like almost every line on that album. It wasn't thought out or anything; it's just the way it came out. I'm never really pessimistic about me, just about seeing things…like people…in a funny light.   —Ian McCulloch, 1981

It's weird, because although [*Crocodiles* has] got that elusive dream-like thing, and it sounds like its based on big-scale things, a lot of it's based on me going walking in the streets and seeing things— seeing people and that. It's basically about my regard of people in general, a lot of it's specific people. I haven't got that much regard

I saw an advert for the army in the TV Times; this fella at a passing-out parade—y'know, 'Happy Death Men.' He probably got his knees blown off the next day. —Will Sergeant, 1979

… a rambling closer which goes nowhere   —*NME*, 1980

… bizarre, unworldly, and faintly disturbing
—*Musicians Only*, 1980

Crocodiles still stands up, I think, though there's a few things on there, like 'Happy Death Men,' where I never had a clue why I was singing it in the first place.
—Ian McCulloch, 2001

Crocodiles is not a concept album, but it's got that feel. It's a sort of semi-concept album. There are themes that link through each track. It's not a contrived sort of doominess. If it's contrived, people are able to give clear explanations and definitions about what they're doing. But we don't totally understand it ourselves, what we're getting at. Like, it's hard to describe what each track's about, because the album's a whole thing, a complete thing.
—Ian McCulloch, 1984

I just think because we're a more intelligent form of rock, people assume it's impenetrable or something, and it's not. It's not my fault if the majority of people are thick.
—Ian McCulloch, 1984

... I couldn't say 'Johnny is a ... slob!' It just comes out more vague than that.   —Ian McCulloch, 1980

I've never written a happy lyric. It's just that you can write better poetry when it's dark and it's not happy—not that it's poetry. But all me favourite stuff is not happy stuff. I like listening to lyrics meself when I'm not sure how to take them. I like Bowie, I like Leonard Cohen, Lou Reed, Iggy Pop (sometimes), Subway Sect, The Fall—they're brilliant. I can't think of a happy song I like, actually ... There's always a sense of humour in my lyrics, but it's not like happy, it's ironic.   —Ian McCulloch, 1980

In a few interviews shortly after the release of *Crocodiles*, Mac and Will attempted to encapsulate the intentions behind the album, and their music in general.

We are one band that can kind of—not educate people, but steer people toward intelligent music. It's what I dreamt about, to be the most intelligent band. Not intelligent-brainy, like Brian Eno, but just a band who make music full of feelings, having every emotion you can think of. We just want to be the best. Just so we know we're not wasting our time. It's hard to define what being the best is.
—Ian McCulloch, 1980

What we're about is making people feel. Maybe to think, but definitely to feel.   —Will Sergeant, 1980

It's got to be honest, you've got to be yourself and write music that gives you goose pimples down your back.   —Ian McCulloch, 1980

It's the fall of man in three easy lessons.   —Ian McCulloch, 1980

Generally, however, the Bunnymen were not so forthcoming to the press. In a hysterical piece for *The Face* in 1980, Mac out-Mitchumed Mitchum by staring blankly at a light bulb in a hotel ceiling, and, between yawns, languidly instructed the hapless writer to "form your own opinions; make it up." Will's contribution to the article was hiding behind a *Star Trek* magazine and refusing to acknowledge that an interview was even occurring.

The Bunnymen's attitude toward journalists turned downright defiant when the press attempted to pigeonhole the band as being on the vanguard of what was dubbed "The New Psychedelia."

Pete: "We're echoed up country and western music, really."
Mac: "Les said we were just 80's music."
Will: "What are we going to be in 1990?"
Pete: "90's music."
Will: "Infinite music."
—*Sounds*, 1981

Whoever the turd was who said that, they should chop his head off! It only takes one person to say it. Somebody could say we were 'wall-to-wall music' and everyone would start saying that. Nobody knows what it means. It doesn't mean anything, 'psychedelic.' Now if rock critics could learn to be as original as we are…   —Ian McCulloch, 1981

You've gotta laugh about these labels sometimes. We've been called wacky, post-modernist, Neil Young, electric folk, bleak industrial.

We're just fish and chip holders, really.   —Will Sergeant, 1980

I don't like psychedelic music.   —Ian McCulloch, 1984

Despite Mac's dislike of psychedelia, he expressed an appreciation for the 60's countercultural revolution, even a moral kinship.

Something happened in the sixties that, if it hadn't been surrounded by all that metaphysical drug crap, something could have changed, y'know? It's a pity that it's shunned by a lot of people, even people who are supposedly intelligent, like the rock press. It was important in that it could have actually done something, and I think it's sad that people try to make me feel embarrassed or guilty about not being part of something that doesn't align itself to anything that matters.   —Ian McCulloch, 1984

Because of their wacky name, the surreal atmospheres on *Crocodiles*, and the druggy album art, the Bunnymen also endured suggestions that they themselves used drugs—namely psychedelics—to inspire them. This they denied as well. Although drink and other consumables would play a role in the future of the group, at this point, their chemical innocence was on a par with the naiveté with which they created music.

Crocodiles was the most 'druggy' album the Bunnymen did and it was done totally straight, a few pints in Monmouth. —Ian McCulloch, 1994

People say, 'What drugs do you take?' and when I tell them I don't they say, 'Aw, come on'—they think I'm joking. Mostly we just go for the occasional bevvy.   —Ian McCulloch, 1980

The music and lyrics aren't at all drug-related; just symbolic, metaphysical. These days, anybody who's got any imagination is thought to be off his head.   —Ian McCulloch, 1984

In another attempt at pigeonholing, some critics accused the Bunnymen of being little more than a thinly disguised homage to The Doors.

The similarities are mainly on the surface. I have that kind of deepish voice and intonation that might be similar to Morrison's. But lyrically, it's quite different. He was the back door man, always having his fires lit. He wrote more about the groin. I'm more cerebral.   —Ian McCulloch, 1984

Will: "I'm goin' electronic disco."
Les: "I'm goin' folk. The next album's gonna be electronic-disco-folk."
Pete: "I'm going ska."
    —*The Bristol Recorder*, 1980

Mac: "It wasn't so much psychedelic drugs. A lot of bevvy, a lot of drink. When we made the records it was all pretty straight, wasn't it?"
Will: "Yeah. You can't make records when you're tripping."
Mac: "The Rolling Stones did it."
Will: "Yeah, the Stones did when they did *Their Satanic Majesties Request*, but The Beatles were all pretty much all right when they did *Sgt. Pepper's Lonely Hearts Club Band*—they must have been. It plays too well. If you listen to the Stones one, it's a bit all over the place, isn't it? It's a bit like you think it's a good idea and you play it later and it's a bit fucked. So we followed The Beatles' example and didn't while we recorded." —*Rolling Stone Raves*, 1995

I don't think we sound like them. Maybe 'Rescue' because it's got that bluesy bass line
  —Ian McCulloch, 1980

When *Crocodiles* came out, everybody said it was like The Doors. I said, 'What do they know? We're nothing like The Doors.' And then I got to like them, so I put 'Light My Fire' in [extended versions of 'Crocodiles'] as soon as we stopped getting compared to them. It's serious, but it's also very tongue-in-cheek.
  —Ian McCulloch, 1983

Jim Morrison never got blanded out—he was the pure rock star. I don't think I could've been like that. I can be naughty in snatches, but he was just *it*, wasn't he? He knew how to stand ... perfect timing ... I'm sure he looked in the mirror a few times.   —Ian McCulloch, 1984

I don't think there are any honest comparisons. The only real likeness I can see is Mac's voice, and I don't even really see that. Keyboards featured very strongly with The Doors, but not with us.
  —Pete de Freitas, 1980

I honestly prefer Abba to The Doors.   —Ian McCulloch, 1984

Although Mac may prefer the glacial pop of Sweden's sweetest to the brooding Brechtian psycho-circus of The Doors, he still professes an admiration of lead singer Jim Morrison.

Jim is probably the best-looking. If rock & roll hadn't existed and someone had explained what rock 'n' roll might be, and you had to draw the picture of the Rock God, it would be him. He wore leather keks like no one has ever worn, and had a great voice. He was in between being clever and stupid, and that was kind of good, because the contrast was what made him fascinating. They thought he was a poet. His poetry was shit, but he was a great rock & roll catchphrase writer, simple lyricist ... he symbolizes rock god-ism. —Ian McCulloch, 1995

Wylie used to play me 'Celebration Of the Lizard' and I'd think, 'What's this 98-minute song with all this crap poetry?' I never really got into the Jim-is-a-poet stuff but I think Morrison was the most complete rock & roll star ever. They were so accessible but so scary with it. Did I ever wear leather trousers? No, if you do you're just a poor man's Jim Morrison. I did try some plassy ones once, but they didn't suit me.
  —Ian McCulloch, 1994

THE PUPPET

Despite the annoyance of journalistic misconceptions, the Bunnymen refused to be hindered. September 14, 1980 saw the release of the band's second major label single, "The Puppet," b/w "Do It Clean." Initially, Warner Brothers intended to release "Villiers Terrace," an obvious choice, but the Bunnymen disagreed, arguing that another single from *Crocodiles* would have "milked" the album excessively.

  It was an unfortunate decision. "The Puppet" only rose to #91 in the UK charts, and, although the song was catchy enough, it lacked the tension and dark textures that made *Crocodiles* such compelling listening. None of the band—not even Mac—particularly liked the single.

Wasn't my fault—I hated 'The Puppet.'   —Ian McCulloch, 1999

THE PUPPET

I practice my fall
For practice makes perfect
Chained to the wall
For maximum hold
The window too far
Too far from my legs
Oh, open the door
And let out the cold

You knew about this
With your head in your hands
All along
I was the puppet
I was the puppet

Trampoline's broken
Ceiling has come down
The ache in my back
Tells me something's gone wrong
Rocking horse rocks
As the wallpaper peels
Curtain would like to know
What he has done

You knew about this
With your head in your hands
All along
I was the puppet
I was the puppet

We're the salt of the earth
And we know what to say
We're the salt of the earth
We know our place

You knew about this
With your head in your hands
All along
I was the puppet
I was the puppet

I never thought it was the greatest thing we ever recorded. I like that opening line, but some of the lyrics are a bit cringe-city. I like 'We are the salt of the earth/And we know what to say/We are the salt of the earth/And we know our place' because with that verse it's a little diverse. It was the element of working class with 'We're the salt of the earth, and we know what to say,' but at the same time '…we know our place.' It's like we can never aspire to anything beyond this because we've got all this bigotry that's involved with being working class; you can't like this, you can't like that. You can't like fellas in ballet tights.
          —Ian McCulloch, 1985

Most people see 'The Puppet' as the Bunnymen's weakest single, bar none.   —*Goldmine,* 1998

Cloaked in the familiar old overcoats, the Bunnymen shuffle out for the second time onto the singles page. 'Rescue' stands alone amongst the year's rock records, but it was a song about nothing while this proclaims their refusal to carry anybody's cross. It lacks versatility, but it does have intensity of a peculiar brooding kind. Something will have to happen to draw them out. They need a good fight—it's no use being angry in a corner.
—*NME*, 1980

CAMO

By not being the most visually exciting outfit in existence (fact is, they have always looked painfully dull), Echo & the Bunnymen often, if not always, had trouble attracting the semi-interested observer ...the inaccessibility of their stage presence detracted from the potentially imposing music.
—*NME*, 1980

The Bunnymen pressed on. On November 12, the Bunnyvan barreled back down to London, where the band performed their third Peel Session. At this point, they were writing prolifically, almost effortlessly. The panoramic grandeur of "Heaven Up Here," "Zimbo," "Turquoise Days," and "That Golden Smile" (an early version of "Show of Strength"), although embryonic, indicated just how far they'd traveled from the more linear, conventional song styles of the *Crocodiles* material. The Bunnymen weren't so much hopping as confidently *vaulting* into previously uncharted regions of rock.

But the furor and dynamic intensity of the new Bunnysongs hadn't yet translated into the live show, which remained a little anonymous and lackluster. During the 12-date UK tour just before *Crocodiles'* release, the shortcomings of the concerts were all too obvious. The Bunnymen's technical naiveté still bordered on the verge of incompetence, and their inexperienced nerves were so rattled that, according to Mac, it resulted in a "no-go ankle situation"; to wit: they barely moved at all onstage. (Even now, it's not uncommon to see a Bunnymen gig where Will stands immobile and statue-like for the majority of the show.) Indeed, beyond Mac's androgynous good looks, the band's stage presence was little more than four shy, vaguely ragged-looking youths standing like frozen rabbits caught in the beams of a particularly terrifying pair of oncoming headlights.

Simply, Echo & the Bunnymen are not the most immediately dynamic performers. They're trenchantly static and even Ian McCulloch, charisma and haircut aside, is about as interesting to watch as a particularly riveting episode of 'Jackonary.'
—*Sounds*, 1980

Clearly, in order to present fans with a more compelling experience during their upcoming three-week tour, the band had to dress up its image.

Drummond and the Bunnymen eventually settled on the idea of using army surplus camouflage clothes and netting to give the live show visual panache. There's a bit of contention regarding who actually originated the camo. Julian Cope insists that after he came up with the notion for the Teardrops, Drummond then stole it and passed it on to the Bunnymen. Although the Bunnymen don't seem sure who came up with what, they don't agree with Cope's version of history.

Mere mention of Cope brings out McCulloch's alter ego, Mac the Mouth, at his most acid-tongued.

[Julian] nicks half my songs so for him to complain about a jacket ... no, it wouldn't have worked with them. 'Ha ha I'm drowning in your love' and *Apocalypse Now* chic? Forget it! I think Bill Drummond had the camo idea, but Will probably suggested the netting.

—Ian McCulloch, 1999

[Julian] tries to mythologize himself above everyone else, when he was just another dude who went to teacher training college and bought a few punk records. He was always a dickhead and still is.

—Ian McCulloch, 1994

Julian goes on about it being his idea for the camouflage thing. It wasn't. It was me and Les,' and then it just grew naturally. We started wearing it—somewhere in Holland—and then the crew wore it and it became our thing. And the camouflage nets on stage were Bill Drummond or Bill Butt's idea.

—Will Sergeant, 1995

Julian Cope is a total twat, and you can quote me on that. He's just a no-mark from Tamworth. We knew him—we knew the real Julian Cope—and he's a total fake. He's a turd ... he has no moral fibre.

—Ian McCulloch, 1994

One journalist went as far as suggesting that the Bunnymen had copped the camo from funkmaster George Clinton, who had used it in his early 70's flamboyant freak show. It became quickly apparent that this was not the case.

Will Sergeant: "George Clinton? Who's he?"
Ian McCulloch: "We don't like westerns."

—*Creem*, 1980

Regardless of the camo idea's genesis, it was ideal for the Bunnymen at this stage of their development. The clothing was distinct and cheap, which at the time was a crucial consideration. Plus, the netting over the stage, meshed with Bill Butt's doomy and dramatic use of back-lighting, turned the previously nondescript stage into a surreal, apocalyptic netherworld. The set imaginatively transformed Bunnymen gigs into *events* that supplemented the moods and atmospheres of the group's stratospheric and emotive sound.

With netting thrown across the stage, a lighting design that turned the band into shadows and silhouettes moving through a hellish landscape, and lashings of dry ice, the Bunnymen flirted for awhile with

[The camo is] nothing political or anything to do with armies. Except for the fact that armies happen to wear the same stuff we do. It goes with the show, the lights, the stage effects. The idea of using camouflage netting on the stage is to make it more intimate. It creates a certain atmosphere that works with the music.

—Pete de Freitas, 1980

We weren't trying to start a fashion. The camo was just practical. We wore it all the time and the older it got, the better it looked. Half the bands now look like they've bought Gary Glitter's cast-offs.

—Les Pattinson, 1983

It was totally unhip. It was so unhip it had to be hip. And the fans all turned up wearing khaki, too, and felt like they were getting into the Bunnymen thing.

—Ian McCulloch, 1982

an *Apocalypse Now*-like chic. The set suited the dark moralities of the songs and emphasized the Bunnymen's gothic tendencies.

—Mark Cooper, *Liverpool Explodes*

The live shows with the camouflage netting overhanging the khaki-clad musicians, the deep, intense stage lighting, and the sometimes Cecil B. Demille-like wall of sound the Bunnymen create ... all suggest an *Apocalypse Now*-like journey into the Heart of Darkness itself, to the primal origins of the unconscious even! This is intensified by the smoke that sporadically pours out about the onstage musicians—some claim that so powerful is the psychic intensity put out by the group that the result is spontaneous combustion all about the stage area. (For some there is no smoke without fire.)

—*NME*, 1980

Bill Butt started doin' the lights and he devised the grotto thing. It was fuckin' amazing, like Bunnyland. Army netting all over the stage, camouflaged up. Everyone went on about it: 'Psychedelic smoke? I thought we'd seen the last of that.' No chance! And it was proper smoke, not dry ice ... [the camouflage netting] became a roof to the whole stage, and you had to get in through a soddin' trap door … We were in our own frightening environment. It was probably the most complete we felt onstage.

—Ian McCulloch, 1999

Butt went as far as proposing that each show open with the crew careening dramatically through the audience in an army jeep and hurling camouflage netting over the PA and stage floor, but this notion was nixed as being slightly too impractical, even for Bill Drummond.

The camo did more than just provide the Bunnymen with a noteworthy visual appeal. It bonded the band and crew together, made them feel part of a team, and gave the fans a sense of involvement, a distinct style for them to emulate. Bunnymen detractors sneered that this was a deliberate attempt to contrive a crass fashion.

Les and I wanted to wear our cowboy gear but the others laughed at us.

—Will Sergeant, 1980

In hindsight, it's easy to see how a touring international band decked out in military gear might stumble across some awkward situations.

Going through the checkpoint in Berlin was a good laugh.

—Ian McCulloch, 1984

SHINE SO HARD

While the Bunnymen were completing the Camo Tour, Bill Drummond had the idea to kickstart 1981 with a secret happening, an event akin to The Beatles' "Magical Mystery Tour." The concept was to transport fans from all over the country to an undisclosed location, where the Bunnymen would play a show in full camouflage regalia within the Faustian nightmare of the stage set. Bill Butt would capture the whole event on film. It would be a celebration of the Bunnymen's successes over the previous year, and an appetizer for future glories.

With characteristic irony, Drummond decided on the Botanical Gardens in Buxton, Derbyshire—perhaps the most un-rock & roll setting in all of England—as the ideal location, and set the date for January 17. An advertisement was placed in the music press: fans who wanted to attend were to write to Zoo Management, who would post a free pass and directions to the venue. For those who didn't have their own transport, coaches were provided, running from London, Liverpool, Manchester, Leeds, and Sheffield, at the relatively small cost of five pounds per seat. The show was scheduled for early evening—5 o'clock—so concert-goers would have time to get home at a decent hour.

Two days before the show, the band and crew split for Buxton to rehearse and to create a video that would culminate with footage of the performance. Butt and Drummond had hastily formed a film company called Atlas Adventures to get an angle, as it were, on the emerging MTV-fueled focus on video within the music industry.

Against the snowy, sleepy rural backdrop of Buxton, Butt shot film snippets of the four individual Bunnymen engaged in activities meant to capture the essence of each person's character. There were clips of a vaguely stunned Will wandering the Gardens, listening to a Walkman, Les jovially playing with a toy boat, and Mac walking along a darkened hallway and preening his coif in a mirror. Pete was filmed eating a meal and reading, sporting a head he'd inexplicably shaved for the upcoming event. The hirsute Mac looked on, askance.

There are bits with Pete reading *The Catcher In the Rye*. He stayed up all night before the movie and shaved his head, and I thought, 'You soddin' pillock. I have to go on tour with this.' Even then he was showing signs of weirdness, setting himself apart. —Ian McCulloch 1994

Despite the pomp and preparation, the concert itself was something of an anti-climax. Due to heavy snow, the show was under-attended, and the

This would be the first in a long line of unique events and tours that were to become a Bunnymen hallmark.

—*Goldmine*, 1998

The whole thing was to do things that no other rock band would contemplate. The tours became events. Will loved that. I loved that. I loved the audience and I wanted them to feel it was just for them.

—Ian McCulloch, 1999

The band lacked power and commitment, the very qualities for
which they'd previously been
championed, and looked as if
they'd lost their way. The rock
press turned on them for the
first time and the band were
shaken.   —Mark Cooper,
                 Liverpool Explodes

I feel a bit let down. You come
all this way and I suppose I
expected a bit more, really. It
wasn't as if there was any mystery 'cos we all knew where the
gig was going to be ages ago.
          —Unnamed attendee, 1981

We've forgotten about it. I'd
like everybody to forget about
it. Our fans aren't so untel-
ligent that they need us to
wear camo for them to enjoy us.
That was just a brief flirta-
tion for them—they could be
like us. But hopefully they
don't need us to dress up in a
specific way for them to feel
part of it.
          —Ian McCulloch, 1981

momentum of the performance was constantly interrupted by lighting and
camera arrangements. The Bunnymen themselves were a little uneasy and
confused by the whole production, and the show reflected their bewilder-
ment. Both fans and journalists took note.

This was meant to be a party ... the party never materialised. The
cameras zoomed in from the side, each song ended with instructions to
the cameraman from a disembodied voice offstage, and I got the feeling we were being used. The Bunnymen tried to inject the dramatic tension and sense of urgency that should be intrinsic to their performance, but it was too close to rock & roll (that sick phrase). Echo &
the Bunnymen should frighten us with their vision, not with their lack
of direction. They should shatter, beak up, and trample over all tradition. Smash and question, irregular, intense, and aware. The
Bunnymen should scratch our souls ... Album tracks, stage favorites,
and singles were played. It was all too safe. It was something of an
event, but no party.   —Journalist Chris Burkham, 1981

After the relative failure of the Buxton performance, the band heeded
the message of the writers and fans and concluded that the novelty of the
camo had grown tired and outworn its use.

We just didn't want to do it anymore. It's like we don't want to have
to end up relying on doing a load of stuff like nets and smoke before
people are interested. Let the music stand on its own.
          —Les Pattinson, 1981

The camo thing was meant to be tongue-in-cheek because we were considered the shy boys next door. Well, maybe we are but don't assume
it. Us, the group with no image, and so the camo was ironic. As we
developed our own image we got the confidence we needed, we struggled
for it. We didn't need the camo. Originally, it made large stages seem
intimate because of the netting, and the kids could wear it and feel
a part, but in the end we wanted sparse everything, so people could
see us sweating and giving emotion.   —Ian McCulloch, 1981

Butt's film, *Shine So Hard,* emerged as an interesting but fairly pretentious 35-minute piece of work.

I didn't like it much. It was really embarrassing to see myself on
film, where everything I did looked unnatural. —Les Pattinson, 1983

Shine So Hard was eventually screened at selected British theaters, and it ran at London's ICA for two weeks, along with Derek Jarman's Marianne Faithful documentary *Broken English*, and Pink Floyd's *Interstellar Overdrive*. It was virtually forgotten until 1994, when Britain's National Film Theater exhibited a series of rock & roll films as part of the "Punk: Before and Beyond" installment. Mac was invited as a celebrity guest to the screening, and offered his opinion of the film to the music press.

I remember thinking it was so pretentious, which shocked me because I always thought we were beyond pretension. But we were so naive, a young band trying to bond with our fans and I think that's what really mattered. You could look at it from outside and see it as pretentious, but it was for the fans as much as anything. It gave them a sense of belonging. Looking back on it, the camouflage isn't embarrassing, but them boots I had on. There's a real close-up shot of them, and they're ridiculous. I walked 'round the world with them boots on; they didn't have any heels on them and it was just felt on the bottom. I remember walking 'round Berlin when it was covered in snow and I just remember wringing my socks out, gaffer taping them up. What a stupid pillock!   —Ian McCulloch, 1994

It would take three hours to do a three-second shot, and it looked that way, too. Still, it's good that we have that camo period on film, because we don't wear it anymore—it was falling apart and getting smelly. —Pete de Freitas, 1982

★★★

Eventually, Drummond and Korova/Sire decided to make the best of the Buxton misadventure and released a live four-track EP from the *Shine So Hard* soundtrack on April 10, 1981. The EP contained "All That Jazz" and "Crocodiles," plus two new songs, "Zimbo" and "Over the Wall." The Bunnymen weren't particularly happy with the idea of the record, either.

We didn't think it was good enough. Actually, we were surprised that we played well on it, that we were in tune and everything. Like, Will said, 'This would make a good EP' and the next thing you know it was out. No one consulted us. It just went too far and we couldn't stop it.   —Ian McCulloch, 1981

We didn't want that released because there's two songs off the new album on it and the new album versions are a million times better.
                              —Pete de Freitas, 1981

Immediately after the Buxton show, the Bunnymen were scheduled to record their follow-up to *Crocodiles*, which had been almost completely written before the band set foot into the studio. It was clear that this sophomore effort would not be as cut-and-dried an affair.

We had a few songs knocking around for about six months and then we knew we had an album to do in three weeks' time and we had to write something like six songs. We wrote those in two weeks and had a week to rehearse the album.　　　　　　　　　—Ian McCulloch, 1981

When the majority of the songs were roughly sketched, they again headed to Rockfield and spent the next four weeks recording. The band hired *Crocodiles* engineer Hugh Jones as producer, rather than The Chameleons, who were partially responsible for the artistic and commercial failure of "The Puppet." These recording sessions were less uptight and rigid than the manic three weeks spent laying down *Crocodiles*. Although most of the new material was at the embryonic stage, the songs were looser, more open to experimentation.

It's like when we do John Peel Sessions; we're told about a week before and we haven't got a clue what we're going to do, so we just get in a rehearsal studio and think of something, and when we do them it turns out really well. It's a great way of doing it.

　　　　　　　　—Will Sergeant, 1981

We had an overall idea and a bit of the stuff was improvised. A lot of the stuff was spontaneous, whereas on the first album everybody knew all the songs.　　　　　　　—Ian McCulloch, 1981

Rather than go in producing songs that have been there for ages, it's like you can develop them as you do them. It's like, I suppose, an artist; if he paints a picture, he does it as he goes along, he doesn't necessarily know how he's going to do it right from the beginning, and it works out much better.　　　—Pete de Freitas, 1981

Whereas most of *Crocodiles* had been written without a live drummer, the Bunnymen took full advantage of Pete de Freitas, and encouraged him to play his kit in his own idiosyncratic manner.

We banned hi-hats and anything else that went 'tsss.' We told him to get stuck into the toms. Budgie [from the Banshees] was the only other drummer doing that stuff at the time, and Pete loved his drumming.

　　　　　　　　—Ian McCulloch, 1995

The new album, provisionally titled *The Rocker*, was *Heaven Up Here*, and was fueled by a maelstrom of insomnia, insect infestation, and cocktails.

Port, Clan Dew, whiskey mac, dry sherry. Going to bed at 10am after a lot of Captain Morgans. Flies everywhere. Shit pubs in Monmouth. But a great atmosphere. That was where the bevvy started kicking in big time.   —Ian McCulloch, 1999

During these sessions, the Bunnymen's schedule was nothing short of insane. For four punishing weeks, they began recording around 10am, finished at 2am, rehearsed for their U.S. tour, collapsed for a couple of dreamless hours, then started all over again. No one particularly minded. The Bunnymen were having a great time, and coming into their own as a group.

We work best under pressure.   —Will Sergeant, 1981

It was all about us being invincible. Making that record was very spiritual, and we knew we were doing something that was fantastic and would really set us apart and make us the best and coolest band in the world. Literally we felt it was 'Heaven up here'; we were on this cloud above everyone else. *Heaven Up Here* was incredible to make; it felt like it was the best we would ever be, and it kind of was. It was so quick and on the spot, it had so many moments.
                                                       —Ian McCulloch, 1994

Heaven up Here was our favourite album to make. Probably the best time of my life.   —Ian McCulloch, 1992

If Mac is to be believed, the lunatic schedule, along with the camaraderie and inspiration provided by the spirits, propelled the Bunnymen's growth.

We did definitely mature, especially during the first week of doing the backing tracks. It was brilliant, we couldn't actually believe what was coming.   —Ian McCulloch, 1981

Relations between the band members were at an all-time high. In a magazine interview, when Mac was asked to list his influences, the only people he would acknowledge beside the Velvet Underground and The Fall were Will Sergeant, Les Pattinson, and Pete de Freitas.

The whole album was done on hot toddies, rum and black … getting bevvied. I'm not exactly Dean Martin, but the drugs thing was getting out of hand, so I switched us to a drinking band. Of course, your average boozer wouldn't understand the lyrics anyway.
                        —Ian McCulloch, 1981

When we were making it, it was like we were all in love with it—we were proud of it. We related to each other for the first time. We've always had this thing that all of us are Bunnymen, and you don't get a Bunnyman every day. But this was the first time that that was really true. We all knew what was going on.
                        —Ian McCulloch, 1981

THE BIG COUNTRY ·

After recording *Heaven Up Here*, the Bunnymen embarked on their first tour of the United States in March 1981. It was a last-minute arrangement—so rushed, in fact, that Mac had to bring his dirty laundry along with him, as he'd had no time to wash it in the UK. The tour was intended as a no-frills, down-and-dirty, low-key affair, an "Eddie and the Hot Rods tour," as Mac put it—just the band and crew in one cramped van. The situation was so tight that Pete had to sleep on a guitar case in the footwell. The tour's purpose was to expose the Bunnymen to American audiences, and to give the group a feel for the U.S., which had just had its first delayed-release taste of *Crocodiles*.

The foursome was both disturbed and confused by its initial impressions of a country they felt was culturally empty, and as haunted as an Edward Hopper painting.

Los Angeles is supposed to be like this sunny paradise and all the palm trees are covered in smog. The sun's just a blur above the smog. We looked at the Hollywood Hills and they're just scum. It's like Huddersfield. You could wipe your finger on the hill and there'd be dust on it.   —Ian McCulloch, 1981

First time you visit, for the first few days it's like noth- ing—zero, zilch, emptiness, a cartoon or something. All the noises outside windows—police cars ... the diversity, size, and culture of non-culture get to you. It's neither good or bad—just totally weird.
          —Ian McCulloch, 1985

The pizzas were dead big. You expect 'em to be eating chili dogs and tacos all the time, but you don't really think they will eat that shit. And they do!   —Will Sergeant, 1981

The fact we came here in the first place was not our wanting. I dunno. I like England ... [but] the burgers are OK.   —Ian McCulloch, 1981

Sounds: "Has America inspired anything that might become a song?"
Les: "I hope not."
Will: "Depression."
Pete: "This is an unreal, happy smiling place. It's false, that happiness."   —*Sounds*, 1981

The Bunnymen's wide-eyed distaste for the U.S. might not have been so extreme if it hadn't been for their resentment of Sire's insistence they impress the stateside market.

We'd rather let what's going to happen happen rather than go out and work at 'cracking' anything. It was just, 'Let's go play in America and see what happens.' Everybody else wanted us to come here and 'crack America'—the record company, etc.   —Pete de Freitas, 1981

I would like us to do well, but when it's a conscious 'cracking' it's a waste of time. Stupid. There's only one way that can end: selling yourself short, one goal in mind, and that's to get yourself known and make money. People say you should crack America and make an impression, because they deserve it, [our] music is better than all the other crap that gets played on the radio, it deserves to go on the radio. But I don't go along with that.   —Ian McCulloch, 1981

Despite his aversion of America, Mac was thrilled to stay at the Tropicana Hotel in L.A., where he rented a room in which Iggy Pop had passed out for six months. Almost as enticing was a bar across the street where Jim Morrison had boozed regularly, although Mac decided it wouldn't be prudent to enter this establishment. It wasn't so much that The Doors comparisons bothered him anymore—but the bar had become a cruising joint for lesbians.

Mac did manage to encounter one member of L.A.'s most revered rock legends. Doors keyboardist Ray Manzarek, his interest piqued by the music papers' constant comparisons of the Bunnymen to his former band, attended a show, and was introduced to Mac afterwards. The singer, collapsed under a table, exhausted after the night's performance, indicated in no uncertain terms that even if he were a fan, he was certainly no sycophant.

I said, 'Hey Ray, aren't you dead? Or what?' I was probably trying to be funny.   —Ian McCulloch, 1995

Although the Bunnymen were ambivalent to the Doors comparisons, and mistrustful of the U.S. itself, they were performing extremely well, laying waste to packed houses all over the states. On several occasions they were enthusiastically informed that they had an "American sound."

We probably have got an American sound, but it's not an American sound like all the bland crap. We do like a lot of American groups—the Velvets, Talking Heads. It's an American sound, but the good American bands, maybe. We're not ripping them off or anything. It's the feeling more than anything. It's because we like them.
                                                —Will Sergeant, 1981

I always felt that if we were an American band from New York, we'd probably have been seen as the greatest band of all time. We'd have had something that American bands have that English bands just can't do.
                                                —Ian McCulloch, 2001

American or not, the Bunnymen's brand of rock was becoming more and more profoundly visceral, a development that the music press happily embraced.

A big-echoing sound—dreamy, dirgey, passionate, majestic. Not the American arena band idea of majesty, an overstated assault that grabs you by the balls and lays like lead on your stomach. This was a quiet majesty, a fascinating, intangible grandness that grips your heart before setting into your brain. You could wring out the air and it would rain emotion.
                —Sounds, 1981

Television is overwhelmingly present here, but I don't see the harm in that ... like the Television of 1976, the thing works on the simplest premises of rhythm, and like Television, the Bunnymen get more grit and feeling into every second of sound than anybody. It's currently the most urgent and accomplished live performance you're likely to see.
                —NME, 1981

Everywhere's weird, it's great. Even France is weird. Everyone talks French there ... it's just *weird*. You don't feel threatened abroad, even though it's probably just as dangerous. Because everyone's foreign, you just think you're in this dream world. You can't read the signs but you find your way around. It's like being a kid. Even goin' to a caff is great.
—Ian McCulloch, 1987

With their first visit to the U.S. completed, the Bunnymen barely had time to change their socks before they embarked on a Spring UK tour, after which they headed to Europe for their first trek through the continent. Bill Butt caught much of this outing on 8mm film, and the resulting *Le Via Lounge: The Last of The Long Days* boasted an eerie soundtrack by Will Sergeant. The film was eventually released on videocassette, coupled with *Shine So Hard*.

The Bunnymen attempted to capture the essence of the tour by audiotaping conversations and tour bus shenanigans, with the idea that these would be transcribed, edited, and released as a book. This volume never materialized, and the subsequent tapes proved to be a lot of in-jokes interspersed with long periods of silence. At this point, the Bunnymen were immune to the clichés of a touring rock band, and where other bands might have been throwing TV sets out hotel windows and choking on their own vomit, the Bunnymen were quite often simply bored shitless, entertaining themselves with whatever their imaginations could provide.

I didn't really bag-off much on the European tour. In fact, I didn't really bag-off at all.   —Will Sergeant, 1981

I had a crap last night and it was like Moby Dick. There were men round the bowl with harpoons. Greenpeace got called in, like, save the whale.   —Will Sergeant, 1981

The European tour was marked by two other outstanding achievements. On June 1st, Mac became engaged to his girlfriend of two years, Lorraine Fox, in Amsterdam. He'd glimpsed her at a Simple Minds show at Eric's just after "The Pictures On My Wall" single had been released, and, after an introduction from a future member of hairmeister band A Flock of Seagulls, the two had become virtually inseparable.

A week after the lovers were engaged, the Bunnymen recorded one of their finest B-sides in Tidestal, Norway. The chilling, eerie drone of "Broke My Neck" sports what is still probably Will's most discordant, savage guitar assault. Although the single on which it appeared, "A Promise," released on July 10, only ascended to #49 in the charts, it was easily the band's most formidable 7-inch to that date.

You said something will change
We were all dressed up
Somewhere to go
No sign of rain
But something will change
You promised

You said nothing will change
We were almost near
Almost far
Down came the rain
But nothing will change
You promised
A promise ...

It's exactly the same
You said it's always the same
But I'll make it change
Into something the same
I promise
A promise ...

Light
On the waves ...

A promise ...

There's light on the water
We could sail on forever

I'd written this two-verse poem that wasn't intended for a song, but it fitted the riff.   —Ian McCulloch, 1985

It's about frustration, really. I just thought I'd certain morals and principles since I was 13 or 14 and I carried them through, but things change. It becomes evident, when you realise you've changed, that the promise wasn't kept.   —Ian McCulloch, 1981

Melody is rarely one of the Bunnymen's strong points, but this one is beautiful—haunted by fine, plaintive vocals that flirt with desperation, almost a broken moan in places (I see Mac as a true Bunny Wailer), sealing the song's status as perhaps the classic Echo track to date.   —*NME*, 1981

'A Promise' was the one where we used to sit there with our 'ot toddies and say, 'This could definitely be the saddest song ever and a worldwide number one.   —Ian McCulloch, 1983

Best track of the year's best LP—simple as that, really. It's the kind of a song that calls for sweeping statements because it *is* a sweeping statement. Soul and emotion, majestic melody, grandeur without pomp. Ian McCulloch and fellow Bunnies have never performed better; they've never had anything better to perform.   —*NME*, 1981

We always used to listen to the backing track of 'A Promise' whenever we had a spare five minutes. And one time we stuck it on and I was sitting there and I was just really sad and I was nearly crying. I dunno why, I was just maybe thinking about something I shouldn't have been. And I said, 'I want to do it now' and I legged in. I'd never thought it was possible to do that—be that involved in the emotion. And the vocals are quite emotional or exasperated or whatever, but when I did that it was like one of the best feelings ever.

—Ian McCulloch, *Never Stop*

I try and change the rules of that standard 'great pop song' into being able to be really emotional. I wanna try and reduce the distance between acting and reality as much as possible but still create that great popness, but so far the gap's quite big between, say, what Jim Morrison really felt and his public persona. Lou Reed was a lot closer.

—Ian McCulloch, 1984

… gives agonised self-pity a stately home   —*The Face*, 1981

Bill Drummond found the most far-out studio he possibly could. It was in the basement of somebody's house. It was kinda strange. And I think I was drinking like some soddin' yak's blood alcohol or gnu droppings or something. I just remember being three sheets to the soddin' northern wind—I was completely off me bongo. Hence not many lyrics and not much singing on that.

—Ian McCulloch, 1999

We were on tour and needed a B-side. Bill Drummond found this studio in Norway halfway up a mountain. It was down this little track, and you couldn't get the bus there. Little shack of a studio. Les used an e-bow on his bass, and I did this Gang of Four-type of guitar. It was great, that one—kind of builds up.   —Will Sergeant, 2001

Mac is mesmerizing. He twist and jerks like some spastic toy…   —No 1, 1984

BROKE MY NECK

I forget
Just what I meant
Broke my neck
Lost respect
It was my fall from grace

I object
Is what I meant
Lost all track
And away I went
No sign of face-to-face
No chance of face-to-face

I helped myself
I couldn't help myself
I helped myself
I couldn't help myself
I tell myself
Go on and help yourself
You can help yourself
I can't help myself

No sign of face-to-face
No chance of face-to-face

... is positively modernist—almost dub-like textures, drones, and brittle metallic guitar. One lyric ('I forget just what I meant') seems to consciously deflate McCulloch's more hammily portentous moments.   —Q, 2001

1981 burdened the Bunnymen with the toughest touring schedule of their career. Over the course of 169 days, the band played 113 shows. By the end of the year, they had slogged through two major UK and U.S. tours, one European jaunt, and a stop-off in Australia and New Zealand. This breakneck pace gelled the band as a live unit.

Roadie Jake Brockman had proven himself as an indispensable "fifth Bunnyman," often guesting on keyboards, and, on occasion, standing in for Mac on rhythm guitar. This helped the singer to develop his skills as a frontman, a task at which he soon excelled. Unhampered by his semi-legendary pink Telecaster "Pinky," he was free to exhibit a stage presence that was both engaging and otherworldly. Having overcome his fear of onstage movement, he'd incorporated an eccentric dance into many of the songs, where he resembled a praying mantis-cum-scarecrow riddled by machine-gun fire.

McCulloch dances like a drunk ballet star trying to stay on a tightrope; he's all bends and curves and angles, half awkward, half graceful.   —Smash Hits, 1984

Oh, that's just how I dance. I freak out a bit and a lot of people say, 'Hey, you're dancing's great' but it's not dancing to me, it's just articulating bodily what I would have done vocally. You can dance to anything if you develop your own thing.   —Ian McCulloch, 1984

The singer also took great pleasure at pleasing and teasing an audience with wry comments, sarcastic quips, and extended ad-lib forays into rock's tattered tapestry, dropping snippets of classic songs into the extended bodies of "Crocodiles" and "Do It Clean." Mac was emerging as a true pop star and pin-up—a role he'd aspired to since the day he first heard "Starman." It's curious, then, that he approached his role with such ambivalence.

Even now, walking around, I feel self-conscious. People coming up to me in the street, I try to be dead nice to them but it does unsettle me. I don't know if I can be that soddin' 'Mac' bloke. There's something about Liverpool; they can see right through you, if you're a charlatan in some way. And I'm not. That's why they like me, but sometimes they need a bit of that stage craft, whether it's onstage or not. I can't deal with people being in my face a lot.

—Ian McCulloch, 1995

What gives me pleasure is being able to do what I've always wanted to do. The celebrity side of it doesn't give me any pleasure, really—it gives me paranoia, I think. It's something that I don't feel that comfortable with ...

—Ian McCulloch, 1984

I still am a puritan, I suppose. I mean, I'm not a star or anything. People in my road don't know anything about Echo & the Bunnymen, and that's great. You still get the teen idol thing, I suppose, but it's nothing to do with charisma. Stardom's a very misused word anyway, 'cos people are called pop stars when they're not.

—Ian McCulloch, 1981

There was no contending that Mac was fronting a band that, over the course of 1981, had become the darlings of a UK music press that was virtually falling over itself in its rush to heap plaudits on the Bunnymen's live show.

Last year, even during the Camo Tour, Bunnymen shows were erratic, fragile events. But where material was stylised it is now swollen with adventure; where it was linear it is now emotionally charged. The Bunnymen ... have the guts and the passion to stand with and above the very best—be that the Stones, Joy Division, The Doors, Iggy, or The Velvet Underground—and they can do it absolutely live. For presentation, Echo rely on simple stuff: no props, just imaginative lighting from Kit Edwards. The initial impression onstage is distinctly gothic medieval with the bells from Paques Chant Gregorian preceding the set. The hesitancy of previous moments has been blown away by a four-way pact that is the essence of any great rock 'n' roll band. McCulloch's pretty face isn't the only focal point anymore, but he's still pretty hard to resist. His vocals are now inspiring and uplifting, soaring and plummeting, whooping and yelling and screaming—in tune. He has controlled power and his performance teeters on the verge

Much of 1981 was spent touring and by the end of the year [the Bunnymen] had transformed themselves from an erratically brilliant live band whose off nights were hidden behind atmospheric staging and lighting to a consistently daunting live force capable of taking all comers. When they are good they have that abandonment, that strut and swagger that is simply spiritually uplifting. On such nights they are irresistible.
—Journalist Mick Houghton, 1984

of madness—the only way to be: ask Jagger or Bowie or Iggy Pop, look at Morrison and Curtis. Added to that is the McCulloch rhythm guitar, a savage driving force that's as vital to the group's unique leap forward as was Keith Richards's on *Aftermath* or Lou Reed's on *White Light/White Heat*. Watch that man! —*NME*, 1981

The band's artistic and critical successes, however, hadn't yet translated into financial profit. Virtually all the money they generated went back into the cost of touring. Each Bunnyman was scraping by on a meager pittance of a mere 35-pound weekly salary. Mac was vexed to find that, in some countries, a bottle of Cuervo Gold cost almost a week's wages. But somehow, the group managed to take its relative poverty in stride.

It just seemed so much more natural and outside of business than any other band that was around. It did seem something special, most particularly after *Heaven Up Here* when the feeling was just so amazing between everybody. And it didn't matter what the financial results were. We arrived back from that tour and we were just absolutely bankrupt. Yet those kind of things simply don't matter when it's special.
—Pete de Freitas, *Never Stop*

I don't know about being successful. I like the feeling of being appreciated, that's self-respect, which is successful enough for me.
—Les Pattinson, 1981

★★★

The Bunnymen were on a spiritual high and they knew it. They had evolved from a nervous, inconsistent group of scruffy Liverpudlian lads into one of the most intense and inventive English groups in recent rock history. Some thought the Bunnymen's musical naiveté and stubbornness—if not laziness—were the keys to their magic.

The Bunnymen don't push themselves very much, and I don't just mean Mac staying in bed all the time; they'll only do something that they know they can do. They have a sort of fear that restrains them. [They have] built themselves up slowly. When they finally get 'round to doing something, they're usually ready. They've never really risked themselves, and as a consequence they've never suffered any major defeats. —David Balfe, 1981

Echo & the Bunnymen proceed cautiously but thoroughly at their own pace, sniffing the air from time to time with that caustic Liverpool suss, making sure they do it clean and don't come a spectacular cropper.   —Mark Cooper, *Liverpool Explodes*

Separately, what they're playing didn't seem that great. But somehow, when the four of them touched together, it ignited the blue paper. You could say to them, 'Play A to D' They'd all join in and play A to D, and it would just sound great. The four of them created some kind of chemical reaction.   —*Mojo*, 1997

Bill Drummond suggested that the Bunnymen's chemistry might spring from more esoteric sources.

It's the interstellar ley line. It comes careering in from outer space, hits the world in Iceland, bounces back up writhing about like a conger eel, then down Mathew Street in Liverpool where the Cavern Club—and latterly Eric's—is. Back up twisting, turning, wriggling across the face of the earth until it reaches the uncharted mountains of new Guinea, where it shoots back into space. Deep space. This interstellar ley line is a mega power one. Iceland, Mathew Street Liverpool, and New Guinea are the only three fixed points on earth it travels through and anywhere else on earth that something happens that is creatively or spiritually mega is because this interstellar ley line is momentarily powering through the territory. Whenever the Bunnymen do a brilliant gig, we know it's because they were on the line. Sometimes it's only there for a couple of songs.
        —Bill Drummond, *From the Shores of Lake Placid and Other Stories*

Another has offered a more earthbound explanation.

The advantage with this group is that we mean it and you could see that.   —Ian McCulloch, 1981

When Will or any of us cocks up onstage is better than when almost any other band gets it right.   —Ian McCulloch, 1984

We get to rehearsals then we have a cup of tea. Then we set the stuff up and then we have a cup of tea. Then we probably have a cup of tea and pick the guitars up or something.
        —Will Sergeant, 1981

It's a total mystery to me that these four individuals, who at times seem to derive no pleasure from what they're doing—particularly the peripheral promotional aspects of being in a successful band—can produce such a vital spirit as a foursome when they come to record or play live. They are still so refreshingly innocent about the music business they're in. They are almost childishly (some would say pig-headedly) single-minded about what they will or won't do, whatever pressure is brought to bear. However much it makes sense to do something, they stubbornly resist. However daft an idea, they'll do it. The Bunnymen are a law unto themselves. Thank God.   —Journalist
        Mick Houghton, 1984

We are the greatest band in the world.   —Ian McCulloch,
                1978-present day

Heaven Up Here was released on May 30, 1981, and rocketed to #10 in the UK charts. The album was met with even more ecstatic press accolades than those *Crocodiles* had received. To many fans and critics, it still remains the band's masterwork.

The Bunnymen of *Heaven Up Here*—a mystically masterful album it should be said right here—are a kind of Clash with a conscience … This is an intensely personal album. From the almost Talking Heads-ish openings of 'Show of Strength' and 'With A Hip' onwards, there is no mistaking that Echo & the Bunnymen are a rock band, but at the very periphery of rock, changing its structures around like the Heads do, doing impossibly new things with its tired body, practically willing it into a few last original corners. And they do it with all that rock has left, the very last breaths of its style. The style is overwhelming … after every listen something new and often startling emerges from Hugh Jones's brilliant production. It all adds up to an enormously rich record … a big quiet form of traditionalism in these times of small loud innovations. Celebrate this misery.   —*Sounds*, 1981

The Bunnyperson's second album is a quiet narcotic. It creeps up and takes over like a heat rash—the high points strong enough to hold interest until the less defined areas slip into focus. David Byrne would be wise to look over his shoulder.   —*The Face*, 1981

… darker yet more passionate [than *Crocodiles*]—where [the Bunnymen] were cautious, detached—and softer yet more powerful. Power, as this music proves, is not the preserve of men with wide mouths and gatecrashing guitars. Power arises out of emotions properly expressed.   —*NME*, 1981

The way *Heaven Up Here* seems to shift in sequence, different songs altering their emphasis, variations in colour and passion changing constantly, speaks of a sophistication hardly ever encountered.   —*NME*, 1983

… a heady blue dive into existential fire. There was a hugeness and otherness there; these songs moved toward an undefinable space …   —*Stylus*, 1999

Liverpool's finest continue to sing the blues, continue to devote themselves to the glossy celebration of existential sadness. *Heaven Up Here* offers an anatomy of melancholy, resplendent with the glamour of doom.   —*Record Mirror*, 1981

At their finest, the Bunnymen are continuing to play majestic, uplifting music that will shine through the dark days ahead of us.   —*Melody Maker*, 1981

The Bunnymen had it all. Their second album *Heaven Up Here* was the essential purchase in a world that was going daft on the post-Human League synth boom, when grown men wore tea-towels. They were the coolest band in the world.   —*GQ*, 1996

… *the* classic LP of the 80's   —*Smash Hits*, 1983

I seriously think that *Heaven Up Here* is one of the most superior articulations of 'rock' form in living memory.   —*NME*, 1981

Echo & the Bunnymen have done for rock what Tamla Motown did for dance music.   —*NME*, 1981

Although the Bunnymen themselves weren't completely satisfied with the record's mix—they were touring while that job was done, and couldn't oversee the process—they were, and still are, pleased with the results.

I don't want it just to be reviewed like your average album because it has profundities about it. It's not just like a dance album , a ska album, a Clash album. It's intelligent, the new album. Just say that we're proud of it.   —Ian McCulloch, 1981

We went off and proved we were going into uncharted territory, where no band of the time could even contemplate going. —Ian McCulloch, 1998

Bill Drummond, still the band's biggest fan and critic, doesn't agree.

The album is as dull as ditchwater. The songs are unformed, the sound uniformly gray.   —*From the Shores of Lake Placid and Other Stories*

In contrast to his cool assessment of the recording, Drummond was affected as profoundly by the mythic properties of *Heaven Up Here*'s sleeve as he was with the cover of *Crocodiles*.

Brian Griffin had taken the cover shots again. He'd taken the band off to some mud flats on the Severn Estuary. The four members of the band, backs to the camera, standing in a line in the middle-distance, rain-coats on, staring into a bleak milky sky. It was a classic photo. Even I could see how it romanticised the essence of the band to great effect ... .It was a while after *Heaven Up Here* had been out that the weird shit began to leak from the cover shot. On the cover of *Crocodiles*, Echo looked benignly on while Will, Mac, Les, and Pete gazed aimless-ly about themselves like innocent children, unaware of the Trickster's presence. On the sleeve of *Heaven Up Here*, Echo had taken to the skies. Off. Gone. In this photograph [the Bunnymen] were seemingly still unaware of Echo, but were aware something had departed, like when a shadow moves across your face and you look around to see what's there. It was as if they'd become aware of a presence only through its depar-ture. They stared up into the skies, wondering what it was. It was a

Heaven ... was the album of the year, as a statement of intent. It's like the Liverpool FC. Even if they come fourth, everybody knows they're the best. But I do equate us with Liverpool FC. We've got our Kop behind us. —Ian McCulloch, 1982

Musically, what we were doing at the time was great. That spikey edge still stands up.
                    —Ian McCulloch, 1995

...*Heaven Up Here* is me favourite.—Will Sergeant, 1995

big something. Not just a little bunny hopping down a hole. This departing presence filled the whole sky.

—Bill Drummond, *From the Shores of Lake Placid and Other Stories*

Drummond wasn't the only one impressed with the album art. At the end of the year, *Heaven Up Here* won "Best Sleeve Award" in the *NME*.

A considerable part of the Bunnymen's splendor came from Mac's increasingly operatic vocalization and his unorthodox word usage. As with *Crocodiles*, both critics and fans expressed curiosity and suspicion about Mac's lyrics, which had grown even more vague and cryptic. In interviews, Mac candidly discussed his lyrical style, and tried to explain what he thought a song's words should convey.

On this album I've been less worried about the way it read; I've been more concerned with the way it sounded. I'm not saying [the lyrics] deserve anything; I don't pretend to be the new Bob Dylan or anything. But I do like the words; there's some very funny ones as well, which I'm pleased about. But the most important thing is that they fit with the music really well.

—Ian McCulloch, 1981

I suppose the songs are always about the possibility of something great and then the breakdown of trust or the breaking up of possibilities.

—Ian McCulloch,
Liverpool Explodes

Intelligence … emotion … shivers down your back … some kind of meaning, even if it's vague, which most of my stuff is. Not intentionally, it just comes out that way; I'll just write a line and it could be really simple language except the words might be in a different order.

—Ian McCulloch, 1981

A lot of it was about people's expectations of me, what they assumed I was like. Some of the lyrics are about people in the press assuming what I am is what they see. I was getting loaded with all kinds of stuff, and the band were too! In the track 'Heaven Up Here' there was 'I' in it quite a lot and 'we' in it quite a lot. 'Where are you now? We're over here.' That was about the change between *Crocodiles* and *Heaven Up Here*. It's about people who pigeonholed us after *Crocodiles*—we went to 'Heaven' while they weren't looking.

—Ian McCulloch, 1984

Perhaps the most concise and accurate assessment of Mac's lyrics came from journalist/author Mark Cooper.

The one constant in Mac's lyrics is a sense of betrayal, of a promise broken, of the disappointment that comes from seeing humans betray their potential over and over. Mac dreams of things being right, of finding life as he dreams it might be, only to find it wrong. The Bunnymen's music records this constant story in its rises and falls, in its search for climaxes and its ebbing away in disappointment.

—*Liverpool Explodes*

★★★

In contrast to the majority, there were a few journalists who vociferously disapproved of the band and what they perceived as *Heaven Up Here*'s intentional obscurity and sense of mystery. This criticism was not mollified by some of Bill Drummond's more fanciful offhand quips to the press. The Bunnymen tried to dispel Drummond's mythmaking as best they could.

Bill Drummond described the band as being 'from the Northern part of the Northern Hemisphere. They represent cold, dampness, darkness.' To which Mac responded in a subsequent interview with the delicately chosen words 'WORRALOADACRAP! Everyone knows we represent fun!'
—*Record Mirror*, 1987

Other criticism expressed discontent with the Bunnymen's use of traditional rock motifs in an era where self-conscious experimentation was becoming the status quo of modern British music. The band didn't deny their love of the past—at this point, they were considering re-releasing Television's long out-of-print *Marquee Moon* on Korova—and attempted to justify their avoidance of weirdness for weirdness's sake.

The trouble with experimentation is that it becomes the hip thing to do, and it's just played out too much. —Pete de Freitas, 1981

People ask us what sort of band we are, and I always say 'We're a rock band.' Because I'm proud of that ... but a lot of people seem to be embarrassed about it. I like rock music. I much prefer good basic drums, bass guitar, guitar, and vocals to good electronic, experimental stuff. I prefer being good or great within that basic format. I like a lot of experimental stuff, but in the end I just prefer basic songs. —Ian McCulloch, 1980

A lot of it just doesn't sound very good. I think the use of basic drums and guitars can be a lot more inventive than the so-called 'experimental' stuff. —Ian McCulloch, 1981

The basic songs on *Heaven Up Here* certainly provided pleasure enough to the swiftly increasing cult of Bunnymen fans. At the year's end, when reader poll results were tallied up, the Bunnymen came in second, just behind The Jam, in the *NME*'s "best group" category. As for the "best album" category, *Heaven Up Here* was perched regally at #1.

It's about trying to be honest with yourself even though you know you're a dishonest turd. It's about somebody obvious and it's about me. Mostly it concerns people who pretend they've got guts and passion when they haven't. When they try to get it from someone else. —Ian McCulloch, 1981

'Show of Strength' deals with damnation; it's about pop stars and pop pundits, it's very Northern and it applies to [un]specific scenes. —*NME,* 1981

Even when I'm being dead honest in a lyric, quite often it'll have this undercutting one-liner, this irony, like 'It's hard to dig it all too happily.' It's true I'm not too happy about anything. I'm pessimistic about large-scale things, but not about me!
—Ian McCulloch,
Liverpool Explodes

SHOW OF STRENGTH

Realistically
It's hard to dig it all too
  happily
But I can see
It's not always that real to me
A funny thing
It's always a funny thing
And those sadly things
Just get in the way

Open to suggestion
Falling over questions

Hopefully
But that's as well as maybe
A shaken hand
Won't transmit all fidelity
Your golden smile
Would shame a politician
Typically
I'll apologize next time

Bonds will break and fade
A snapping all in two
The lies that bind and tie
Come sailing out of you

Realistically
Hard to dig it all too happily
But I can see
Not always that real to me
A funny thing
Is always a funny thing
And those sadly things
It's always a sadly thing

Bonds will break and fade
A snapping all in two
The lies that bind and tie
Come sailing out of you

A show of strength
Is all you want
You can never set it down
Guts and passion
Those things you can't
Even set down
All those things
You think might count
You can never set them down
Don't ever set them down
Never set them down

Hey I came in right on cue
One is me and one is you
Hey I came in
Right on cue
One is me
And one
Is
You

This was written in Northern Sweden. It was very cold. We always felt that people from cold climates are made of sterner stuff.
—Ian McCulloch, 1992

WITH A HIP

Halt
Nobody's allowed
Strictly verboten
Out out out out
Bounds
Of course we know no bounds
Until, at least, and then
Trespass all the way down
They got it
And I want some
I can handle it
And I want some

Relax
Feel the pleasure inside
Error and trial
Collide, collide
You'll listen
I don't expect you to
We've lost
And something's all we can do
With a hip-hip-hop
And a flip-flap-flop
Gonna steal some bananas
From the grocer's shop
With your head in the clouds
And your trousers undone
Gonna shit on the carpet
Just like everyone

This is the one for the money
This is the one for the trees
This is the one called Heaven
And this is the one for me

You've yet to discover
Discover the difference
The difference between
The moral and motto

They've got it
And I had some
I couldn't handle it
But I had some

Hold it in the light and see
    right through it
For God's sake make a decision
Take it for a walk and hold it
    hold it
Pin it on the wall and fasten
    onto
Move into the bathroom oh yes oh
    yes
Do what must be done and don't
    say maybe

This is the one for the money
This is the one for the trees
This is the one called Heaven
And this is the one for me

We are the most hip unhip band in the world.

—Ian McCulloch, 1982

'With a Hip' is about knowing your limitations. It's nothing to do with hipness, although I like the idea that people might think it is. I like it when people analyse the words and get something out of them. That's a compliment.

—Ian McCulloch, 1981

There was only the Talking Heads that we felt any kinship with. I know I was influenced by *Remain In Light*. We had it and played it to death. That was a definite influence over the choppier, funkier things on *Heaven Up Here*.

—Ian McCulloch, 1999

I didn't think of it as an anthem. It was just something to do with escaping the barriers in your brain, not a rallying call to the moronic masses.
—Ian McCulloch, 1984

... resonates with the austere, apocalyptic spirit of its age—a time when newspapers were full of 'scenarios' where squadrons of Warsaw Pact tanks rushed across the West German Plain to be met with a 'tactical nuclear response.' —Q, 2001

The mood is shamelessly romantic, but it works because the band have incorporated flesh and blood. When McCulloch rolls something like 'I'm walking in the rain to celebrate this misery' around his tongue, his pitching and conviction shunt the line a long way from embarrassment. It's how the character of the song feels; sentiment becomes more important than significance.
—The Face, 1981

'Over the Wall," an Echo classic ... was drawn out, eerie, and intensely psychedelic, with the band taking its 'ebbs and flows' aesthetic to the limit.
—The Vibe, 1997

OVER THE WALL

The man at the back has a question
His tongue's involved with
  solutions
But the monkey on my back
Won't stop laughing

Over the wall
Hand in hand
Over the wall
Watch us fall

There's something to be said for you
And your hopes of higher ruling
But the slug on my neck
Won't stop chewing

Over the wall
Hand in hand
Over the wall
Watch us fall

I'm walking in the rain
To end this misery
I'm walking in the rain
To celebrate this misery

What's that you say?
Speak up I can't hear
What did you say?
I couldn't hear

Over the wall
Hand In hand
Over the wall
Watch us fall

Pounding the road
Coast to coast
Pounding the road
Coast to coast
Come over the wall ...

I can't sleep at night
How I wish you'd hold me tight
I can't sleep at night
Come on and hold me tight ...

Hold me tight
To the logical limit

A song about mind over matter. This one set us apart from the rest of the pack. None of the bands around then came anywhere near it.
—Ian McCulloch, 1992

Les wrote two poems which are in the background on 'Over the Wall.' You're not meant to hear 'em properly, but I wish you could hear what he says a bit. They're dreamy and sort of funny. —Will Sergeant, 1981

Wasn't 'Over the Wall' a great song though? It was just so Bunnymen. That was the chemistry of the four of us.   —Ian McCulloch, 1990

IT WAS A PLEASURE

Let's get rid of the shit
I know you like that, too
The stuff that undermines
The best of me and you

It was a pleasure to meet you
You slapped me right on the back
Just a pleasure to meet you
You got it almost exact

No discussion now
No bad dreams now
No reason now
No excuses now

If I knock it all back
Just like you said I do
Would it confirm the suspect?
The suspicion will do

It was a pleasure to meet you
You slapped me right on the back
Just a pleasure to meet you
You got it almost exact

No discussion now
No allusion now
No dilution now
No excuses now

Let's get rid of the shit
I know you like that, too
The stuff that undermines
The best of me and you

Failure to do so will result in
    the failure
Failure to do so will result in
    the failure

'It was a Pleasure' was written because I thought we were
going to get slagged. It was
like a pre-backlash thing.
                —Ian McCulloch, 1987

If people think we're hip, that's a mistake. If they want that they can go see a Scottish band. Once one of these hip bands plays to an audience that hasn't read the right articles, they're gonna be in trouble. We were bracketed with the hip Liverpool scene because we brought out an independent single that had nothing to do with hipness. Intelligence was acknowledged and some kind of thought. We're an attack against hipness, although I do think we're the hippest band in the world. The title song on *Heaven* ... is about being in that position. The press saying, 'Where are the Bunnymen now?' and us saying, 'We're over here.' Because if these writers think they are hip, then they're crazy. It changes— *everything* is hip. You've only got to read the *NME* to realize that hipness is a pile of crap.
—Ian McCulloch, 1981

... hilarious, sending up the band's 'groovy' connotations ... the music dances and kicks through some wild outer limits of debauchery.   *—NME,* 1981

HEAVEN UP HERE

Where are you now?
We're over here
We've got those empty pockets
And we can't afford the beer
We're smoking holes
And we've got only dreams
And we're so damn drunk
We can't see to steer

The applecart upset my head's
    little brain
This little moon in the sky upset
    my head's little brain

I saw, yippee, I did, I swear
Walking through the hallway
Crawling on the stairs
Abebe baby ... Bekila
I'm giving up on whiskey
Taking up with tequila

I'm on my own in my blind alley
I turn myself around so it's
    swallowing me

Groovy groovy people
We're all
Groovy groovy people ...

F-F-Faustus
You've got nothing to fear
It may be hell down there
'Cos it's Heaven up here
I'd have given forever
For a few good years
But too much of a muchness
Is too much you hear?

The hammer on my chest was an
    abominable pain
The anvil on my belly was an
    abdominal strain
You got the bottle
Gonna take the bottle
Gonna take a sip

On 'Heaven Up Here,' which features a richly rhythmic pulsebeat, McCulloch's vocal exclamation have reached fever pitch intensity, and guitarist Will Sergeant punctuates with slashing fills reminiscent of The Gang of Four.   *—CMJ New Music Report,* 1999

The song is about pride, objectively escaping from the image people have of you.
—Ian McCulloch, 1981

THE DISEASE

My life's the disease
That could always change
With comparative ease
Just given the chance

My life is the earth
'Twixt muscle and spade
We wait for the worth
Digging for just one chance

As prospects diminish
As nightmares swell
Some pray for Heaven while
We live in hell

My life's the disease
My life's the disease

If you get yours
From Heaven
Don't waste them ...

The rhythm of the track, the tempo, was set up by the buckets swinging over. It had a natural feel to it.
—Les Pattinson, 1987

... wouldn't seem out of place on Leonard Cohen's Greatest Hits.
—*NME*, 1981

... damned uncomfortable listening wherever you sat.
—*Melody Maker*, 1984

'The Disease' is short, morbid, and strange.
—*NME*, 1981

I wrote 'The Disease' as a kind of anthem for the Liverpool suppressed, for those who see their potential in human terms, and not in terms of having or not having a job. —Ian McCulloch, 1982

Jake, who plays keyboards with us now, went out to the docks in Bristol and recorded a dredger, before anyone had heard of sampling. It ended up on 'The Disease.' —Will Sergeant, 1987

ZIMBO (ALL MY COLOURS)

Flying
And I know I'm not coming down
You're trying
But you know you must soon go down
All my colours turn to clouds
All my colours turn to clouds

Zimbo ...

What d'you say
When your heart's in pieces?
How d'you play
Those cards in sequence?

That box you gave me burned nicely
That box you gave me burned nicely

Zimbo ...

Flying down
Flying down
All my colours turn to clouds ...

Hey, I've flown away
Hey, I'm blown away

'Zimbo' is about the loss of someone and the fact that people hold on to things that have already gone.
—Ian McCulloch, 1981

...our first soul song...the first song where we proved we could connect emotionally.
—Ian McCulloch, 1997

...builds and rises until it ceases to remain merely a song and takes on properties of an hypnotic chant or mantra.
—*Sounds*, 1981

In 'Zimbo,' centered upon an Indian war drum beat and an acoustic guitar, McCulloch slowly builds the song to a devastating level through the simple yet powerful device of word repetition. Strong emotions equals strong music.
—*CMJ New Music Report*, 1999

...a billowing epiphany of smoke and ghosts   —*NME*, 1983

'No Dark Things' aches with an obvious and intense honesty; as a statement of the band's widest intent it couldn't be bettered. It's a communication.
—*NME*, 1981

...in Japan there's a metaphysical book called *Zimbo* which tied in really closely with something ... [although I'd] never heard of it ... .you sort of think you have. And it makes you feel good. You think, 'Maybe I was writing about the same thing'—'it's all part of the cosmos' thing.
—Ian McCulloch, 1987

The chorus ... we were in rehearsal, and I was singin' in this low voice, not knowing what the bloody hell was going on, whether what I was doing was right, and I just started singin', tongue-in-cheek to meself, 'Jimbo Jimbo Jimbo,' meaning Jim Morrison … and the other three are diggin' it 'cos I'm givin' it moody croonin', and I'm thinkin' I'm just doing a bad imitation of Jim Morrison. And then it became 'Zimbo' and everyone went 'That's great, that! What're ya singin' Ian?'
—Ian McCulloch, 2001

Q: "What does 'Zimbo' mean?"
Ian McCulloch: "It's an anagram of 'mozib,' an old African word."
Q: "What does 'mozib' mean?"
Ian McCulloch: "Zimbo."   —MTV Online interview, 1995

NO DARK THINGS

I like it
My hands clean
No head shaved
It's quite safe
Compromise
Discovery
It's just an
It's only

Oh my god
Oh you misconstrue all
The tactics
You must learn
To distinguish error
From my bait

Really don't think it's funny
But he's beginning to accept the
    facts

Into the middle of the floor
You walked over
In the middle of the wall
The picture was still hanging
From the corner of my eye
You stick the pins in
In the middle of the floor
I fell over

We have no dark things
Nothing to hide or that
Just some heads and a wish
Something to sing about
We have no dark things
Nothing to hide or that
Just some heads and a wish
Something to scream about

No dark things
No dark things

Just when the thought occurs the
    panic will pass
And the smell of the fields
    never lasts
Put your faith in those
    crimson nights
Set sail in those turquoise days
We've got a problem
Come on over
We got a problem
Come on over

It's not for glory, it's not
    for honor
Just something someone said
It's not for love, it's not
    for war
Just hands clasped together
It's not for living, it's not
    for hunger
Just lips locked tight
It's not rebellion, it's not
    suffering
It's just the way it is
And my pistols packed
And my God goes with me
I fell easy
And I want it
And I need it
And I've got it

It's not for this, it's not
    for that
It's not any of it
Did you say knowledge?
Did you say prayer?
Did you say anything?
If not for good
If not for better
If not the way it is

Just when the thought occurs the
    panic will pass
And the smell of the fields
    never lasts
We'll place our faith in those
    crimson nights
Set sail in those turquoise days
Place your faith in those
    crimson nights
Set sail in those turquoise days
You've got a problem?
Come on over
You've got a problem?
Come on over

Now I think I know just what
    to say …

That's about the human race today. It's people not understanding
everything they do and all the motives for doing things. They think
it's for things like love, glory, war, and all that, but it's not—
it's abut something else which I haven't figured out yet. 'It's just
the way it is.' I mean, that one viewpoint on my philosophy can be
different from my viewpoint on another part of my philosophy.
'Turquoise Days' and 'Disease' are two sides of the same coin.

—Ian McCulloch, 1984

Sometimes you get a line or a tune out of ad-libbing. 'All I Want' came from an ad-lib. Sometimes it works and sometimes it doesn't.

—Ian McCulloch, 1981

ALL I WANT

I began to feel so bad
Waking up laughing so rare
Up and down and down the stairs
Set myself up in the chair

And said all I love
Is all I love
All I want
Is all I want

If we make
The same mistake
Who could we blame?
When we make
The same mistake
Who will we blame?
What will we blame?

We blame all I love
All I love
All we want
All we want

I had a helpful discussion
I had to sleep in a chair
I laid my head on a cushion
Because it was there

Up and down and down the stairs
Set myself up in the chair

And said all I love
All I love
All I want
Is all I want

Got the hands
To hold the key

… one of the most purely powerful songs ever written, building up from the archly concealed Doors quote to a chorus almost frightening in its cinematic frenzy.   —NME, 1981

... one of the most startling love songs I've heard. Pete de Freitas's drumming is a racing pulse of scattered and shattered rhythm that propels the song like a rush of blood to the brain. The guitars juggle on a nerve-ending of terrible tension. The voice and guitars are often at variance, held together by the thinnest and tautest of threads.
                                                            —NME, 1981

1982: ON THE CHOPPING BLOCK

Will Sergeant themes for 'GRIND'

The problem with highs, as anyone with a proclivity for drugs or drink will tell you, is the inevitable comedown. If 1981 found the Bunnymen high on their own self-belief, the next year watched them crash-land into a hung over hell. The band met the dawn of '82 by careening at Concorde speed into a stultifying writing block. Although they spent five days a week jamming at their Liverpool rehearsal studio, The Ministry, the well of inspiration that had fueled *Heaven Up Here* had simply evaporated. The frustrated foursome found itself banging its head against a wall of dead-end block-chord riffs— mostly in D.

The devil-may-care brotherhood that defined 1981 Bunnyspirit had vanished and replaced itself with an air of interpersonal tension, due quite probably (and not just a little ironically) to the same breakneck schedule that had produced the sense of camaraderie in the first place.

The problem was compounded by shifting priorities. Mac was still dedicated to the Bunnymen mission, which was essentially—or arrogantly—to be the Best Band in the World.

I think we'd like to be the best band at everything. When we go on holidays we should be the best band. Best band who smoke cigarettes. Best at everything. When you're a Bunnyman you should become more aware of yourself—like, when you go on tour it's like a small human race, us and the crew, which works without causing wars with each other.   —Ian McCulloch, 1983

    ... Mac had wild ambition on the way we should live and tour, and that got in the way   —Les Pattinson, 1992

Mac's a very jealous person. If he thinks people aren't chipping in, he freaks out.   —Will Sergeant, 1997

When you're a Bunnyman, you're a Bunnyman to the end.
                                          —Ian McCulloch, 1997

I'm ambitious in that I've always wanted to got down in history as being important, as being great, as having something. Not necessarily just on the music side, but to stamp our personality and individuality as people.
                                          —Ian McCulloch, 1987

The rest of the band wasn't so single-minded. Les repeatedly expressed his *ennui* with the music industry, and yearned for his former proper job of boatbuilding. Pete's eyes swerved from the Bunnymen mission at least long enough to produce and provide drums for The Wild Swans' debut single "Revolutionary Spirit" under the pseudonym Louis Vincent, his two middle names. The Wild Swans were the new project of Paul Simpson, who had left

The Teardrop Explodes just before their first album was recorded. Will had strayed so far as to create an entire solo LP: *Themes for 'Grind'* contained 11 instrumentals, recorded on a four-track.

Bill Butt wanted to make this film called *Grind*, and he asked me to do the music. I said, 'Yeah' and did all this music, and then he got all of his film stuff robbed out of his car, so that was the end of it.
—Will Sergeant, 1998

It's a solo LP in the way that I did everything on it, but I don't want to think of it as a solo LP like Steve Howard would do ... it's fairly boring background music—it's no big deal. It's not ... whizz-out guitar freakouts, it's just background ambiance. If you wanted guitar freakouts, 'Weird as Fish' is the one—but I'm afraid it's unavailable at the moment.
—Will Sergeant, 1982

Themes For 'Grind,' released in March 1982 through Rough Trade Distribution on Will's own "92 Happy Customers" label, sold 2000 copies, considerably more than 92. Whether many of those customers were actually happy with the album, however, remains uncertain. Will himself described the cryptic collection of atmospheres and textures as "a bit naff." Critics largely agreed.

The impetus need some pop musicians feel to diversify rarely amounts to any more than their undoing. What makes Will Sergeant, the Bunnymen's intelligently dramatic guitarist, think a record of his electric ambient music will stimulate us or inform us more variously about his ideas and expressive powers than the Echo records? *Themes for 'Grind'* suggests his homemade music is best kept for his own four walls.
—*NME*, 1982

At least one voice of dissent is Frank Coleman, creator and former manager of the Bunnymen's website, who insists that it's a work of unparalleled genius. But the limited commercial and artistic appeal of *'Grind'* didn't prevent Will from considering a soundtrack project in the future.

If it's on an 8-track, it will probably be twice as good! Then it will only be crap.
—Will Sergeant, *Never Stop*

There's one track on it that I always imagine as cave dwellers; it sounds like industrial troglodytes. Some of the sounds on there are really amazing, considering I really didn't know what I was doing.
—Will Sergeant, 1998

In 1997, *Themes For 'Grind'* was re-released on Ochre and Spiffing Records, with an additional track, "Favourite Branches." The reissue prompted both Will and reviewers to reassess its value.

Themes For 'Grind' pretty much paints the unfinished film itself; urban decay, industrial wastelands, factories belching smoke, inner city blues. An electronic urban Ry Cooder, its eighties-ness is so unmistakable you could almost imagine Cabaret Voltaire or Joy

Division nodding their approval. Its rarity value far outstrips its musical content—which isn't to say *Themes For 'Grind'* is a lost cause, far from it. If bleak, out-there electronica appeals, this is worth a listen. Just don't expect any lost Bunnymen classics.

—*NME*, 1997

Back in 1982, Bunnymen classics were exactly what Mac was aiming for, and he was beginning to doubt the dedication of his bandmates. Despite this, when speaking to the press, he attempted to conceal the group's lack of work-in-progress with some bravado and offhand humor.

I always said the second album would be a hundred times better than *Crocodiles* and it was. This one is gong to be better than Da Vinci or Michelangelo. Even Hieronymous Bosch ... well … maybe not … we've written sod-all for this album.   —Ian McCulloch, 1982

The Bunnymen managed to pound enough rough material together for their fourth Peel Session on February 8th. They played three tracks: a doomy, sketchy little rumble called "No Hands," built around Les's intro to live versions of "With a Hip"; the dirgey "Smack in the Middle," which evolved into "Higher Hell"; and the comparatively upbeat "Taking Advantage." The latter track was the last shred of musical spontaneity the lapine Liverpudlians would encounter for some time.

We wrote [the song] in a day and then went down to do this Peel Session with no lyrics or anything and Mac wrote them there and then.

—Pete de Freitas, 1983

"Taking Advantage" was the only song of the three that sounded like it had potential to be the single that WEA was demanding. Although the Bunnymen were still fairly happy with the sound of *Heaven Up Here*, they wanted to stay insular regarding a producer, possibly due to insecurity about the quality of their new material, and their natural suspicion of big-name music biz types. It was decided that *Crocodiles* co-producer and Will Seargent flatmate Ian "Kingbird" Broudie would sit behind the booth.

Broudie decided to bring strings—big, bold, hard strings—into the song's arrangement, which resulted in a grandiose, panoramic sound that would became a virtual Bunnymen signature for the next few years. Although the recording of the song itself—which was retitled "Back of Love" in-studio—went fairly smoothly, the strained relations between the Bunnymen had reached critical mass. Broudie recollected that during the recording session, all four Bunnymen stumbled around the studio in sunglasses, either arguing

We just had a riff, just a chord structure ... we rehearsed it and everything happened at once.

—Will Sergeant, 1983

They were hard work sometimes ... they were a really close group but they'd have fierce arguments. Mac would come in saying he'd written something and the rest would refuse to play it. Will would spend hours on a guitar solo and Mac would dismiss it instantly.

—Ian Broudie, 1997

vehemently or refusing to speak to each other at all.

Bill Drummond was aware of the tension, and he agreed with the group that the new material wasn't up to snuff. He sensed that the Bunnymen needed to communicate more as friends, and, as ever, to work harder at writing proper songs. To this end, he sent the four on an impromptu no-frills tour of Scotland in April; just the Bunnymen and Jake squeezed into a van, without so much as an extra lightbulb between them, never mind a PA.

The idea of the Scottish tour was to reduce everything to basics. We even humped our own gear and played tiny villages that tours never usually go to. I think the locals appreciated the gesture, but I'm not sure how much they enjoyed us.
   —Ian McCulloch, 1983

Will: "It was like the audience would be one punk, one skin, one greaser, one hippy ... "
Mac: "One sheep."
Will: "One of everything."
Mac: "One welder."
Les: "And he wasn't a real welder. Found the glasses on a tip."
Mac: "And the sheep would be the only one who'd get into it."
   —Hot Press, 1997

At least one or two of those sheep must have been moonlighting as music journalists, as the press's love affair with the Bunnymen continued unabated.

Worshipped by the faithfuls, the Bunnymen are a secret to the TOTP audience. This has not frustrated or diverted them. The Bunnymen remain concerned with the larger issues: faith, betrayal, the rest. Taking themselves seriously, they're never pompous and never trivial. Instead, they keep growing like a natural force, slowly, deadly, irresistibly. When they triumph, it will be on their own terms … if pop can include more moods than smiles and has no fear of feeling, the Bunnymen won't be a secret much longer. And that's a promise.
   —Journalist Mark Cooper, 1982

The promise of the live show notwithstanding, the intentions behind the Scottish tour weren't realized. The Bunnymen were still barely on speaking terms, and they only managed to force out a couple of new songs—two tortured slabs of spiritual pychotica called "Clay" and "My White Devil." Mac in particular was becoming more frustrated with the situation, to the point where he was considering quitting the band entirely.

BACK OF LOVE

On a more positive note, the hell-for-leather caterwaul of "Back of Love," b/w "The Subject" and "Fuel" was released on May 21, 1982, and rose immediately to number 19 in the UK charts. Mac was proud of the single, particularly his vocals and the obvious message contained within the lyrics.

That was the [best] vocal that I ever did…I really believed every syllable and meant every syllable.   —Ian McCulloch, 1983

BACK OF LOVE

I'm on the chopping block
Chopping off my stopping thoughts
Self-doubt and selfism
Were the cheapest things I
    ever bought

When you say it's love
D'ya mean the back of love?
When you say it's love
D'ya mean the back of love?

We're taking advantage of
Breaking the back of love
We're taken advantage of
Breaking the back of love

Easier said than done you said
But it's more difficult to say
With eyes bigger than our bellies
We want to but we can't look away

What were you thinking of
When you dreamt that up?
What were you thinking of
When you dreamt that up?

Taking advantage of
Breaking the back of love

When you're surrounded by a
    simple chain of events
Eventually you'll shack those
    shackles off

We can't tell our left from right
But we know we love extremes
Getting to grips with the
    ups and downs
Because there's nothing
    in between

When you say it's love
D'ya mean the back of love?
When you say that's love
D'ya mean the back of love?

Taking advantage of
Breaking the back of love
What were you thinking of
When you dreamt that up?

We're taking advantage of
Breaking the back of love
Breaking the back
Of love

Love—that has to be the most abused word ever. You get people like Gary Crowley talking about 'soul' on the telly and he plays these horrible disco records with this crap woman singer and this divvy from Scotland who wouldn't know 'soul' if it smacked him 'round the head a few times.
    —Ian McCulloch, 1984

All these chart groups seemed to be writing about love in a very surface way, and I wanted to sing about it as a real emotional thing, not some scummy trash.
    —Ian McCulloch, 1983

An urgent song, always seeming to be half a beat into the next second even as the preceding one is being played … [the Bunnymen are] moving away from the 'psychedelic' tag into an area governed by more unusual sound mixtures. What has not changed, though, is the McCulloch way of looking at the world through grey tinted glasses. It's hardly the stuff of a happy song. But Echo have never been a happy band, merely a necessary one. An arresting piece of music. Echo & the Bunnymen make you think while they make you move, a talent in danger of being lost by the majority of today's generation of songsters.
—Journalist Jim Kozlowski, 1982

… one of the best songs I've ever heard, let alone written. What was in there was agony, and it was very real.

—Ian McCulloch, 2001

The future of rock & roll (British section), I presume? Like the idea or loathe it, it's not far from the truth, so it's encouraging that the lap-ine ones are dispatching us such high-quality goods from their northern lair. More commercial and taken at a more spirited pace than one has come to expect of these gents, 'Back of Love' boasts a hummable refrain and strings, as well as an intriguing lyric, delivered with suitable self-righteous passion by young Mr. McCulloch. There's a strength to it that makes much of the competition sound downright flimsy.

—*Melody Maker,* 1982

A best-forgotten extra B-side. It had terrible words and a rubbish tune. It was done in a rush and it shows. Utter crap.

—Ian McCulloch, 1999

A lot of the time I think I'm being really direct. Like, with 'Back of Love' … I mean, you can't sing, 'When you say that's love/You mean exactly the opposite of what you're talking about when you say love,' because it doesn't fit the song, so I said 'the back of love.' It's just a way of writing. I'm not trying to be vague so that people will think I'm some enigmatic writer.

—Ian McCulloch, 1983

Most people would have taken the chords of 'Back of Love' at half the speed the Bunnymen do. I thought it one of 1982's best crude blowouts.

—*NME,* 1983

… like a breath of fresh air—there wasn't a song to touch it last year. It was a simple thing done simply—it was punky, but with an extra essence that punk never had.

—Ian McCulloch, 1983

I love 'Back of Love' because it did just what it was designed to. People seem to have forgotten about things sounding raw. I like things which are simple but which last. Songs like 'Twist and Shout' and The Doors' 'Light My Fire' you can still listen to now. I think 'Back of Love' is like that. You could probably do the twist or even pogo to 'Back of Love' but it's just not hip.

—Ian McCulloch, 1983

Liverpool's lushest discard their murky air of mystery, throw caution to the wind, and stray near something like a tune. Sadly this sounds like one hell of a mess to me ... the Bunnymen strike a bright atti-tude with a clumsy playfulness that's distinctly unseductive. Muddy brass lies buried somewhere beneath the general untidy jumble while Mac reels around some variations of his theme of awestruck inarticu-lacy.

—*Sounds,* 1982

THE SUBJECT

You know exactly what is good for
   you
Bottle love and no dictionary
Shoving your face into anyone
Skating around the subject
With your skin undone
Rubbing your fingers into anyone

So far so good but what's good
   for me?

You know just exactly what is
   good for you
Bottle love and no dictionary
Tell me what you're thinking is
   good for me
Bottle love and no dictionary

Skating around the subject
Is my skin undone?
Mating with the subject
Subject, anyone?

FUEL

There is an easier route ...

Have you had enough
Of your infancy, well?
Would you pass me the bit
Between Heaven and hell?
There's an easier route
The hypotenuse
By bypassing the tongue
Home and dry and unstuck

Come and get me
I'm coming ready or not
I can learn you
A few minor things
A hymn to learn and sing

Falling over ourselves
Never bothered to choose
Do they laugh at your need?
Are they changing to you?

There's a book on the floor
Many pages for me
I can fit it too well
Do you know what that means?

Come and get me
I'm coming ready or not
Falling over myself
Getting ahead of you ...

Have you had enough
Of your infancy, well?
Are you planning the move
Between Heaven and hell?

You can teach me
A few major things
Some animal things
Some hymns to learn and sing
Come and get me
I'm coming ready or not ...

It was done in my bedroom on a 4-track, where I did the *Grind* soundtrack and all my weird stuff. Pete had this marimba thing he'd got in Paris. Made that one up on the spot ... we used to open the set with that live sometimes. It's one people are always trying to get hold of.   —Will Sergeant, 2001

WOMAD

Shortly after the release of "Back of Love," the Bunnymen were invited to headline Peter Gabriel's ambitious but financially disastrous World Of Music, Arts, and Dance (WOMAD) Festival, held at Shepton Mallet, near Bath, on July 17th. Pleased to take part in the multicultural event, and to exhibit their own proclivities towards the exotic, the band highlighted their set by pounding out a tribal version of "Zimbo" accompanied by the Royal Burundi Drummers.

That was the whole point of that thing, all sorts of bands from different cultures playing together and hanging out. Nobody else did it except for us. I just said, 'Why don't we get the Burundi Drummers?' because I'd seen them, and they were brilliant. —Will Sergeant, 1998

The Burundi Drummers were great—the good thing was, they wanted to do it ... that was the only point where all the WOMAD stuff 'bout cultures meeting really happened. 'Twas like being on another planet.
—Ian McCulloch, 1985

To commemorate the event, a WOMAD album was subsequently released, featuring selections from artists at the festival. The record didn't contain any Bunnymen songs—although the sleeve art pictured a Burundi drummer proudly sporting a Bunnymen T-shirt—but instead included an atmospheric Will Sergeant solo composition called "Favourite Branches."

I think they just asked me to record it, because I was into the whole concept of the festival, and was into Indian music and all that kind of stuff.
—Will Sergeant, 1998

The song was also released as a split 7-inch single with Bill Loveday's "Himalaya." This quickly became a rare collector's item, eventually tagged on at the end of the Ochre/Spiffing CD re-release of *Themes For 'Grind'* in 1997.

SELF-DOUBT AND SELFISM

After the WOMAD festival, the Bunnymen went back to the job of writing and recording their third album, provisionally titled *The Happy Loss*. The title was eventually changed to *Porcupine* "to show that we throw out spines," Mac explained. The recording process was extremely slow and painful, not only due to the Bunnymen's creative block, but the influences—alcoholic and otherwise—under which they were writing.

Porcupine was very hard to actually write and record ... it's that inevitable point you reach when you start to question what you do, and you start to think, 'Hang on—is this good anymore?' When you start to do that it's very hard to be confident in what you do. *Heaven Up Here* was pure confidence, we did it really quickly; we had a great time doing it—but this one was like we had to drag it out of ourselves, almost.
—Pete de Freitas, 1983

It was probably the first album where the bev was kicking in ... us becoming distanced from one another.
—Ian McCulloch, 1999

The first two records were done with a lot more naiveté. With *Porcupine*, we questioned what we were doing for the first time, whether it was right or not. The composition of the music was the first thing, and from there we went on to question our abilities in the writing of songs, or why we were even doing it, basically. Nothing seemed so intuitive as it used to, and I always thought it *had* to be intuitive.
—Ian McCulloch, 1983

When the Bunnymen finally presented the troubled LP to WEA, the record company rejected it as being "too uncommercial." Surprisingly, the band agreed, and were willing to re-record it—except for Will, whose musical tastes were fairly uncommercial anyway. Never one for compromise, Will has always been vociferous with his distaste towards record label bureaucracy.

We can argue with them and try to say what we think, but they are basically a bunch of tossers, and have never liked anything we've ever done anyway.   —Will Sergeant, 1983

The record company uses us and we use them, and it's who can us the other to the best advantage, and that's all it is. And there's no friendship or nothing like that. No artistic integrity.—Will Sergeant, 1985

Despite Will's protests, the album was redone, with the original recording acting as a rough blueprint. Selections from the scrapped version eventually made it to vinyl: "Wrapped In Paper," one of the Bunnymen's most intensely paranoid moments, was retitled "Way Out and Up We Go" and released as a B-side, as were "Drop In the Ocean" and "Heads Will Roll [Summer Version].")

With the template of the rejected album to work from, the recording went more smoothly the second time around. Many songs were only slightly altered and given a brighter production. Bill Drummond recruited Indian violinist Shankar (not Ravi) to add texture and mood to the songs, and to build on the success of the strings used on "Back of Love."

Overall, the record was extremely expensive and time-costly—seven months of work from start to finish—to the point where a planned tour had to be rescheduled. Much of the final version of the album was invented with just a week of recording time left in the studio. Les in particular enjoyed this, a shade of the musical spontaneity he adored about recording *Heaven Up Here*.

SEFTON PARK/REYKJAVIK

In November 1982, just months after *Porcupine* was pounded out, 20,000 fans were treated to a free Bunnymen show in Liverpool's Sefton Park as part of the city's "Larks In the Park" festival. The concert was filmed as part of BBC2's "Pop Carnival" series. Shankar sat in on strings, adding exotic touches to the Aigburth experience. In contrast to or perhaps because of the strain within the band, their live show was more invigorating and powerful than in recent memory.

★★★

To the *Star Trek* tune, a well bevvied Bunnyband took the stage. Had they been at the fabled Seffy Park magic mushrooms? Was this REALLY the new Woodstock? Should I have worn a kaftan? All fears that they were the 'ultimate trip' were shattered as the Bunnydrunks produced an immaculate, forceful hour of rock music. Both the New Punk and HM sheep in wolves' clothing should come and see Bunnyhead to see what Real Power is about … the Bunnyidols are the epitome of all that is good about rock … a vital performance. ` *—NME*, 1982

The photo session for *Porcupine*, that main waterfall, we were lucky with that because it's not frozen over that much; like, if we had gone in summer it wouldn't have been frozen over, but because it was it meant we could get into locations on the whole waterfall that we couldn't have otherwise. It was really dangerous … I was really scared, I didn't enjoy that at all. [But] it was impressive, standing up there and being a part of that, 'cos we were the only people there. —Bill Butt, 1983

After the Sefton Park show, Warner Brothers asked the Bunnymen to create three promo videos and album art for *Porcupine* with the relatively tiny budget of 16,000 pounds. The frugal and inventive Bill Butt insisted that he could create an LP cover *plus* a complete half-hour film for that kind of money.

To accentuate the frigid feel of the album, Butt wanted to go to Scotland and film the band in icy environs. The late November weather forecast in kilt country didn't look good, so the group decided to go where snow would be guaranteed. With Butt and a film crew, the Bunnymen threw caution and an unhealthy amount of the budget to the wind and flew to Iceland. Filming took place by a waterfall called Gorfolos, in Reykjavik, surrounded by volcanic ash roads in below-zero temperatures. Fittingly, the filming proved to be nearly as traumatic as the creation of the LP itself. No one was prepared for the harsh environment, and all involved inadvertently and literally risked their lives in the name of—ahem—*art*.

It was really dangerous; that ledge we were on … wasn't that wide. If we had slipped there wasn't anything for hundreds of feet below us … you could easily die of exposure. It was dangerous in all kinds of ways; if the cars hadn't been working, we would have probably frozen to death … we almost did. —Ian McCulloch, 1983

It was November in Iceland, so the sun barely appeared the whole time we were there. To walk, stand up, or just think seemed a massive effort. But beyond the conditions, in technical terms, the shoot was very easy. The most difficult thing was Ian McCulloch's hair. Even though we were freezing to death, Mac still had to spend a few light years making sure his hair was in the right formation. —Brian Griffin, 2001

The album sleeve proved worth the risk.

That was such a great cover. It would have been an even better cover if it hadn't been minus 20 degrees. —Ian McCulloch, 1990

In my head it had to be another full bleed shot of the band on location. But this time, the Bunnymen, the four followers of Echo, would be off on the journey to find Echo, to seek his wisdom. They ame back with a shot of the Bunnymen wandering along the edges oᵣ ₁ frozen canyon. [It was] a perfect cover. —Bill Drummond, *From the Shores of Lake Placid and Other Stories*

The *Porcupine* cover is the epitome of rock band as heroic archetype—young men on some ill-defined but glorious mission, one easily as timeless as the stars and the sea.
—*Q*, 2001

Returning to Liverpool in December, Butt filmed the Bunnymen performing songs from *Porcupine* at the Ministry, with clips from a Russian film, *The Man With the Movie Camera,* interspersed throughout to underscore the Far Eastern vibe of the music. Given the band's love of Soviet graphics and imagery, one wonders if they ever considered touring that sector of the world. Apparently not.

We were asked a lot to got to Eastern Europe, but we couldn't be arsed. Too many invasions and stuff, and getting paid in boiled potatoes.
—Ian McCulloch, 1995

No potatoes—in fact, no groceries of any kind—were harmed in the making of Butt's video, in which he placed psychedelic watercolor effects projected over the band—perhaps a nod to The Velvet Underground's legendary "Exploding Plastic Inevitable" 1966 stint at New York's Dom. The half-hour film, eventually released under Atlas Adventures, featured promo videos for six psychedelic slices of soul-searching: "The Cutter," "Back of Love," "My White Devil," "Porcupine," "Heads Will Roll," and "In Bluer Skies."

It's a surprisingly flat-footed compilation; Mac and the chaps strumming along to the tracks in a variety of basements, attics, warehouses, and rehearsal rooms with inter-cut footage of glaciers, ice-caps, and the group cavorting in the snow, none of it at all inspiring... Butt … fails conspicuously to match the classic grandeur of pieces like 'The Cutter' with any kind of appropriate visual impact.
—*Melody Maker*, 1984

Porcupine dates from the Bunnies' late, great constructivist infatuation days. The Red worker look—plastered all over this tape—has since been dropped … *Porcupine* is the Bunnymen performing the LP in a grey garage. There are a few Icelandic cutaways and much, much Sovietism. The music is brilliant.
—Journalist Desa Fox, 1984

THE CUTTER

On January 14, 1983, "The Cutter" single was released, b/w "Way Out and Up We Go" and "Zimbo" with the Royal Burundi Drummers. (Initial pressings of the record came with a poster of a still from the Reykjavik shoot, plus a free cassette of the Bunnymen's first Peel Session.) Featuring a Moslem prayer intro, a singalong chorus and a soaring middle eight, "The Cutter" was perhaps the Bunnymen's most crafted song to date.

The full impact of the song's resolution was not the Bunnymen's doing. When Drummond presented the single to the executives at Warner Brothers, they thought it sounded somehow incomplete, and suggested that trumpets be added. This Drummond did, without informing the band. When the

Bunnymen eventually heard the results, they were furious that their work had been tampered with, but grudgingly agreed that it sounded fantastic. Drummond has since referred to this little bit of duplicity as the best thing that he ever did for the band on a commercial level.

Lyrically, the song was one of Mac's most vague, although he's tried to clarify the essence of the words to the press.

The lyric was making out that people were so thick that if Jesus came back a second time [they] would ignore him or ridicule him.

—Ian McCulloch, 1994

Someone said to me a few years ago, 'It's about a drug dealer, innit? "Spare us the cutter — don't put too much of this shite in!' I thought that made a lot more sense in the 20th century than some kind of rehash of Jesus, the second coming, and the savior figure.

—Ian McCulloch, 1998

[The Cutter is] a person who's got a job to do, an important job ... of cutting out all the crap in the world. A lot of people thought it was the 'grim reaper' or something stupid like that. [But the Cutter is] somebody who cuts all the crap out, a ruthless person. I think there should be a person—a politician, whatever—who cuts away all the crap in the world. But the 'spare us the cutter' bit—the majority of people don't want that person, 'cos they don't want what's good for them, generally. They always want what's safe for them, or bad for them. Somebody like the cutter would be good for them, but they wouldn't be able to cope with it. It's not me talking, it's other people, but I believe there should be a cutter.   —Ian McCulloch, 1983

I wanna strip away the masks that people wear, and that people make us wear as well.   —Ian McCulloch, 1983

THE CUTTER

Who's on the seventh floor
Brewing alternatives?
What's in the bottom drawer
Waiting for things to give?

Spare us the cutter
Spare us the cutter
Couldn't cut the mustard

Conquering myself until
I see another hurdle approaching
Say we can, say we will
Not just another
Drop in the ocean

Come to the free-for-all
With sellotape and knives
Some of us six feet tall
We will escape our lives

Spare us the cutter
Spare us the cutter
Couldn't cut the mustard

Conquering myself until
I see another hurdle approaching
Say we can, say we will
Not just another
Drop in the ocean

Am I the happy loss?
Will I still recoil
When the skin is lost?
Am I the happy cross?
Will I still be soiled
When the dirt is off?

Conquering myself until
I see another hurdle approaching
Say we can, say we will
Not just another
Drop in the ocean
Ocean ...

Watch the fingers close
When the hands are cold

Am I the happy loss?
Will I still recoil
When the skin is lost?
Am I the worthy cross?
Will I still be soiled
When the dirt is off?

Our first perfect song. The key to 'The Cutter,' for me, is having the best middle eight of the 80's.   —Ian McCulloch, 1992

'The Cutter' may be the best pop utilization of Indian strings since fellow Liverpudlians the Beatles got into the mystic.
                                        —*Rolling Stone*, 2001

Will somebody please tell Radiohead that this is what miserabilism [sic] should sound like?   —*Melody Maker*, 1998

   ... apart from an exaggeratedly Bowie-esque bridge passage—a pastiche of 'Heroes'—the song (which may or may not be concerned with death's scythe) is hopelessly lacking in the poppy intensity of 'Back of Love.' And aside from the sitar introduction, the sound is striking only in its ordinariness.   —*NME*, 1983

No greater charge has been experienced this 45 year than 'The Cutter'
                                        —*NME*, 1983

WAY OUT AND UP WE GO

When I asked for money
You would give me alcohol
Wasn't being funny
When I said no ifs at all

I'm thinking thoughts too late
No linking
I won't wait

When I wanted coffee
You insist on alcohol
When I said no maybes
You would give me ifs, that's all

A message wrapped in paper
Each passage wrapped in paper
Wrapped in paper made for us
Wrapped in paper made for us

Some meaning sent to someone
Each read it, passed it on
Passed it on to one of us
Passed it on to one of us

Crumpled on the mattress
Best you cover up
Hardly in the bad day
When you don't get up

He made it
Wrapped in sackcloth
Afraid of it
Had to back off
Backed off into one of us
Backed off into one of us

Ten seconds
You can't see it
Old record
Laugh my way out

Way out and up we go
Out of the way and up we go

… is about three different aspects of this man, the cutter. I'm six foot tall, so that's a clue.
                    —Ian McCulloch, 1983

Will: "Broudie did some of the guitar bits. You know where it goes 'Spare us the cutter' and then it goes 'chang?' He did that big 'chang.' I still don't know how he did it. I just do a 'D.'"
Goldmine Magazine: "He never showed you how?"
Will: "I never asked him."
                    —*Goldmine*, 1998

A brilliant song, powerful, yet vulnerable, with some memorable guitar work.
                    —*Goldmine*, 1998

"The Cutter" entered the UK charts at #27. The song solidified the Bunnymen's emergence as cult, critical, and commercial contenders for 1983's rock & roll throne.

I think 'The Cutter,' was a big turning point. We just grew naturally as a band. We built up a following, it evolved, and we became a
real group with real chemistry that knew no bounds. We were scared of
doing uncool things and making crap music, which is fine, but we
weren,t scared of experimenting. We worked within our own limitations
and made them seem kind of limitless.   —Ian McCulloch, 1998

'The Cutter,' was the first one where you,d get other people, maybe
older people saying, 'Oh yeah, love that song.' Me and Pete were
changing money in an airport, and this French woman came over—she was
maybe 50, working in the building—and she said, 'Did you do that song?
Can I have your autograph?' I loved it ... I used to be into The Doors,
and I've just been over to France to see Jim Morrison's grave.' Weird.
That song did that ... it didn't cross over into another market, [but]
maybe people who were around in the 60's appreciated it more than any
of our other stuff.   —Ian McCulloch, 1984

At the beginning of the year, with The Jam recently dissolved, the only other competitors in pop's premier league were U2, a Dublin band whose stadium-bound anthems superficially echoed the Bunnymen's stratospheric style. Their single "New Year's Day," released the same day as "The Cutter," entered the charts at #23. The same week, Mac's old mate Pete Wylie and his group The Mighty Wah! were turning heads with a character-istically over-the-top foray into orchestrated soul, "The Story of the Blues," which made the top 10 on the week of its release. All three of these bands were guests on "Top of the Pops" within a few weeks of each other. U2 and the Bunnymen actually performed on the same evening. This marked the first time Mac would encounter the band's singer, Paul "Bono Vox" Hewson.

Bono is penguining around the studio, wearing his big Orson Welles hat
and these ridiculous Cuban heels. So then he sidles right up to me
and says, 'It's great that we're both on the show. You know what it
means? We're going to change the whole world. This is our mission,

y'know.' And I'm thinking, 'See you later, Fatso.' Not that he was fat
exactly. But he was a squatty little turd. And I thought, 'What the
hell's he going on about anyway? We've just got nothing at all to do
with what he's doing.'   —Ian McCulloch, 1997

During the Bunnymen's mime through "The Cutter," an inebriated Mac
inexplicably pulled his safety-pinned shirt down, exposing a few inches of
pale torso. Although some thought this was an attempt to upstage his Irish
rivals, Mac had ulterior motives for the gesture.

I thought it was funny when I pulled me shirt down, even if some people did think it was crap. What they might not know is that I did it
for a reason. All the bands that appear on the show have to come down
and do a backing track specifically for the show. But it's a fact that
everyone swaps tapes for prerecorded ones. But when we did our track,
this bloke came down and we couldn't swap them around. And that's
where the shirt pullin' helped. It distracted people away from the
racket we were making.   —Ian McCulloch, 1984

Regardless of its rationale, this drunken display of skin helped drive
"The Cutter" up the charts, where it peaked at #8, becoming the Bunnymen's
most successful single thus far.

On February 4, 1983, three weeks after the release of "The Cutter," *Porcupine* was finally released. Although it immediately ascended to #2 in the UK charts, it was savaged by the majority of critics for being self-indulgent, overly doomy, lyrically incomprehensible, and, overall, unbearably difficult listening.

Porcupine takes the Bunnymen as far beyond their Doors-meets-Television happy death pop as is either conceivable or desirable … [it] groans behind bars, an animal trapped by its own defences. To Mac must I say… 'end your groan and come away.' —*NME*, 1983

Supposedly Mac's 'personal' album, it wanders through an arctic wasteland, a nightmare of twitching acoustic guitars, skidding strings, and self-doubt. —*Record Mirror*, 1987

Cheap Quills: the Bunnymen still lack that special something that makes and sometimes breaks a great band ... these Bunnymen sound older than I'll ever be —*Sounds*, 1983

There's something cruel about the way Mac's vivid poetry embraces ambiguity, because these songs are virtually intolerable in their exposition of pain without specifying anything. There is no clear hook to hang a sob onto. —*NME*, 1983

Echo remain criminally conservative. Problem is, Mac just can't tear his group away from his own juvenile obsession with doom and gloom. He's caught up in an interminable dark tunnel that simply refuses to let in even a modicum of optimistic light. Consequently, the Bunnymen remain stunted, overwhelmingly pessimistic, and perversely unable to develop artistically … I suggest these Bunnies hurry underground for (their own) good. —*Melody Maker*, 1983

Some adopted a less analytical approach to the record's faults.

The album was shit.
—Bill Drummond, *From the Shores of Lake Placid and Other Stories*

A few journalists, while recognizing the pained and painful quality of the album, did commend *Porcupine* for its unrelenting emotional honesty and relatively profound themes.

One of the most intensely difficult records likely to be released in this or any other year. *Porcupine* growls and roars, and there is an awful beauty about it; but it takes time to squeeze past the outer quills … its seems to me that few records have been so accurately titled. —*NME*, 1983

The Bunnymen were playing too loud for Mac, too intensely in block chords instead of chord progressions, in the wrong structures, in the wrong key. He wasn't singing, he was straining, and how could he blame folks like me for missing out on his humor when the whole aura of the songs was overwhelmingly, if unintentionally, self-important?
—*Melody Maker*, 1984

Porcupine, a blurred storm of isolation and enlightenment, found [the Bunnymen] at their brilliant weirdest.   —*Stylus*, 1999

One of the most emotionally effective records ever made —*Sounds*, 1983

The third album may be traditionally problematic, but you have to wipe the cold sweat of this one before you can even play it. Fortunately, *Porcupine* has enough invention and sheer vigour to carry it off. This may mean dipping into old revolutions, backwards guitar, eastern drones, and The Velvet Underground, but it's all deftly merged into the inspirations of hungry adventurers. Ian McCulloch's enigmatic lyrics dwell as usual on the elusive dignity of man and his many absurdities … as well as the expected wordplays around the life and times of a troubled ego ... Its intention to confess remain admirable if uncompleted.   —*Melody Maker*, 1983

Porcupine is probably the hardest record in the world to listen to at one sitting. Denser than the thickest forest, giving little, expecting less. It seems to last forever. I have reason to believe that it is a work of genius.   —*Jamming*, 1985

The Bunnymen's own Black Album ... *Porcupine* has an overpowering sense of dread, claustrophobia, and collapse that reflected difficulties in the band. Although it stands out like a sore, broken thumb in the Echo canon, *Porcupine* has a certain Satanic majesty that sounds eerily in tune with the current pre-millennial blues ...
—*Uncut*, 1999

Porcupine was a long time coming, the labour pains were severe, and the child, it seemed, was still-born. So much soul searching went into *Porcupine* that its enduring worth took several months to appreciate. It remains, to my mind, Mac's most consistent body of lyrics, and, as an album, almost up there with that other great third LP, by the Velvets.
—Journalist Mick Houghton, 1984

That "work of genius" contained Mac's most autobiographical and ambitious body of lyrics to date. Although couched in metaphysical metaphor and religious symbolism, the words directly reflected Mac's own personal and spiritual crises.

It *is* an autobiographical record. I wrote these lyrics because I was more or less going through all those things I was writing about, as the band was, and the world was, on different levels.
—Ian McCulloch, 1983

I think *Porcupine* is politically the best album we've done so far. It's like a diary in that it is very personal, but it definitely takes on a range of subject matter far beyond what we've done before.
—Ian McCulloch, 1984

Despite Mac's insistence that the album was autobiographical, many detractors accused Mac of lyrical pretense, willfully assuming an overly

A lot of it is a confessional thing, an exorcism of things you go through. It's definitely a baring of soul.
—Ian McCulloch, 1983

...suicide material...music to swing to … by a rope…
—Ian McCulloch, 1984

Generally, I don't treat what I put into the songs as being outside my own experience. Echo is not a pretence, a fantasy, or a lie; it's very real.
—Ian McCulloch, 1983

romanticized tortured artist pose. Mac vehemently testified to his lyrical and vocal honesty, although he was willing to admit that *Porcupine* provided a pretty tough listen—albeit one worth the struggle.

I think *Porcupine* was a classic autobiographical album, the most honest thing that I'd every written or sung. Now I think people have realized it's great but it's too late to matter now. I know it's brilliant. The thing is ... .it didn't make me happy. How could it when it was so autobiographical? I found material from it really heavy to play—like, really oppressive. That's the only reason why I didn't like the album. The songs were great but it didn't make me happy. An' if it doesn't, then there's no point. —Ian McCulloch, 1984

Porcupine is probably ... the most *Bunnymen*, way beyond *Crocodiles* and *Heaven Up Here*. But it was horrible to make and nasty to listen to.
—Ian McCulloch, 1999

I'm 24. It's old enough to be world-weary these days.
—Ian McCulloch, 1983

John Webster was
One of the best there was
He was the author of
Two major tragedies
The White Devil and
The Duchess of Malfi ...

Change in the never
Do I get the choice?
Chancing forever
When do we get the spoils?

Now that love is upside down
It's down to us to say that
Our monkey brains
Content to laugh
When laughing wanes
It's time to change

Me on the when
I will be him
You on the then
We will be them

Here it comes again
Knocking on its feet
Here it comes again
Knocking on its feet

Don't say it's like
On the barrier ...

Is it enough now
To tell me you matter
When you haven't a clue how
To bring me to tears?
How many leaves must you crumble
'Til you believe what I told you?
That your lies are just
    stumbles?
Breaking your legs on the way to

Changing the never
Do I get the choice?
Chance in forever
When do we get the spoils?

In 'My White Devil' I sing 'The Duchess of Malfio' because it fits the meter better, and Julian Cope said in an interview around the time, 'Look at that, he says "Malfio" and he doesn't even know it is "The Duchess of Malfi."' I thought, 'Don't be a soddin' cretin.' I couldn't believe that, typical Julian. He embarrasses everyone who has ever heard his songs. He just isn't weird and yet has spent a lifetime trying to be weird. To me, he is still just a tosser who went to teacher's training college.
                        —Ian McCulloch, 1994

...one of my least favorite on the album. That 'John Webster' thing—we had the riff, but I didn't have any lyrics. I was finding it difficult, and me girlfriend had an old exercise book with one page of writing in it. It was about this bloke John Webster who I hadn't heard of—not being that great an English student—and the first line was 'John Webster was' and it all fitted like that! I was always gonna change it, but then I thought, 'Why should I?' It's supposed to be a joke, because it's totally separate from what the rest of the song is. The *NME* review of the album was based around it, and they imagined I was some great literary freak or something!   —Ian McCulloch, 1983

'Oh, isn't it nice/When your heart is made out of ice' ... I didn't have a lyric for that bit on 'Clay,' and I just like the sound of that Lou Reed lyric. I sang it once in rehearsal and everybody liked it, so it stuck … I wanted to do a backing vocal where I went, 'Thanks, Lou' in the background, but I never got 'round to it.

—Ian McCulloch, 1983

I like exposing the contradictions in myself and in other people.

—Ian McCulloch, 1987

… another torture chamber opening and a discordant clash between Mac's diffident vocal and Sergeant's guitar twisting below like a knife in the stomach.

—*NME*, 1983

CLAY

Am I the half of half and half
Or am I the half that's whole?
Got to be one with all
    my halves
Is my worthy earthly goal ...

Are you the heavy half
Of the lighter me?
Are you the ready part
Of the lighter me?

When I came apart
I wasn't made of sand
When you fell apart
Clay crumbled in my hands

On with a life-low
Statues and halos
Am I the half of half and half
Or am I the half that's whole?
Am I the half that's whole? ...

Are you the wrongful half
Of the rightful me?
Are you the Mongol half
Of the cerebral me?

When I came apart
I wasn't made of sand
When you fell apart
Clay crumbled in my hands

If we exercise just some control
When we exercise our sum control

Oh isn't it nice
When your heart is made out of
    ice? ...

Are you the heavy half
Of the lighter me?
Are you the ready part
Of the hesitant me?

Am I the "shall" in potential
Or am I the "suck" in "cess"?
Pools of delusion deluge me
Am I the more or less? ...

When I came apart
I wasn't made of sand
When you fell apart
Clay crumbled in my hands
When I came apart
I wasn't made of sand

When I was the Cain
You were the Abel

When I came apart
Clay crumbled in my hands

I used to listen to [David Bowie's] 'Quicksand,' and me brother who was older once said, 'What do you think that's about?' And I said, 'I don't know, I just really like it.' And he said, 'I think it's about being attracted to extremes.' And in a way that's what I'm like—'torn between the light and dark.' I suppose that's a lot of what I'm on about, seeing things that attract and at the same time repel. A lot of songs are about coming to terms with the opposites in me.

—Ian McCulloch, 1984

PORCUPINE

There is no comparison
Between things about to happen
Missing the point of our mission
Will we become misshapen?

A change of heart
Will force the veil
Nailed to the door
To all avail

There are no divisions
Between things about to collide
Hitting the floor with our vision
A focus at some point arrives

A change of mind
Will force the veil
To hit the head
And set the sails

A change of skin
Will shed the tail
Hung on the wall
For use again

A change of heart
Will force the veil ...
There is no comparison
Between things about to happen

Sick as a pig this pork is mine
I'm pining for the pork of
    the porcupine
I'd best be on my best behavior
Best behave yourself, you hear?

Sick as a pig
This pork is mine
Pine for the pork of
    the porcupine ...

I'm beginning to see the light
Beginning to see the light

It was meant to be about the world, I suppose, about the fact that nobody has yet grasped what the mission is for the human race, because there is, obviously, a mission—not a religious thing or anything, but a reason—and that's how it set out ... and then I realised, 'Bloody hell! This is applying to the band as well! And to me as an individual!'

—Ian McCulloch, 1983

I was getting things totally out of proportion, and thought we were on this great musical crusade in search of some musical holy grail, except I wasn't sure if the band were coming on that journey with me. The first line of that track is 'There is no comparison between things about to happen, missing the point of our mission, will we become misshapen?' All very operatic and very tenuous rhymes, which I have always liked. I'd bend the word and make some real dubious rhyme sound like Pavarotti, but it worked! I knew I was going 'round the bend, but I was into that because I thought that was all part of the myth. The rhymes were going 'round the bend and so was I!

—Ian McCulloch, 1994

... the most shockingly dispirited thing Echo & the Bunnymen have ever done ... a kind of 'All My Colours' on a bad trip, its final exhausted throes are as draining (and as moving) as the bleakest moments on [The Fall's] *Hex Induction Hour*, but devoid of the Fall's humour; just a voice crying against nothing, a beat banging into the void.

—*NME*, 1983

What cryptic message is hidden at the tail-end of 'Porcupine'? You'll have to put on your red pajamas and find out.

—Anonymous phone call
to the author, 2001

There were a lot of coded messages, but like any code you don't reveal how to crack it. Which can cause problems ... but I've always liked cryptic crosswords, I've always done them. I like to keep things cryptic ... not as much lyrically [anymore]. But old cryptic codes I never reveal; it's like espionage.

—Ian McCulloch, 2001

'Heads Will Roll' commences like a Mamas and Papas drug song before plunging into an enervated echo of Bowie.   —*NME*, 1983

'Heads Will Roll' at first slipped past almost unnoticed, but after a while its ruthless guitar dynamics and runaway-train momentum began to make plenty of sense.

—*Melody Maker*, 1984

Through me life I've always felt ...not a calling, but there were things speaking to me, not any kind of Christian God thing, but I always felt that I was picked out or sumthin'. It's just a simple thing … y'know, 'What do I do when those voices stop?'

—Ian McCulloch, 1995

The Bunnymen mission ... I have an inkling but it's not one I can describe in words. It's like a feeling; something that doesn't involve going to the pub, getting drunk, watching telly, institutions. There's something in *Childhood's End* by Arthur C. Clarke, there's an essence to it which is similar to what I think. At the end of the book, all the children that have been born after a certain time all become like amoeba-type things and float off into space, and become part of the whole thing. And all human beings had been worrying about themselves as this thing called the human race when all it was, in the end, was part of something bigger. I hope that there is something bigger than the human race ... it's something to share, a feeling you can share, a common ground where you can get on with people and communicate.

—Ian McCulloch, 1983

HEADS WILL ROLL

Partly politic
Heads will roll
Mostly politic
God must call
'Til the winning hand
Does belong to me

What if no one's calling?
God, then, must be falling

If I ever met you
In a private place
I would stare you
You into the ground
That's how I articulate
The value of one face
The value of my face

What if no one's calling?
God, then, must be falling ...

When all the bottom has
   dropped out
And sadly times are the times
   I love
That's when all of the lights
   go out
Oh yes, did you know I came
   so close?

Partly politic
Heads must roll
Mostly politic
God must call
'Til the ruling hand
Does belong to me

What if no one's calling?
God, then, must be falling

RIPENESS

I found a thing
In a bad room
Changed the shape of
    the world for long enough
Got the boat to
As far as I could afford
    it to take me
It was far enough

Mature you said
At the wrong time
Broke my aging skin
'Cos age was mine
Had a field day
Smelt like roses
Harvesting my thought
'Cos up was time

When you asked the question
Did you miss the meaning?
When you met your challenge
Did you go out fighting?

We will discover
Ripeness twice over

Sing your salt
Worth its weight
In God gold
Curse its fate

When you asked the question
Did you miss the meaning?
When you met your challenge
Did you go out fighting?

How will we recover
Ripeness when it's over?

I lost something
In a big room
Changed the shape of
    the world for long enough

When you asked the question
Did you miss the meaning?
When you met your challenge
Did you go out fighting?
When you climbed on top
Did you fall on shadows?
When clambering off
Did you fall on rainbows? ...

How will we recover
Ripeness when it's over?

Are you fuel for the fire?

'Ripeness' I love, I think it
could have been a classic, but
it was just recorded so poorly.
—Ian McCulloch, 1983

A bloodletting of 'A Promise.'
—*NME*, 1983

… just a play on words. It's about creating your own Heaven and hell, a joke about God's orders.

—Ian McCulloch, 1983

HIGHER HELL

Smack in the middle of today
Got to learn new words
Merely got to simply say
I think we all misheard

Cracked in the middle of me
Have to find my heart
Smiling equates with happy
But I know they're miles apart

Just like my
Lower Heaven
You know so well
My higher hell

When confronted by
Continuing the course
Will you open up
Or do I have to force
The words right out
Of your stubborn mouth
Stunted of course
Guilty in their growth

Just like my
Lower Heaven
You know so well
My higher hell

Crashed through the floor today
I couldn't find my legs
I suppose you live and learn
Learn it again and again

Smack in the middle of today
Got to find new words
Merely got to simply say
I think we all misheard

Just like my
Lower Heaven
You know so well
My higher hell

I couldn't understand how we got to writing something like 'Higher Hell' which, to me, was just a dirge. I mean, I like it—it one of the best pieces of dirge you could write ...   —Ian McCulloch, 1984

I probably never knew who the sod I was ever since I was a teenager. As soon as the Bunnymen started, I was just thrust into soddin' Overcoatsville and Camoland, and I was just The Dude With The Lips, who was singing all this shite about 'higher hell.' What the sod was *that* about? I was having a great time.   —Ian McCulloch, 1999

How can you pretend
When there's so much at stake
That it's a different world
And your hands don't shake?

At the end of the room
In front of the bar
We knew that soon
We'd be making our mark
(Mark my words)

Why do you defend
The part you have to take
With your fingers on the world
Hoping your hands don't shake?

When you get the time
Why not think about
Connecting yours and mine
And turning in to out?
(Out of it and into it)

Back to the bar
I was feeling it
The hole in the floor
Was where I would sit

Positions will be lost
Things will fall in place
The falling will not stop
'Til we have found our face
(Let's face it, we're in Heaven)

Oh will you mention
My name
To one
Oh, will you mention
My name
To me

Gods will be gods but my one
    forgot I was made out of skin
And bones will be bones but when
    I came home there was no one in
So where were you staying
While I was out praying?
Was nobody laying
The foundations?
The fulfilling
Of our killing

How can you pretend
That there's so much at stake
When it's a different world
And everything shakes?

Shake baby shake
Roll baby roll
Gonna hit the highest heights and
Never be told to
Roll baby roll
Shake baby shake
Gonna hit the highest heights and
Make a mistake

If you can work out 'Gods Will
Be Gods,' you're a better man
than I am … it's very direct
when we do it live, but on
record it's a bit of a wash of
tinny noise. It's alright, but
the way we do it live is really powerful and precise.
                —Ian McCulloch, 1983

I played 'Gods Will Be Gods'
the other day. Worst-sounding
track I've heard in me life.
                —Ian McCulloch, 1987

One night we were playing 'Gods
Will Be Gods.' Instead of
singing 'the hole in the
floor,' I wanted to sing 'the
hole in my arse.' I thought it
was hysterical, cos I was on
this bevvy. Every time I got to
that bit I couldn't stop laughing. It went on for about ten
minutes. But I never got so
bevvied that I'd fall over.
Well ... once, in Belfast.
                —Ian McCulloch, 1995

Try listening to 'Gods Will Be
Gods' on headphones in the dark
without thinking, 'This is
fucked up.' I don't ever wanna
go back there.
                —Ian McCulloch, 1999

… it's about walking off to a better sky. I felt like I was living in a Delux advert where the sky goes black, and I personally thought we should be looking for something a lot lighter. It was the last song we wrote and recorded for the album, and it leaves a lot more space than the others.
—Ian McCulloch, 1983

... a very obvious lyric, because I did find myself on the verge of falling apart. I don't think I ever discovered insanity, but I discovered just grooving along with how it was going.
—Ian McCulloch, 1983

IN BLUER SKIES

What needs must be, I realize
I'm walking out from
    blackened skies
You say belief is in our eyes
But how can I believe in
    blind lies?

I'm counting on your heavy heart
Could it keep me from
    falling apart?

Have we been born to follow
Tied to a bitter reign?
Or will we begin to grow
Bound by this simple chain?
Will we evolve tonight
Sparkle of brittle stars?
Can we dissolve tonight
Held by your hungry arms?

I'm counting on your heavy heart
Could it keep me from
    falling apart?

Why weren't you ready
Ready to grow?
Was your heart heavy
Heavy with sorrow?
Hurting and heavy
We could have both been grown
Now your heart's heavy
Heavy with sorrow

I'm counting on your heavy heart
Could it keep me from
    falling apart?

What needs have been,
    you'll realize
I found myself in bluer skies
I know belief is in your eyes
But we can't believe in
    blind lies

I'm counting on your heavy heart
To keep me from falling apart

***

We think that *Porcupine* represents a beginning and an end. The end of a trilogy, and the beginning of a new period, a new course which will lead the group to carry out things which don't have anything to do with the past. —Will Sergeant, 1983

As "Bluer Skies" foretold, albeit underhandedly, a long-overdue sense of positivity and vigor finally descended on the Bunnymen after *Porcupine*'s release. The swagger of old was back. To Mac and Will, the catharsis of *Porcupine* was worth it for this reason alone, and the Bunnymen were ready to take on new challenges, to change the world with a defter touch.

I've gotta be optimistic—if you're not, you might as well give up.
—Ian McCulloch, 1983

Whether the album's liked or not, I think it was essential for us and our growth. The album is really simple, but it's done in a complicated way. I want us to get simple again ... to do simple things simply.
—Ian McCulloch, 1983

Despite the critical potshots leveled at *Porcupine*, even the most jaded rock writers agreed that the Bunnymen still provided a thrilling, virtually irresistible live show, able to whip up an almost religious intensity out of thin air. Their winter UK tour produced the standard rapturous reactions.

I always half expect Echo & the Bunnymen to disappoint me, but they never, never do; in a swirl of fog and Gregorian chant they hit the stage and burst into 'Going Up,' keeping you fascinated and entertained for the next hour with the mix of solid pumping rhythms and powerfully seductive dreaminess, all the while boosted by the strength of the songs themselves and the charm of the people playing them. Rather than the sustained rant of the past, the mid-'83 Bunnymen are condensing intensity within individual songs. Never has their gift for turning out distinctive and memorable tunes been more evident; still all are channeled through the Bunnymen's immediately charming, fluid, spontaneous, seemingly improvisational style. —*Sounds*, 1983

... a rock sound affrighted by romance, delighted at a form of transcendent despair ... memory will enshrine a tremendous vision: four wafer-boned, strangely askew figures, silhouetted against artificial clouds, driving across an eclectic music glittering with shards of melody dipped in the most bittersweet of chalices ... Some of the most thrilling music to come from an English stage —*NME*, 1983

NEVER STOP

After the tour, Warner Brothers wanted to release "Heads Will Roll" as a follow-up. The Bunnymen were eager to produce another single, but balked at pulling another song from *Porcupine*. They desperately wanted to extract themselves from the difficulty of that record, and didn't want to be seen as milking an album. They also reasoned that too much time had passed since the release of "The Cutter," and, as most Bunnymen fans already owned *Porcupine*, the single would stiff.

Still, the band was willing to compromise—up to a point. In the late spring of 1983, they entered London's RAK studios with the intention of recording a completely new version of "Heads Will Roll," and possibly a recent composition titled "Do You Love Him?" Once inside the studio, Mac rewrote the lyrics to the latter, and the title was changed to "Never Stop." Excited by the new song, the Bunnymen quickly discarded any intention of updating "Heads Will Roll."

Unbeknownst to the band, Bill Drummond had assigned Steve Lillywhite, a seasoned producer of the likes of U2, to helm the sessions. Drummond wanted the single rush-released to coincide with a summer tour he was arranging. This proved to be a grave error. When Lillywhite entered

RAK, he was greeted with blank stares and a "why don't you go and make a cup of tea?" Lillywhite perceived this as "fuck off," and never returned.

Despite this hiccup of negativity, things couldn't have been more optimistic in the Bunnymen camp. The new songs that were so elusive during the *Porcupine* sessions were finally flowing thick and fast, with a lightness and sense of melody absent from the previous LP. Several factors contributed to this: on April 16th, after nearly four years of courtship, Mac and Lorraine were married in Lorraine's hometown of Warrington, and, following a brief honeymoon in the south of France, the newlyweds returned to Liverpool to live together in their own flat. The other Bunnymen—including Jake—had moved into a Victorian mansion on Aigburth Drive, which provided the band with a warmer, more comfortable and relaxed atmosphere in which to compose and scheme, in sharp contrast with the cold confines of The Ministry.

***

I think that it's probably the best, most well-thought-out political song since Bob Dylan, 'cos it isn't one-dimensional ... what provoked it? I think it was old age pensioners more than anything. 'Cos I'd seen these old grannies and that on the news and it was like, 'Well, dear, who are you gonna vote for?' 'Labour.' 'Why's that?' 'More money at Christmas.' And that's what it comes down to. An extra two quid in the Christmas pension. Nobody gives a shite, really, do they? All anyone wants is a bit extra, and that's it. Thank you very much.

—Ian McCulloch, 1990

"Never Stop" b/w "Heads Will Roll (Summer Version)" and "Drop In the Ocean (The Original Cutter)" was released on July 8, 1983, and immediately burst into the UK top 30, peaking at #15. The song was far removed, both musically and lyrically, from the dense, tortured introspection of *Porcupine*, and had an dancey, electronic feel, with an expanded arrangement that included congas, marimbas, violins, and cellos. Lyrically, the song captured Mac swaggering and on the attack, spitting venom outward, rather that self-immolating in a pit of tortured soul-searching.

Although Mac described "Never Stop" as a "post-election protest song," he denied that the lyrics were an assault on the recently reelected Margaret Thatcher.

I wouldn't give her the honour of one of my lyrics. It's about people as they always are.   —Ian McCulloch, 1983

'Never Stop' was my song for the common man, telling him not to be so common. Don't just accept your position, change it. Like, you can wallow in having dirt in your fingernails for so long, but in the end, it just means you've got dirty fingernails. I hate people who wallow in their own ignorance and limitations. I hate people who romanticize the working class; there's nothing romantic about being working class.
                    —Ian McCulloch, 1984

The attitude today is you've gotta be average, that's the noble thing, and it's the most disgusting attitude that prevails throughout the world. There's just so much scum throughout every class in every coun-

try, and I'm accused of being right wing and pompous and self-opin-
ionated because I think that certain things matter.

—Ian McCulloch, 1984

I thought it was the best thing we'd ever done ... we all loved it.

—Ian McCulloch, 2001

The press, too, were pleased.

... scathing, vitriolic, loud, but not overburdened; it sounded mean,
compact, to the damned point. The timing of its release set its outraged howl in the context of Thatcher's landslide at the polls.

—*Melody Maker*, 1984

The rediscovered Bunnymen swagger didn't stop with the song. Interviews
found Mac speaking again of the band with newfound pride.

Ian McCulloch: "We are the only important band."
Melody Maker: "Qualify that, Mac?"
Ian McCulloch: "Well, you know what 'only' means, don't yer? And you
know what 'important' means?"   —*Melody Maker*, 1983

NEVER STOP

Good God, you said, is that the only thing you care about
Splitting up the money and share it out
The cake's being eaten straight through the mouth
Poison poised to come back in season
For all the ones who lack reason

Measure by measure, drop by drop
And pound for pound, we're taking stock
Of all the treasures still unlocked
The love you found must never stop

The king is dead and long live the people who aim above
All the simple stuff never understood
Like right from bad and wrong from good
Deny that you were ever tempted by the lie
That there's an answer in the sky

... Ian Bunnyman has a great
appearance and approach, like a
guardian angel pushed beyond
breaking point ... magnifique!

—*NME*, "Single of the Week," 1983

I think the Bunnymen are a lot
better than David Bowie. I've
looked up to him all my life
but now I think he should look
up to us. We are the greatest
band in the world.

—Ian McCulloch, 1983

I knew it had to start with
'Good God' 'cos I'd seen *On
Golden Pond*. In that, Henry
Fonda keeps on saying 'Good
Gaaad" in this great voice.

—Ian McCulloch, 1983

I get really wound up with people not being able to tell the difference between good and bad. It could be politics, music—anything. The reason the word 'good' was invented was because some things *are* good; there can't be that many differences in taste.

—Ian McCulloch, 1984

Measure by measure, drop by drop
And pound for pound, we're taking stock
Of all the treasures still unlocked
The love you found must never stop ...

Never stop ...

We'd spent a long time doing 'Never Stop.' Another shed of a song—two minutes forty—but I liked it lyrically. I remember Rob [Dickens] going, 'Look, it's a top 5. I know these things.' But it wasn't. I think it went in at 15, although Julie Burchill said it sounded like 'the black angel.' Looking back, I think that gave us a kick up the arse ... it was time to make something that was truly unstoppable.

—Ian McCulloch, 1999

A chance to see my favourite group in my favourite part of the world. —Bill Drummond, 1983

OUTER HEBRIDES TOUR

While "Never Stop" was in the works, Bill Drummond was scheming a special summer tour for the Bunnymen. Rather than have the group play the touring game and plug away, he wanted them to do the coolest, most interesting or bizarre tour he could imagine. To that end, Drummond devised an outing that would kick off in New York in June, then head directly to Iceland, followed by a quick stop-over to Denmark for the annual Roskilde Festival. The band would then play the remote Outer Hebrides Islands in Scotland, travel down to the Northwest of England, and return to London for a series of triumphant gigs at The Royal Albert Hall.

The notion of playing in the Hebrides grew out of various conversations. I'm Scottish anyway, and I'd been there as a teenager. I was particularly impressed by the circle of standing stones on Callanish and Lewis. It seemed like a romantic thing to do. —Bill Drummond, 1997

Drummond hopes the islands and highlands will influence the group in some positive, semi-spiritual way. A group like The Jam, he theorises, aspire to a housing estate outlook, and Wham! for example, reflect the inner city—but the Bunnymen, in Drummond's eyes, are tapping 'more glorious' sources—hence the exotic settings that have become a feature of their LP sleeves and videos. —*NME*, 1983

Capitalizing on the expanded sound of "Never Stop," the band drafted "The Bunnymen Orchestra," which featured percussionist Tim Whittaker, string players Adams Peters and Nick Barnard, former Psychedelic Furs guitarist Mike Mooney, and the ever-present Jake Brockman.

The reason we are using other musicians on the tour this time is purely and simply because we wanted to see how a nine-piece worked. It is just an experiment ... because we've been working as a four-piece so long, it was necessary to have a change.   —Ian McCulloch, 1983

This was going to be a unique and unusual journey, even for a band already regarded as markedly unique and unusual. As the Bunnymen were departing for the Outer Hebrides, scores of fans turned up at the ferry, prepared to follow the rest of the tour. It was like a flashback to Ken Kesey's Merry Pranksters or Dylan's Rolling Thunder Revue.

It had more of the atmosphere of a holiday than a rock tour. Most bands on tour will hole up in the hotel and indulge their whims, but not the Bunnymen. They made the most of a trip like that. Les Pattinson brought his fishing gear, and Will Sergeant had a pair of binoculars for bird-watching. It was a wonderfully relaxed atmosphere. You felt as if everybody knew everybody else. I had the feeling too that a lot of people weren't even Bunnymen fans. They'd come because it was an event, like going out to see a traveling circus.
          —Journalist Max Bell, Q, 1997

One interesting thing was how the band welcomed us in. Even though we were outsiders, we were made to feel like part of an extended family. When we walked from the hotel to the gig in the afternoon for the sound check, it was a bit like a scene from High Noon. There were little clusters of local people staring at us like we were aliens, and we stared back at them.   —Journalist Jonathan Ashby, Q, 1997

If the Bunnymen and their fans were perceived as aliens, at least they came in peace. On the Island of Skye, the band was polite enough to postpone their show until a church service next door was completed, and both the fans and group were very gracious to the locals.

When I came down for breakfast next morning, Will was sitting there with his sewing kit, offering to fix buttons on for anybody. That is a typical Bunnymen thing. Will never went anywhere without his sewing kit.   —Journalist Mick Houghton, 1997

The [Bunnymen were] fantastic. The entire back wall seemed to be filled with stacks of speakers, and you could feel the whole hall shaking with the noise. They had a brilliant liquid light show, and the total effect was overwhelming. You felt like you were somehow inside the performance.
          —Journalist
          Jonathan Ashby, Q, 1997

Onstage, however, the Bunnymen were playing with a savage ferocity that had reached its zenith.

During the summer of 1983, it is feasible to claim that Echo & the Bunnymen were indeed great, and yes, probably the greatest. Everything about them was demonstrably perfect. Drummer Pete de Freitas's angular, metronomic style had compelled the band's sound to scale the heights of new wave psychedelic symphonia ... it seemed that he was orchestrating the music so drenched in fear, fury and feeling. Bass player Les Pattinson held his guitar like a rifle. Will Sergeant wore the permanently startled look of a fellow given to meeting aliens in his back garden, and he played guitar accordingly. In the midst of this maelstrom stood Ian McCulloch, a tall, skinny thing who looked like he read Rimbaud for breakfast, talked like an especially leery docker, and sang like an angel with a broken heart. They looked cool, said cool things, but, most importantly, they were making glorious music. It was their time and they knew it.

—Journalist Keith Cameron, 1997

Some people treat you like you are an Aunt Sally.
—Ian McCulloch, 1983

I get very angry. I always feel like smashing someone's face in. I hate getting lip from anyone and being treated like an idiot by an idiot, even if it's some yobbo sneering at the way I might look. It doesn't happen that much anymore 'cos a lot of people recognise me. But if it happens in another country where they don't know who I am, I'll just stare them out or … I wouldn't not fight someone.
—Ian McCulloch, 1984

Only one incident marred the glory of the tour. After a show on the Isle of Lewis, (where the band played a hotel dining room!), Mac was approached by a drunk oil rigger who objected to the supposedly anti-Thatcherite content of "Never Stop," among other things.

In the recreation area of the hotel, Mac was holding court with a bunch of fans, and an older guy from the island starting chiding him about the fact that he was wearing ballet shoes and no socks. The suggestion was that [Mac] was homosexual. Mac must have taken exception, because the next thing was this scuffle and punches being thrown in the middle of the room.
—Journalist Mick Houghton, 1997

… I chased him down this long corridor and grounded him with a Jackie Chan-style karate kick. When he turned 'round I gave him a real rotor blade smack in the nose, of the kind I've never used before or since.
—Ian McCulloch, 1999

While Mac was blackening eyes, Bill Drummond had stars in his. After the show, the mystic manager had convinced Will Sergeant and a few journalists to experience the island's Standing Stones of Callanish.

Will, myself, and Bill walked down until we found the circle. We had to clamber over some of the stones, and I was taken aback to see Bill jump into a trench in the middle of the circle and lie down. It was very cold and damp, and yet he lay there for what must have been a good ten minutes, presumably basking in some sort of magical emanations. When we got back to the car, the battery had mysteriously gone flat, and there was the general agreement that this was because we had been tampering with powerful forces. Then, just as unexpectedly, the battery came back up again and we set off. By now, though, a dense mist had come down, and we could barely see ahead of us. That was the moment a little bunny rabbit chose to wander out in front of the car and, instead of scampering back into the night, it ran ahead of the car for what seemed like miles. Bill, of course, immediately concluded that this was one of the minions of Echo, The Rabbit God, sent to lead his followers safely back to their hotel. —Paul Du Noyer, *Q*, 1997

LAY DOWN THY RAINCOAT AND GROOVE

On July 18th and 19th, presumably without the aid of a live rabbit mascot, the tour thundered to its conclusion at the Royal Albert Hall. In an effort to transcend the image of doom-and-gloom merchants that they had created for themselves, the Bunnymen printed T-shirts and programs sporting the legend "Lay Down Thy Raincoat and Groove."

People always think of us as a 'serious man's band'—in a lot of ways I suppose we are, but there is a fun side to it too. Music is about enjoyment, really. If you can't enjoy it, why bother playing it or going to hear it?   —Ian McCulloch, 1984

A lot of our followers wanted our songs to be depressing, and they wanted us to be dressed in black. But now we have these other people who just think we have good songs, and maybe like the way we look and stuff. And that's a lot easier than being expected to be a tortured artist.   —Ian McCulloch, 1984

The venue doors opened at 6:45pm. Forty-five minutes later, Mendelssohn's "The Hebrides (Fingal's Cave)" aired over the PA in honor of the Isles on which the band had just played, and to set the mood for the oceanic feel of the new material they had been writing. At 7:40, organist Simon Russell performed a recital, which was quickly followed by Bach's "Fugue in D Minor" and H. Mullet's "Carillon Sortie." Intermission followed

What I always wanted was a band that wasn't about rock myth or bashing guitars. I wanted songs that captured all the different elements of a human being—romantic, sarcastic ... I can't even think what all the ingredients are. I always think that Echo & the Bunnymen should be a balanced thing; if we are doomy and gloomy, that should just be a part of us, and we should also be funny and cocky.

—Ian McCulloch, 1984

A true milestone in the group's career. If there were any doubts about the Bunnymen's rise to stardom, this put them to rest.   —*Goldmine*, 1998

The two shows were brilliant. The Bunnymen were now one of the greatest live bands ever.
              —Bill Drummond,
*From the Shores of Lake Placid
              and Other Stories*

Our gigs at the Royal Albert Hall were the live peaks of the Bunnymen's career. It felt like God was there, conducting.
              —Ian McCulloch, 1992

WHAT A WAY TO SPEND EASTER

It's funny, we're just a group writing songs and yet we have all this holy stuff written about us. The thing is, I half believe it.
              —Ian McCulloch, 1983

at 8 o'clock, and at 8:20, the nine-piece Bunnymen took the stage.

Although Hall management had asked the Bunnymen to play it cool and urge fans to remain in their seats, Mac did as any good rock & roller should and encouraged the audience to dance. They complied, and quickly broke on through the Hall's barriers, adding a nice touch of insurrection to the proceedings. One can imagine that this ability to manipulate a huge crowd with a mere offhand suggestion added immeasurably to Mac's already bursting confidence as a frontman.

Many critics and fans state that this sense of abandon, along with the Hall's own transcendent atmosphere and the band's almost punk performance, might have created the very best couple of gigs of the Bunnymen's career. It's quite possible. The group blasted through their catalogue—even dusting off old obscurities like "Simple Stuff" —and encored with a version of The Velvet Underground's "Heroin."

Echo & the Bunnymen succeed in transforming the gargantuan splendour of the hallowed ground known as The Albert Hall into a place of genuine musical worship. The solid foundation of Pete's tortured drumming and Les's driving methodical bass surge ahead of the flanks. Will simply goes mad, wrenching awesome sounds out of his guitar and array of effects pedals. And Mac is left to stumble around like a rag doll dressed all in black. Sometimes he rambles like a majestic fool, other times he waxes lyrical with the sharpest tongue this side of the man he calls 'Billy Shakespeare.' Like the rest of the Bunnymen, he stretches himself to the limit. Tonight everything came together and it proved to be the best concert I've seen all year. —*Smash Hits*, 1983

GODS WILL BE GODS

Some at this point began to regard the Bunnymen with a religious reverence. Mac in particular had a messianic image, a beatnik Jesus to his eager acolytes. The band was slightly diffident about their fans' worship as rock saviors.

Looking back, the whole 'rock god' thing was sort of created around me. And I suppose I reached a point where I thought, 'Yeah, why not, I'll have a bit of that.' Interviewers would tell me that I was some kind of messiah, or some kind of metaphysical being, and I just went along with it. At the start, it was just sort of tongue-in-cheek. Then it gets on a roll and you can't stop it.   —Ian McCulloch, 1997

... [our music] makes people more aware … of something that's bigger than themselves, and bigger than Echo & the Bunnymen. It's like an electricity between people, like communication I suppose. Sometimes a Bunnymen concert can be really awesome, but it's not awesome in the way that a Bowie gig is supposed to be awesome, where he's the star and the crowd are the crowd. It's to do with awe, the whole thing. The world is really awesome because it's the world, not because one nation's bigger than another, or because one government has total control over its people. At a Bunnymen gig, we're onstage, but we're not the governing body, particularly. We don't try and put ourselves on a pedestal. We have presence, but so do other people from the crowd. I don't think we artificially create anything. Sometimes the force is with us, and sometimes it's not.   —Ian McCulloch, 1983

It's all cracked up to be something sacred, but it doesn't mean anything in the real world. It's like a painting, people can either look at it or walk past. And that's the way it is. You could be doing a painting and thinking, 'This is brilliant, this is going to change mankind,' and it will end up on a chocolate box. —Will Sergeant, 1985

There was a time when I had idols too, but you shouldn't really—you should set your own example, I think.   —Ian McCulloch, 1983

    Messiah or not, there was no point in denying Mac's frequent use of spiritual and metaphysical metaphor. Mac has attempted to explain his religious motifs, and to underscore that they aren't intended for literal interpretation.

I never like being pinned down about why I mention Heaven a lot, or why I mention God a lot. *Heaven Up Here* was a spiritual thing with the Bunnymen, but it was more about a belonging, which I think is the basis of mostly Eastern religions. Western religions always seem to have to have an end product, like a capitalist religion. It's typified in America where, if white, middle-class citizens are going to be bothered with going to church every Sunday and praying to God, you've got to get something out of it. You've got to live forever. Whereas it seems to me that the Eastern religions are more about belonging, and being at peace with something. Which I'm into.
—Ian McCulloch, *Never Stop*

I kind of always did use the concepts of religion, but metaphorically. But now, I do feel that it has become a part of my expression,

We have no interest in willful obscurity. One thing I always wanted to avoid was an audience/performer barrier and I'm conscious of that all the time because I'm not interested in that kind of elitism. That's why we encourage people to come backstage after and talk, to deflate all that. We're just there, and I'll be slumped in a chair—we're nothing, y'know, other than just people, that's all.   —Ian McCulloch, 1983

I always thought we had this big spiritual kind of thing. That was why people liked us; not just 'cos we were 'a good rock band.' It was that mood, that mystery, I suppose, and the nearest thing you could equate that to was ... .God. But it wasn't really Biblical; it was always metaphorical. *Heaven Up Here* wasn't about religion...
—Ian McCulloch, 1987

I'm not a religious person, but what I've done with the Bunnymen is surround them with a religious thing that isn't religion. It's applied in a totally different way. I've used words like 'God' in that religious way—'Gods will be gods but my one forgot that I'm made out of skin'—but that's got more to do with conventional attitudes than religion.   —Ian McCulloch, 1983

because I think maybe I have allowed myself to believe something a bit more. Maybe it is because of things like my parents dying. My dad died in '88 and my mom died in '96. I think about them a lot. Maybe it is somehow connected. I don't analyze it, really. I still don't know what I am touching on, exactly. But I know that, through experience, things happen in your life that turn you towards some kind of spirituality.

—Ian McCulloch, 2001

It's got something to do with understanding the wind and cloud formations. It's like walking down the road and seeing a cloud formation and thinking it means something, and that cloud formation is there because you've dreamt it up. I've got a lot of time for the weather. It's great. Keeps me happy for hours.

—Ian McCulloch, 1989

The Bunnymen have always delighted in the unusual and unexpected. And what could be more unexpected than a post-punk band playing The Royal Shakespeare Theater at Stratford-on-Avon? So, that's precisely what they did.

—*Goldmine*, 1998

HIPPY HIPPY SHAKESPEARE

For a few months after the Royal Albert Hall shows, the Bunnymen relaxed and continued writing songs in Liverpool. Delighted with their performances and reaction to "Never Stop," they were determined to ensure that 1983 end on a high note. The opportunity came when they were invited to play on October 23 headlining a two-week youth festival. The location, true to form, was unusual: The Royal Shakespeare Theater at Stratford-on-Avon.

The band bested both *Hamlet* and *Macbeth* by being the fastest sell-out in the history of the theater. Tickets were in such demand that the venue had to add a matinee show. Mac, in a nod to that other sarcastic Scouser John Lennon, announced that the group was now "bigger than Henry the 5th."

To ensure that they not fly in the face of history, however, the Bunnymen made efforts to pay their respects to the great bard. In the programs for the performances, the band was presented in a manner similar to Shakespearean characters: Mac was dubbed "The Duke of Norris Green," Will, "A Woodsman," Les, "Sir Thomas Leslie, a Knight with a Mission," and Pete, "Louie de Freitas, the Traveler."

In the continued effort to shed their heavy image, the Bunnnymen invited comedian Ben Elton to introduce both gigs with "Friends, Romans, and Bunnymen, lend me your ears." At the end of each set, another comic, Hugh Laurie, was ushered onstage to recite the lyrics to "Villiers Terrace" in a faux dramatic style worthy of Sir John Gielgud at the tail end of the song. The gesture was perfect—fitting, cheeky, self-deprecating, and extremely humorous theatre.

The humour in the songs is all too often overlooked. There is both seriousness and humour in what we do and generally the humour balances everything out. I mean, we are the funniest band going! I would like to get that across more.   —Ian McCulloch, 1983

Overall, the two shows divided themselves down the middle. The matinee was something of a mess. New songs, such as "The Killing Moon," "Seven Seas," and "Silver" were rather uncertainly unveiled, and Mac was nervous (and alcohol-free). Record company representatives—and Mac's mother—were watching.

Mac seemed tentative and reticent, and frequently sang out of tune. He spent the remainder of the afternoon in seclusion, consoled by the ever-faithful Lorraine. For the evening's concert, Mac's mom and record company execs were absent, the band more confident, and they'd found time to knock back a few cocktails. As a result, the Bunnymen were in murderous form, and surged through the performance, which had the same set list as the matinee, in reverse.

The day after the Stratford-On-Avon gigs, BBC Radio One aired the Bunnymen's sixth Peel Session, which had been recorded a few weeks earlier. They played four new compositions—"Nocturnal Me," "Ocean Rain," "My Kingdom," and "Watch Out Below," an early version of "The Yo Yo Man." As planned, the songs were notably different than what listeners had come to expect from the Bunnymen.

The Peel Sessions were to unveil the Bunnymen with a new-found simplicity of approach, a brave directness, and a blooming pop vitality. [The songs] hint at a readjustment and a period of new positive recovery.   —*Jamming*, 1983

PLAY AT HOME/THE TUBE

After the Shakespearean shows, the Bunnymen, along with Siouxie and the Banshees and New Order, were invited to film their own television specials for the BBC. While the other two bands decided to create big productions—the Banshees going so far as to remake *Alice In Wonderland*—the Bunnymen decided to capitalize on their bohemian image, and filmed the goings-on at Brian's Diner on Stanley Street, a café where they hung out. The program revolved around a day in the life of Brian, an ex-boxer, who in his heyday had the fastest recorded punch in the UK.

The film also gave the Bunnymen a chance to test-drive some of their new material: a joyous, uplifting "Silver" and a sketchy "The Killing Moon," which was faster and lacked the scope of the studio version. They also delved into older material, performing a wilted rasp of "Stars Are Stars" with an elegant harpsichord lead, and perhaps the most unique version of "Villiers

Terrace" they've ever played. It was a laid-back acoustic strum through the song, not as intensely performed as the lyrics might warrant, with a bongo and sax intro. In a nod to the Fab Four, the Bunnymen performed an approximation of "All You Need Is Love" in Liverpool's Anglican cathedral.

The arrangements of these songs—acoustic guitars, brushed drums, a thrumming upright bass, added exotic extras—laid down the blueprint for their next LP, *Ocean Rain*, which was to be, for the world at large, the Bunnymen's most effective statement ever.

```
Yeah—we invented 'Unplugged.'              —Ian McCulloch, 1995
```

The Bunnymen's 1983 concluded with a live appearance on "The Tube," where they gave what is arguably their best televised performance. They discarded all old material and instead focused on versions of "The Killing Moon," "Ocean Rain," reworked from a poppy breeze into a heart-stopping ballad, and a new song, tentatively titled "Thorn of Crowns," or, possibly, "Cucumber." The final performance captured the band at its most intense: Mac threw himself at the mic like a man possessed, Iggy Pop with a fright wig, while Les pulsed on the upright bass. Pete virtually attacked his drums with brushes, and Will tore his guitar to fiery pieces. It was a perfect way to end the Bunnymen's year. Even the notoriously dour Will was grinning broadly.

On November 15, the Bunnymen turned five years old. What of Bill Drummond's insistence that the band break up on that date?

```
... there was a notion that at one point that would be right to do.
But then we decided that it may not be right. We'd decided that in the
five years we'd do a lot of certain things and we'd do them well, and
it's just ... we haven't got some of these things done yet. It's taken
longer than we thought. We'll now go as far as fate will let us.
                                             —Ian McCulloch, 1984
```

```
It's a weird question. Like 'when are you going to kill yourself?'
With rock music, it has to end at a certain point. Otherwise, you
become Rod Stewart. I don't think we are that clichéd rock thing that
has to die before it gets old. I think we're more like a Leonard Cohen-
y thing, which doesn't really have a time limit. —Ian McCulloch, 1987
```

PARIS

As they entered 1984, their resolve to redefine rock in an original, distinctive way was as strong as ever. The Bunnymen had proved themselves more confident and convincing that their home rivals The Teardrop Explodes and Wah! Their humor, creative ambition, and fierce pride might stem largely from the great mythology of their Liverpool roots. The sense of adventure, drama, and emotion in their music, however, were more typical of a rock tradition that has given birth to the likes of The Doors, The Velvet Underground, and Joy Division. Echo & the Bunnymen were among those few bands in the 80's making rock music of rare, consuming rapture and lyrical depth.

—*History of Rock,* 1984

As 1983 drew to a close, the Bunnymen finished constructing the material for their fourth album. As the previous Peel Sessions indicated, these songs displayed a conscious withdrawal from the heaviness of *Porcupine* and the involved production and technology behind "Never Stop." The intention was to sail into lighter, brighter waters, steered by a simpler, warmer approach.

After *Porcupine,* which was intense and complicated, we wanted to write *songs,* and wrote them in our flat in Liverpool or 'round each other's houses, with acoustic guitars a lot of the time. I suppose we were looking for a more melodic thing.   —Pete de Freitas, 1984

During writing of *Ocean Rain,* Will got into the guitar style of the Violent Femmes, Les went a bit jazzy, Pete took up brushes, and Mac sweated the rock Messiah role out of his system. —*Melody Maker,* 1984

The Bunnymen were determined make a statement as far removed from the Bic lighter–waving pomp of Big Country/U2/Simple Minds with which they had become associated since the success of "The Cutter." These comparisons disgusted and infuriated Mac, as he despised these groups and all they stood for.

In England everybody goes on TV to push their records, and it's like selling dishwashing liquid. It's very artificial. It's that childish need for fame and money. These groups are saying 'look at me, watch me, like me.' It's disgusting. It's one of the more pointless things to want to do. They're selling themselves all the time, and the

I felt comfortable doing the heavy thing, but really I like fragile things. I don't want to make people bang their heads anymore—I want to make them smile.   —Ian McCulloch, 1984

I simplified things quite a lot ... because you can get too involved in writing a work of art and miss it completely. I used to worry that I didn't have enough lyrics for a song but when you think back to 'Villiers Terrace,' there's only about three different lines in it. I've gone full circle.

—Ian McCulloch, 1984

I think that rather than write Pied Piper music, where people are supposed to follow or lead and go to this great congregation in the Hammersmith Odeon, our songs lead people more into themselves, more introspective. That is a big difference. All that positive attitude stuff implies that everything's all right with the individual. It's like, let's all go wherever the hell we're supposed to be going and they haven't even been within themselves. There's no self analysis there at all. And that is true pomp when it doesn't even question anything let alone themselves.

—Ian McCulloch, 1984

A lot of people knew we were the best live band in the world, and we were probably better live than on record. We were considered to be a rock band that played electric guitars, we were always tipped to be the biggest stadium band, but we never wanted it. I think we were scared of that, maybe, because at the time it wasn't so much the stadium, but the bands that generally played them that made the whole thing unappealing and frightening. There was so much bad showmanship going down, and crowd-pandering. Everyone saying "how you doing out there? —from Bono to Bruce Springsteen—and those are words that I never said. No Cuban heels and no flags, those were two of the golden rules.

—Ian McCulloch, 1998

records start sounding like an extension of this 'please like me' syndrome. It's sad. All that matters is getting your face on this and that. Maybe it's always been like that. But I thought that in the 60's there was this genuine aim to write music. There were so many more great singers then, it was something they were born to do. My vocation is singing and writing words, and that is what I do best. I think I would have survived in the 60's with my voice, but I don't know how many others would've. There's a lack of good people around now. John Lennon, Jim Morrison, even Lou Reed, they all had great voices because they were original. Mick Jagger, Paul McCartney, the Spector singers and all that soul stuff … but name the great singers today. Bowie's got some quality in his voice, but he was knocking around in the 60's anyway. It's a definite worry!   —Ian McCulloch, 1984

I'd like people to understand that we're not doing this to sell records. We're doing this to compete with Shakespeare, Hieronymous Bosch and Vincent Van Gogh instead of Jim Kerr or Boy George, because I don't think they're in the same sphere. I'm in the position of being able to say things like that and get away with it because people will know I'm not an idiot. I think I'm the first one who has come out and said these things because everyone else is too modest. Or they're not that good. —Ian McCulloch, 1984

The Bunnymen are as superior to your U2s and whatever as a peacock is to its turds.   —NME, 1984

We'd become this rock band, having hits, where people said we were gonna be bigger than the biggest group of our generation. And I just thought, 'Sod it. Let's go on a tangent. Let's do something that these bastards wouldn't think of in a million years.' They were too busy trying to get to bigger stadia.   —Ian McCulloch, 1997

Bill Drummond had his own colossal concept for the next album.

The Bunnymen's fourth album was to be their last. The final record would be greater than any album ever recorded by any band anywhere. It would be perfection. It would contain proper songs with lyrics that weren't shrouded in bogus mystery. The meaning would be direct. The wisdom of Echo would have been received. The Bunnymen would be on the sleeve, head on, holding us firmly in their stare, confident and strong. The Bunnymen would never have to write another song again. Everything that needed to be said would have been said. They would become the biggest band in the world and exist completely outside the recognised music industry. Their status would become mythical. Their legend would be spread by word of mouth across the continents.

—Bill Drummond, *From the Shores of Lake Placid and Other Stories*

But at the recording stage, the foursome wasn't so much concerned with crossing continents as it was with simply crossing the English Channel.

I remember phoning up Rob Dickens, the head of the company, and saying 'I want to do this one in Paris.' And he said 'Aw, come on, why? Because you want to just go drink in bars, famed Parisian whatever.' I said, 'No, you know Paris, imagine me walking around Paris and then going in to do a vocal.' So we upped and went to Paris and did *Ocean Rain*.
—Ian McCulloch, 1998

Paris is the most beautiful city in the world. I thought it was really weird the first time I went there, just like London. But then a week later I realised I'd fallen in love with it. It's such a varied city. I just love going down all the little side streets and into the bars.
—Ian McCulloch, 1984

Although once again interband relations were strained—due in particular to Mac's emergence as a genuine pop star heartthrob, and the attention that went along with it, by and large, the recording went extremely well. The band loved the vibe and studios of Paris.

The best part in going to Paris was the atmosphere, the change for ourselves. We'd been in English studios for some time, so we went there and the engineer was a laid-back French man who couldn't speak much English, so everything happened quite slowly. He just did everything he was told to do. The orchestra was intended as a French orchestra. It was nice to record it in Paris for the feel.
—Pete de Freitas, 1984

We took the ferry from Liverpool rather than fly. It was all very romantic, very literary. We were all in there hitting bells and playing accordions, double bass, and acoustics. Springtime in Paris. They'd booked this studio with some French runt who couldn't speak a word of English. Nice studio, but there was a handy sort of restaurant/bar with the new Beaujolais. So I was hanging out there, working on the lyrics. They were doing all those things like sticking amps in echo chambers, but I wasn't into that. I knew the notes! I found a

The material suggested an atmospheric location. I really wanted to do it there and the others sort of went along with it. The songs that we've got are warm. They give me the ... not the sound of the city, but the colours. I really think that'll be reflected in the album. It won't be that marked a thing but the colours'll be there. Paris in winter.
—Ian McCulloch, 1984

I function best in romantic places.   —Ian McCulloch, 1984

The album sounded great while we were there, because they had all these old reverb units, huge things, that you just don't get in studios. They're from the 50s or something. They also had an echo chamber, a proper tiled room. I remember doing my guitar in it. It sounded amazing, better than the actual board where we mixed it, as we mixed it in an ordinary studio. I remember it sounded loads better in Paris, because a lot of the sounds are through these reverb units, they were dead warm, dead big sound, a real Jacques Brel/Scott Walker feel to it. We liked Jacques Brel and stuff like that, so we went there to capture that sound. It's still a great LP, but it would've been great to have mixed there.
—Will Sergeant, 1998

When you say you've used an orchestra, people think 'bloody hell' but on *Ocean Rain* we still did it with a fragility in mind, and we produced it ourselves, which stopped it from going over the top. We wrote the songs and then thought about the strings, so it meant we could play the song in a pub without strings and it'd still sound really good.
—Ian McCulloch, 1985

nice little cozy bar was the best place for me. I was discovering Paris. I must have been in that studio, but I can't really remember. So next they booked this other place, Da Vu, which was very famous for Jacques Brel and Edith Piaf and all them people. Turned up there and it was a total shed, like someone's front room in Huddersfield. And in some shit part of Paris. I said 'I can't see Jacques Brel hanging out here. Have they moved it or summat?' So I'm in there and it's like 'Jesus!' I actually tried the first verse of 'Ocean Rain' and it sounded rubbish. Condensation, shit. Either that or I was just banjaxed! I said 'I'm not seeing this' and disappeared off to the bar. Didn't come back for about six hours. We got Gil Norton over to produce it—he had a great time, but he didn't do anything except laugh his head off when I decided ... not to show up! Eventually, we ran out of time, came home, and I sang the lot in Liverpool. I didn't record a note in Paris. —Ian McCulloch, 1999

The Bunnymen's love affair with strings, begun with "Back of Love," continued during the *Ocean Rain* sessions, where they used a 35-piece orchestra.

For a band like the Bunnymen—brought up on punk—this embrace of lush orchestration, violins, horns, and woodwind was a fearless move. Previous attempts by rock bands to work with orchestras had, for instance, been mostly disastrous embarrassments, much derided. Think of the risible prog arrogance of Deep Purple, The Nice, Emerson Lake and Palmer, and Rick Wakeman. *Ocean Rain* effortlessly overcame this prejudice, beautifully, unapologetically, and with admirable disdain for critical preconceptions.
—*Uncut*, 2001

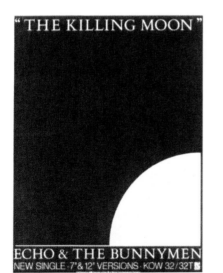

THE KILLING MOON

The first song to emerge from these studio sessions was "The Killing Moon," which the Bunnymen co-produced with David Lord. One can't help but suspect that, given the implicit spirituality of Bunnymen music, the group had chosen him simply on the basis of his name. A year later, Siouxie and the Banshees picked a producer just because they thought his surname, Churchyard, fitted their dark, gothic image.

Mac's first choice was David Bowie, or, failing him, Libyan leader Moammar Gadhafi. The rest of the album was self-produced.

It had to be, otherwise it would have been like Shakespeare giving his plays to an editor and saying, 'Ponce 'em up a bit and make 'em commercial.
                                                            —Ian McCulloch, 1984

"The Killing Moon" was released on January 24, 1984, and entered the charts at #17. As a song, it remains possibly the Bunnymen's greatest. Before, as Mac has remarked, the Bunnymen created *cool* music, but this song was a true timeless classic, one for the ages, a song that could have been covered by both Sinatra and Jim Morrison. The strings swooned and Mac crooned. Indeed, the mood of the song was a romantic celebration that few if any post-punk bands would have tried. *Au revoir* dour Northern industrialist Bunnymen; *bonjour* heady Parisian soul-stirrers.

THE KILLING MOON

Under blue moon I saw you
So soon you'll take me up in your arms
Too late to beg you or cancel it
Though I know it must be the killing time
Unwillingly mine

Fate up against your will
Through the thick and thin
He will wait until you give yourself to him

In starlit nights I saw you
So cruelly you kissed me
Your lips a magic world
Your sky all hung with jewels
The killing moon will come too soon

Fate up against your will
Through the thick and thin
He will wait until you give yourself to him

... hints at unimaginably passionate encounters under starry, Moroccan skies.
                                                            —*Melody Maker*, 1998

'The Killing Moon' came out one morning, just like that. I woke up in my house and thought 'Fate up against your will' and I knew the tune in my head straight away. I had some chords for the verse already so I tried them out. I got out of bed and picked up my acoustic and sang

I still think 'The Killing Moon' is worth a whole album. Even now nobody has released anything like that. And it was so easy to write. I can't believe people can't write like that. Actually, I can. I think it's the best song by a group since the 60's. The best ballad, at least.
                                                            —Ian McCulloch, 1987

I thought at least a coupla million would understand 'The Killing Moon.' I thought that, at the time, it was so obvious. It was about God, or, if you're going downstairs, about the devil. And people thought it was a love song about two dudes under a lamplight.
                                                            —Ian McCulloch, 1999

... it was all about predestiny, and the fact that even when you think you've made a choice, it was the one that you were always going to make.
                                                            —Ian McCulloch, 1997

'The Killing Moon' is just great; it's like listening to the sea.   —Ian McCulloch, 1995

...a small, curious perfection, so cryptic and elliptical, the perfectly wrought rock equivalent of Keats's masterpiece of form 'Ode to a Grecian Urn.' Mac, doubtless, would chuckle 'pretentious shite' at such lofty comparisons, but the simile stands; at this elevated songwriting altitude, symmetry and textures matter.

—*Melody Maker*, 1992

... shows off the qualities that are the Bunnymen's long suit: big, articulate gobs of romance in a setting of melancholy pop loaded with dynamic tension.

—*Smash Hits*, 1984

the words through. I worked out it was a five fret job and it just worked. Lou Reed said that five fret chords are the best and he was right. The Velvets were always such an influence when we were writing—not specific chords, but a feeling. When 'The Killing Moon' hit me out of the blue like that it was beautiful, and I will never forget that moment. Lots of people don't think it's that amazing, but it is definitely the best song the Bunnymen ever wrote. 'The Killing Moon' was the shining jewel in all of the 80's songwriting.

—Ian McCulloch, 1994

'The Killing Moon' must have made a lot of people shiver when they heard it. It made me shiver to sing it.   —Ian McCulloch, 1984

It just seems like a weird idea, the idea that if you play a load of notes it makes the song better. I remember, whatsisface, the drummer of The Police—Stewart Copeland—reviewed 'The Killing Moon,' on the radio, and he said, "I think it's about time they stopped playing one finger guitar solos.' I mean, if you're saying that, you just don't get it, do you? It's not how many fingers you use, it's about the atmosphere. That's a typical muso attitude from a typical muso band.

—Will Sergeant, 1997

★★★

Between the release of "The Killing Moon" and the follow-up "Silver," the Bunnymen toured Japan for the first time, and did their first full-length jaunt through the U.S., a country they'd slowly grown to enjoy. They'd certainly become popular there—"Never Stop" had been a hit single, and their live dates were, at this point, guaranteed sellouts.

During this tour, the band took some time out and revisited their 60's roots in San Francisco, where they recorded the B-side "Angels and Devils," a shameless Velvet Underground rip-off—ironic, considering the Velvets were a speed-fueled New York band that actively attacked the West Coast flower power vibe.

"Silver" was released on April 13, 1984, paving the way for *Ocean Rain*. It only reached #30 in the UK charts—odd, considering it was easily as commercial as anything the Bunnymen had ever done, and was certainly their most radio-friendly song thus far. It's possible that this single—"the one that wasn't," according to Mac—didn't do well because no video was made to promote it. By 1984, video had reached the point where it was the primary music marketing tool, often considered more important than the songs themselves.

SILVER

Swung from a chandelier
My planet sweet on a silver
    salver
Bailed out my worst fears
'Cos man has to be his own
    saviour
Blind sailors
Imprisoned jailers
God tamers
No one to blame us

The sky is blue
My hands untied
A world that's true
Through our clean eyes
Just look at you
With burning lips
You're living proof
At my fingertips

Walked on a tidal wave
Laughed in the face of a brand
    new day
Food for survival thought
Mapped out the place where I
    planned to stay
All the way
Well-behaved
Just in case it slips away

The sky is blue
My hands untied
A world that's true
Through our clean eyes
Just look at you
With burning lips
You're living proof
At my fingertips

Yeah, 'man has to be his own saviour.' I found there's no such thing as God. But it seems like this is Heaven, and we're here, and it's great. I don't want to go to Heaven. Everyone's got permed blonde hair ... and there's too many strings on the harp.   —Ian McCulloch, 1987

At last it seems the Bunnymen are returning to the song instead of those over-worked atmospherics and drone-the-house-down vocals. 'Silver' is far closer to 'Rescue' and the first album than anything they've done since, and is all the better for it. It's also ridiculously fresh and optimistic; another song for the season, and more proof that spring or something must be in the air. Distinguished by a breezy string arrangement and Will Sergeant's Eastern-flavoured guitar, 'Silver' eschews the theatrical menace of 'The Cutter' for something altogether more believable and meaningful. Once more—if you're going to Toxteth be sure to wear some flowers in your hair ... the summer of love part two. *—Melody Maker, 1984*

Being married, and happily married, made me write lines like 'you're living proof at my fingertips.' A lot of people would say a lyric like that was cheap poetry, but I think it's a dead good line. —Ian McCulloch, 1984

I've always felt at one with the Silver Surfer. He's the loner, locked in the force fields in the Earth's atmosphere. The color silver is icy. If you walk into a club and you're silver, you're cool. If you're gold, you might as well pack it in and go home ... I was born to be what I am, the Silver Surfer.
            —Ian McCulloch, 1990

Man has to be his own savior. This is the flash of enlightenment to which the Bunnymen have been privileged after suffering quietly by standing around in all those snowy places and next to all those horrible cold lakes. No wonder you never see them without their overcoats. Actually, I'm being malicious because only one overcoat is visible on the cover. 'Silver' belts along fueled by lots and lots of strings ... and much of Mr. Sergeant's electric 12-string, which—remarkable in these post-Byrds times—attempts a discreet raga-rock exercise towards the end. It all sounds very important indeed.
            —NME, 1984

Great, classic.
                —Will Sergeant, 1985

Between the sheets of Heaven
and Hell—what a song—
San Francisco!
                —Les Pattinson, 1985

I love that song. The words are
important, and the voice.
Obviously, you can see I'm a
bit of a philosopher on the
side, and I know what I'm on
about.   —Ian McCulloch, 1987

ANGELS AND DEVILS

Call it a day
When night becomes a mad escape
Forgetting the things you mean
    to say
When all the right words come
    too late
And everything falls out of place
Under the pillow
Out of the race
Out of the window

Devils on my shoulder

So so happy
When happiness spells misery
And mister me
Hoping to be
Where ugliness meets beauty
And if you'll see
The demon in you
The angel in me
The Jesus in you
The devil in me

Angels on my shoulder

Called it a day
When night became my bad escape
Forgetting the things I meant
    to say
When all the right words came
    too late
And everything fell out of place
Under the pillow
Out of the race
Out of the window

Devils on my shoulder
Angels coming closer

MAC THE MOUTH

I always set out to alienate a certain type of person.
                —Ian McCulloch, 1985

By 1984, Mac had far outgrown the shy, taciturn nature of his early youth, and had transformed himself into "Mac the Mouth," a/k/a "The Liverpool Lip," a character capable of spitting withering criticisms, extra-dry slags, and sly observations, all coupled with a wicked humor and an insistence on the Bunnymen's "obvious" superiority. At this point, Mac's outrageous quotability was matchless. He had become just as entertaining within the pages of a pop weekly as he was onstage.

No. 1 magazine arranged an interview between Mac and Morrissey, the unique and outspoken lead singer of The Smiths, an emerging Mancunian pop group. The meeting, which occurred in the plush environs of Liverpool's famed Adelphi Hotel, provided some interesting insights on the part of both performers, punctuated by several moments of sheer hilarity.

While Mac swilled bitter, Morrissey gingerly sipped orange juice, and the two attempted to see if they had anything in common. Mac inquired about Morrissey's Christian name, to which the other singer responded "Stephen." Mac replied "I knew it was either that or Jim." He subsequently called Morrissey "Steve" for the rest of the interview, to which the effeminate Mancunian initially shrieked and good-naturedly feigned collapse. While discussing their band names, Morrissey said that he had intended his to sound as basic and deflationary as possible. Mac cocked an eyebrow. "What about Fred? The Freds? Jack?"

Such sarcastic cheekiness, combined with Mac's distinct porcupine hair, long overcoats, and opaque shades, made him one of the most recognizable pop stars of the early to mid-80's. Although his appearance has changed slightly over the years, Mac the Mouth's garrulous gob has remained intact.

He was as wet as they come, Morrissey. Like, if in doubt, eat vegetables. Sod off. 'Meat is Murder.' What a soddin' paltry, pathetic thing to say. I mean, try telling that to a cow. —Ian McCulloch, 1989

Elvis Costello? Bloody terrible. Have you seen him on the telly? All fat and sweaty. Looks horrible. Can't dance, either.
—Ian McCulloch, 1994

I hate anything I hear by Culture Club. His voice really gets on my wick. He's just an old soddin' queen mincing 'round like some sickening Danny La Rue. Billy Idol's even worse.   —Ian McCulloch, 1984

I can't believe it. [Those groups] are all so much bigger than us, and yet all of them would love to be seen the same way as us. I read in this French magazine Jim Kerr saying that I say all these things about them because I'm insecure. That's ridiculous. He regarded us as the black sheep of the family—the family being us, U2, Simple Minds, and Big Country. I thought that was telling. In order for that family to mean anything it has to have us in it. We give them credibility. We've just been lumped in with them through no fault of our own. The others are all in the same colostomy bag. And as for Bono, he needs a colostomy bag for his mouth.   —Ian McCulloch, 1984

What a twat [Nick Cave] was. I remember in the NME they used to have these 'death lists' and on the top of Cave's was The Crucial Three. And I was at some festival in Holland, and he was there, and I thought, 'Come on, kill me.' But he never had a go. What a twat. I'd have concreted him. He'd be in the Hudson Bay now. You can tell him, if I'm still on his death list he can try it and I'll soddin' kill him. Twat. Australian, dingo-shagging turd. And he's a fake, and he can't sing. Fucking has-been junkie. He can't even OD. But anyway ... Nick babe, I fucking love you. You fucking Antipodean twat. Kangaroo is all he is. Delusions of syringe-dom.

—Ian McCulloch, 1989

Who buys U2 records anyway? It's just music for plumbers and bricklayers. Bono, what a slob. You'd think with all that climbing about he does, he'd look real fit and that. But he's real fat, y'know. Reminds me of a soddin' mountain goat …
—Ian McCulloch, 1984

All you need to be successful these days is a Gibson Les Paul and a Marshall amp with some bloke wailing away about 'in excelsis Deo.' Anyone can write an anthem like U2. We don't need to condescend and wave flags around. Our music isn't meant to save anyone's soul; it's more meant to make their ears bleed.
—Ian McCulloch, 1983

It's all very well finding answers to questions, but when the question only amounts to, 'Shall we play a benefit concert for the miners?' And the answer is, 'Yeah, let's play a benefit concert for the miners,' then I don't think anybody's asking or answering enough questions. Nothing's that simple.
—Ian McCulloch, 1984

You've got to hand it to Paul Weller. He's come up with two of the worst names of all time. Three—if you count 'Paul Weller' which is, let's face it, a crap name for a singer.
—Ian McCulloch, 1997

If I saw Bono walking down the street, I would just think he was one of the worst-dressed men I'd ever seen.
—Ian McCulloch, 1990

I remember in an interview with Bono once, he talked about becoming a madman. Well, he's to blame for that. To want to look that bad must say something. He really looks shit. Mind you, U2 always looked shit.
—Ian McCulloch, 1987

I wouldn't have thought any band could make it with a W.C. Fields lookalike for a singer. If Jim Morrison had looked like Jim Kerr he'd still be alive.
—Ian McCulloch, 1984

Mac reserved his most contemptuous comments for Paul Weller, former lead singer and guitarist of The Jam and leader of working-class soul merchants The Style Council.

Paul Weller was a Tory five years ago but now he's like Ken Livingstone's mannequin. I just think he's as thick as two short planks, he's a non-entity. There was a headline in one of the music papers the other day—'Paul Weller angry at death of taxi driver' or something. Who cares if Paul Weller's angry about it? Obviously it was a bad thing to happen, but you don't have to issue statements saying how angry you are. People who are attracted by that are just little soddin' deadbeats who need someone like him to give them an excuse for being the scum of the earth. People are so soddin' thick and selfish. I'm selfish but at least I admit it.   —Ian McCulloch, 1984

Paul Weller … he's the biggest divvy of them all. Saw him on the telly with that Mick Talbot, y'know, one of the greatest geniuses of our time. It was from Paris or somewhere and they were talking about *Café Bleu* or something … ha! He's probably bought a packet of Gitanes once in his life, and he doesn't like the taste but the packet looks better than a packet of Rothmans … he wouldn't know a paving stone if it hit him on the head … he's just a skinny twat who has the worst haircuts going. Totally asexual. How he's got the nerve to compare himself to Tamla Motown? He's trying to set up the new Motown and he gets Tracie … I've seen more soul in an ice cube. He's like the kid at school who was in the remedial class and he'd have spit between his two top teeth and then flicked his cigarette over the school fence as a sign of rebellion. And he was always the turd who, when *Animal Farm* came around in the third year and he was supposed to read it, he'd be scratching his name on the top of his desk. It's all very well maturing at 26, but when you're just maturing into a fifth form remedial, what's the point? —Ian McCulloch, 1984

Mac, on the other hand, professed nothing but pride for himself and the Bunnymen.

Whatever I do is capable of being a classic. I could probably mumble anything and somebody would think 'Great, that. Passionate.'
—Ian McCulloch, 1984

I am the king of rock & roll. —Ian McCulloch, 1997

I know John Lennon compared himself to Jesus Christ but that wasn't quite the same as saying *better*. —Ian McCulloch, 1984

I'm the Son of God. —Ian McCulloch, 1984

Bill Drummond, Les, and Pete, were, in general and at best, a little uncertain about Mac's vociferousness.

He's not a spokesman for the band—he's a spokesman for himself. I like a lot of what he says, but there's a lot I don't.
—Pete de Freitas, 1985

I generally respect what he says, but when he tries to align the band to great art by comparing them to Picasso and Michelangelo, he only makes himself seem like a dickhead. I know why he wants to elevate them to a higher plane, but that isn't what he understands best. Still, we all say things that make us look daft. —Bill Drummond, 1984

When you're on tour and you have to do one interview after the other you run out of different thing to say and end up talking crap.
—Les Pattinson, 1985

Will adopted a less philosophical stance towards Mac's missives.

Shiiit, Maaaac! You stupid, stupid, stupid bastaaaard! Why, oh why, can't you keep your fuckin' mouth shut?!? —Will Sergeant, 1985

When caught in candid moments by the press, Mac has attempted to justify his tirades.

It's difficult for us not to be the best. There's so much rubbish about, we can't help standing out. There are a lot of Jacks-of-all-trades about, and no master.
—Ian McCulloch, 1983

The only inferiority complex I've got is about other people being inferior.
—Ian McCulloch, 1984

I've got great lips. I've got a great face. It's not my fault.
—Ian McCulloch, 1984

Never trust a thin-lipped bastard. —Ian McCulloch, 1989

I do think you've gotta have a *swagger*. It's like, you can't be in a football team and think that the other side's as good, or you're gonna get beat. Like, Bill Shankly, he had this sign that said 'This is Anfield.' And teams'd have to go under that before they went out on the pitch to play Liverpool. All I ever tried to do is make that point— THIS IS ECHO & THE BUNNYMEN. So when people go down that tunnel to see Liverpool or the Bunnymen, they know what they're gonna get. The best.   —Ian McCulloch, 1984

I think it's fairly obvious why I say those things; it comes from a person who does think his own opinion is the right one. All that ego thing, the things I've said, a lot of it was culled from me rather than me proffering it forth. A lot of groups are easy meat 'cos they're so transparently not very good, and because I've got a certain gift of one-line burials. It's like second nature. And it is, like, a Scouse thing. It might be Liverpudlian gobrot, but it's a lot better than any other kind of gobrot. It's like the Bill Shankly era of Liverpool. A lot of people resent the fact that Liverpool was the best team even when they weren't winning things. And we're the best, whether we sell 2,000 records or two million. Everybody knows it, that's why they don't like it.   —Ian McCulloch, 1984

I'll just say anything that comes to my head. Normally I'll try and lie a bit.   —Ian McCulloch, 1985

I see my role as partly to be a star. I think that's what people want, and it's not my fault that I pull it off.   —Ian McCulloch, 1987

I'll do anything and say anything to avoid being boring. The actor George Sanders wrote a suicide note which said, 'Life is intolerable but boredom is unforgivable.' That's how I feel, basically. Nice people are ten-a-penny. You need people who'll shake things up a bit. That's the way it's always been for me and the band. The bottom line is that we were always having a fucking good laugh ... sure, you want to make people connect with your music and all the rest of it. But if you can't have a soddin' good laugh while you're doing it, then you might as well fuck off home.   —Ian McCulloch, 1997

While some of the press and public derided Mac's comments as annoying arrogance, others attempted to rationalize it.

Mac can back up his lip with the certain conviction that he is as good as he says he is, and that it's all an ambiguously self-deflating joke, anyway. He knows he's good copy, and enjoys rambling on even if he's not sure what he's talking about.   —NME, 1984

McCulloch has a head the size of your average barrage balloon and an uncanny knack of alienating everyone in sight just by uttering one or two of his infamous barbed comments. But his egotistical sparring matches with the press, whether they aggravate or entertain, are infinitely more interesting than the self-effacing modesty of lesser mortals. There might even be a grain of truth in there somewhere—the fun comes in trying to find it without treading in all the strategically-laid bullshit. Whatever happens, McCulloch will inevitably get the last laugh.   —Journalist Caroline Watson, 1984

For all his arrogance, McCulloch has always been an immensely likable individual. What is usually missing from reports of his comments is the twinkle with which they are delivered. —The Observer, 1997

Ian McCulloch has the knack of making vast claims and looking completely baffled at the same time. It's a good knack to have.   —Melody Maker, 1987

The Mac the Mouth image came to a head in mid-1985, during an interview with *Smash Hits* magazine. His house had just been burgled for the sixth time, and he couldn't contain his fury.

I've been talking about Liverpool for the past seven years, saying how great it is, and it's not. It's a disgusting place and I hate it. Fifty percent of the people there, at least, are scum.
                    —Ian McCulloch, 1985

The Liverpool Echo caught wind of Mac's comments and printed POP STAR SAYS YOU ARE SCUM as a banner headline. The citizens were outraged, and demanded a public apology, a request to which Mac partially acquiesced. Angry at having his words manipulated, and probably slightly embarrassed about the whole affair, Mac attempted to bury the whole image.

A lot of what I said was quite hurtful, so I'll just leave it alone—'Mac the Mouth' and that. I'll just be a bit more clever.
                    —Ian McCulloch, 1985

After the smoke had cleared and tempers had quieted down, Mac expressed his true feelings about his hometown onstage, at the end of a gig at The Royal Court.

By the way ... I love Liverpool.   —Ian McCulloch, 1985

NME cover, November 1980

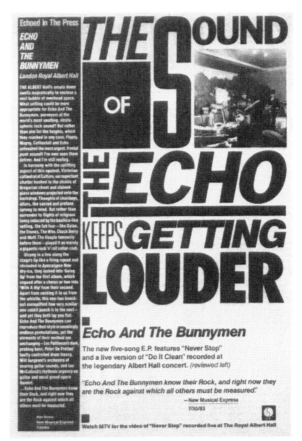

Sire Records promotional ad, 1983

Live in Liverpool, 1982 (photo: Gary Lornie)

Will. Door. (photo: Jim Kutler)

Live, 1988 (photo: Jim Kutler)

Mac, 1988 (photo: Jim Kutler)

Les, 1988 (photo: Jim Kutler)

Will, 1988 (photo: Jim Kutler)

Pete, London, 1985 (photo: Jim Kutler)

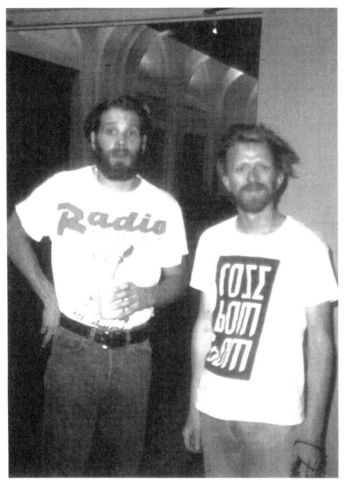

Pete and Jake, 1988 (photo: Jim Kutler)

Les, 1985 (photo: Steve Doughty)

Euphoric Records logo, 1991

Mac, "Scando" tour, 1985 (photo: Birgit Gunnarsson)

Echo and the Burundi Men, WOMAD Festival 1982
(photo: Musicfoto.com)

Pete, 1988 (photo: Jim Kutler)

Will, 1988 (photo: Jim Kutler)

Ocean Rain was released on May 5th, 1984, Mac's 25th birthday. To promote the album, Warner Brothers designed posters and purchased full-page ads in the weekly music papers, which announced that this Bunnymen recording was "the greatest album ever made."

... when Mac described *Ocean Rain* as 'the greatest album ever made' it sounded less like hyperbole than statement of fact ...
                                                              —*Uncut,* 1999

That wasn't my idea! I was on the phone to Rob, just joshing, and I said 'Oh, it's the greatest album ever made.' And he used it on the poster. It was all very Bill Shankly, you know—trash the opposition, take no prisoners!   —Ian McCulloch, 1999

The greatest album ever made? Another touch of irony that was misunderstood. The greatest orchestrated rock album ever made? Yes.
—Journalist Mick Houghton, 1984

'The Greatest Album Ever Made'? History might judge otherwise, but the record remains as close as the Bunnymen ever came.   —*Mojo,* 1997

The sleeve for the album was again as evocative as its contents. A photo of the band in Paris would have been the obvious choice, but as the Bunnymen saw their catalog as a sort of "deck of cards," they wanted to retain the elemental theme determined by the previous trio of album covers. So the art pictured the band in a rowboat, drifting along a lake inside an underground English cave.

At last, Liverpool's latter-day Fab Four had found their own Cavern.
                                                              —*Q,* 2001

At the skiff's helm was Mac as Narcissus, gazing into the water, index finger gliding over his reflection, a man falling in love with his own image. Will sat directly behind the singer, staring blankly at the viewer, as endearingly uncomfortable as Warhol ever was. Les and Pete stood in back, oars in their hands—the stalwart working boys. It was a perfect visual representation of arguably the Bunnymen's finest album.

Our best yet. There are plenty of vocals on it, for a change. It's fast and bully music, but you can hear the words.
        —Ian McCulloch, 1984

The album is, in post-paranoia, our definitive statement.
                                                  —Ian McCulloch, 1984

It's the best album yet by about a light year. It's Jacques and the Brellymen. I mean, if Hieronymous Bosch has been 50 years younger, he'd have sounded like this.   —Ian McCulloch, 1984

My singing on this new album is pretty good. Not quite Jacques Brel—he had one of the best voices around—but a lot better than Big Country and U2.   —Ian McCulloch, 1984

   Most of the music press agreed, and the album has aged well over the years.

Ocean Rain was the culmination of all that had gone before, yet moving even further into the future. Mixing exquisite pop with heady atmospheres both dark and bright, the album had the density of *Heaven Up Here*, the risk-taking of *Porcupine*, and the drive of *Crocodiles*, but wrapped in a warm sound that vibrated across the tracks.
                                                    —*Goldmine*, 1998

...in which Captain McCulloch steers the H.M.S. Echo away from the jagged ice of *Porcupine* into almost Mediterranean waters … the Bunnymen at their most romantic. The lyrics are full of starry skies, golden views, and April showers, and in 'Thorn of Crowns' McCulloch turns his martyred artist image on its head. A consistently thrilling demonstration of how to be epic without being pompous. Not 'The Greatest Album Ever Made,' but certainly the saltiest.
                                                —*Record Mirror*, 1997

Soul equals emotion—and Echo & the Bunnymen are dripping with that. *Ocean Rain* dribbles and pours with passion … close to the bone, straight from the heart, jangling and beating to your ears. No sell out, nor carefully positioned (throwaway) dance beats, no guitar histrionics, just Echo & the Bunnymen being Echo & the Bunnymen, the only way they know how. *Ocean Rain* is an album to live with.
                                                       —*Sounds*, 1984

The album shows a marked departure from its predecessor, *Porcupine*. It finds the Bunnymen in a more romantic mood typified by the lavish 'The Killing Moon.' The result is a more spacious and tuneful set of songs than we've had yet from the Bunnymen, with "Big" Mac McCulloch stepping into the spotlight with his new-grown killing croon to test out territory previously only occupied by the likes of Lou Reed and Jim Morrison.   —*Melody Maker*, 1984

Ocean Rain [the Bunnymen's] most charming and friendly album yet, sails in warm and intoxicating Mediterranean waters, Homer's wine dark sea. But the men from Liverpool don't bask in the torpid heat; there

I think it shows that we can create an element of magic without pandering to current tastes. *Ocean Rain* is kissing music, songs to fall in love to.   —Ian McCulloch, 1984

Produced at the legendary Studio Des Dames, where both Edith Piaf and Jacques Brel had made their names, the Bunnymen employed its house orchestra to bejewel the bares bones of their music with similar baroque drama; music of the gods incarnate ... here was a phantasmagoric pop riddle of trembling cellos, Arabic melodies, spirit-soaring pizzicato, and Mac's 'dream-like' visions of blue moons and stalagmites ... Though clearly of its time, *Ocean Rain* is a Byzantine musical feast which possesses a majestic classicism which hasn't dated ... no album since has matched its unique synergy of acidic pop mysticism which full-on orchestral panache.
                              —*Uncut*, 2001

Ocean Rain is one of the most transcendent acoustic records ever made. A profoundly human work, it was easily the most singable record of its time.
                           —*Stylus*, 1999

Ocean Rain made me laugh and cry quite a bit. It was certainly wittier, healthier, even sexier than we had any right to expect.　　　　*—Jamming,* 1985

is a squalling undercurrent of desperation and violence that cuts through those plush tunes. A thrilling equilibrium of rapture, mystery, and humor rises above the waves. And the living proof, of course, is at my fingertips.　　　　*—NME,* 1984

Even Bill Drummond agreed that the album captured the band at a creative peak.

It was not the earth-stopping album I had wanted, with songs that said, 'Now these ones have been written, there is no point in anybody else ever writing any more songs ever again.' Instead, the band had made a pretty good record. I knew this was not the album I had hoped to complete the series, the one where Echo was found and his wisdom and truth revealed. Something had been completed in me. A level reached. A cycle turned. The power of Echo lay not in his material revelation but in his eternal mystery. That is why for me the *Ocean Rain* album was so perfect. It retained the mystery without relying on adolescent pretensions to wisdom. The sleeve portrayed the band once more adrift. But to be adrift is the only way to travel on the glorious journey. It was as if Echo were turning 'round and saying, 'I'm not so easily nailed down, called to account.'
　　　—Bill Drummond, *From the Shores of Lake Placid and Other Stories*

There were also detractors, such as Biba Kopf, who wrote a scathing review in the *NME*.

… everything on *Ocean Rain* has been designed to buttress the notion of the group's importance. Not unnaturally the results have the opposite effect. Where before they had some grasp on mystery, now they're grasping after it. Once cupidly impressionistic, they've become culpably impressionable. And the surreal touches Big Mac endeavors to bring his lyrics through tired juxtapositions of mysterious buzzwords, nonsense, and banality carry all the conviction of a Roger Dean Yes cover. I perceive no real irony in his portentous delivery of them—he's too wantonly cuddly to be a wicked messenger. Indeed the Echo of *Ocean Rain* presents me with a stock Dean-style fantasy of Big Mac as a vainglorious knight errant, his vocal astride a Bunnymen music comfortably maintaining an even canter through Xanadu-misty landscapes conjured up by the mellotron-style wash of strings and bleating wood winds ... [*Ocean Rain*] is wasted on one of contemporary rock's more worthless quests: to relocate the Chord [sic] the Moody Blues lost a decade ago. Sad to report Echo & the Bunnymen have found it.　*—NME,* 1984

Naturally, Mac had a response.

Ocean Rain's an album that conjures up beauty and you either see if or you don't. You either think its totally wonderful or hippy music, '5th form poetry.' I was always aware of what 5th form poetry was. And it's not. It's probably more 1st form poetry. —Ian McCulloch, 1984

... some people got it and some people didn't; the ones that didn't were fools.
—Ian McCulloch, 1998

There's no question that a lot of people got it. The album entered the UK charts at #4, and the Bunnymen found that they'd inadvertently become something they'd never really intended: fully-fledged international rock stars. And on no one's terms but their own.

***

NOCTURNAL ME

An icecap fire, old burning wood
In a world of wire
Ignites our dreams of starry skies
It's you and me
Us realized our bigger themes

Take me internally
Forever yours
Nocturnal me

Do or die, what's done is done
True beauty lies on the blue horizon
Who or why? What's won is one
In pure disguise of vulgar suns

Take me internally
Forever yours
Nocturnal me

Whatever burns burns eternally
So take me in turns, internally
When I'm on fire, my body will be
Forever yours
Nocturnal me

'Nocturnal Me' succumbs fatally to a ghastly bombastic arrangement, comically reminiscent of Tom Jones's 'Delilah.' —*Melody Maker*, 1984

...a positive song ... it intimidates in a positive way. It makes me smile when I'm playing it. —Ian McCulloch, 1984

The lyrics of that song are nothing at all. Nocturnal me, writing songs about me staying up all night. That's not going to do anything.
—Ian McCulloch, 1997

... boasts a strong melody and some wiry guitar from Will, which could profitably have been remixed into a much brighter brew.

—*Melody Maker*, 1984

People imagine that we're a cold, icy band. I don't think that we are. I think our music is all about sunshine.

—Ian McCulloch, 1987

I like 'Crystal Days' more than anything on that first side.

—Ian McCulloch, 1999

'I'm the yo-yo man, always up and down'—that's the most accurate description I can give of me. —Ian McCulloch, 1984

CRYSTAL DAYS

Here am I
Whole at last with a golden view
Looking for hope and I hope
   it's you
Splitting my heart cracked right
   in two
The pleasure of pain endured
To purify our misfit ways
And magnify our crystal days

Where are you?
Shadows only I can see
Looking for hope and you hope
   it's me
Tattered and torn and born to be
Building a world where we can
Purify our misfit ways
And magnify our crystal days

Purity magnify

Here am I
Whole at last with a golden view
Looking for hope and I know
   it's you
Splitting my heart cracked right
   in two
The pleasure of pain and joy to
Purify our misfit ways
And magnify our crystal days

THE YO-YO MAN

Froze to the bone in my
   igloo home
Counting the days 'til the ice
   turns green
You know when Heaven and hell
   collide
There are no in-betweens

Flames on your skin of snow
   turn cold
Cold as the wind that blows
Through my headstone

Collecting the bones of my
   friends tonight
Sowing the seeds in a fruitless land
You know when prayers all hit
   the ground
There is no higher hand

Flames on your skin of snow
   turn cold
Cold as the wind that blows
Through my headstone

I'm the yo-yo man, always up
   and down
So take me to the end of
   your tether

Flames on your skin of snow
   turn cold
Cold as the wind that blows
Through our headstones

Aaaah-ahhh
Aaaah-ahhh

You set my teeth on edge
You set my teeth on edge
You think you're a vegetable
Never come out of the fridge

C-c-c-cucumber
C-c-c-cabbage
C-c-c-cauliflower
Men on Mars
April showers

Aaaah-ahhh
Aaaah-ahhh

You are a dying breed
You are a dying breed
You once was an Inca
Now you're a Cherokee

C-c-c-cucumber
C-c-c-cabbage
C-c-c-cauliflower
Men on Mars
April showers

You kick it
Kick it

Wait for me on the blue horizon
Blue horizon for everyone
Wait for me on a new horizon
New horizons for everyone

I wanna be one times one with you
I wanna be one times one with you

Aaaah-ahhh
Aaaah-ahhh

I've decided
To wear my thorn of crowns
I've decided
To wear my thorn of crowns
Inside out
Back to front
Upside down
All the way around
Down...

It's weird, isn't it? When a dark-haired Liverpudlian has got the nerve to get up on stage and sing 'C-c-c-cucumber, c-c-c-cabbage, c-c-c-cauliflower' and not only get away with it, but be hailed as the new messiah by a legion of faithful fans. —*Blitz*, 1984

The Bunnysound is a shimmering, spikey landscape, sometimes it tangles and traps you, then just as effortlessly twists and leaves you with a handful of dust. Everything and nothing.   —*Jamming*, 1985

... almost like a demonstration track of how little you need to make something great. Basically, it's about nothing—but everything. Going 'aaa-ah' can be worth more than a hundred words. It's like the beginning of 'Baby Love'—really great. I think 'Thorn of Crowns' is really sexy, and I suppose words like 'cucumber' fit in with that. It's also self-deflating, it wasn't meant to sound serious. All that 'I've decided to wear my thorn of crowns' is meant to be not taken seriously—but very seriously at the same time. All that 'inside out, back to front'—I thought it was fairly obvious that it was meant to be anti-messianic. But obviously, for the people who hate us, it was more fuel to the fire.
—Ian McCulloch, 1984

... although I'll make an effort to pretend to make myself into some kind of deity ... it's meant to be tongue-in-cheek; it's meant to deflate myself as much as elevate myself. But a lot of people take it at face value
—Ian McCulloch, 1984

Get into comedy. The best thing you can do is cry tears of laughter. Learn to have a sense of humor about yourself.
—Ian McCulloch, 1999

... clucking 'c-c-c-cucumber!' while screechy-scratchy guitars made the finest forays into controlled noise since the Velvets.   —*Uncut*, 1999

... where Arabic melodies entwine over an ominous percussion rumble, then give way to raw-scrubbed guitar over which Mac waxes mystical—'You are a dying breed/You once was an Inca/Now you're a Cherokee.' Admirers of the much-plundered Doors might find themselves altering Mac's 'wait for me on the blue horizon' to 'meet me at the back of the blue bus.' Fits perfectly.
                    —*Melody Maker*, 1984

Why so may aquatic references? Well, all the nice girls love a sailor, as the saying goes— though I'm no sailor. I used to love taking the ferry to Europe instead of flying. I find that whenever I'm near water, it's just, I suppose, calming.
                    —Ian McCulloch, 1997

...hits transcendental, ocean-shimmering peaks
                    —*Melody Maker*, 1997

...the most accessible song they've ever recorded
                    —*Melody Maker*, 1984

If your underpants size is getting bigger over the years, instead of saying 'I have to buy bigger underpants, I tend to put it in a religious setting and call it 'Thorn of Crowns.' My thorn of crowns is really my underpants. It is semi-spiritual, but it also puts it in an environment that can maybe challenge, so it's not just *me* I'm talking about. To somebody in Africa, who cares about me? You've got to connect with other people, and a spiritual thing is something everybody at some point thinks about. A lot of people say they write religious lyrics, but they're not really.   —Ian McCulloch, 1987

McCulloch has often been compared to the late Jim Morrison, and he's rarely been pleased about it. Echo's long and winding 'Thorn of Crowns' worked on its own terms, and also as a wicked Doors parody. 'I've decided to wear my thorn of crowns/I've decided to take my trousers down,' sang McCulloch, lancing Morrison's artistic pretensions by pairing it with his infamous, on-stage exposure indecent.
                    —*The Boston Globe*, 1984

... a garage-band epic, almost like The Leaves trying to do 'A Day In the Life' under conditions of intense personal pressure. —*NME*, 1984

SEVEN SEAS

Stab a sorry heart with your
    favourite finger
Paint the whole world blue
And stop your tears from stinging
Hear the cavemen singing
Good news they're bringing

Seven seas, swimming them so well
Glad to see my face among them
Kissing the tortoise shell

A longing for some fresher feeling
Belonging or just forever kneeling
Where's the sense in stealing
Without the grace to be it?

Seven seas, swimming them so well
Glad to see my face among them
Kissing the tortoise shell

Burning my bridges and smashing
    my mirrors
Turning to see if you're cowardly
Burning the witches with mother
    religious
You'll strike the matches and
    shower me in
Water games
Washing the rocks below
Taught and tamed
In time with tear flow

Seven seas, swimming them so well
Glad to see my face among them
Kissing the tortoise shell

MY KINGDOM

I chop and I change
And the mystery thickens
There's blood on my hands
And you want me to listen?
To brawn or to brain
When the truth's in the middle
Born of the grain
Like all good riddles

B-b-burn the skin off
And climb the rooftop
Thy will be done
B-b-bite the nose off
And make it the most of
Your kingdom

You kill when you talk
And the enemy weakens
Your words start to walk
When you're not even speaking
If my heart is a war
Its soldiers are bleeding
If my heart is a war,
Its soldiers are dead

B-b-burn the skin off
And climb the rooftop
Thy will be done
B-b-bite the nose off
And make it the most of
Your kingdom

I've lost and I've gained
And while I was thinking
You cut off my hands
When I wanted to twist
If you know how to dance
To bony moroney
He's doing the ballet
On both of his wrists

B-b-burn the skin off
And climb the rooftop
Thy will be done
B-b-bite the nose off
And make it the most of
Your kingdom

You're a between-the-lines person
And your death is well overdue
You suck the foot that kicks you
You kiss the hand that hits you

Ten-a-penny ...

'My Kingdom' has probably got a lot more bite than 'Villiers Terrace'; there's a lot of venom in it which you would normally associate with youth. I don't think you lose that bite and venom, because it's part of who you are.
—Ian McCulloch, 1985

I think 'My Kingdom' is a barrel of laughs, but it was meant to be.   —Ian McCulloch, 1984

An overlooked track from my favourite Bunnymen album.
—Ian McCulloch, 1992

...a triumphant affirmation, fragile and roaring by turns ... plays off the soliloquy-like intimacy of Mac's vocal against a sudden torrent of lead guitar from Sergeant which comes storming out of the song's hymnal chorus like Neil Young on re-heat.   —*Melody Maker*, 1984

'Ocean Rain' slips gently onto a moonlit sea via its mystically hushed opening. 'All at sea again' mutters Mac wearily, and you can almost hear the creaking of the rigging. Built around a cello figure of fragile beauty, 'Ocean Rain' is the jewel in the crown, walking a tightrope between melodrama and majesty. It's both sinister and alluring. —*Melody Maker*, 1984

A song like 'Ocean Rain,' it's ahead of its time so if it's nostalgia, then it's nostalgia for the future. Or it's—a favorite expression of mine— 'ahead of its timelessness.'
—Ian McCulloch, 1999

It's the greatest song we ever wrote. If there's one song I want to die singing, it's that one.   —Ian McCulloch, 2001

OCEAN RAIN

All at sea again
And now my hurricanes
Have brought down this ocean rain
To bathe me again
My ship's a-sail
Can you hear its tender frame
Screaming from beneath the waves
Screaming from beneath the waves

All hands on deck at dawn
Sailing to sadder shores
Your port in my heavy storms
Harbors the blackest thoughts

I'm at sea again
And now your hurricanes
Have brought down this ocean rain
To bathe me again
My ship's a-sail
Can you hear its tender frame
Screaming from beneath the waves
Screaming from beneath the waves...

I'm glad I was born with the voice I've got. 'Cos it can sing 'All at sea again/And now your hurricanes/Have brought down this ocean rain' and it's brilliant—it's *believable*. It comes not just from my appreciation of the ocean, but it's a song *for* the ocean. That sounds stupid, but, y'know, the elements ... I suppose it's a bit Wordsworthian; he felt all those elements were actually speaking, and I suppose I do.
—Ian McCulloch, 1984

... the slow, awesome sound of a thousand chandeliers tinkling in the breeze ...   —*Liverpool Hoopla*, 1999

...a bittersweet, touching song, the seduction is complete. Like staring at brown eyes and strolling through cities at 2am, you just *fall*.
—Journalist Ian Drury, 1997

 ... one of the finest songs ever written, it's good enough to justify McCulloch's rampant arrogance on its own.   —*Melody Maker*, 1997

A CRYSTAL DAY

On May 12, 1984, one week after the release of *Ocean Rain*, the Bunnymen staged what may be the crowning achievement of their career. Earlier in the year, Mac had come up with the notion of playing the under-used St. George's Hall, just opposite the Lime Street train station in Liverpool.

'Crystal Day' was really my idea. I really fancied playing the St. George's Hall because I'd heard from me dad that the building was being cleaned out, and I decided it would be a great place to play.
—Ian McCulloch, 1984

Eventually, with the help of Bill Drummond, Mac's idea blossomed into the notion of arranging a day's worth of happenings in Liverpool.

We could have either done a proper tour up and down the country, or gone for something different at the risk of falling flat on our faces. We were willing to take that risk. It came down to choosing somewhere we were familiar with and places we'd have permission to visit. Mac was also keen to play St. George's Hall, last played by The Beatles, so we settled on Liverpool.   —Bill Drummond, 1984

Actually, the Hall was not last played by The Beatles. According to Mac, they "used a bit of license." "I don't know what kind," he said. "But it sounds better than saying the last group that played there was Judas Priest."

The *NME* announced "A Crystal Day." If nothing else, the event indicated the Bunnymen's fierce pride in their hometown, a pride they've retained through the thick and thin. The whole idea behind 'A Crystal Day' was to showcase the myriad charms of Liverpool. After all, why go through the hassle and expense of playing the Outer Hebrides and similar "Atlas Adventures," while avoiding "the greatest city in the world"?

It portrays Liverpool in a better light than people reading about muggers killing old women, y'know? It's the antithesis of that scummy side of Liverpool. It's meant to be a celebration of the good things in life. —Ian McCulloch, 1984

Mac still lives in the city, just a fairly short cab ride from the city center, and he can be frequently spotted at various nightspots around town. His love of Liverpool has, if anything, increased over time.

I get a weird pleasure from knowing that Liverpool has the highest unemployment rate in England and the highest car theft rate and the dirtiest river ... I quite enjoy that image. Liverpool is the best place going, and I think it always will be.

   —Ian McCulloch, 1983

I can't see us leaving Liverpool. There's something about the city that inspires the best in us. Absurd, isn't it?   —Ian McCulloch, 1987

Liverpudlians never kiss arse, which is basically why we're still here.

   —Ian McCulloch, 2000

The reason the Bunnymen are special is to do with Liverpool. It's the epicenter of the world. It's the quickest place on the planet, 'cos before you've a chance to stick your smartarse joke in, the other feller's already shot you down in flames. It's a magical place.

   —Ian McCulloch, 2001

I think Liverpool should be like Amsterdam or Hamburg—you know, fucking, prostitution, and gambling. What we're good at is a bit of music, footie, and just entertaining. People always have a great time up there with us, so we should play to our strengths. That's why everyone hates us, 'cos they know it's the best place. All this Scottish independence stuff—it should be 'Scouse independence.' I've got this idea to invent a really long saw and saw Liverpool off from the rest of the country one night when no one's watching. Just float it off to the soddin' Pacific; We should call it Scouse Islands.

   —Ian McCulloch, 1992

Presumably unable to find a saw of the proportions necessary for such a grand-scale situationist gesture, Bill Drummond and the band sat down at the Bunnymen flat in Aigburth and conceptualized what would constitute an ideal Bunnymen day in Liverpool. A ferry ride across the Mersey River to Birkenhead was obvious—you couldn't *not* do it, given the river's historic role in the city, and the Gerry and the Pacemakers hit. Plus, the band wanted to provide financial aid to the threatened institution, which was in danger of being shut down. The concert was to be given at the end of the day. But what else? Bill Drummond, as always, had a few ideas.

... each event dripped heavily with ritualistic symbolism. With the passing of time I can't remember what these events were. I do recall something going on at the old cathedral, and a vast amount of blue and yellow balloons being released—blue and yellow being the colors of the label of the Bunnymen's first single. But for me the pivot of the daytime events was actually a cycle ride around the city. What I had done was to draw out an outline of Echo, the rabbit god character—as depicted on the 'Pictures of My Wall' single sleeve—on a map of the city of Liverpool, the manhole cover at the bottom of Mathew Street being Echo's navel. The bike trip followed this outline.

  —Bill *Drummond, From the Shores of Lake Placid and Other Stories*

Beside the bicycle journey and ferry ride (including a banana fight), the events comprising "A Crystal Day" were as follows: Reveille above Brian's Café, and a visit to the Diner itself to provide a struggling Brian and his family with enough money to keep the café alive. Fans had to queue outside Brian's and purchase a meal, indicated by a stamped ticket, or they wouldn't be allowed into the evening's show. (Toward the end of the day, this stipulation was discarded.)

Then there was a visit to Victor's hair salon, where all the Bunnymen except for the Lorraine-styled Mac had their hair cut. From there it was a visit to the Anglican Cathedral, "the most powerful building known to mankind, and the largest single chamber in Europe" according to the event's program, and where Scouser Ian Tracy, "the world's greatest classical organist under thirty" would perform a recital. For the actual gig, the Bunnymen would play three sets, each separated by a performance from the play "The Monkey King Subdues The White Bone Demon" by the Chinese troupe "Dancers of the Pagoda of 100 Harmonies." A Crystal Day would officially conclude with the announcement of The Last Post from the rooftop of St. George's Hall.

The blueprint for the day spanned the historic, the transcendental, the humorous, the exotic, and the just plain daft. In short, it spelled BUNNYMEN in large capital letters.

Fifteen hundred fans showed up for the events. Amazingly, everything went without a hitch, with the possible exception of the bicycle ride. Drummond's hastily sketched route didn't particularly correspond to any actual streets; instead, the map demanded that fans plow straight through the Anglican Cathedral, which would have no doubt upset organist Ian Tracy, not to mention the Church of England. The map also implied that bicyclists speed into a large body of water, which would have drowned the more literal-minded and dedicated Bunnyfans. Luckily, Will and Les participated in the ride, their guidance potentially sparing the lives of hundreds of fans. Mac himself had decided not to attend most of the events.

I'll probably be washing me hair. Anyway, I can go out to Pier Head or see the cathedral any time.   —Ian McCulloch, 1984

When he and Lorraine eventually emerged for the ferry ride, they were swarmed by hordes of autograph seekers. No doubt Mac would have preferred to be at Anfield, where, that day, Liverpool FC won the league championship for the third year running. If any day existed to prove "the quality of Mersey is not strained," it was clearly this one.

The Bunnymen blazed mightily through the three sets, performing a total of 25 songs, spanning *Crocodiles* through *Ocean Rain*.

Musically, the Bunnymen were at their best, striking the perfect balance between thrusting aggression and crystalline beauty. The searing

The Bunnymen... invariably answer all their critics when they play live. 'A Crystal Day' was no exception. A lot of people wanted to see the group with egg all over their faces. In the end, though, [the Bunnymen] played as well at St. George's Hall as they did at Albert's—subtler, but just as sure. The only egg that day was to be found at Brian's Diner, if you could be bothered to queue for it.   —Journalist Mick Houghton, 1984

... another blistering performance from one of the greatest
rock bands of the decade.
—Soundcheck, 1984

When the band took the stage,
St. George's Hall shook.
Quadraphonic thunder rolled,
edged with bending, distorted,
and lead sounds, frilled with
acoustic strumming, focused on
a loud, forward singing voice.
It was hard to be certain at
first who was roaring louder,
Mac or the crowd.
—Hot Press, 1984

passion of 'Pictures On My Wall,' 'Read It In Books,' 'Stars Are
Stars,' 'Crocodiles,' and 'Monkeys' was bowled home in fully husky
voice, driven by Les's manic bass lines and peppered with whiplash
drum frenzy. In contrast were the glittering splinters of 'All My
Colours,' 'Turquoise Days,' 'Thorn of Crowns,' and the shivery magic
of 'The Killing Moon.' It has to be said (again) that when the Bunnies
break out of consuming self-indulgence and wailing ego trips, they're
still far and away the best rock band. *—NME, 1984*

One of the most perfect Echo & the Bunnymen shows ever to be performed. *—Tony Fletcher, Never Stop, 1987*

The new limited edition double pack SEVEN SEAS
and LIFE AT BRIANS –LEAN AND HUNGRY The soundtrack including all
acoustic live versions of ALL YOU NEED IS LOVE. STARS ARE STARS
THE KILLING MOON and VILLIERS TERRACE

SEVEN SEAS

Although they had never pulled more than two singles off an album, the
Bunnymen decided that they should release one more from *Ocean Rain*. On
July 6th the "Seven Seas" EP hit the streets, made available as both a 12-
inch single and double-pack 45, titled "Life At Brian's: Lean and Hungry."
The B-sides were "Stars Are Stars," "The Killing Moon," "Villiers Terrace,"
and "All You Need Is Love," all recorded for the Play at Home special.

Determined not to make the mistake they'd made with "Silver," the
Bunnymen hired Anton Corbijn to film a video for the single. Eager to high-
light the humor of the band, Corbijn drafted a script that cast Will as a fish,
Les as a penguin, and Mac tarting it up in drag as an Amsterdam prostitute.
The Bunnymen loved the script, and exhorted him to make it even weirder.
This he did, and when it was completed, it was forwarded for approval to the
Warner Brothers top brass, who promptly freaked out.

Here they were, already faced with the proposition of trying to sell a difficult band with a silly name, and they're presented with a bizarre video that
calls for the guitar hero to don the guise of a flounder! Arguing that this
would destroy the marketability of a band who were already perceived as a
tough sell, the company rejected the script. This infuriated the Bunnymen,
who speared down to London for an impromptu meeting, where both parties
screamed blue bloody murder at each other. Warners refused to finance the
video, and told the band that they could put up the money for the film themselves; if the company decided that the final product was acceptable, they'd

buy it from the Bunnymen. Much to WEA's surprise, that's just what the band did. When the film was completed, the Bunnymen brought it, beaming, to the record company, and aired a private screening. Warner Brothers was overjoyed with the video, and promptly purchased it.

... it was great—when I'd got the make-up done and the wig put on, I looked in the mirror and it looked totally weird. When I walked out with the wig and the lipstick on [the other Bunnymen] couldn't believe it. I think Will thought it was a bit frightening. It was meant to be a skit on all them soddin' gender benders ... It was just that heritage of Bowie and Jagger and stuff. I thought I walked so much better than all of them other turds who do it seriously, and dye their hair yellow and put the Max Factor on and think they look really pretty and stuff. None of them seem to carry it off well, and I just thought that wiggle that I did was better than anything I'd seen. I suppose it was from when I used to like Bowie a lot, and there were all them people wearing make-up, and I suppose at the time I thought, 'God, I'd love to be able to dye my hair orange and get the lippy on' and stuff, just to see what'd I'd look like. So it was the first time I'd ever tried something like that. It was all being 13 again, living out what I'd never lived out when it was all happening.

—Ian McCulloch, 1984

I've always thought I would've made a prettier girl than, er, most girls, really.

—Ian McCulloch, 1989

With the aid of this promotional snippet, "Seven Seas" eventually rose to #16 in the UK charts.

The Bunnymen then hopped over to the U.S. for a quick trek through some of the major cities. Instead of playing in the standard triangular "rock" formation onstage, the band presented themselves in a dramatic straight line, with Pete playing stage right. Most thought it was an original and impressive set-up—although Mac was a little dubious.

That was an intentional move, presenting ourselves that way. It looked great [but] it sounded crap on stage—I couldn't hear a soddin' thing. Christ knows what it sounded like out front. All these people keep talking about classic Bunnymen gigs, but, to be honest, they all sounded like shite from where I was standing.   —Ian McCulloch, 1997

Stateside writers disagreed.

Echo & the Bunnymen indeed confirm their reputation as ferocious live performers. Bassist Les Pattinson and drummer Pete de Freitas lock into a throbbing groove of powerhouse locomotion, anchoring

For one tour ... it was alright ... on a visual level, more than anything ... [but] the perfect thing is to have the drummer in the back and the singer in the middle. I was always cued to one side by accident. I didn't have any room to groove about or do anything. I just think drum kits look horrible. And having cymbal stands at the front of the stage is horrible. It should be like the father, the son, and the holy ghost, with the drummer in the back.

—Ian McCulloch, 1988

There is nothing hesitant about their attack, with Will Sergeant's frantic "ostrich" guitar (very Velvets) and bull-dozing crescendos urging McCulloch's inky rasps into a desperate wail … For all their epic drive, the Bunnymen still haven't forfeited their humor and humanity … The show's dizzy climax shows us just how great a pop band the Bunnymen really are.
—Journalist David Fricke, 1984

In many ways, it's a relief when they quit the stage. Their intensity, their sheer, pluck, and dash and nerve is exhaust-ing, leaves so many highlights to come to terms with, to accommodate, size up, and define. I couldn't put the spectacle of their performance in perspective then, and I can't now. Spanning high drama and ironic subterfuge, this was a monumental address to the faithful that also witnessed the final conversion of this dubious skeptic. This head rolled. —Melody Maker, 1984

McCulloch's clenched rhythms. Will Sergeant's Telecaster betrays an obvious Tom Verlaine influence, shifting from spacious ringing leads … to shuddering wads of white noise. The set is both frantic and precise. —Record, 1984

Returning to the UK in September, the band immediately embarked on an extensive tour, which received the same superlatives as the U.S. shows. This tour proved to be the Bunnymen's most successful thus far, to the point where Drummond had to keep adding shows to accommodate Bunnyfan demand.

The series of gigs concluded on a bad note when, for the final show, the group headlined the annual York Festival. The Bunnymen didn't play partic-ularly well, the weather was foul, and the security was unreasonably heavy. During the usual encore of an extended "Do It Clean," rapturous fans attempted to rush the stage, and were brutally beaten back by bouncers. This infuriated both Mac and Will, who took such abuse of their audience person-ally. Will attempted to smack one overzealous bouncer with a guitar, while Mac started lashing his microphone stand toward another bouncer named Roger Newby. After the song ended, Newby attacked Mac backstage, punch-ing him repeatedly for a full minute, blackening Mac's eye and shredding his shirt. Both Will and Les witnessed the assault, but bouncers restrained them from the melee. When it was over, an aching and angry Mac flopped down and guzzled most of a bottle of Jack Daniels while waiting for police to arrive. As one might suspect, they weren't too impressed with the sight of a drunk-en pop star crying foul. In his post-show comments to the press, Mac tried to play the whole incident off glibly.

My shirt was completely ripped, which did worry me. I mean I was wor-ried about my ale gut showing. —Ian McCulloch, 1984

The singer was affronted enough to file a lawsuit against Newby, which went to court in 1985. One witness, a co-worker of Newby's, stated that Mac was trying to incite a riot, while Mac had trouble identifying Newby, pre-sumably due to his poor eyesight—and the fact that the most he saw of Newby was his fist. Mac's backstage inebriation was used against him, as was the Isle of Lewis incident. The case was dismissed.

THE PICTURES ON MY WALL VIDEO

'From Erics to the World'
ECHO & THE BUNNYMEN

At the end of 1984, WEA released *The Pictures On My Wall*, an hour-long collection of promo videos, plus clips from *Shine So Hard*, "A Crystal Day," The Royal Albert Hall shows, and candid footage. Although it's an enjoyable enough collection, it seemed to indicate that, up to this point, video wasn't the Bunnymen's strongest medium.

Weird that, for all Mac's arrogance and innate sense of style, the Bunnymen have never discovered any visual empathy for their surreal- ist rocking. Remember the embarrassing *Apocalypse Now* camo chic? Remember Bill Butt's sub-art school exercises, lots of people eating and cars passing, trees posed as profundity? Well, the whole story's here. *The Pictures On My Wall* is a frustratingly edited scrapbook of the Bunnies magnificent follies from well before the Buxton fiasco right through to Anton Corbijn's memorable 'Seven Seas' Victorian panto. Most of this stuff is alarmingly po-faced—all Russian graph- ics, soaring seagulls, and shadowy cellars—and it's left to the live footage ... to capture any essence of magic. Best of the premeditat- ed stuff is the aforementioned 'Seven Seas,' Mac doing a great Bowie- as-tart routine (wiggling hips and lipstick lips). Here, at last, is some manifestation of the band's inherent scathing wit. All in all, though, *The Pictures On My Wall* exhumes the past pretty honestly and, following this visual line of argument, the Bunnies' best is still to come.   *—NME*, 1985

The Pictures On My Wall video has remained out of print and can be obtained only on auction Web sites. Why the Bunnymen haven't produced another video collection remains something of a mystery. Both "A Crystal Day" and the Royal Albert Hall shows were captured on film, and there have been more than enough promotional clips over the years to warrant another compilation from the warren. Whether any of these will ever be released for retail is anyone's guess.

You didn't have to make videos in the good old days ... I don't like linking a song to visuals, because it becomes trapped in a video instead of just being a song. I mean, no one made a video of 'My Way.' As soon as you put a video on it, it becomes one specific visual.   —Ian McCulloch, 1984

"Oh it's a long while from May to December"

September Song
a single by
IAN McCULLOCH
available on 7 & limited edition 12" version with poster

This year I'll have to make a solo LP—real Scott Walker stuff. That should sell a few.
                                        —Ian McCulloch, 1984

Just say if there's a soul album next year, that'll be the one.
                                        —Ian McCulloch, 1984

The idea of doing a solo project had been developing at the back of Mac's mind for some time, and, during his time off after the *Ocean Rain* tours, he decided the time had come. The initial idea was to record four singles, or possibly an album, with different players and producers. Mac expressed interest in working with Barney from New Order and, possibly, Charlie Watts from the Rolling Stones, using Benny and Bjorn from Abba as producers. He also wanted to collaborate again with Ian Broudie, and the two eventually wrote and recorded some demos. A Mac-less version of one of these songs, "Persuasion," eventually emerged as a B-side for Broudie's band, The Lightning Seeds. The nonexistent LP's working title? "Songs For Swinging Suicides."

I've thought about doing a cover version of the *Thriller* album. I wouldn't mind selling 25,000,000 albums.
                    —Ian McCulloch, 1984

Rob Dickens, impressed by Mac's swooning croon on *Ocean Rain,* suggested that he record a version of the Kurt Weill/Max Anderson classic "September Song," from the 1938 musical *Knickerbocker Holiday*. Mac liked the song, and agreed to do it as a sort of Christmas present for his mom (and for the fee of five thousand pounds). He entered the studio with producers Colin Fairley and Clive Langer, (the latter formerly of Deaf School) plus an orchestra arranged by David Bedford. In addition to "September Song," Mac recorded a take on "Cockles and Mussels," a traditional Irish song.

Mac attacks 'Cockles and Mussels' with a bawdy drinking song delivery. Our charming Bunnyperson wants nothing more than to be seen as the last great British eccentric genius, and this sets him well on the way to fulfilling that ambition.   *—NME,* 1984

I've always fancied doing a sea shanty.   —Ian McCulloch, 1984

Mac didn't have any real solo ambitions—he just considered the single a one-off experiment, and treated the whole thing as such in his comments to a curious music press.

Somebody left a horse's head in me bed one day, and I had to do it.
                                        —Ian McCulloch, 1984

Will loves my single, and that has made me feel great, more than I could explain. I think he can tell I've done something I needed to do, to get a little bit of crooning out of my system. People say it's a Christmas single, but that's not my intention. Plus, all the sleigh-bells at the hire company were hired out on Slade records. And Redskins follow-up records. —Ian McCulloch, 1984

Rob Dickens might have had more serious motivations. The other Bunnymen were difficult and insular, but, by appealing to Mac's ego, he might be able to mollify him and suck him into the star machine. If these were indeed Dickens's plans, they certainly backfired. When "September Song" was released on December 7, reviews were quick to indicate its faults.

Excruciating. —*Melody Maker*, 1984

Mac's rendering relishes the song's style without quite getting inside its essence. —*NME*, 1984

While Will apparently loved the recording, Pete and Les seemed fairly disinterested, if not bemused by the whole affair.

I thought it was a bit weird. I didn't even know anything about it for awhile. I thought the song might be bad, but it was OK. —Les Pattinson, 1985

"September Song" was little more than an odd anomaly in the Bunnymen's history, a quaint little curiosity. Although its portents of an immanent McCulloch solo career never came to pass, it did indicate that the singer harbored sentiments not comfortably expressed within the parameters of a rock & roll band.

Crooner McCulloch fails to embrace all the nooks and nuances of [the song] simply because he fails to make the effort. —*NME*, 1984

From the sublime to ... well, you've got to admit, Ian, it *is* faintly ridiculous ... —*Melody Maker*, 1984

Do you know Lou Reed has just released a version of 'September Song'? Someone said that it's loads better than Mac's. —Pete de Freitas, 1985

THE YEAR OFF

Perhaps more disturbing than Mac's solo single was the concurrent announcement that the Bunnymen were taking a year off from touring, writing, and recording.

This break is a way of putting people off so they don't see the Bunnymen as another band with a career. We were never into making a career for ourselves. The point was to be the best band in the world. —Ian McCulloch, 1984

The idea was Drummond's, who thought that the year off would help the

band write different kinds of songs, and allow them to stretch out as individuals. Most of the Bunnymen liked the notion. Pete wanted to travel to Spain and France on his beloved Ducati motorbike, and Les yearned to work on a boat he'd purchased. This would leave Mac free to pursue any solo projects, or, if he chose, to sleep all day—something he often did anyway. Will didn't want an extended holiday.

I thought that taking a year off was a daft idea. I didn't see the point of it. It was like we'd go away and then we'd come back. Big deal.   —Will Sergeant, 1985

In the end, the band took just under half a year off. Pete did his traveling, and Les puttered on his motorboat and had a daughter, Rebecca, with his girlfriend Yvonne. Mac caught up on his sleep and spent time with Lorraine, and Will did little but sit around and rent videos. Not that he was initially willing to admit it.

I've been extremely busy. I've played with the Sutherland Brothers and Quivver, and Phil Collins came round for a jam. I made me triple concept album, *Tales of Topographic Onions*.   —Will Sergeant, 1985

Will did manage to get away from his VCR long enough to make an appearance on Radio Merseyside, playing some of his favorite records. These included The Mel-O-Tones' "Bugs Bunny Bendy Toy," Syd Barrett's "Vegetable Man," Bowie's "There Is a Happy Land," The Velvets' "Foggy Notion," Pere Ubu's "Final Solution," Captain Beefheart's "Drop-Out Boogie," and The Residents' "Constantinople." In addition, both Will and Les aided Liverpudlian band Surreal Estate with the recording of their debut EP, *Midas Touch*, on Probe Plus Records.

As it turned out, Will's instincts about the year off being a daft idea weren't far from the truth.

That was just a pose to show people how famous we were. You can have a year off and not tell anybody about it ... but we never got our momentum back, afterward. The thought was, we'd peaked.
                                                                    —Ian McCulloch, 1992

IT'S ALL OVER NOW, BABY BILL

At the end of 1984, Bill Drummond abandoned his post as the Bunnymen's manager. The decision was mutual. Although Drummond was a conceptual genius, and his off-the-wall ideas lent a weird edge to the Bunnymen, he was never much of a businessman.

I've never been happy with the straightforward thing. One of the reasons for Echo & the Bunnymen not being U2 or Simple Minds is my attitude. If I'd been managing The Beatles, instead of playing Shea Stadium, I'd have had them playing a week of dates wherever Buddy Holly's plane crashed, to a few cows, in celebration of Buddy Holly. Shea Stadium can wait.   —Bill Drummond, 1997

Mac in particular had become impatient with Drummond.

He was inspired, but his head wasn't in business or direction, so we were self-destructive—mythically so.   —Ian McCulloch, 1990

He started working for the record company, moved down South. He wanted to hedge his bets with a long-term career. It never comes out, all that shit, but his loyalties were divided. When he was in Liverpool, he would say things about the songs, but once he was sitting in an office next to Rob Dickens, it was wrong. Again, this never comes out, but I summoned a meeting and told him it was over.
—Ian McCulloch, 1999

He took us down blind alleys. It was all part of the mythologizing of the group. Twenty years later, we haven't exactly gone down with Thor, Icarus and all of them dudes.
—Ian McCulloch, 2001

The bottom line was that the Bunnymen weren't making any money. Something had to give. The band needed a manager who was more down to earth. They might lose a little bit of their quirkiness and charm, but it had come to the point where the foursome simply needed cash to survive. And Drummond felt that, after *Ocean Rain*, there was nowhere left for the Bunnymen to go but to be massively successful. Cleary not the man to tackle that job, he threw down his hand at the behest of Mac, and former Duran Duran tour manager Mick Hancock was promptly drafted in to fill the vacancy.

After a few idle months, the Bunnymen got bored with their holiday and decided to regroup for yet another unique tour. In the late spring of 1985, they went to Scandinavia, where they were both the support act and the headliners of their show. They'd play one blistering set of songs by their favorite artists, go offstage for an intermission, and return for an equally incendiary selection of their own classics. Forgoing the standard big-time rock production that was expected of any band of the Bunnymen's stature, they decided to play the most minimal, primitive punk shows they could get away with. Simple stuff.

By doing all these vintage songs, it sort of helped us to *think* primitive. And it meant we could approach it less intensely, y'know? It was just like the old days. No coaches and stuff, just a van. Just rocking out with little practice amps, y'know? It's what a proper band should do. And [the audience] loved it.   —Ian McCulloch, 1985

That Scandinavian tour in 1985 was great. I used a practice amp, this crappy little Roland Cube thing. The idea was for everyone to 'Cube out,' have rehearsal set-up ...
                —Ian McCulloch, 1995

Doing the covers made it easier to get back together and think about writing new songs.   —Pete de Freitas, 1985

The reason we did these particular songs was ... to get us in the right spiritual ... groove.   —Ian McCulloch, 1985

This was by far the loosest Bunnymen tour yet—to the point where the band played several shows just for free drinks—and drink, particularly Scandinavia's mind-numbing "Easter Brew," flowed heavily. On several inebriated occasions, songs were performed so poorly that they had to be aborted. In a display of uncharacteristic pragmatism, the Bunnymen later programmed a sample of canned laughter into their Emulator synthesizer, should similar occasions arise in the future.

The Scandinavian tour revealed many of the Bunnymen's influences, all of which indicated that they were indeed steeped in the tradition of the finest rock & roll, and not just some Goth Band—a tag they'd probably received due to Mac's hairstyle as much as anything else. In an interview with the *NME*, the Bunnymen discussed their choices of cover songs.

The Litter's "Action Woman"
Will: "It's just a thrash, like something out of the 60's."
Mac: "We wanted to do this [because] we were riding 'round [on tour] listening to these tapes Will had made of *Pebbles and Nuggets* and

stuff. And we really got into them and the sun was shining, and it just made us have a good laugh ... "

The Doors' "Take It as It Comes" and "Soul Kitchen":
Mac: "We could have done other Doors songs but they were too hard. So we tried to pick ones that were … "
Will: " ... groovy."
Mac: "'Soul Kitchen' was the first song I ever liked by The Doors. I like their stuff when it's straightforward—y'know, four-minute classics. I'm not keen on the psychedelic stuff."

Talking Heads' "The Big Country":
Will: "I just love it. I love it where he says 'I wouldn't live there if you paid me. No siree.' That's great, that."
Mac: "I would have thought it was probably the least likely, of all of them, for us to do. It's one of my favorites."

Wilson Pickett's "In the Midnight Hour":
Will: "It'll never get better if you Wilson it."
Mac: "I've always liked it, but I just thought that it was one that nobody would ever think we'd do. And it doesn't even sound like that song, actually. It sounds like Television or something."
Will: "There's a bit that I don't know how to play, so I just do my Tom Verlaine rip-off."

Jonathan Richman and the Modern Lovers' "She Cracked":
Will: "Classic. It's just power. They did it in 1972, and it was like punk before its time."
Mac: "I can take or leave Jonathan Richman. I like 'Roadrunner,' but I think he's a bit twee—though 'She Cracked' isn't twee. It's just dead easy and makes you feel like soddin' ... a god ... when you walk on and it just starts 'ding-ding-ding ding.' It's just like playing with no hands."

The band also performed covers of The Rolling Stones' "Paint It Black," Bob Dylan's "It's All Over Now, Baby Blue," and Television's "Friction," which, as journalist Steve Sutherland accurately remarked, "could have been written for Will Sergeant's guitar."

At a warm-up show before the tour at Liverpool's Café Berlin, the Bunnymen also played a hushed version of "The Partisan" to accommodate Mac's love of Leonard Cohen. Although they never aired the Cohen cover again, Mac remains a big fan.

... Leonard never lies with his lyrics, he just nails it. And he's such a heart-throb ... 'Famous Blue Raincoat' was my favourite song. 'There's music on Clinton Street all through the evening.' I'm there.

—Ian McCulloch, 1994

Leonard Cohen, to me, is my spirit guide. 'Suzanne' is the most perfect song I've heard in my life. Every chord in that song is exactly where you want it to go, it just resolves at the end. It's beautiful. In nearly all of his songs I find something, apart from 'Jazz Police,' which was shit. I couldn't believe he'd written that for us. He's allowed one in a lifetime.

—Ian McCulloch, 1995

I like the way he's had the same suit for 20 years.

—Ian McCulloch, 1987

I first saw him when I went to see the film *Bird On a Wire* in 1973. It's a live documentary filmed in Berlin and Jerusalem. In Jerusalem he goes offstage because the vibe isn't right. He just stops playing and he goes and has a shave, and then comes back because the vibe came back after he had a shave. Weird. I like him because he has a great charisma in his voice. People say he can't sing but his voice is brilliant. I followed his tour 'round in 1985 and cornered him in a hotel foyer in Dublin. I gave him a tape of *Ocean Rain* and told him he was great. I was really bombed out on Guinness, really embarrassed. I've met him a few times backstage since that; he's charming, cadges ciggies and drinks red wine. I don't really understand why he's still around. I think it's something to do with him wearing a pin-striped suit and a black T-shirt. He has a certain timeless cool. I just love his lyrics, he conjures up things that you think you've been through or things that might happen. He does something that no-one else does, he's able to put me in situations. It sounds posey but I feel that I've lived life through his music. —Ian McCulloch, 1991

I just think I've learned a lot from him over the years. I like his dignity and he's a funny bastard as well. The first time I met him I was crapping myself, there was this wave of ... not fear; I was a kid again. Anyway, he's like 'Hey, Ian, people tell me you're a great poet' and I'm like, 'Shut up.' But meeting him taught me how to deal with people—to try and be nice. No head butts. —Ian McCulloch, 1997

Cohen has reciprocated.

I know Ian McCulloch quite well. If I'm ever in his part of the world when I'm touring, he always comes on the bus for a few days and hangs out with us and the band. He's a very sweet man ... a good man. I've always been fond of him. —Leonard Cohen, 1992

The Scandinavian tour also gave the Bunnymen the chance to perform covers of several songs by The Velvet Underground. Few Bunnymen sets are complete without a desultory nod to the Velvets; in fact, the band has probably covered more of Lou Reed's songs than any other group in existence. Over the course of their career, they've performed versions of "Pale Blue Eyes," "What Goes On," "There She Goes Again," "Heroin," "Sweet Jane," "Walk On the Wild Side," "Sister Ray," "Run Run Run," and "Foggy Notion." Jimmy Brown, from the Velvets' "Oh! Sweet Nuthin'" made an appearance in the Bunnymen's "Bring On the Dancing Horses."

Possibly more than any other thing, The Velvet Underground are impor- tant to Echo & the Bunnymen. The capacity for writing something like 'Pale Blue Eyes' and yet being able to write 'Sister Ray' as well. And the Bunnymen write things like 'Over the Wall' and they also write 'Zimbo.' There was something about The Velvets that is hard to explain. It's the same with the Bunnymen ... the two groups are linked in that way.   —Ian McCulloch, 1984

I think [*The Velvet Underground & Nico*] is actually the greatest album ever made. I play the third album more but this is frightening ... The Beatles or the Stones can't touch this. It covers the complete spectrum between weird drug songs and seemingly innocent love songs, but even with 'Sunday Morning' there's an undercurrent of weirdness, mainly due to Lou Reed's voice. Perfect.   —Ian McCulloch, 1994

There's a lot of average stuff to wade through with Reed, but at his best he's unbeatable. Think of *Transformer*, *Street Hassle*, or *New York*. What's great about Lou Reed is that when you go to New York, you realise it's exactly how he writes about it. He doesn't make any- thing up, his songs are like a documentary about the place. A lot of what appears to be throwaway references are really pretty sound. He always sounds detached from what he's singin', but he's actually right in the thick of it.   —Ian McCulloch, 1998

They were just the epitome of the weird group, weren't they? And they looked good as well. I think they're great. I mean, most groups you can say some- thing bad about after a period of time. Like with The Doors you could laugh at Ray Manzarek's haircut or some- thing. But the Velvets seem untouchable in that way.
—Ian McCulloch, 1985

I like the vulnerability of Lou Reed. I still think the first Velvet Underground album with the Andy Warhol cover is his best, but my personal favorite is the third. The one with 'Pale Blue Eyes' and 'Beginning to See the Light.'
—Ian McCulloch, 1983

David Bowie, who turned Mac on to the Velvets, remains something of a hero for Mac, but the man's impact isn't exactly what it used to be.

Bowie has influenced me the most, or at least 1972 Bowie ... I've never wanted to be like Bowie, though. He's a dilettante who gets a lot of respect for his intelligence, which is a bit dubious to me.
—Ian McCulloch, 1984

I stayed loyal to what was good about Bowie, or the little bit that is still good about Bowie, but I never believed in staying loyal to anyone. Bowie, he could've been so much better than he is. I like the good side of Bowie, not the successful side. I mean, I'll still defend him against any criticism, 'cos I always feel that I'm the only per- son authoritative enough to criticize him. Because I'm smug.
—Ian McCulloch, 1984

I still think he was the best. I think he was so under-rated because of his image; people just see him as this bloke with different hairstyles, but he was the best pop-rock writer that Britain's ever produced. He's written so many classic songs that people don't seem to focus on. They make him out to be cleverer than he is, but primarily to me it just made me shiver when he sang. Without Bowie, I'd probably be on the dole now ...
—Ian McCulloch, 1994

Ian McCulloch's
"Desert Island Discs"
circa 1984
"Marieke" —Jacques Brel
"Famous Blue Raincoat" and
    "Hey, That's No Way To Say
    Goodbye" —Leonard Cohen
"Je Ne Regrette Rien"
    —Edith Piaf
"Indian Summer" —The Doors
"Pale Blue Eyes"
    —The Velvet Underground
Ziggy Stardust-David Bowie
"Twist and Shout" —The Beatles
"A Promise"
    —Echo & the Bunnymen
"Be My Baby" —The Ronettes

Mac's favorite hit singles, circa 1997

"Starman" —Bowie: "This is my favorite single of all time. It changed my life and it's where I came in."

"God Save The Queen" —The Sex Pistols: "One of the most explosive records ever. I preferred it to 'Anarchy,' which I also loved."

"Be My Baby" —The Ronettes: "If there's such a thing as perfect pop than this is it—Ronnie Spector's voice is incredible."

"American Pie" —Don McClean: "A masterpiece—beyond the Mona Lisa."

"Walk On the Wild Side" —Lou Reed: "The coolest single in history. How could Lou go onto have the uncoolest hairdo in history? He's still one of my main inspirations."

"Fake Plastic Trees" —Radiohead: "I love this song. For me, *The Bends*, along with *Nevermind* and *Automatic For the People*, is one of the best albums of the last 10 years. Probably my favorite band in the world, along with the Fun Lovin' Crims."

"Suzanne" —Leonard Cohen: "The most perfect song ever written. I'm not sure if Leonard's version was a hit but someone's was. An absolutely beautiful song."

"Champagne Supernova" —Oasis: "To me this is one of the top rock songs ever, along with 'Gimme Shelter,' 'Sympathy for the Devil,' and 'The End.' 'Where were you while we were getting high' is a fantastic line."

"Smells Like Teen Spirit" —Nirvana: "Another song in the same league. Like 'Anarchy in the UK' it blew everything apart. Kurt Cobain was special."

"Heroes" —David Bowie: "This only made it to number 25, I think, but it grew in stature to become his anthem. A true gem."

"Find the River" —R.E.M.: "This is my favorite track off *Automatic for the People* and the only single [off that album] that stiffed. One of the few songs to ever make me cry."

Will's Favorite Records, circa 1994

Their Satanic Majesties Request—The Rolling Stones: "The first record I ever bought was 'Gimme Shelter.' I got a Dansette as well. I actually went out to buy *Who's Next* but they'd sold out. I prefer *Their Satanic Majesties Request*. It's a bit crap here and there, but I like '2,000 Light Years' and 'She's a Rainbow.' I've got the 3-D sleeve, in mono."

The Best of Pink Floyd: "This includes a lot of the early Syd Barrett stuff. I've also got a blue vinyl bootleg of 'Vegetable Man' and 'Scream Thy Last Scream' on Angry Taxman. Three quid! Pete Jenner told me in was gonna be their next single, but Syd flipped his wig! Great song and I love its rarity value."

Barbarella—Bob Crewe Generation: "Excellent soundtrack album, which I paid about fifteen quid for, and I have a single 'An Angel is Love' in a picture cover."

Ogden's Nut Gone Flake—The Small Faces: "One of them quirky LPs. Usually, albums with talking on them get on your wick a bit, but not this one. Great stuff."

Living in the Past—Jethro Tull: "Their early stuff had a real strange atmosphere, with a thin, distorted voice effect. I remember them vividly on Top of the Pops, doing 'Witch's Promise.' Tull are a nostalgia trip. When I was 12, everybody was into them. Or they were skinheads into Tamla."

Biff Bang Pow!—The Creation: "I've just got that *How Does It Feel To Feel* compilation and the single 'Biff Bang Pow!,' and that reissue single with 'Uncle Bert' on it on Edsel. I generally push out the middles for my jukebox, but the Planet single I can't bear to do that to."

Strange Days—The Doors: "When punk came along, you weren't allowed to like The Doors. It was unhip old crap. It was only because I played them all the time that Ian McCulloch started to like them. *Strange Days* is the one. Like Ogdens, it's got its own atmosphere, a strange vibe with little funky keyboard sounds—spooky, and a bit disturbing. 'When the Music's Over' is my favourite, with its big guitar solo which sounds like two at once. The Doors were a big influence on my guitar playing."

Will's Desert Island Discs circa 1984

"My White Bicycle" —Tomorrow
"Circles," "A Quick One," "Sell Out"—The Who
"Tripmaker" —the Seeds
"A House is Not a Motel" —Love
"Painterman" —The Creation
"Piper At the Gates of Dawn" —Pink Floyd
"Mr. Soul"—Buffalo Springfield
"She Said, She Said" —The Beatles
"Paper Sun" —Traffic
Nuggets and *Pebbles* LP's
"Early Days of Pearly Spencer" —David MacWilliam
"Bend Me, Shape Me" —The American Breed
"Kites" —Simon Dupree and the Big Sound
"In the Year 2525" —Zager and Evans
"I Want to Hold your Hand" —The Moving Sidewalks
"Horse Latitudes —The Doors
The Residents
The Velvet Underground

Favourite guitarists:
Townshend, Hendrix, Verlaine, Marr, Roddy Frame on 'Oblivious,' The Byrds.

Chocolate Soup for Diabetics—Various Artists: "If I had to choose a psych compilation, it'd be the purple volume with the Voice's 'Train To Disaster' on it—the best riff going. The pressing is crap but I recently bought the CD. It's got the Crazy World of Arthur Brown's 'I am the God of Hellfire' at the beginning. I [also] like 'Father's Name is Dad' by Fire."

Troubadour—The Definitive Collection '64 - '76—Donovan: "This is always lying around because it doesn't fit the CD rack! You get a book that tells you who played on the tracks; like 'Hurdy Gurdy Man' is Led Zeppelin without Robert Plant, and 'Babarajagal' had Jeff Beck, Micky Hopkins, and Suzi Quatro, Madeline Bell, and Leslie Duncan on vocals. I might as well go for this: it's long, if I'm stuck on a desert island!"

Sell Out—The Who: "I love 'Armenia City in the Sky,' where it's all backwards; and the little advert links. When I make up tapes, I always throw in a couple of tracks. I used to have *Backtrack 5*, Hendrix and the Who, with 'Tattoo,' and 'Mary Anne With the Shaky Hand' on it."

Easter Everywhere—13th Floor Elevators: "I've also got their debut, *Psychedelic Sounds Of ...* , but I think this is better, with 'Slip Inside This House' and 'Slide Machine,' which has a strange vibe. 'Earthquake' is a corker. 'Fire Engine' on the first one is excellent. Television did that. We used to cover the Chocolate Watchband version of 'It's All Over Now Baby Blue' with that twiddly guitar."

Forever Changes—Love: "I deejayed at one of Arthur Lee's gigs in Liverpool. The band, Shack, were great 'cos they were all into it. He could have got a load of wanky session men! Me faves are on this: 'Alone Again Or' and that one about a motel."

Marquee Moon—Television: "The guitar playing of Tom Verlaine and Richard Lloyd was a big influence on the Bunnymen. I love the solo on the title track."

Andy Warhol's Velvet Underground—The Velvet Underground: "My first Velvets record, with the Coke bottle on the gatefold. I bought it in the early 70's 'cos I liked the cover—I'd never heard of the band! It's got 'Sunday Morning' and 'All Tomorrow's Parties,' but me favourites are 'Pale Blue Eyes,' 'European Son,' and 'Sister Ray.'"

An Electric Storm–White Noise: "It's brilliant, quite disturbing–trancey, like. Some if it's dead muffled and distant, and then there's real crisp bits, like gibbering and orgasms, over the top, and strange, synthy sounds flying around. Nice singing but strange rhythms in the background–an eerie twist."

★★★

GLASTONBURY

After the low-key warm-up of the Scandinavian Tour, the Bunnymen returned in full force when they headlined the Glastonbury Festival before a crowd of 50,000 on June 21. One would think that the band would have been as professional as possible for such a prestigious gig, but, contrary to the cnd, they were still relaxed in Scandinavian mode. Hitting the stage without so much as a set-list, they opened up with a savage take on Jonathan Richman's "She Cracked." Throughout the rest of the performance, they interspersed cover songs they had mastered on the Scandinavian tour with ferocious versions of their own material. The band also unveiled a couple of new compositions: a hell-for-leather rocker called "Satellite," and "All In Your Mind," which, at this stage, sounded remarkably like the "Batman" TV show theme. Reviewers clearly expressed that standing in the rain, knee-deep in muck was a small price for such a gloriously wanton and primitive performance.

The Bunnymen are made for cold wind and rainy occasions. Moreover, this being their only major show of the year, they needed to be good. Instead they were magnificent, and transformed a potential disaster into a celebration. McCulloch shook the audience by the hip and bit the nose off any moaner with a vocal performance to match with classic Echo. The band ripped apart golden oldies like The Rolling Stones' 'Paint It Black,' Bob Dylan's 'It's All Over Now Baby Blue' (sung with a perfect Jagger drawl), The Cramps' 'Garbage Man,' James Brown's 'Sex Machine,' and The Doors' 'Soul Kitchen' and made them sound better than the originals. It was pitch black and pouring rain when they left the stage at 9p.m., but Noah could been have building his Ark for all the crowd cared. No one would have bothered to get on. *–No. 1,* 1985

The Mac pack are nothing if not surprising. They shunted the fabulous PA up to behemoth levels, and played a mixture–sometimes in the same song–of covers and originals. They were quite splendid. Their recent [Scandinavian] tour has rejuvenated them. By letting their roots grow out they've abandoned both their epic glaciality (*Crocodiles* to *Heaven Up Here*) and their cavernous reverbatory cycles (*Ocean Rain*) in favour of a nail-hard, dare I say it, punk sound. *–NME,* 1985

After only half a year off, the Bunnymen were back, writing together, and ready to record a few new songs. They had the two they'd played at Glastonbury, another garage-rock blast called "Like a Rollercoaster," and a quirky little ballad titled "Jimmy Brown" or, possibly, "Brittle Heart."

Although old stand-bys Ian Broudie and Clive Langer were summoned for their production expertise, nothing of note resulted from these sessions. Broudie did, however, introduce Mac to The Stranglers' most recent single, "Skin Deep." Mac considered it a great pop song, and he particularly appreciated the sharp, shimmering clarity of Laurie Latham's production. After briefly debating on the possibility of using dub producer Eddy "Electric Avenue" Grant, or the production team behind Abba's sound, the Bunnymen settled on Latham. The band and producer met in Brussels and recorded "All In Your Mind," "Like a Rollercoaster," and "Jimmy Brown," which was eventually retitled "Bring On the Dancing Horses," and eventually selected as an A-side.

While the song itself was pretty typical Bunnymen fare, the production added a rich, luscious texture to the song that made Echo & the Bunnymen sound infinitely more commercial than ever before.

—Tony Fletcher, *Never Stop*

It's not as raw as New Order, but it's got that danceability to it. Smooth? I don't think it is. I think as soon as I sing on something it stops being smooth. But we did want to try something different and get tongues wagging. I think it's really funny that we got live reviews from Glastonbury … saying that we sounded like a punk band, which we did. But probably more of a New York punk band than The Sex Pistols.   —Ian McCulloch, 1985

"Bring On the Dancing Horses" b/w "Over Your Shoulder" and "Bedbugs and Ballyhoo" was released on October 7, 1985. The song's production contrasted with the Glastonbury performances.

I think it sounds a bit flat ... it's absolutely polished. I prefer the demo. That's got an edge to it.   —Pete de Freitas, 1985

Some disappointed writers accused the Bunnymen of deliberately trying to create a top 10 single, a charge that the band didn't completely deny.

We sat down earlier this year and decided it would be nice to be millionaires.

—Ian McCulloch, 1985

You can stick to your principles too much and you end up where everyone thinks you're a dickhead. I don't want to be some divvy in a poxy cult band from the late 70's on 'Pop Quiz' one day. That's what you're destined to be, a question on 'Pop Quiz.'   —Will Sergeant, 1985

If becoming millionaires was the Bunnymen's intention, it failed miserably. The single only made it to #21 in the UK charts, despite the fact that the band were "playing ball" with the record company, doing as many interviews and television appearances as they could. Some die-hards understandably screamed sell-out. The Bunnymen attempted to rationalize the conventionality that "Dancing Horses" and its subsequent promotion openly embraced.

When pop gets too broad it just becomes dull and crap. The Velvet Underground for me were about as far as you can go. And they did it within the confines of good tunes, good songs. I feel the same about paintings. If you want to go and look at something, you shouldn't be presented with too much of a riddle which looks horrible, y'know, even if some turd says it looks good. Well, he's wrong. I don't understand all this striving after weirdness. Things don't always have to be that different. I think there's a line where things get too avant-garde. Take the LP *Porcupine*. It's rock music, but it's got a different slant to it.   —Ian McCulloch, 1985

    Although the sound of "Dancing Horses" was hyper-accessible, the single presented Mac's lyrics at their most bedeviling or pretentious.

... it was meant to be a song about—I don't really know … Sometimes I do have a definite idea of what's behind a song, but not this one.
—Ian McCulloch, 1985

It's really no fun to talk about what songs mean. What's the point of writing them, then?   —Ian McCulloch, 1984

Mac: "Art's always been an island, but surely you can either say something's pretentious or you love it—everything that's ever been done in the art world is open to ridicule. I think Vincent Van Gogh chopping his ear off was probably the best thing anyone ever did. Except he should've chopped his painting hand off. He was mad, wasn't he?"
Will: "Mad? He was furious!"   —*Melody Maker*, 1987

★★★

Echo's 12-month sabbatical seems also to have sharpened their commercial instincts. Without resorting to any kind of crass commercial strategy, 'Bring On the Dancing Horses' sounds like it's been aimed straight for the top; it's as if Mac's finally decided that it's time to fully assert the Bunnymen's natural superiority over largely inferior competition. Echo continue to sound grand, but while their musical gestures remain epic, they also sound effortless. Graced by a phe-

We've decided to be a bit more co-operative lately ... we've told the record company that we'll cooperate if they get behind us. It's a very crappy thing to have to say, but it's the truth ... we're still basically going to be the same, but we're just going to bend a little bit, not much. We're not all of a sudden going to ponce around on stage or anything like that. We're going to do more interviews, more photo sessions. That's all it boils down to really. We'll still be writing songs that we like.
—Will Sergeant, 1985

It's a bit like a nice little fairytale.—Ian McCulloch, 1985

... A lover's classic.

        —*Sounds,* 1985

Poignant.

  —poet Maya Angelou (!), 1985

'Dancing Horses' is floating, like a poem. Like a painting, it's something in itself. It's the mood of the song, rather than the meaning.

    —Anton Corbijn, *Never Stop*

Almost perfect—melodic, romantic, assured, and authoritative. Deeply fabulous and shamefully under-bought. Single of the year.

      —*Melody Maker,* 1985

… our techno-ballad.

      —Ian McCulloch, 1990

A slick electro-kaleidoscope.

       —*Sounds,* 1985

A modern Spectorish sort of thing. A big sound.

    —Pete de Freitas, 1985

Not so much a song as a requiem. Our last great moment together. Recorded in Brussels—the first place we ever played on foreign soil—where sadness hangs in the air.   —Ian McCulloch, 1992

...pivotal, foreshadowing the more melodic, melancholic sound that would dominate [the Bunnymen's] later work.

    —*Record Collector,* 2001

nomenal vocal performance from Mac, that has the grandeur and nobility of, say, David Bowie's 'Heroes' or the heart-wrenching emotional gravity of Joy Division's 'Love Will Tear Us Apart.' Like both of those records, I'm sure it will be quickly recognized as a classic. Will's guitar spans continents behind Mac's pleading, windswept vocal tracks ... spectacular magnificence. Monumentally moving. —*NME,* 1985

BRING ON THE DANCING HORSES

Jimmy Brown
Made of stone
Charlie Clown
No way home

Bring on the dancing horses
Headless and all alone
Shiver and say the words
Of every lie you've heard

First I'm gonna make it
Then I'm gonna break it
'Til it falls apart
Hating all the faking
And shaking while I'm breaking
Your brittle heart

Billy stands
All alone
Sinking sand
Skin and bone

Bring on the dancing horses
Wherever they may roam
Shiver and say the words
Of every lie you've heard

First I'm gonna make it
Then I'm gonna break it
'Til it falls apart
Hating all the faking

And shaking while I'm breaking
Your brittle heart
Brittle heart ...
And my little heart goes ...

Jimmy Brown
Made of stone
Charlie clown
No way home

Bring on the headless horses
Wherever they may roam
Shiver and say the words
Of every lie you've heard

First I'm gonna make it
Then I'm gonna break it
'Til it falls apart
Hating all the faking
And shaking while you're breaking
My brittle heart
Brittle heart ...
And our little hearts go ...

Bring on the new messiah
Wherever he may roam
Bring on the new messiah
Wherever he may roam
First I'm gonna break him
Then I'm gonna make him
Find his own way home

BEDBUGS AND BALLYHOO

Buffalo and bison
Bison and buffalo
Cannonball and rifle
Rifle and cannonball
That's the way the thunder rumbles
That's the way the thunder rumbles
Rumbles

Down on your knees again
Saying please again
Yeah yeah yeah

Kangaroos and chipmunks
Chipmunks and kangaroos
Ballyhoo and bedbugs
Bedbugs and ballyhoo
That's the way the bee bumbles
That's the way the bee bumbles
Bumbles...

Down on your knees again
Saying please again
No no no

Buffalo and bison
Bison and buffalo
Cannonball and rifle
Rifle and cannonball
That's the way the thunder rumbles
That's the way the thunder rumbles
Rumbles ...

'Bedbugs ... ' was like, we didn't have anything. We just went in and did it. It's my favorite track we've done in ages.   —Les Pattinson, 1985

Fabulously innovative.
                    —*Goldmine*, 1998

... a Disney-ized take on The Doors.   —*Rolling Stone*, 1987

We were doing B-sides for 'Bring On the Dancing Horses.' We'd had a bit to drink and I was trying to do some impromptu off-the-cuff stuff, as we often did … I was humming along this idea for a melody when I realised that 'buffalo' and 'bison' had the right amount of syllables, then 'cannonball' and 'rifle.' Pretty soon after that I had the whole lyric. It was mega-fast—even though I write lyrics quickly, that was really fast. The chorus of 'down on your knees again, saying please again' was ... the usual self-rebuttal, as much as I thought I was God's gift. It made the song turn on its head after all that nonsense. I sang it in one take and Will was most impressed. He said, 'That imagery's great, I love it,' and I thought, 'You dickhead, what are you on about? I have written poetry for you and you haven't spotted it, and now you think this is great!' We had this roadie ... and one night after a gig he said to me, 'That "Bedbugs and Ballyhoo," it's shite, isn't it?' and straight away I said, 'I'm afraid it isn't, it's the most exact lyric I have ever written. I know exactly what that lyric is about and I am going to go through every line for you.' Off the top of my head I made up some weird political overture about America and all this shite, how the Buffalo and Bison represented some weird American involvement in the wars of the world. The funny thing was it all made perfect sense to me at the time. —Ian McCulloch, 1994

…seemed to be a deliberate attempt to remind flavor of the month The Jesus and Mary Chain who could rip off The Velvet Underground best.

—Tony Fletcher, *Never Stop*

OVER YOUR SHOULDER

Look over your shoulder
I'm here
The face on your head looks older
We're here

Never gonna change
Never gonna disappear
Stars shine down on me tonight
Doors close tight

The day of departure
Is near
The ears on your head
Don't hear

Never gonna change
Never gonna disappear
Stars shine down on me tonight
Doors close tight

Victims fall
Ghosts descend
You get scared and I'll defend
I really care then I'll pretend
The good and bad right to the end

Look in the cellar
We're here
I've been meaning to tell you
I'm here

Never gonna change
Never gonna disappear
Stars shine down on me tonight
Doors close tight

Victims fall
Ghosts descend
You get scared and I'll pretend
I don't really care but I'll
    defend
The good and band right to the
    end
End ...

Look over your shoulder
I'm here
The face on your head looks over
We're here
Never gonna change
Never gonna disappear ...

It was just that we had to do it quick, and that was the easiest way of covering up our not knowing whether we were going to like it when we finished the song. We just made it up on the spot, really, so putting ... this distortion or whatever on the guitar … it sounded alright, y'know.   —Ian McCulloch, 1985

SONGS TO LEARN AND SING

Although the single hadn't fared as well as hoped for, WEA still loved 'Bring On the Dancing Horses," and decided to release a greatest hits package with the song included on it. The Bunnymen were dubious, but Bill Drummond, now working behind a desk at Warner Brothers, liked it, and eventually convinced the Bunnymen that such a collection might have its merits.

It's a good opener for people. The first Leonard Cohen LP I bought was a greatest hits thingy, and it doesn't stop me from being a bigger fan than those who were into him in the 60's. —Ian McCulloch, 1985

The only good thing about this new greatest hits LP is that it will make us some money.   —Will Sergeant, 1985

On November 15, seven years to the day after the Bunnymen's first gig, *Songs to Learn and Sing*, boasting a title swiped from a bastardized line in "Fuel" was released. A repressing of the "Pictures On My Wall" single came shrink-wrapped in the LP. The album was the band's biggest yet, selling over 200,000 copies in the UK alone, while, Stateside, it became a staple for virtually every college dormitory room.

The album also marked the first time that Mac's lyrics were printed within the sleeve, an idea Mac had always balked at in the past.

Some of [the lyrics] might stand up just as words, but a lot of them are only written to go with the music. We never put them on the record, because it's then difficult to get people to approach it as just a record.   —Ian McCulloch 1985

You shouldn't have to worry about how lyrics look written down. A lot of the stuff I do, I just string things together—any old stuff I think sounds good. They usually mean something to me, though I don't know whether they should mean anything at all.   —Ian McCulloch, 1985

Meaningful lyrics or not, critics loved the collection. To this day, it stands as testament to the fact that, at the very least, the Bunnymen were a damn fine *pop* band.

Thank you, God, for Echo & the Bunnymen. Arrogant, stubborn, uncommunicative, and amazingly single-purposed, the Bunnymen have taken the

I thought it was a good album because we knew we wouldn't be having another out for a while, and it possibly plays better than every other album because every song is different. Quite often with our albums I'll only play a few tracks.
                    —Ian McCulloch, 1987

The company want us to reach a broader audience, and it's their idea of a way to do it. They think it'll help.
             —Pete de Freitas, 1985

... a stunningly strong collection of singles ... makes you wonder how on Earth the Bunnymen have managed to keep themselves obscured so effectively.   —*Melody Maker*, 1985

I love all the bits. I love the posey lyric sheet and I love the bonus 7-inch of the original versions of the classic 'Pictures On My Wall' and the even more classic 'I've Read It In Books.' I love the absurd notion of a 'best of the Bunnymen' LP because it means that I am definitely not too young to get served in pubs. I love the chronology, and the profound and funny continuity from 'is this the blues I'm singing?' to 'bring on the new messiah, wherever he may roam.' I love the bitchy, vicious meaninglessness of 'Do It Clean' and the way 'Never Stop' makes me turn the volume up till I forget all those subjective sentimentalities. I love these songs. If I get time at the weekend, I fully intend to play this record. I love it. I hate The Doors. Stellar and statuesque. Little sister's Christmas present.*—Sounds, 1985*

I'd [like to] do something else, like make pottery.
—Will Sergeant, 1985

slings and arrows, taken the slag-offs and the plaudits, and above all they've taken the piss. Now they've released this wonderful collection of singles and things. You're left wondering why the Bunnymen aren't up there in the American charts with people like U2 and Simple Minds. There isn't a duff song here ... *Songs to Learn and Sing* makes damn splendid listening whether you're sitting, standing, or comatose ... this collection is a fine testament to painstaking achievement. Mac, it's your round.
—*Melody Maker*, 1985

The early stuff, collected on *Songs to Learn and Sing* remains a testament to haunted youth. In a real sense, [the Bunnymen were] The Cure who drank beer.
—*Liverpool Hoopla*, 1999

Despite the success of the collection, as 1985 drew to a close, relations within the Bunnymen camp were disintegrating rapidly. Conflict was now at an all-time high. One factor behind this was the band's lack of purpose. What to do after you've already created the greatest album ever made?

I think, after *Ocean Rain* ... we had done four albums, like a pack of cards: diamonds, hearts, clubs, and spades. It was hard to know where to go after it.
—Ian McCulloch, 1996

Will became increasingly negative about the idea of being in a group at all, and made a point of expressing his growing disinterest in the whole business of making music.

I never have a guitar at my flat, ever. I don't sit around tinkering tunes.
—Will Sergeant, 1985

It's a weird thing to do, y'know, be in a group. You never seem to get settled. I feel weird all the time—unsettled and not at ease. I think we all need psychiatric help. You know all those weirdo 'rock' people? Well, we're turning into them. We'll be walking 'round with plastic bags on our heads and fish down our jumpers soon ...
—Will Sergeant, 1985

Even the usually upbeat Les was expressing his misgivings.

It's all money. I hate this business, to be honest. How long will I stick with it? Well, now, how deep is the ocean? That is a good question. So is 'how long is a piece of string?'   —Les Pattinson, 1985

When everyone's happy in this band, we work so well together. But that's getting rarer and rarer. We used to be a diplomatic group, but these days Mac makes all the decisions. It's not equal anymore.

—Les Pattinson, 1985

Even Bunnyman-to-the-end Mac acknowledged the growing tensions within the band, and expressed his own frustrations.

Les is always saying rubbish about me ... it's weird. I always thought he liked me, but sometimes I think he hates me. —Ian McCulloch, 1985

Sometimes I've really hated the others onstage. But the others feel the same sometimes—particularly Will. Because we depend on each other, we sometimes do resent each other, and blame each other for things that are our own fault, or things that have nothing to do with the band. —Ian McCulloch, 1985

But perhaps no one was growing more dissatisfied with the Bunnymen and the music business than the perennial outsider, Pete.

I still feel like I want to get out every other minute. If you're working closely with the same people all the time, it's obvious that you're going to get fed up. —Pete de Freitas, 1985

I'd rather be riding me bike. —Pete de Freitas, 1985

Basically, [record companies are] like agents. They've no idea what's a hit or what's not a hit. The only thing they do is dampen your enthusiasm for making a great record. They try and turn it into something that's recognisable on their wavelength. They try and talk you into being that one thing, and meantime you lose your originality.

—Les Pattinson, 1985

They resented me for doin' soddin' everything. I resented them for doing bugger all. They had a work ethic that said rehearsing was work but the hardest part of all—writing songs—wasn't. I never got around to saying 'You soddin' try all this.' But imagine them doing magazines in America: 'Looking forward to playing Philadelphia?' 'Nah, sooner be home.' —Ian McCulloch, 1999

SEX GOD

He's probably the calmest in the group—the most rational, anyway. Which I can dislike when I'm being really irrational.

—Ian McCulloch, 1984

I wasn't capable of being callous enough to walk out, so I suppose I had to go a bit crazy before I could do it. —Pete de Freitas, 1987

Bunnymen tensions exploded when, a day before he was to become the godfather of Les's new daughter at a New Year's Day christening, Pete went AWOL and flew to New Orleans. Pete somehow thought Les would find this funny. He took along the Bunnymen road crew of Tim Whittaker, Andy Eastwood, and Steve "Johnno" Johnson, plus Tim O'Shea, of Liverpudlian pop group Send No Flowers. They decided they would form a group called The Sex Gods, a title which Pete equated with "rhythm and greatness," even though some thought it was a ridiculous name for a rock band. Pete disagreed.

You're going out, and they put some James Brown on, and you're getting into it and dancing in front of some girl you're totally into— you feel like a Sex God! Does 'Echo & the Bunnymen' sound any more sensible?   —Pete de Freitas, 1986

I wanted to get away on holiday and come back with more than just memories and having spent a lot of money and very big hangovers. I wanted to come back with something positive.
—Pete de Freitas, 1986

In this group, the multitalented Pete would sing and play guitar instead of drums. The idea behind The Sex Gods was a lunatic lost weekend. They wanted, as de Freitas said, "to work totally off chance—to go away with nothing and come back with everything." The concept of the trip was loosely based on the film *The Dice Man,* a culty lunatic semi-religion called Bokanism, and the notion of "The Duck." The Duck was a symbol for the ridiculous, and Pete shakily reasoned that, since "life is ridiculous, and everyone's insane, the philosophy of the ridiculous/insane was all that really made sense." Ummm ... *yeah.*

I was philosophizing with a sledgehammer. I just decided that I had to do something, and force out certain issues in my own mind. What occurred was an awful lot of weirdness. I was very much involved with what I was thinking, which, I guess, was bordering on insanity. I just thought I'd take it to its limit ...   —Pete de Freitas, 1986

The band set up camp at a friend's house in The Big Easy, and were joined by occasional Bunnymen extra Mike Mooney and Psychedelic Furs saxophonist Mars Williams. This ragged crew hung out, occasionally worked on songs, and documented the whole thing on super 8 film, and in a book called *The Godlogs.*

In fact, the trip wasn't nearly so much about creation as it was destruction. Pete wasn't eating, plus he was ingesting vast quantities of LSD, cocaine, Ecstacy, and alcohol, and crashing vehicles at a furious pace. Pete totaled Jake's and Andy Eastwood's motorcycles, and he did the same with a 1950 Dodge and a 1972 Vista Cruiser. And he wasn't sleeping at all.

Liking New Orleans's nocturnal pace, but unwilling to risk missing any of the daytime, de Freitas and Eastwood agreed they wouldn't sleep. They bought new socks and T-shirts every morning and showered three

times a day to fend off the scratching, insects-under-the-skin sensations of manic sleeplessness ... de Freitas ... stayed up for eighteen days on the trot. To avoid the possibility of falling asleep acci-
dentally, [he] decided to never sit down. He stood constantly—or, more
usually, paced—filling notebooks with his thoughts. He wore shades day
and night.   —Q, 1998

Pete's phone calls back to Liverpool were equally disturbing. He
announced his official departure from the Bunnymen, and demanded that
Mac send him 15,000 pounds, for all the cigarettes Mac had cadged from him
over the years. Mac did not send the requested sum—instead, he shipped
over a few cartons of smokes, along with a request that Pete return home.
Pete was clearly not himself at this point, any more than The Sex Gods were
really a rock group.

Pete was a pretty strange dude. He was pretty quiet, kind of kept to
himself a lot of the time, but then every once in a while he'd open up,
party, and hang out. He was singing, and also decided he was going to
play guitar. We rehearsed a bit in the house, wrote and worked on songs,
and then we went into the studio and recorded some of it. The thing
that was really bad about the band was that Pete should've been playing drums, because he was a great drummer, and the guy that was playing drums wasn't. And Pete was not a good guitarist, so who knows what
he was trying to do. It was more like Pete's friends hanging out; it
was a garage band, or, in this case, a living room band. We'd get drunk,
sit around, smoke pot, and play. It was weird.   —Mars Williams, 1998

He was doing E before the Happy Mondays. He was the E King. He was
inventing a persona for himself he felt he needed. His problem was he
thought he was never one of us. But he was. He was a Bunnyman.
                                            —Ian McCulloch, 1997

We were meant to be going away to do a tour; he ... wigged-out big-
time ... you just couldn't get any sense out of him. He'd lost the
plot completely, he'd gone a bit loopy ...   —Ian McCulloch, 1998

It just suddenly went weird.
[Pete] was hanging out with
people ... who thought motor-
bikes were a good idea. It was
all that grubby soddin' ... it
wasn't 'Bunnymen.' He blew all
his money ... and thought he
was invincible. He was doing
loads of Ecstasy, crashing
motorcycles, crashing cars. The
maddest phone calls. He wanted
Les's [engineer] dad to build a
phone to talk to aliens ...
            —Ian McCulloch, 1999

[Pete] had a mission to accom-
plish. He wanted to change the
world by April. I told him it
will take at least until June.
            —Ian McCulloch, 1997

Mac in particular was furious with Pete's irresponsibility, and thought
the road crew were taking advantage of him.

I thought it was my job, goin' mad! No, I thought, 'The cheeky fucker. We invited him into this thing, and he's tarnishing the Bunnymen.'

It was at a time when we couldn't afford to fragment. I thought he was an idiot. He was being sucked dry by people who were supposed to be his mates. On the other hand, if you're on the dole and some bloke with a penchant for ... madness offers you free drugs, drink, and accommodation, you're gonna go.   —Ian McCulloch, 1999

Tales of Pete's madness concerned Bill Drummond to the point where he flew over to New Orleans to check on the wayward drummer. Instead of annoyance or concern, Drummond felt inspiration.

He was literally king of the world out there, calling himself 'Mad Louis,' living this extraordinary dissolute lifestyle straight out of a Jack Kerouac novel in which anything was possible. And it really was until the money ran out and he had to come home to reality. The experience changed my life. I thought to myself, 'Is this what rock & roll is really all about?' I started seeing things in a different light, and when I came back I chucked my job in the mainstream music business and decided to record my own album, which was something I'd been vaguely thinking about for some time. There's even a track on it called 'Ballad For a Sex God,' which was my 'thank you' to Pete. I wanted him to produce it, but he felt that he couldn't. At that time he was just a burnt-out shell ...   —Bill Drummond, 1989

As Pete's finances dwindled, members of The Sex Gods began drifting home one-by-one, each expressing concern about Pete's mental health. Once his cash was practically exhausted, Pete took his last hard-earned money and flew, somewhat sheepishly, back to Liverpool. Although he wasn't exhibiting signs of true madness any longer, he wasn't quite the same as before he'd left.

After a few months at home, Pete mentioned his misgivings to Bunnymen biographer Tony Fletcher.

He came back slightly changed. Something had been lost. He was trying to find something and came back with less. Everything was different after that.
—Ian McCulloch, 1999

I went very stupid, actually. I don't know what happened. It's very weird … it was very much my life, being in the Bunnymen … perhaps too much in a way … I've found myself a bit lost now that I'm out of it. It was an all-consuming thing … I have regretted [leaving] at various moments, actually.   —Pete de Freitas, 1986

While Pete was wailing away in his Kero-wackian adventure, the Bunnymen had business to take care of. There was a U.S. tour slotted that couldn't be canceled, and an album to record with producer Gil Norton, who'd helped with the arrangements on *Ocean Rain.*

Once Pete had announced his departure, the Bunnymen drafted former Haircut 100 stickman Blair Cunningham to fill in on the tour. Although Cunningham was an adept musician, he was a strange choice for the Bunnymen. His former band's teenybop appeal was certainly at odds with the darker tendencies of the Bunnymen, and his skills behind the kit lacked Pete's attack and inventiveness. On a personal level, Cunningham and Mac seemed to get along, but neither the guitarist nor the bassist could relate to him on any level.

The Game

Echo & The Bunnymen

7" & 12"

Les and Will can't play without [Pete]. Will wasn't happy and Les was freakin' out.   —Ian McCulloch, 1987

[Cunningham] used to throw his sticks into the crowd at the end of the set.   —Will Sergeant, 1995

Despite Cunningham's incompatibility, the band's sixth U.S. tour in early spring, 1986, was their most successful thus far, due largely to the sales of *Songs to Learn and Sing* and *Pretty in Pink*, a film soundtrack that featured "Bring On the Dancing Horses." Cunningham could sense that he didn't really belong in the Bunnymen, and, when he received an offer from The Pretenders at the end of the tour, he promptly accepted. The Bunnymen quickly drafted former ABC drummer David Palmer for the recording of their next album. Although Palmer made some contributions, by July 1986, he, too, quickly concluded that he really didn't want to be a Bunnyman, just as Pete decided that he wanted to rejoin.

Although the Bunnymen were initially tentative, concerned about Pete's mental health and his betrayal, they eventually allowed him back into the warren—albeit this time as a paid hand, rather than a fully-fledged member.

The first Bunnymen performance with Pete back on board was for the BBC's "Rock Around the Clock" marathon on September 20th 1986. They played a couple of new songs titled "The Game" and "Lips Like Sugar," and were joined by Billy Bragg (with whom they'd toured the states in 1984) for a version of The Velvet Underground's "Run, Run, Run," with a bit of Sinatra's "One For My Baby" thrown in for the hell of it.

Shortly thereafter, both Warner Brothers and the band determined that

It was a mutual kind of thing—
we wanted to carry on because
we really wanted to do it with
Gil, but it became obvious that
it wasn't going to work out.
We'd done too much to sort out
what had gone wrong. It was
easier to start again than to
change what we already had.

—Jake Brockman, 1987

they weren't particularly happy with the results of the sessions with Gil
Norton and David Palmer. The group was also eager to record once again
with Pete back behind the kit. They decided to scrap the Norton tapes and
proceed to record an entirely new LP with Laurie Latham, whom WEA had
initially suggested.

Despite these setbacks, the Bunnymen were chomping at the bit to
record. Will and Les, excited and relieved by the return of newly nicknamed
"Boomerang Pete" informed the press that they were ready to play a pop festival on Mars, and Mac was looking forward to creating an album of classic,
direct, unpretentious pop songs.

The group started rerecording the new LP with Latham in Cologne.
From there they moved to Brussels, then Germany, and then to London. It
became apparent that this album wasn't going to be the hoped-for collection
of simple songs. Latham was a very specific, exacting producer, who would
work on one song for as long as a month at a time. Even worse, Mac had
become almost totally alienated from the rest of the band, due in part to the
star treatment he received, and his increasingly heavy drinking. No one—
including Mac—was happy with this turn of events.

I was a paranoid schizo mer-
chant. I only trusted my own
judgment but I knew I was losing it. I was on another planet but then I didn't want to be
on the one [the other Bunnymen]
were on.

—Ian McCulloch, 1997

I was staying in some Hofbrauhaus in Germany. Not speaking to anyone
for weeks on end. Coming in bevvied out of me head every night because
I'd stayed in the studio, or going down to the Lowdown, a local club,
with two people in there. One a policeman, probably. Pete was living
in the loft, with pigeons. It always seemed dark. I thought 'This is
as bad as it can get.' But we ended up in the Old Kent Road in London,
next to the Henry Cooper pub, and that was dismal ...

—Ian McCulloch, 1999

Mac used to go for your weaker
points. You'd cruise along
thinking that he was your best
mate, and then he'd come out
with something, like you could-
n't spell a certain word that
he could spell when he was
five, and he'd get you wound up
about it. He was a master of
that.

—Les Pattinson, 1997

Mac had distanced himself from everyone else and he was getting different treatment from the rest of us. Not that we wanted the treatment he was getting; we just found it all ridiculous. He had people
running around behind him, basically wiping his arse ... he had started to act like a turd.   —Will Sergeant, 1995

It would always start with these little divisions. Even going to the
bar, Mac needed some eyes, someone who could see, 'cos he wouldn't
wear glasses. Quaint in a way, but it got a bit much. He was always
getting drunk and talking about how we were going to make the greatest thing ever—and the next day he just had a hangover. I'm sure not
even Jacques Brel got so pissed that he couldn't think what he was
doing the next day.   —Les Pattinson, 1997

[Alcohol abuse] seemed way out of hand. I was living on 15 minutes of not even kip a night, just lying down with me arms crossed, just in case, for embalming purposes ... y'know, shifting me out of the body-bag. The greatest folly is people in groups think [excessive drinking] can help you escape from this claustrophobic cocoon. They never tell you it wraps about 10 more shells around you. So you can't get out of the first one, and then those other 10 layers are Fort Knoxed up.　　　　　　　　　　　　　　　　　　—Ian McCulloch, 1999

A little relief was provided when former Doors keyboardist Ray Manzarek visited the studio to aid in the recording of a new version of "Bedbugs and Ballyhoo" and a cover of The Doors' "People Are Strange." Both Pete and Les wanted to re-do "Bedbugs" because they felt that it had been wasted as a B-side, and director John Hughes had asked the band to contribute the latter for a film, following the success of *Pretty In Pink*. Although the band was initially hesitant about recording a Doors song, they decided that they couldn't pass up the opportunity.

It's a nice little version, a bit more cabaret than The Doors' version.　　　　　　　　　　　　　　　　　—Ian McCulloch, 1987

They're one of my favorite bands. Ian McCulloch is an excellent poet. He's dark and moody and mysterious.　　　　　　　—Ray Manzarek, 1987

In fact, Mac's lyric-writing capabilities were about as far from poetic as they'd ever be. By many accounts, he couldn't be dragged away from Lorraine and their newborn child, Candy Lou, named after Lou Reed's "Candy Says." Will was so distressed with Mac's lyrical reticence that he even attempted to write some words of his own for the LP. The crux of the matter was Mac's heart just wasn't with the Bunnymen anymore, and this ennui was reflected both in the songs and Mac's confidence.

Mac didn't have any firm ideas of what he wanted, so he just kept changing the lyrics, and we had to keep changing the music to fit them. So in the end it was just washed out and everyone was fed up with it.　　　　　　　　　　　　　　　　—Will Sergeant, 1990

(Inexplicably, when the album was released, it was the first collection of new Bunnymen songs to come with a full lyric sheet—arguably their only record that *wouldn't* have benefited from one.)

To add to the Bunnymen's troubles, manager Mick Hancock quit during the recording. WEA quickly signed on Steve Jensen and Martin Kirkup,

I was feeling maybe I'd got out of my head too many times. I remember thinking, "I can't do this anymore,' that I was going to jump out a window or something.　　　—Ian McCulloch, 1994

'People are Strange' was recorded at Amazon and I was glad we did it in the end. It sounds pretty much the same as The Doors original ... a bit more cabaret. It wasn't one of my favorite Doors songs anyway. 'Indian Summer' I would have liked to have done. It was just nice working with Ray, who's a really good laugh; he was like a friend after a couple of days.　　　—Ian McCulloch, 1987

I enjoyed making all of the Bunnymen records, apart from the last one.
　　　　　　—Ian McCulloch, 1992

I'd thought I'd lost it all ... I thought that I would never write a decent lyric again.
　　　　　　—Ian McCulloch, 1988

I think that everybody thinks that there's something not there that should be.
—Ian McCulloch, 1987

It wasn't the album we should have made. In the back of our minds, I think we felt guilty. We didn't want to play the songs. It was shite.
—Ian McCulloch; 1999

There were bits that were alright, but it was too nice; the whole thing was just too produced and perfect.
—Will Sergeant, 1997

It's an overcooked fish.
—Will Sergeant, 1987

It doesn't have whatever the other four had. And I felt if we made another one like that, it would be very hard to strive for magic again in music. I think just settling for a kind of trans-Atlantic approach to writing would have crept in, and we would have been stuffed ... it would be very hard to do something that was artistically motivated.
—Ian McCulloch, 1990

known collectively as Direct Management. The duo was a businesslike, LA-based team with an office in London. It was evident that WEA were no longer willing to deal with the Bunnymen's quirkiness, which they no longer considered quaint; the management had been hired to turn the weird and difficult group into conventional, stadium-filling rock superstars, like their contemporaries U2 and Simple Minds.

It was Direct Management's decision to have the LP mixed in America by industry heavyweight Bruce Lampcov, which just contributed to the problems of an already troubled suite of songs that even Mac candidly admitted were "50% bullshit." Les, who'd wanted the album to sound like "The Killing Moon," conservatively estimated that the resulting flat and linear recordings were "crap." Over the years, the band has stood vociferously behind its distaste for the LP.

By the time we finished the album ... I didn't wanna soddin' hear it. Checked the mixes down the phone.
—Ian McCulloch, 1999

I liked the songs, just hated the mixes.
—Les Pattinson, 1987

It still sounds crap.
—Ian McCulloch, 1995

***

Despite interband divisions and the Bunnymen's unhappiness with their latest recordings, a mood of optimism briefly prevailed in early 1987 as they ventured on a sold-out tour of Brazil, a country they'd never previously visited.

We played Porte Allegre, San Paulo, and Rio. They were great. You didn't expect people out there to know us and it came as a complete surprise [that they did]. This was the first time we'd played with Pete after the break, and everything seemed to fit into place. We were playing great and the audiences were brilliant. —Les Pattinson, 1987

It was the best place we could have gone to start playing again, because we weren't that rehearsed before we went, but we didn't have to be. It was like the best we've played since probably Heaven ... because it wasn't like playing the Hammersmith Odeon, where everyone's expecting a certain thing, and it just made us relax. —Ian McCulloch, 1987

While the band were in Brazil, Anton Corbijn was called in to direct a video for the forthcoming single, "The Game." In a beautifully shot piece of 8mm film, Corbijn caught the group at its most natural and relaxed. Mac spent a good amount of the video as the bastard child of Leonard Cohen and Carmen Miranda, sporting a black suit and shades complemented by a straw hat overflowing with colorful fruits, while Will mimed the song's guitar solo with his acoustic held in front of his face. The only turmoil experienced during this shoot came from an outward source.

I was nearly decapitated by ten military policemen in Brazil. We were shooting the video for 'The Game' and the police were doing a drugs raid on this flavella where we were. They made us take our shoes and socks off. I thought, 'What a way to go. What will the missus think?'
—Ian McCulloch, 1999

Eventually escaping bullet-free to the UK, the Bunnymen were determined to maintain the light-hearted air they'd enjoyed in Brazil. When an interviewer asked what had kept the band together for so long, they unanimously shouted "Super Glue!" Upon further prodding from the hapless writer, they changed their response to "money." And why did they need the money? "To buy Super Glue!"

Les: "I went to Bolton last week."
Will: "Jamaica?"
Les: "No, she went of her own accord."
Mac: "Why? Is there a Bolton in Jamaica?"
Les: "No." —*Melody Maker*, 1987

★★★

The Funnymen broke almost two years of silence on June 1st, 1987, when they released "The Game," b/w "Ship of Fools" and "Lost and Found." While the A-side overall was an unsurprising yet pleasant autumnal strum, the lyrics were Mac's most revealing yet.

The words to 'The Game' talked of a pride and a proud refusal to seek approval. That's probably as close as McCulloch has ever come to explaining the Bunny view of themselves. A kind of 'My Way' in Bunny-talk. —*Record Mirror*, 1987

'The Game' was a kind of summary of where I felt the Bunnymen were at. I wanted it to be the key song of the album. 'Pride/A proud refusal/And I refuse to need your approval.' That was a way of saying, 'We're coming back and I don't care if you like it.' For a few years, I thought I was living out the fantasy of these 15-year-old boys in overcoats—that I have, in a way, created a generation of people in overcoats with sticking-up hair, weight of the world on their shoulders—and I wanted to say, 'I'm not going to live that out for you anymore.' I haven't got the weight of the world on my shoulders, and I don't want it. —Ian McCulloch, 1987

I used to think that in order to be a real serious musician, I had to have hang-ups, so I used to force some on myself. I used to think that it was my job to have the weight of the world on my shoulders, and I didn't have any of it, actually, except if my hair didn't stick up properly, or if I had a spot on my nose or something. I used to take that and pretend things were bad.
—Ian McCulloch, 1987

On the eve of the single's release, it was announced that the following LP would be simply, blandly titled *Echo & the Bunnymen*. The band had considered calling the album "The Game," but balked because Queen had already released an LP of that name in 1980. Interviews made it clear that the band was ready to strip itself of its image as mysterious, contrary, super-serious rock missionaries.

It's different now. On the first four albums, it was always that thing of being intense ... 'this is the be-all and end-all of the human race.' But with this album, we thought every track was dead good, but without being holy about it.

—Ian McCulloch, 1987

I think now we're old enough or mature enough to realise that playing countries at the time the record comes out there, to sell more of it, isn't such a bad thing. We'd do something that'd mean we'd sell less records, then wonder why we didn't have any money. And now we're just ... I dunno ... there's less pretension and self-consciousness there.

—Ian McCulloch, 1987

We'll be a bit humbler this time around, a bit quieter.

—Ian McCulloch, 1987

I usually come up with titles that are weird or that are animals. Like nobody knows why I've called it *Porcupine* or ... something a bit more mysterious like *Ocean Rain* or *Heaven Up Here*. On this album I just wanted it to be 'Echo & the Bunnymen.' A lot of the titles are just straightforward 'cos I wanted to get away from the mysterious side a bit.   —Ian McCulloch, 1987

... Half of you [is] thinking it is all serious and important, and the other half is thinking it's just a game. Going onstage and being all moody, then coming off and shouting 'Where's the bevvies?' You come off and it's a totally different thing ... the only act is in channeling all that 'moodiness' into one-and-a-half hours. It's something you feel normally in your life, but you're compressing it into short bursts, so sometimes a song can be overdramatic. It's always dangerous to think you're more serious about your life than anybody else is about theirs. You might be more articulate when it comes to putting it across, but you should never think it's more important ... [We're] closer to realising that there's no use thinking there is a 'Big Answer.' Well, everyone knows that! You write a song, and a year later, you realise you've said something everyone thinks. Which is probably a good thing. But quite often you think: 'God! I've just hit on something nobody else has ever thought of!' But ... they have.

—Ian McCulloch, 1987

A lot of people say it's a mellowing thing but I don't think so. I think that's the wrong choice of words. It's just a nicer way of being a human being, to not want to inflict some kind of sarcasm on someone just for the benefit of proving that you know how to put someone down and make them feel awkward about being in a room with you. I think that kind of game is mad.   —Ian McCulloch, 1987

Initially, this nicer, enigma-free version of the Bunnymen did not translate into record sales. "The Game" stuttered humbly to #28 in the UK charts, and vanished rapidly.

THE GAME

A sense of duty was my one intention
And an ugly beauty was my
    own invention
Pride, a proud refusal
And I refuse to need
    your approval
Too many seekers, too few beacons
But through the fog we'll keep
    on beaming
Through the crying hours of your
    glitter years
All the living out of your
    tinsel tears
And the midnight trains I
    never made
'Cos I'd already played the game

Everybody's got their own
    good reason
Why their favorite season is
    their favorite season
Winter winners and those
    summer suns
Aren't good for everyone, aren't
    good for everyone
Spring has sprung and autumn's
    so well done
So well done

And it's a better thing that
    we do now
Forgetting everything, the
    whys and hows
While you reminisce
About the things you miss
You won't be ready to kiss
Goodbye

The Earth is a world
The world is a ball
A ball in a game
With no rules at all
And just as I wonder

At the beauty of it all
You go and drop it
And it breaks when it falls

I'll never understand why you
    thought I would
Need to be reassured and
    be understood
When I always knew that your
    bad's my good
And I was ready
Ready to be loved

Born under Mars
With Jupiter rising
Fallen from stars
That lit my horizon

I'll never understand why you
    thought I would
Need to be reassured and understood
When I always knew that your
    bad's my good
And I was ready
To be

Through the crying hours of your
    glitter years
All the living out of your
    tinsel tears
And the midnight trains I never made
'Cos I'd already played

It's a better thing that we do now
Forgetting everything
The whys and hows
'Cos while you reminisce
About the things you miss
You won't be ready to kiss
Goodbye

… a great song, almost country and western for us. I pretty much wrote that as a kind of anti-Bunnymen song; it was very reflective. It was a statement of intent in the negative, but a statement of what I was about, rather than the group. Prior to that it had always been 'we.' 'The Game' was really the first solo record I made …
—Ian McCulloch, 1994

'The Game' is a dignified, almost serene, stroll-cum-scroll from the ambassadors of all things good and grand. It's a song … which Tom Jones might cover before you can say 'Gene Pitney's better.' The philosophy is sound—all rhyme and little reason—and Mac sings with a perfect degree of sleepy angst-tinted poise which shows Bono up for the windy buffoon he is. The Bunnymen still manage to sound truculently composed. Deft as daggers.
—*Melody Maker*, 1987

I was singing 'The Game' in my head the other day and it's a brilliant song.
—Ian McCulloch, 1995

... much dirtier than 'The Game'—
all discreet handballs and cun-
ning late tackles; an episodic
summer breeze.
                    —*Melody Maker*, 1987

LOST AND FOUND

I was standing in a graveyard
Under silver studded skies
In a forest burning ashes
On the bonfires of our lives

As the sky fell down
I was lost and found
Saw my world spin 'round
'Round and 'round

All the ghosts have gathered
     'round me
Come to tell me of a change
In the darkness that surrounds me
I am falling down again

On this haunted ground
I was lost and found

Lost
Lost and found ...

She will tell you her cathedral
Has no windows and no doors
And you know she doesn't need you
And that's why you want her more
As your heart melts down
You are lost not found

Lost
Lost and found ...

I was counting all the tombstones
Of the buried boys and girls
As the wind blew in like ice
And froze this cemetery world

And we all fell down
We were lost and found
And the sun went down
We were lost and found

Lost
Lost and found

SHIP OF FOOLS

In the bedroom you will find her
All your life is dead
Everything you do reminds her
Step lightly and beware

Hark the herald angels singing
All the holy bells are ringing
Hark the herald angels singing
Singing singing singing

Every journey, every station
Every twist and every turn
Signposts your destination
Rivers of no return

Hark the herald angels singing
All the holy bells are ringing
Hark the herald angels singing
Singing singing singing

All aboard
Ship of fools ...

Head in the stars, you're
     heading for home
In search of dreams that you can
     call your own
Call your own

In the bedroom you will find her
All your life returned
She sucked you in and lit the fire
Struck you up and watched you burn

Hark the herald angels singing
All the holy bells are ringing
Hark the herald angels singing
Singing singing singing

All aboard
Ship of fools ...

Head in the stars
Heading for home

On July 6th, 1987, the release date of *Echo & the Bunnymen,* the band previewed the album with a brief set atop the HMV Record shop on Oxford Street in London, mimicking The Beatles' rooftop concert on The Apple Records building almost two decades earlier. In another homage to the Fab Four, they closed the performance with a delightfully ramshackle thrash through "Twist and Shout." Eighty feet in the air, the band still managed to bring traffic to a standstill on the sweltering streets below. The Bunnymen were trying to maintain their tradition of unusual gestures, but Oxford Street was hardly The Outer Hebrides. Still, fans reasoned, it was better than nothing. Assessments of the album were just as abject.

… appears with little but the rush of vocal and guitar melodies that has always been the band's stamp of quality. It is scattered with shreds of expected class, but after such a long time coming, the result is disappointingly conservative and lacks progression.   *—NME,* 1987

...that eponymous collection suggested that the band had been reduced to re-treading their finest moments for the American market. *—Q,* 1989

　　In an attempt to cherry on, an almost sheepish Mac half-heartedly tried to defend the "new" Bunnymen to the press—and, probably, himself.

… we can't go on like we were in 1981. You can't get by because 'we're the coolest group in the world' or whatever. We have to change as well, because all of the audience are changing. The minute you try to recreate something that's gone before, that's when somebody who has seen you a lot will think, 'Hang On, this ain't as good as it was.'
　　　　　　　　　　　　　　　　　　　　　—Ian McCulloch, 1987

I used to come to America and read reviews that would say 'Echo & the Bunnymen sound like they could be great but they're too self-conscious,' and I used to say, 'Hey man, that's just our attitude.' I'm not denying my past at all because I love going through self-consciousness, sitting in the recording studio thinking that I've just re-invented the meaning of life. But I can see why it confused a lot of people. I still think our new album is as weird as any album we've done because it's us doing it, but I do think that a lot of the pretend-highbrow stuff is missing, and the music is a lot more direct and quite intelligent, without saying it.　　　　—Ian McCulloch, 1987

Initial impressions led to the conclusion that this may be the weakest offering in the Bunnymen canon. The guitars sound less caustic and the keyboards too prominent, resulting in a softer, more polished rock than what we've come to expect from the band.
　　　　　　　　　—*Creem,* 1987

… mostly horrible, lacking focus and with hardly a hint of the Existential Groove that was Bunnymusic.　*—Stylus,* 1999

The record's too quiet ... the production doesn't do the material any justice at all. (Either that or something got lost in the mix.) The crispness and fragility that made *Ocean Rain* such an essential purchase isn't anywhere near as apparent on *EATB.* The most worrying thing is that the whole record smacks of a loss of creative ability ... there isn't a 'Back of Love,' a 'Killing Moon,' or an 'Over the Wall' in evidence. Shame.　　*—Bluer Skies,* 1987

Echo & The Bunnymen

OVER YOU

Jump right in
Take the call
Were you pushed or did you fall?
Fell apart
Feeling low
Happy ride, the merry-go

And I always hear them singing
And complaining about the world
And my chiming bells are ringing out
The word, the word, the word

Love rebounds
Heart goes snap
Is she ever coming back?
Let her down
Break her fall
Never ever felt so small

And I always hear them singing
And complaining about the world
But my chiming bells are ringing out
The word, the word, the word

Feeling good again
Always hoped I would
Never believed that I ever could
Feeling blue again
Never wanted to
Under the weather
And it's over you

When there's a hole in the holy
And a crack in our hearts
It's love and love only
That sets our world apart
Worlds apart
Joined at the heart

Jump right in
Take the call
Were you pushed or did you fall?
Fell apart
Feeling low
Happy ride, the merry-go

And I always hear them singing
And complaining about the world
And my chiming bells are ringing out
The word, the word, the word

Feeling good again
Always hoped I would
Never believed that I ever could
Feeling blue again
Never wanted to
Under the weather
And it's over you

And a dream is a means to the end
    of the things
That will tempt you away
From the path to the true way in

ALL IN YOUR MIND

You say you're proud to be one of the people
Hands on the money and your feet on the ground
Shouting out loud from the top of the steeple
Counting the flock while collecting their pounds
All you thieving wheeler-dealers in the healing
    zone
Giving me fever fever fever fever
Down to my bones

I pray
And nothing happens
Jesus
It's all in my mind
You say
Stop looking for answers
And reasons
They're all in your mind
All in your mind

Covered in flies and smothered in lava
I can't scratch my itches with these pumice stone hands
I dream of my days as a desert farmer
Living my life on the fat of the sand
All you thieving wheeler-dealers in the healing zone
Giving me fever fever fever fever
Down to my bones

I pray
And nothing happens
Jesus
It's all in my mind
You say
Stop looking for answers
And reasons
They're all in your mind
All in your mind

Stuck in a world losing its way and wonder
I wonder what happened to the world we knew
Splitting the atom and feeling its thunder
Could never ever make me feel the way you do
You give me fever fever fever fever
Down to my bones
Wheel me wheel me wheel me
To the healing zone

I pray
And nothing happens
Jesus
It's all in my mind
You say
Stop looking for answers
And reasons
They're all in your mind
All in your mind

The rabbit-punch bass line punctuation of 'All In Your Mind' juts through the coiling pulse, catching McCulloch with his voice draped around his knees as the toilet door of religion is sledgehammered and home-truths dissolve. The [Bunnymen's] tireless quest for answers has matured into a ceaseless hunt for questions. There is beauty in such confusion.

—*Melody Maker,* 1987

Organized religion ... it's pseudo-religion.

—Ian McCulloch, 1987

I think people spend too much time thinking about [religion]. I just find it funny that people spend so much time thinking about something they can't prove exists. I can understand wondering. I wonder what happens and why we are here. But to bother building churches and organizations, it seems, well ... it gets a lot of people in jobs, and I can understand that. [But] it seems a lot of concrete and work involved with something that's just a notion. —Ian McCulloch, 1987

You never see God down at the pub. You can't have a drink with God and tell him how you feel and stuff. You have to kneel down. It's this need to be inferior and obsequious in the human race, as though somebody else has got the answers to your problems. I think the whole point of living is to enjoy them problems, and to unravel them and solve them. It's like one big crossword. Sometimes you finish and sometimes you don't. And that's the beauty of it. —Ian McCulloch, 1987

   ... the manic Will Sergeant guitar solo on 'All In Your Mind' ... screeches like an antelope with a nitric acid suppository.

—*Melody Maker,* 1987

The other night in a hotel room in Aberdeen, I was in my room and I thought, 'This is so boring. I'm gonna get the Holy Bible out of my drawer.' And I flipped it open. I forget what soddin' chapter it was, but I must have seen what looked like about a hundred different names on one page that I was supposed to take in. And they were all in some mad language. Who knows what anyone was saying? And you're supposed to read that crap and believe it? I think it's wrong.

—Ian McCulloch, 1997

BOMBER'S BAY

The word went 'round in no-dream town
They shut us up and shutters down
The planes flew in
And laid the ground
We built upon
And spun around
God's one miracle
Lost in circles

On the march
Berlin to Bomber's Bay
Traveling dark
On the road to Mandalay

Cannon fire came to call
Stood us up and watched us fall
The way we were
And now outworn
Our costumes changed to uniforms
Black black days
Here to stay

On the march
Madrid to Bomber's Bay
Traveling dark
On the road to Mandalay

Pack up your troubles and you'll
    all get by
Smile boys, that's the style
Pack up your troubles and you'll
    all get by
Smile ...

They give us hope and teach us well
With magic moons that cast a spell
And hypnotise, and draw us in
I believe
I'm believing
God's one miracle
Moves in circles

On the march
Berlin to Bombers Bay
Traveling dark
On the road to Mandalay

Black black days
Where the flying fishes play

... a chewy chunk of profound pop, luxurious in guitar and keyboard collages and the stirring of strings, lyrically precise and incisive.
—*The Buzz*, 1987...

... like Jacques Brel and Kurt Weill.   —Ian McCulloch, 1995

It's vaguely political and it's about war, but ... it's also about beauty in the face of war, and all the structures and obstacles of life, and the order of life ... I don't know ... I don't know what it's about. That's probably why I love it, because I haven't quite worked out what I'm on about. It's like a freedom song, an innocent song. It's really hard to capture that innocence. —Ian McCulloch, 1997

I think the singing on it is the best on the album. I like the voice and the words, and it goes on, sails on where it should sail.
—Ian McCulloch, 1987

A true Bunnymen classic, with a sublime guitar line, a yearning verse, and a soaringly gorgeous chorus.

—*Goldmine*, 1998

A bulldog rocker highlighted by the booming Duane Eddy twang of Will Sergeant

—*Melody Maker*, 1986

Unrepentantly saccharine ...

—*Rolling Stone*, 1987

... could be either a romantic ode to an adored woman or McCulloch's valentine to himself.

—*Denver Westworld*, 1987

'Lips Like Sugar' found the band falling into the candy-pop trap, giving McCulloch little to do but play the dangerous heartthrob.

—*The Boston Globe*, 1988

LIPS LIKE SUGAR

She floats like a swan
Grace on the water
Lips like sugar
Lips like sugar
Just when you think you've caught her
She glides across the water
She calls for you tonight
To share her moonlight

You'll flow down her river
She'll ask and you'll give her
Lips like sugar
Sugar kisses
Lips like sugar
Sugar kisses

She knows what she knows
I know what she's thinking
Sugar kisses
Sugar kisses
Just when you think she's yours
She's flown to other shores

To laugh at how you break
And melt into her lake

You'll flow down her river
But you'll never give her
Lips like sugar
Sugar kisses
Lips like sugar
Sugar kisses

She'll be my mirror
Reflect what I am
A loser and winner
The king of Siam I am
And my Siamese twin
Alone on the river
Mirror kisses
Mirror kisses

Lips like sugar
Sugar kisses
Lips like sugar
Sugar kisses

The plaintive cries of 'Lips Like Sugar' project *Crocodiles* onto the windscreen with verses coated with saccharine and spiked with ball bearings and ecstasy, and a chorus that feels like you're standing directly beneath Niagara Falls.   —*Melody Maker*, 1987

A return to form for Mac and the boys, who were always unmatched at this sort of highly romanticised dramaticism. They have the enviable ability to string unlikely lyrics together in a way that sets the gut twisting with emotion while getting the feet moving too—and thankfully, unlike 'The Game,' this has all those prime qualities. Sweet, sweet music.   —*Record Mirror*, 1987

NEW DIRECTION

Out on a limb
Did you see what the cat dragged in?
Take it on the chin
Catching fire on a roof of tin

You've learned to speak and you're professing
The right to teach us our direction
But I found out on close inspection
True imperfection

I'm looking for a new direction
Where in the world am I?
I took the word, the word was resurrection
And then you took me out to climb

Higher and higher ...
Kissing the spires
Higher and higher ...
Soul's on fire

Inside of my head
I heard what the good lord said
Beware he said
If you don't you might end up dead
You suck the air right out of me
But though you suck you cannot see
That life and living is not free
Though you live, you do not breathe

I'm looking for a new direction
Where in the world am I?
I took the word, the word was resurrection
And then you took me out to climb

Higher and higher ...
Kissing the spires
Higher and higher ...
Soul's on fire

I have changed but still my heart remains intact
And true love stays but will our hearts retain
    their lack of
No sense and no direction
Who in the world am I?
I took the word, the word was resurrection
And then you took me out to climb

Higher and higher ...
Kissing the spires
Higher and higher ...
Soul's on fire

I was told when I was seven
All good things must go to Heaven
All my evils would be blessed
If to God I did confess
He'd wipe the slate of sin and fire
Ate the bread and drank the wine
So as your leaving all the fake processions
Just grab a bottle and start confessing
Start confessing
Get to Heaven

One in a million
One and the same
Looking for freedom
Born to be tamed
Once in a lifetime
One of these days
Gonna grab me a lifeline
Swinging my way

I'm swimming out on a blue
    blue ocean
You're sailing out on a blue
    blue sea
Silhouettes and a vulture hoping
He's gonna pick the bones of you
    and me
You and me

Hearts of ice
Hearts of bone
Beating stronger
Beating home
Where there's wanting
There is need
Where there's having
There is greed

I'm swimming out on a blue
    blue ocean
You're sailing out on a blue
    blue sea
Silhouettes and a vulture hoping
He's gonna pick the bones of you
    and me
You and me

Girl
I want the gold dust
In your fingers
And your klondyke touch
Girl
I want the goldmine
As it shimmers
In your solemn eyes

I'm swimming out on a blue
    blue ocean
You're sailing out on a blue
    blue sea
Silhouettes and a vulture hoping
Licking the bones of you and me
I'm swimming out on a blue
    blue ocean
You're sailing out on the blue
    blue sea
Blue blue sea

SATELLITE

Moonlight starlight
Insight out of sight
Something's certain
Draw the curtains, draw them

One out all out
In doubt far out
Wheels in motion
Take the potion

Take the night
When it calls
Take the night
When it falls ...

Take the night
When it calls
Take the night
When it falls ...

You will, I might
Talking satellites
Rockets, comets
Something's coming

Moonlight
Starlight
Insight
Out of sight

Take the night
When it calls
Take the night
When it falls ...

Take the night
When it calls
Take the night
When it falls ...

The lyrics are about sod all—
it was just dead exciting.
—Ian McCulloch, 1987

... frantic and exhilarating ...
—*Melody Maker*, 1985

... like The Gang of Four doing
'The End' by The Doors.
—*Melody Maker*, 1986

ALL MY LIFE

Oh how the times have changed us
Sure and now uncertain
Men not devils have claimed us
Purity deserting
God's one miracle
Lost in circles

All my all my life
Revolves around
Laughter and crying
As my life turns
'Round and 'round

All my all my life
Revolves around
Laughter and crying
As my life turns
'Round and 'round

Songs for life's lost lovers
Bittersweet their healing
Their prayers prayed under covers
Need not kneeling
God's one miracle
Moves in circles

Cannon fire burning
On the hillside
You and I are
Side by side
Listen
Tin soldiers playing our tune

All my all my life
Revolves around
Laughter and crying
As my life turns
Round and round

We had this song called 'Rollercoaster' and everyone thought it'd be a smash. It was a real good rocker. We thought, 'Let's do this as a single.' We did it about five times and it took us a year.

       —Ian McCulloch, 1987

The first version was the best, the demo. You do something once and you can't recapture it.

       —Les Pattinson, 1987

… a great B-side, but there's nothing there, lyrically. I spend a lot of time trying to get the lyrics right but I never found them. I like the chord sequences, though.

       —Ian McCulloch, 1987

ROLLERCOASTER

Let's go
Do the caterpillar
Freak show
In a hall of mirrors
Move on 'til there's nothing left
Do the levitation on the wall
    of death

Move a little closer
Move a little closer
Move a little closer
Ride the rollercoaster

Enter this world of mine
To find me
Leave it while your downhill slides
Behind me

Hip-hop
Do ya understand me?
Flip-flop
I've got to go
Got me
Got me where you want me
Don't I
Don't I just know?

Move a little closer
Move a little closer
Move a little closer
Ride the rollercoaster

I'm laughing about the things
    you're attacking
Keep saying what you say, it's
all been said before
It doesn't really matter when you
    chitter chitter chatter
'Cos all it is is talking…

Ghost train
Stopping at my station
Helter skelter down the wheel of life
Gotcha!
Got the motivation
Motive's
Braking tonight

Move a little closer
Move a little closer
Move a little closer
Ride the rollercoaster

Changing this world of mine
With sparkle and shine
Out of orbit and out of time
This world will be mine

Tell me it's true
Ride boldly ride
Planet to planet
Shoreline to sky

Of all the things
In all this world
The saddest thing's
The saddest girl
Don't you just know?…

Move a little closer
Move a little closer
Move a little closer
Ride the rollercoaster…

★★★

Despite Mac's crying foul at the album's lukewarm reviews, the record just reflected the band's lack of purpose and direction, and they all knew it. Mac was tired of writing on behalf of angst-ridden youths and a band he barely communicated with, and Les just wanted to quit the business entirely and go back to the boat yard. Pete, never completely recovered from his lost weekend as a Sex God, regarded the Bunnymen as just a day job, and Will was eager to concentrate on his personal life. On August 10th, Will married his girlfriend, Paula. He was justifiably furious when, just a few short weeks before the wedding, he discovered he wouldn't be able to go on a honeymoon, as the band were booked to embark on a large-scale August-September stadium tour of the United States.

Over the previous two or three years, American audiences had warmed to UK pop in general, especially U2, Simple Minds, The Cure, and The Smiths. To capitalize on this trend, tour organizers paired the Bunnymen with Mancunians New Order. It was an intelligent enough decision: both bands were notorious for their insular, stubborn nature, and both had the potential for massive Stateside appeal. Despite the largely football-based Liverpool/Manchester rivalry, they were friends from as far back as 1979, when New Order were still known as Joy Division, and had a habit of mooning the Bunnymen whenever they passed them on the motorway. New Order's singer Barney was a big fan of Mac's, and Mac loved New Order's couldn't-give-a-shit attitude and their proclivity for the odd drink. Mac had appeared at Manchester's Gmex festival the previous year, guesting on vocals for a version of New Order's "Ceremony."

It's me favourite New Order song, great ... [before the set] I had one of [New Order bassist] Peter Hook's 'Headaches.' He mixed me a pint of Pernod, orange, and something else—the most disgusting combination you could have. I was bevvied out of me skull. I only drank half a pint and I was totally out of me head, crapping meself before going on. But doing it was great, with Hooky coming up and singing backing vocals. I cocked it up a bit and forgot the words. I love the way Hooky stands and plays bass and what he plays as well—great bass player.
                                                            —Ian McCulloch, 1987

To prevent any clash of egos, the bands were billed as co-headliners, each acting as the other's support on alternate shows. The opening act was glam-pop outfit Gene Loves Jezebel, a group that both the Bunnymen and New Order detested. This shared disgust added to the bond between the co-headliners.

Yeah, hated those shites! I wanted them thrown off the tour, the dumb bastards. And they were ugly as well. If you're gonna throw the makeup on, you need to have the plastic surgery done first.

　　　　　　　—Ian McCulloch, 1997

We were heading towards that 'bland.' Our live performances were becoming so polished and choreographed.

　　　—Will Sergeant, 1995

Mac hasn't got the nerve he had when he would go on about seeing *The Man Who Fell to Earth* 428 times. He grew up into a decent bloke with a living to make. What he needs is a healthy dose of personal pain ... damage. Violence and damage. They should rip it all up, sell all their equipment, move to Harlem or Naples, forget the word 'ocean,' and rediscover 'Fuel' or 'The Disease.' Take a chance. Until then, the Bunnymen are just a very enjoyable, professional, sensible show. So 'well-done.' That's all.

　　　—Melody Maker, 1987

The tour itself wasn't particularly problematic, but it was evident that the Bunnymen were just a shell of their former selves. Each performance was fraught with a soulless, predictable professionalism; a mundane atmosphere of showbiz competence a million miles removed from the heights of, say, The Royal Albert Hall concerts. The only real dramas on the tour were the risible costumes, the posturing buffoonery of Gene Loves Jezebel, and the occasional encore, where the Bunnymen and New Order would conclude the evening with a largely ad-libbed thrash through The Velvet Underground's "Sister Ray." Surprise guest appearances by Ray Manzarek for versions of "Bedbugs and Ballyhoo" and "Soul Kitchen" and, one bizarre evening in Colorado, John Denver, did little to dispel the humdrum, "business as usual" air of these shows. Even the broken ankle Mac sustained by pirouetting over an on-stage monitor in Santa Barbara, California—which, due to a blood clot, almost resulted in amputation—couldn't provide any real sense of rock & roll danger or transcendence.

American audiences didn't seem to mind. The tour was a sell-out, largely due to the cuddly teeny-bop appeal of "Lips Like Sugar"—but, upon returning to the UK for an autumn tour, the Bunnymen suffered a critical backlash, remarkable not so much for its venom as its almost profound disinterest.

Endgames: Learning to cope with the inevitable, struggling to succumb to the spectacle, Echo & the Bunnymen came to Wembley equipped with their history and a distant murmur of mystery and, when that was patently not enough, resorted to habit and habitat. It really shouldn't have come to this, to *here*, but where else could it end? When the party's over, when the promise has been fulfilled, there's nothing left but the swallowed pride, the pomp, and prattling about ... The show that used to venture into no-man's land when the fancy took them is now nothing but a show. Just a surrender to the necessary, a bit more in the bank ... Echo & the Bunnymen played Wembley and it didn't matter because they don't matter anymore. A shame and all but there it is.
　　　　　　　　　　　　—Melody Maker, 1987

The Bunnymen are like watching reruns of classic cup finals—you know where the goals are coming—and after a while that can get a little boring.
　　　　　　　　　—Record Mirror, 1987

Even long-time fans agreed that the shows were fairly hollow affairs. The inclusion of a new song, "Start Again," while enjoyable enough, seemed like an empty promise. It was obvious to all—including the Bunnymen—that they were a band in name only. In an interview from this period, a mortified Will indicated that the only ambition he had left was "to die with dignity."

Frustrations came to a head on October 27th at Manchester's Free Trade Hall, where a pissed off and pissed Mac trashed the city, their football team, and their beloved Smiths. The fans responded with fury. But there was a method behind Mac's madness.

```
... I was trying to rip it apart, but in public. I was totally out
of me mind on brandy and said to the crowd, 'Yer all Manc wankers and
yer gay, and yer footy teams are shit.' The crowd turned on me.
Afterwards, Lorraine comes in—and she never swears—and just said,
'What the fuck are you doing?' I said, 'Don't you know? I'm trying to
kill it. Proper job, not with a whimper.'           —Ian McCulloch, 1999
```

Despite Mac's efforts, the Bunnygod proved an elusive target for drunken deicide. Emerging scarred (and, eventually, sober) from their critical beating, the band was determined not to make the same mistakes they'd made over the past year.

Although Mac initially stated that he'd like the follow-up LP to "sound like a cross between Billie Holiday and Kraftwerk," the real plan was for the Bunnymen to quickly write and record an album of "savage rock" in an attempt to redeem themselves. The self-produced album would be recorded virtually live, as soon as the band's touring schedule was clear.

Early in 1988, the Bunnymen embarked on yet another UK jaunt, and followed that up with an additional visit to the US. These shows proved to be the best the group had played since their date at Glastonbury. With a stage set that uncannily—and probably intentionally—resembled the *Crocodiles* cover, the Bunnymen played with edgy abandon. Will in particular was finally beginning to enjoy touring, and he played with more fury than ever before.

```
Will Sergeant was superb, moving in a trice from squalls of angry
sound to playing with such care and subtlety that there were whispered
asides from his guitar that I would have sworn only he and I had heard.
Such attention to detail is rare indeed.            —John Peel, 1988
```

In March, 1988, "People Are Strange" b/w "Friction," "Run Run Run," and "Paint It Black" (the B-sides recorded on the Scandinavian tour) was released. Although this covers EP put the Bunnymen back into the UK top 30, critics weren't overly impressed.

```
I can think of funnier ways of desecrating Doors' songs than this ran-
cid effort.                                    —Melody Maker, 1987
```

```
Will Sergeant is wearing the
worst jumper in the world. The
man who once uttered the immor-
tal line 'I've never seen an
American pissing before' lit-
erally steals the show. Will
Sergeant is the Shakespeare of
the guitar world—complete with
spelling mistakes.
                    —Bluer Skies, 1988
```

```
Echo & the Bunnymen had clear-
ly thrown in the towel by the
time they were tossing off
Doors covers for American
soundtracks.           —Q, 1989
```

Despite the band's excellent performances, tentative future plans, and Will's new lust for life, Mac hadn't regained his passion for the Bunnymen. When a journalist asked if the band were "moving on to new fields," Mac dryly replied, "Yeah, Sefton Park," and left it at that. Although his interest in songwriting hadn't waned, cryptic comments to the press made it apparent that Mac wasn't all too sure with whom he'd be writing.

I want to work with classical musicians. Classical stuff like Jacques Brel and Edit Piaf, but not like Barclay James Harvest. Edith Piaf if she was alive.
                    —Ian McCulloch, 1988

We're gonna write some songs, but I want things to change. Echo & the Bunnymen is a name, it's not a philosophy. Things change. It's like a football team; footballers come and footballers go. I just want things to change—not necessarily people, but if people can't change, people must go. Don't quote me on that.   —Ian McCulloch, 1988

When the Bunnymen toured Japan in April, Mac drunkenly revealed his true intentions in a radio interview.

We're gonna split up next week, though; as soon as we finish Japan, we're gonna break up for about five years and then come back again
                                        —Ian McCulloch, 1988

Fans and the other Bunnymen assumed Mac wasn't being serious—Will in particular thought he would eventually come around. But this time, there was no irony or glibness behind the gob.

On April 26th, after the final gig of the tour at The Kousie Nenkin Kaikan in Osaka, Mac flew home alone with the intention of visiting his ailing father, who had just had his second heart attack within a short time span. Bob McCulloch had been suffering from angina for some time, but his condition had worsened considerably in recent months. Just a few minutes before Mac's plane touched down in Liverpool, his father passed away. That show in Japan would be the last time all four original Bunnymen ever played together.

We'd all changed. We'd been these shy teenagers who'd somehow got together this thing that could do anything—or so we thought. That was why it was so good and why we all needed each other. But then we got to a point where we all knew, more or less at the same time, that we no longer had that for each other, that we didn't have that magic between us.
                    —Ian McCulloch, 1989

I knew it was going to be the last gig. I knew anyway. To get the news about my dad was just double-weird. I saw it, in a kind of poetic way, as more than a coincidence—he died the day after the last Bunnymen gig.   —Ian McCulloch, 1997

It seemed so symbolic that the two most important things in my life, the two things that gave me personality, had gone.
                                        —Ian McCulloch, 1997

For five months, rumors circulated about a split within the band. Bunnymen spokespeople denied this, and stated that the group was writing a new LP (which they weren't) and planning a special series of 10th anniversary shows. All last-minute hopes were dashed when Mac called a meeting between himself and the other Bunnymen in September.

I said, 'Let's all get together and get totally bevvied up one afternoon. I wanna talk about things.' And I basically said we should knock it on the head. We'd sold more records of that last one than any other album by far. And I thought, 'That's perfect.' I was getting phone calls from Rob Dickens saying, 'All you've got to do is make one more record, it'll sell millions in America alone.' But I couldn't be arsed. I just didn't have the energy anymore. I was probably being dictatorial, but I felt that everything was getting so flabby that someone had to say, 'This is what we do.' We left the pub that day all pretty much agreeing that was it.   —Ian McCulloch, 1997

I didn't actually leave, I just put it to the others that it was time to stop. I think hearing The Sugarcubes' album made me come to a decision. Looking back on it, it seems like a very dated album, but at the time I thought it was amazing. Then there was U2's album, *The Joshua Tree*, and I remember thinking, 'They're making records that are better than ours' and that really scared me.'   —Ian McCulloch, 1997

Will and Les had markedly different reactions to Mac's pronouncement.

We were riding on the crest of a wave. I think we would have broken through. At that point, Mac was my least favorite person in the world. But I tried to convince him not to go, because I thought it was a crap idea. We'd done a lot of work to get to that point.
—Will Sergeant, 1997

I'd been quite content to let it go. That was it, the end of an era.
—Les Pattinson, 1997

It wasn't a heavy thing. It was nice. We went out for a pint and got totally drunk. And I explained me reasons. And they were obviously a bit stunned. But it was a nice way to do it. It wasn't weird ... well, it was a bit weird. But we had a good drink, anyway.
—Ian McCulloch, 1990

We wasted our opportunity. I never wanted the Bunnymen to end.   —Will Sergeant, 1994

Mac was unmoved by Will's subsequent repeated requests that he remain a Bunnyman. Rob Dickens, too, wasn't convinced that the split was necessarily permanent. He thought the Bunnymen might come back "after a long lay-off, but in a different form with different people. Mac and Will Sergeant are very much the creative force and I think they will stick together." Apparently, Mac was thinking along those lines as well.

I wouldn't have minded carrying on doing stuff with Will, but it would have been a bit like John and Paul without George and Ringo. —Ian McCulloch 1989

Initially, Mac's plans were to record a solo LP, then hopefully continue working with Will within the context of a new project. Mac had already spent late September and early October working on demos at Liverpool's Amazon studios. Essentially, he just wanted time and space to work some things out of his system, and to reassess what he'd done and where he was going. And he was determined to regain the legendary self-confidence that he'd lost over the previous two tours.

I was the best frontman, easy, and then suddenly I wasn't. I went all Frankie Vaughan. I started sounding like *Sunday Night at the London Palladium*. In 1988, I just wasn't seeing it any more. My hair had gone all Brillo pad. I was wearing shite clobber, Paul Young keks and all this, and I was out of my soddin' bongo all the time. It was everything. It was all out of control.   —Ian McCulloch, 1999

He was also clearly happy at the prospect of creating something new for himself, while distancing himself from the albatross Echo & the Bunnymen had become.

I know I'm capable of being as excited as I was. I want whatever I do to sound like it's in my blood. —Ian McCulloch, 1988

I loved the Bunnymen; it was the most exciting time of my life. Then it suddenly wasn't exciting anymore and the idea of me doing it on me own was.   —Ian McCulloch, 1990

As Mac understood it, Will was planning on writing some solo material, while Les was concentrating on boat-building, and Pete was drumming for a Liverpudlian group called The Divine Thunderbolt Corps. So one can imagine Mac's shock and disappointment when Will phoned him up and announced that the trio planned on continuing together without him.

If they'd said, 'We're carrying on with a different name,' that would have been fine. Because then maybe in a year's time we could have all done some more stuff as the Bunnymen. But it's sort of spoilt any notion of that.   —Ian McCulloch, 1988

... when they said they were gonna carry on, I must've thought they would change the name. Will never actually told me they were going to get a new singer. When I worked it out I was really hurt.
          —Ian McCulloch, 1997

I was teed-off. To me, it was like being married to someone, getting divorced, and then your ex-wife marries again but still carries on using your name. I mean, I felt hurt and disappointed, mate. My feelings were hurt—I thought I meant more to the band than that.
          —Ian McCulloch, 1995

Will and Les offered a different perspective.

Les Pattinson: "If we got a brilliant singer that could replace Mac, and he looked as good as Mac did—and sang in tune—imagine how it would be! It would just be brilliant. You'd wanna keep the name. [Or] maybe drop the 'Echo' and just have 'The Bunnymen.'"
Will Sergeant: "It seems logical; the stuff we're doing already sounds like the Bunnymen."   —*Spin*, 1988

The Bunnymen's publicity agent did his best to cushion the split (i.e., lie) in a press release.

Basically, they were very tired after the two American tours. They originally planned to take a long time off. When it came to it, during the lay-off, they decided that they just didn't want to carry on anymore. I guess they didn't want to end up like Status Quo. There's no animosity between them and both camps are wishing each other well with whatever they do.   —Brassneck Publicity, 1988

Fifth Bunnyman Jake Brockman also attempted to make light of the break-up in an issue of the Bunnymen's fan newsletter.

The story so far is that Will and Les and Pete (and me as well I suppose) have decided to resurrect the Bunnymen from the grave and get the next album going. The cloud to this silver lining is that Ian is going to press on with his solo work so we will next appear with a new vocalist. Meanwhile upstairs in the eight-track studio, the teach-yourself chord books are all out and the tape machine is blinking in the harsh light of a Liverpool winter after being dragged out from a pile of old camo netting. Still, we've given it a squirt of oil and a serious talking to, and the album is now underway.'
                                          —Jake Brockman, 1988

The Mac-less Bunnymen (or "Bunnymen Mark II," as fans eventually dubbed them) planned to finish the year by doing a one-off single with a mystery guest vocalist. In their first official press announcement since Mac's departure, they quashed rumors by stating that the singer was "not Cilla Black, or, indeed, Pete Wylie or Julian Cope." Rumors that it might be Andrew Eldritch from the Sisters of Mercy went unanswered. The intended mystery vocalist was in fact two vocalists—Kate Pierson and Cindy Wilson from the B-52's. This collaboration never resulted, due to scheduling conflicts while the B-52's remixed their hugely successful *Cosmic Thing* album. With that plan on the rocks, the Bunnymen placed an ad for a full-time singer, someone to "fill a pair of used crocodile shoes—serious applicants only, please, i.e., no divvies!"

1988 closed with the Bunnymen receiving demo tapes by the bucketload, while Mac quietly seethed and worked in isolation on his solo material.

... it was awful. Will and I were crying on each other's shoulders, but at the same time not talking.

—Ian McCulloch, 1995

THE DEATH OF PETE DE FREITAS

For the first half of 1989, there was nothing but silence from both the Bunnymen Mark II and Mac. This silence was shattered on Wednesday, June 14th. Pete de Freitas was heading to Liverpool on his Ducati 900cc from his home in North London. At approximately four in the afternoon, on the A51 in Longdon Green, Staffordshire, his motorcycle collided with a car at a notorious black spot on the road. The 27-year-old drummer died of multiple injuries before he reached the hospital.

Pete was survived by his girlfriend Johnson and their infant daughter, Lucie. Mac and the remaining Bunnymen were all stunned with grief, and declined to speak to the press. As one would expect, the funeral was an extremely emotional affair.

Les was behind me. I think he was the first to crack, then we all just started making animal noises, like you do when your crying is hysterical.
—Ian McCulloch, 1998

The last time I just blubbered uncontrollably was at Pete's funeral. It was just one collective mass blubbering session, where you don't care what you look like or what people will be thinking of you.
—Ian McCulloch, 1994

The following week, both Bill Drummond and Julian Cope expressed their feelings about Pete in the music press.

I always felt Pete was the real organiser within the group. He was the one who could talk to each of them when they weren't talking to each other. And he always loved being in a rock & roll band, living in hotels and all that, while the others loathed touring and only wanted to get back to Liverpool. But Pete had the knack of finding the best of whatever was going on, whether he was living it up in Paris or staying in some grotty little Italian town.
—Bill Drummond, 1989

```
Pete Louis Vincent you are my brother
And I love you and I miss you
Would be very nice if someone could have warned us
And now it's not the same
I'm so very very angry
Love you,
Julian
```
                                                            —Julian Cope, 1989

On August 2nd, a memorial service for Pete and former Pale Fountain Chris McCaffery (a friend of the Bunnymen who'd died suddenly of a brain hemorrhage) was held at Liverpool's Anglican Cathedral. Hundreds of fans, family members, and friends turned up. During the service, "Bedbugs and Ballyhoo" was reverently aired to showcase Pete's drumming talents.

Over a dozen years have passed, and the memory of Pete still looms large with the other Bunnymen.

```
... I think Pete was possibly the greatest rock drummer in the world,
and I wish I'd told him that when he was alive. —Ian McCulloch, 1997
```

```
He was just a top gent. He was young but he was wise. He was a bit
spaced-out, but he'd give you his last quid. Obviously, he was a bril-
liant drummer, but it's more as a mate that I miss him, really.
                                        —Will Sergeant, 2001
```

```
We lived together for two years ... I still think of him every day.
The longer you live, the more people die around you, and you can't
describe it to anyone. Heaven is a place in people's heads. I'm always
thinking of Pete, so that's my Heaven for him. When Pete died I had
this image of him, at the funeral, that he was bouncing from every
star, like a satellite, from Australia and back. —Les Pattinson, 1997
```

Jake Brockman described his time with the Bunnymen as 'the best of times and the worst of times.' "But I would give up every minute of it to be sat on a beach for a few hours, drinking a beer and smoking a spliff with Pete."

Mac had spent most of late 1988 and early 1989 writing and demoing songs, and considering what kind of approach to take with his new material.

I thought, 'I'll write a whole load of weird shit and people'll think I'm still cool and groovy.' But then I thought, 'What's the point?' Most of the people who though I was cool and groovy were dickheads, and they proved themselves to be dickheads, 'cos they're so fickle, and they don't understand concepts, and the journey of songs. That fan mentality, where they're into one group or another, they don't just let that group be a *part* of their life ...   —Ian McCulloch, 1989

Cool, groovy, or otherwise, Mac was certain about two things: he wanted his solo work to emphasize both his vocal abilities and strengths as a writer of intimate, confessional lyrics—something he had rarely attempted in the Bunnymen.

Initially, I thought I'd go European, as a reaction to all that American 'Lips Like Sugar' stuff. I had an idea of using Bulgarian instruments. Then I thought I'd go to Spain and recruit Spaniards in bars.
—Ian McCulloch, 1992

I decided that I wanted to write good lyrics that were about me, that are about something rather than lyrics that were poetic or metaphysical. In music, if you've got an English A-level you're the Poet Laureate ...
—Ian McCulloch, 1994

I don't want to piss about now. I want to be seen as the greatest white male singer.
—Ian McCulloch, 1990

With the Bunnymen, there were songs that were personal to me, especially at the time, because I was enmeshed in them, and would believe every line, but now I can't picture what was going through my head when I wrote them. That is the difference between writing a classic and writing a really cool song. As the Bunnymen, we always wrote really cool stuff, and a few of them were classics. I think the Bunnymen stuff has longevity, but not those elements of songs that can relate to everybody and stand the test of time. I wrote from a more personal angle for the solo material and I can relate to those songs much more now.   —Ian McCulloch, 1994

Mac started recording his first solo album in the spring and summer of 1989. Tracks were laid down at Eurythmics' Church Studio in North London, Orinoco Studios, Tower Bridge Studios, and The Grande Arms, in Paris. Mac played 90% of the guitar parts—"unless I was too bevvied to do me stuff"— in which case producer Ray Schulman took over. Schulman also provided most of the bass, keyboards, and programming. Cure drummer Boris Williams guested on a few tracks, and former Bunnymen roadie Mike "Curly" Jobson sat in on bass for a couple of songs. Honey-voiced Elizabeth Fraser of the Cocteau Twins was called in to provide some backing vocals.

The first results of these sessions were released on August 21, 1989. "Proud To Fall" b/w "Pots of Gold" and "The Dead End" only made it to #51 in the UK charts. (A few weeks later, a version of the single b/w "Everything

Is Real" and a cover of Joni Mitchell's "The Circle Game" failed to increase the record's popularity.) Critical reaction was mixed but largely, surprisingly, supportive.

... a simple, exuberant loveliness that the old Bunnymen, up on their pedestal as 'serious rock artists' would have been hard-pushed to achieve, [with a] sweetly perfect chorus culminating in the tiny, breathy fragment 'inside it all.'   —*NME*, 1989

'Proud To Fall' is a belated and thrilling acknowledgment and celebration of [the Bunnymen's] headstrong uniqueness, a lingering casting-off of the last Bunnymen vestment.   —*NME*, 1989

Mac was uncharacteristically candid to the press about the message behind his new single.

'Proud To Fall' is me saying 'Here I am again.' It's about why I left the band, and abut why anybody has to leave and face up to what they're becoming.   —Ian McCulloch, 1990

... it's about being proud of the lows as much as the highs, and that I actually did it. The line 'I never really told you who I was/it must have been because, because, because' I really like. Because I think that's what I've tried to do ... give a little bit more of myself to the listener. I think, in that line, I was also kind of singing to meself as well. 'Cos I think of how I've juggled about with different, not personas, but angles of meself. Even in interviews, one minute I'm doing this heavy kind of sincere, sensitive thing. And the next I'm sounding pissed out of me head, slagging everyone off.   —Ian McCulloch, 1990

In the past McCulloch has deserved—and abused—his position as one of pop's most charismatic figures, combining rebel-boy sexiness with almost vampyric [sic] otherness. Unfortunately, 'Proud To Fall' sounds like he's got ready and gone public without checking his hair in the mirror first.   —*Melody Maker*, 1989

PROUD TO FALL

Here you come again
Acting like a saviour
There you go again
Talking like a stranger
You said we all must learn to face
What we're becoming
And then I saw you in the distance
Off and running

But from start to finish
I was proud to fall
And I fell so deep within it
I got lost inside it all
Inside it all
Inside it all

Looks like rain again
Feels like it's rained forever
Can't remember when
Don't remember whether
I ever really told you who I was
It must have been because because
Because

From start to finish
I was proud to fall
And I fell so deep within it
I got lost inside it all
Inside it all
Inside it all

I fell between the bruises
And the red curtain call
I prayed you'd light the fuses
And we'd burn and torch it all

Long day's journey into
Long night's journey out
Knee-deep, so deep within you
I kept and keep without

You said we all must learn to face
What we're becoming
And then I saw you in the mirror
Off and running

But from start to finish ...

POTS OF GOLD

I'm gonna roll down the mountain
I tried so hard to climb
And choose a different ambition
This time

One by one goes everyone
In search of little pots of gold
When each little pot is gone
They look for something else to hold
Heads in the sand
Sinking sand

I'm gonna jump in that fountain
And drink it 'til it's dry
'Til all that I've been missing
Is mine

One by one goes everyone
Believe it all, we're taught and told
The human race in the marketplace
I'll be bought and you'll be sold
Heads in the sand
Sinking sand

Don't tell me that you're happy
No one's happy with themselves
We all want to be somebody
Somebody else

Pots of gold

THE DEAD END

Is it real or imitation
Life, the big and black dead end
All these hand-me-down emotions
Just a mask to help pretend
That I'm gonna leave this station
A happy man among sad men

Take your chance
It's now or never
And then it's passed
Forever

Are you planning to remain
On the outside looking in
'Cos everything be all in vain
And all the chances be so slim
Sad to see you all still waiting
For your boat to come back in

Take your chance
It's now or never
And then it's passed
Forever
Hold this time
And capture it
And make your final wish

EVERYTHING IS REAL

Don't try to hide, don't try to run
We can and shall overcome
Never conceal but don't
    you reveal
What you think and believe

Nothing lasts forever
Everything is real ...

Blow up balloons, blow up the world
It's the same old heartache
Just as I thought, it just goes
    to show
I wish I knew then, 'cos now I
    know

Nothing lasts forever
Everything is true ...
    Oh God, where am I now?

I don't care anymore. I'm great, I'm the best liar in the world. It's great being a good liar, and especially being sexy with it. At the end of the day, you've got to be sexy. Anyway, that last hour, that's the best interview there's ever been. Go home and transcribe that. I am that man. Again.
        —Ian McCulloch, 1989

Mac loved his new single, and, armed with that pride, he once more uncaged his ferocious ego and razor wit.

I'll probably be the greatest legend in the world. I'll be the next Lou Reed with the mellowness of Leonard Cohen. I'm a multi-schizophrenic; there are about fifteen Ian McCullochs—but only three of them are in the room at the moment.
        —Ian McCulloch, 1990

I'm sure this time next year I'll be reinstated as the icon of ... icons. I think I've gotta lead the nation. Again. Out of these dark times. Such a long summer as well. It's time for some bleak. The next album title: 'Loadsa Bleak.'
        —Ian McCulloch, 1989

By the time the single hit the streets, Mac had formed a backing band. The Prodigal Sons consisted of four relative unknowns: Edgar Summertime on bass, Mike Mooney on lead guitar, John McCevoy on rhythm guitar and keyboards, and Steve Humphries on drums. Since most of the hastily recruited group were considerably younger than Mac, it was suggested that he was attempting to feed off fresh blood, in the hopes that it would provide an inspiration and vitality that he himself had lost.

Nope. I didn't want it to be vampirical. They're nice fellows and they respect me, but it's mutual. I let them do their thing, but I also want it to be tight, not overplayed. It's their garagey approach and my experience in crafting songs which gives it the energy, something I was missing at the end of the Bunnymen.   —Ian McCulloch, 1990

From the start, Mac the Knife and His Eight-Legged Groove Machine were determined to distance themselves from the dense, brooding sound and ominous image that were still considered Bunnymen trademarks.

With the Bunnymen, there was a fight to be heard. The new songs haven't got the clutter and I've got more space.   —Ian McCulloch, 1990

I think this band is a lot warmer than the Bunnymen were. There's more communication. That's the big difference. In the Bunnymen concerts, we'd come out to the sounds of Gregorian monk chants. This time around, [we'll] come out to stuff from *The Sound of Music*. It works.
          —Ian McCulloch, 1990

Although he was shedding some of the oppressive vestments of the past, Mac wasn't willing to dispose completely of the image that he'd spent years carefully cultivating: the legendary gravity-defying hairstyle would remain aloft. In fact, when Mac heard that Aero-Tek, his favorite brand of hairspray, might be taken off the market, due to the damage it was causing the ozone layer, he promptly went out and purchased 24 cases of the stuff.

The ozone layer ... we're all supposed to be worried about that. But spraying me hair—it's probably in me Top 10 favourite things to do. I don't give a crap what I spray on me head. So asking me to be worried abut the soddin' greenhouse effect, it's crap. Sod it. You begin to think 'Is everybody really waiting for me to write a song about pollution?' It'd be like soddin' Beethoven sitting down to knock something out and thinking 'I wonder what the ozone layer's doing today?'
          —Ian McCulloch, 1989

CANDLELAND

On September 15, Mac's first solo album, *Candleland*—dedicated to Pete de Freitas, Chris McCaffery, and Bob McCulloch—was unveiled by WEA. Critical pens were tentative but laudatory.

… to keep the head held high remains the guiding principle of McCulloch's first solo venture, even if the record is positively autumnal in its sense of palpable regret … [a] sense of wonder, of deep contemplation runs throughout these songs. The tunes and lyrics on *Candleland* are McCulloch's best since *Ocean Rain*, and his vocals pull off the difficult task of evoking wonder in a style usually reserved for world-weariness. *Candleland* is an enormously charming record …   —*Q*, 1989

… a tremendous record; not an exercise in morbidity but rather the product of experience. An album full of the dark, majestic presence of the past, but alive with newer qualities: maturity, self-mastery, grace. *Candleland* is everything you wanted it to be and more. What has gone in the way of young buck braggadocio has been replaced by a clear-eyed sense of resolve.   —*NME*, 1989

Reviewers picked up on the mature tone and melancholy themes of reflection and resignation that wove themselves throughout the album. This was a different Mac than the slagging, swaggering, bitter-swilling youth they'd grown accustomed to.

The Liverpool Lip, scattergun dispenser of prickly pop propaganda and raucous rock rhetoric … self-absorbed sex kitten numero uno … the Mona Lisa in a gray gabardine, notorious over-indulger … all 'round self-appointed el scally supremo, the big cheese, the kingpin, the top dog, God's bleedin' gift and then some … has changed. He is still the sporter of the finest and most influential haircut in popular music, and the trademark army greatcoat has survived, too. [But] the owner of rock's greatest-ever lips, and the biggest kid in pop, has grown up.   —*NME*, 1989

Mac agreed.

Although [the album] is reflective, it's not whinging. That's the good thing about growing older. I never set out to make a concept LP, but

… a barren, vacant LP. Not in the sense of a lack of tunes or feelings; rather it's terminally, gravely open, an expanse of empty sound. Given the grief he's been through, this is perhaps the only album Mac could have made right now, the emotions it conjures the only ones he has been left with.
—*Sounds*, 1989

Majestic, magical, and mysterious. —*Time Out*, 1989

I've been through times when you're a kid who feels like a star, and been a star feeling like a kid, and now I have become a man—whatever that is.
—Ian McCulloch, 1989

Candleland was sort of an end to a period in my life—sort of an epitaph or whatever for the Bunnymen from age 20 to 30.
—Ian McCulloch, 1992

obviously it has got a theme. It's about me at various stages really. It starts with 'The Flickering Wall,' which has me as a child of nine in that bedroom in Norris Green, and so on. There's a kind of chronology, but it's not a sad growing old or anything like that, just a sort of journey ...
—Ian McCulloch, 1989

Candleland is partially dealing with the loss of a lot of things, and a lot of hope. It wasn't entirely dedicated to Pete or me dad; most of it was dedicated to me.
—Ian McCulloch, 1990

Mac's lyrics, printed in their entirety on the inner sleeve, were especially praised for their poetic, candid intimacy. If nothing else, *Candleland* marked a crucial turning point with Mac's approach to song words.

With the Bunnymen I never felt that easy about writing personal lyrics. It was always cloaked in otherworldliness. I felt pressure from Will more than anyone, because I think he shied away from that side of stuff. I wrote the way I wanted to, by and large, but there were certain times ...
—Ian McCulloch, 1990

[Songwriting is] therapeutic ... certainly *Candleland* was. Since that album I decided that I want my songs to matter to me. Well, they have always mattered, but now I need to be in there with the thick of the lyrics, and know exactly what I am writing about. I have gone through that phase of using snappy lines that I did in the Bunnymen. Will used to say 'I love all that imagery you use, all that weird stuff' and I would think, 'What's he soddin' on about?' —Ian McCulloch, 1994

The voice that used to border on the religious is now more human that holy, and the lyrics that used to storm hell now paint a more realistic picture.
—*CMJ New Music Report*, 1989

That album, to me, has the best set of lyrics that I have ever written. It's all about me, from boyhood to Bunnymen, then thrown into this wilderness where my dad died and I left the band. It was a weird, confused time, and although I felt dead weak, I was really rejuvenated—and my dad was with me all the way.
—Ian McCulloch, 1994

Although the album was similar, stylistically, to some of the more song-oriented Echo & the Bunnymen material, it was also markedly quieter, almost hushed.

The softness of the album wasn't intentional, but it wasn't unintentional. It just came out that way. I didn't really want to come out with an album full of bluster. If it's tentative at all, it's because that's what I was feeling, and a lot of the feelings were tentative. It's meant to be ... enchanting.
—Ian McCulloch, 1990

Candleland was the most introspective I've ever been. I didn't realize it at the time. I knew I was writing songs that were personal, lyrics that were detailed and about specific emotional things, but while I was doin' it, I thought I was rockin' out. 'Cos when you're in the studio, you're playing loud. But when I listen to it now, if and when I play it, I can see how introspective it was. Which is fine, but I can see why people who buy records prefer things that give them a kick.
—Ian McCulloch, 1992

The artistic strengths of the album were not matched by sales. Although it came in strongly at #18 in the UK charts, it quickly descended to #40, then to #69, before disappearing entirely. It was clear that, without the Bunnymen name behind him, and the growing focus on the dance-oriented baggy rave culture, Mac's star status was not quite what it used to be. Mac was well aware of this.

I have my public to think of, you know—all 300 of 'em.
—Ian McCulloch, 1990

For all I know, people aren't interested anymore in emotive, confessional writing.
—Ian McCulloch, 1989

THE FLICKERING WALL

In my world, my little world
Life lies upon the floor
The wind blows in and out again
Through windows and through doors
And it's there I'll look and it's
    there I'll find
What it was I started after
When I mistook what I had in mind
For something made to matter

I heard the footsteps in the street
I saw the lights on the
    flickering wall
I moved my lips but I couldn't speak
Choked on the wonder of it all
Choked on the wonder
Of it all

In my dreams, recurring dreams
But I was never there
Life so still invisible
Just needing to be where
With any luck I might just find
What it was I started after
When I undertook what I had
    in mind
When everything mattered

When I saw the gods up in the sky
I saw the lights on the
    flickering wall
I saw the world through hazel eyes
And choked on the wonder of it all
Choked on the wonder
Of it all

'The Flickering Wall' opens the album boldly and in a shower of light. A raid on the storehouse of McCulloch's memory. Some things you notice immediately: the voice hasn't sounded this good in five years; it's acquired a warm, lived-in gravity that makes the central phrase 'choked on the wonder of it all' instantly memorable.
—*NME*, 1989

... a somber, mournful, yet surprisingly uptempo mesh of brushed drums and light fingered bass, it's not so much obsessed by death as with the space and emotional vacuum such loss creates. It's as though a violently personal revelation is taking place. —*Sounds*, 1989

'The White Hotel' clearly owes more than its title to D.M. Thomas's novel of several years ago. Enigmatic images of alpine peaks and railway carriages and a great, ringing chorus at the song's heart.   —*NME*, 1989

D.M. Thomas's *The White Hotel* is fantastic and I have recommended it to people around the world. It's about a woman who meets Sigmund Freud's son on a train going through Europe and she writes letters to Sigmund telling him all about it. Then it goes into this really long poem. It's so beautiful, sexy, and mad that I re-read it all the time.

     —Ian McCulloch, 2001

'The Cape' falls flat. Here the full meshing of keyboards and guitars evokes dread memories of Ultravox. A pedestrian affair with ideas above its station.

     —*NME*, 1989

THE WHITE HOTEL

I want to be on that white-capped
     mountain peak
Above the lake, above my station
A moving carriage
The perfect marriage
Of life apart from destination

Ringing all the bells
Down at the white hotel
Tonight

I want to write the letters of
     persecution
To someone I don't know who
     doesn't know me
I want to be the dust inside
     a vacuum
An ice cube frozen in the melting sea

Ringing all the bells
Down at the white hotel
Ringing all the bells
Down at the white hotel
Tonight

'The White Hotel' [offers] a smattering of Blue Oyster Cult, a cataract of chopping chords, and a melody that swerves off-kilter at all the right times. If it doesn't exactly roar, at least it purrs with some purpose.   —*Melody Maker*, 1989

THE CAPE

All confused and all-consuming
Scaled the heights of dizzy love
Didn't know how vertigo
Could leave me in the balance of
My heart and all the gods above
Stung and all strung up

It's only navigation
So I'm moving overground
Past the cape of levitation
I'll keep hanging in when all the
     chips are down

Wooden houses, telegraph poles
Gave me reason and my shape
Casting shadows, marking pathways
Signposts showing our escape
Signposts showing our escape
The day, the time, the place

It's only navigation
So I'm moving overground
Past the cape of all temptation
I'll keep hanging in when all
     the chips are down

All aboard and all or nothing
All for one and one for all
The information must be hidden
Not not not for one and all
Not not not for one and all
One push and we will fall

It's only navigation
So I'm moving overground
Past the cape of levitation
I'll keep hanging in
When all the chips are down

CANDLELAND

Get your handful of remembrance
For you to sprinkle through your life
In between the penance
That you carry by your side
With the make-belief and miracles
That only come alive

In Candleland
Candleland

Wear your guilt like skin
And keep your sins disguised
Take some salt and sugar
And rub it in your eyes
You'll know that something's left you
Just as you arrive

In Candleland
Candleland

I walked back inside me
I'd gone back for my youth
As I came down the fire escape
It must have stayed up on the roof
They say you just know
And that knowing is the proof

Of Candleland
Candleland

It's one of the most lyrically honest and least obscure things I've ever written. Candleland is a place where you go to shed your skin every time it needs shedding. It's a place where you go to change, and it's a nice place, but it's a sad place as well.
—Ian McCulloch, 1990

Childlike innocence and mystery, a twinkling maze of fairly lights. Somewhere between a carol, a lullaby, and Lou Reed. Exquisite.   —NME, 1989

With my dad dying, there were references to that Aboriginal place, that place where I am hopefully going but have been there all my life, where I find out who I am. That magical feeling you get. I used to get that feeling a lot when I was a kid, almost like a flashback, say certain smells, that transport you back for a split second. 'Candleland' was about that place that I have left, but every now and then I get taken back to. There's a lot of guilt in there ... Catholic guilt about nothing, just something you are born with. I don't know ... it's basically just the blues.   —Ian McCulloch, 1994

… recalls the halcyon days of the Bunnymen. Powerful, dramatic cadences dovetailed with the incandescent, orchestral figures that made 'Silver' and 'Seven Seas' such great singles. —*NME,* 1989

It deals with clues that are scattered through your life that largely go ignored until it's too late.
—Ian McCulloch, 1990

… a startlingly frank song about death. —*The San Diego Union Tribune,* 1990

HORSE'S HEAD

A single rose
The curtains closed
A stranger's clothes
Were all I found
The great unknown
The tightrope show
A world below
Don't look down
Don't look down
Don't look down

Horse's head found in a bed
Broke the code and braved
    the weather
Wore a gown of chestnut brown
Fingers crossed that there's
    a Heaven
Heaven ...

Found a scroll
And ancient bones

A million ghosts
Were all around
The great unknown
The tightrope show
A world below
Don't look down
Don't look down
Don't look down

Horse's head found in a bed
Broke the code and changed
    the weather
Wore a gown of chestnut brown
Fingers crossed that there's
    a Heaven
Heaven ...

I found a scroll
And ancient bones
A million ghosts were all
    around ...

FAITH AND HEALING

Everyone was running scared
Someone talked and someone heard
The twisted end to all the words
That I'd hung on to
One more time inside the dream
Where nothing has to be this real
And I don't ever have to feel
What I don't want to

You once said I thought too much
But never thought enough to touch
Eyes so sad
Evergreen
The saddest eyes I've ever seen

Lost all reason and belonging
Can't do right for doing wrong and
I don't like the way I'm feeling
Need your faith healing
    healing healing
Faith and healing ...

Pick me up and hold me there
Leave me hanging in the air
'Til I promise I will care
The way I used to
Diamonds in the pool tonight
Reminds me of what nights were like
Before I fell into a life
That I got used to

The shining sea, the silver sky
A perfect world before my eyes
Don't be scared, don't you cry
If all the world goes passing by

Lost all reason and belonging
Can't do right for doing wrong and
I don't like the way I'm feeling
Need your faith, faith and healing
Faith and healing ...

You once said I thought too much
But never thought enough to touch

… a stab at the pale-boy-beneath-the-strobes of New Order, but nobody's heart is really in it, and the song is soon exposed as a tired rehash of wilted post-punk mannerisms. —*Melody Maker,* 1990

'Faith and Healing' is built around an unremitting cybernetic pulse and some clanging guitar shapes reminiscent of New Order, though it discards the Mancunians' detachment in favor of a rueful gusto for life.
—*NME*, 1989

I KNOW YOU WELL

Is your mind made up or willing
To be changed or to stay true?
Are you primed to make
    the killing
Or too scared to follow through?
When all the blood is spilling
Will it be to real for you?

I know you well
I know you well
I know you well
Yes I know you well

When everything is hollow
Holiness will call for you
And I will have to follow
And you will follow too
Will all those silver dollars
Be enough to see us through?

They know us well
They know us well
They know us well
Yes they know us well

Is your mind made up or willing
To be changed, stay true?
Are you primed to make
    the killing
Or too scared to follow through?
When all the blood is spilling
Will it pour right out of you?

You know me well
You know me well
You know me well
Yes you know me well

You know me well

Songs like the guilt-edged and cello-riddled 'I Know You Well' make brave motions towards wistful elegance, but all you want to do is press 10p into the man's hand and run a mile.
—*Melody Maker*, 1989

... a solemn, poignant tune under-pinned by a luxuriant string arrangement —*NME*, 1989

IN BLOOM

Think twice
And do it
Stale life
Don't chew it
Cloud lands
Fog reason
Blue skies
Wrong season

So soon
Vanishing days
Perfume
Of old bouquets

Rice fields
Feet soaking
Minefields
Here's hoping

So soon
Vanishing days
Perfume
Of old bouquets

In bloom ...

Think twice
And do it
Stale life
Don't chew it
Cloud lands
Fog reason
Blue skies
Wrong season

So soon
Vanishing days
Perfume
Of dead bouquets

In bloom ...

McCulloch sounds as if he's cocked an ear to My Bloody Valentine, Spacemen 3, and the like and thought, 'Pah, upstarts.' A howling raga of trance-dance rock with lyrics that combine silliness and luminosity. —*NME*, 1989

Here, a choking, empty guitar straight out of *Porcupine* slaps into another jaunty guitar and blends with the pulse of Schulman's disco beat.
—*Sounds*, 1989

An effortlessly touching reflection on the passage of time that evokes the sleeve dedications to Ian's dad, Pete de Freitas, and Chris of the Pale Fountains. Framed as it is amidst pizzicato strings and an autumnal tide of keyboards, it's a perfect ending.

—*NME*, 1989

There's a line that I didn't write, it just came out of my mouth in the middle eight. It goes 'nothing dies, nothing ever dies' and I'm living proof of that; me dad hasn't died, he lives in me.

—Ian McCulloch, 1989

A kind of 'All My Life' for strings and nylon-strung guitar

—*Q*, 1989

START AGAIN

Woke up sad
When am I ever gonna learn?
It's in my head
But I can't say the words

I had it in my hands
Lost my nerve
Gave it and I got it
In return

One day
I'll come around
Wonder when
I'll turn around
And start again

My fingerprints
Have left their traces
On all the things
The people and the places

I ever felt
And felt a part of
I touched the life
And kissed the heart of

One day
I'll come around
Wonder when
I'll turn around
And start again

Nothing dies
Nothing ever dies

Woke up sad
When am I ever gonna learn?
It's in my head
Time to take my turn

I had it in my hands
Lost my nerve
Gave it and I got it
In return

One day
I'll come around
Wonder when
I'll turn around
And start again

Wonder when ...

... something happened after the initial mourning period. I felt that [my Dad] was with me all the time, an even stronger bond. I can't really invite him over for tea anymore, but every time I eat a meal, he's gonna be eating it with me, and that way he will be over for tea.

—Ian McCulloch, 1990

With the solo stuff I was very much more fragile and I was looking for help, for real things, much less self-mythologising. I knew then that I am as fragile as the next bloke. That's why *Candleland* is the most autobiographical album, and, on that record, 'Start Again' is *the* track.

—Ian McCulloch, 1994

TOAD

Feeling strange and unsure
In the place where I'm standing
Feeling stained and impure
And I'm frightened of landing
Tie a flag on my head
Take a walk on a moonbeam
Just forget what she said
She doesn't know what she means

Five fingers and four divisions
That was all I ever counted
Love provided with all provisions
That was all I ever wanted

No escape from the truth
No return from the deep
Just a failure in faith
And a hunch in a heap
Stop the light coming in
Tell the day not to break
Let the night draw me in
And the walls not to shake

Call out the fire engines
Let's go down in a blaze of glory
Turn all the hosepipes on and
Bring in the hanging jury
Hang 'em high

We're cleaning the city now

I've become a cynic again, which I'm glad about. 'Cos I've got a target again. All the turds in the world who think they know something that they don't ... on one of the B-sides there's a line that goes 'Turn all the hosepipes on and bring in the hanging jury,' and I do believe that we've got to clear all this shite up. It's a call for some vigilantism, I suppose.   —Ian McCulloch, 1989

FEAR OF THE KNOWN

When the night descends because
    of you
And the darkness is your point of view
Loneliness belongs only to you
Nothing is the only thing to do

Fear of the known
Walking the pavement

When the road's a voyage you
    can't make
And the role's a part you've had
    to fake
When godliness has sucked away
    your hope
And hopelessness is hanging by a rope

When will it happen?
How does it end?
Never to happen
Ever again

Fear of the known
Walking the pavement
Fear of the known
Slipping and sliding

Loneliness belongs only to you
Nothing is the only thing to do

When will it happen?
How does it end?
Never to happen
Ever again

... swings and swivels so suavely and self-assuredly ... it has the same effect as 'Bedbugs and Ballyhoo,' only with a completely different sway rhythm. The stabbing, distorted, spindly guitar in the choruses both soars and cuts, which is a great effect.
        —The Big Takeover, 1990

... a great song, the most rockin' thing Mac has recorded since he left Echo.
—*The Big Takeover*, 1990

ROCKET SHIP

Walls close in and scrutinize
The shape I'm in, all paralyzed
Under my skin I'm hypnotized
In the spirit
Just want to fly

On a rocket ship
To the great beyond
Gonna take a trip
Getting so far gone
'Cos you make me weak
And you make me strong
Until I almost feel
I could be someone
Be someone

All the things I never used
Had the choice, I couldn't choose
Roads so long, black avenues

On a rocket ship
To the great beyond
Gonna take a trip
Getting so far gone

'Cos you make me weak
And you make me strong
Until I almost feel
I could be someone
Be someone

Take what's yours and take it boldly
Boldly go and tread so coldly
The drop is sheer and never holy
Just you and you alone
Ride the wave when it comes crashing
Be the knight in a shining costume
Slay the dragons if they're asking
For what you've always known

Armies in control, soldiers on
    the march
Sentries on patrol, danger in the dark
Optimism-isms, heard but never seen
Swept ashore somewhere, desert
    island dream

On a rocketship
To the great beyond
Gonna take a trip
Getting so far gone
So far gone

BIG DAYS

There I was
Read the news out of a comic
D'you remember us?
We had dreams just like
    those rockets
And were heading for the moon
They were heading for the moon

Home is where the house is
House where the toys stay
The sky always blue
With the noises of big days

In true low
I was hotter than the others
In a world below
They were floating down the gutters
And the tide was coming in
And the tide was coming in

Home is where the house is
House where the toys stay
The sky always blue
With the noises of big days

Big days
All my big days ...
All mine

THE WORLD IS FLAT

Soul sucked and drowned
Woodchips on the sidings
Phased and dazed I found
My star was out and smiling
Life's song, and shining

You say you're gonna be someone
Ian's gonna make you smile
Still waiting for the day
    to come
'Til then you'll be a
    Wednesday's child

Opposites attract
Nothing's ever chosen
Gravity is fact
And every moment frozen
A gilded golden

You tell me that you know someone
Who says that you're his
    favorite girl
He's gonna give you all you want
'Cos all you want's his little world

The world is flat ...

I was in a dream
With beauty dressed, and
    I killed
Some babies born in boxes
And Jesus on a hill
And I felt evil

You said you know the world is flat
Nothings gonna change your mind
You know the only way is back
To gather what you've
    left behind

The world is flat ...
For Wednesday's child

WASSAILING IN THE NIGHT

One of these days, one of these
    bad days
You're gonna see me smile
One of those days, one of those
    good days
I'll be out in style
Out of the shadows
Out of the rain
Over the rainbow
Over all the pain

In my own glow, in my own lifetime
You make the world go 'round
Walking the road, walking
    the high wire
With my world so far down
Never the same
Never will be
Never again
Heaven for me
Me

Stopped being scared of
    getting older
I must've changed inside
The weight of the world off
    my shoulders
Traveling light and blind
Sick of defending
Who I became
Tired of pretending
I'd never change
Change

Make it all come true

★★★

In October 1989, Mac kicked off his first UK, European, and U.S. tours at Liverpool's Bluecoat Chambers. Although the shows were a little rough around the edges, they acted as both a nod to the past and a determined gaze toward the future. More structured Bunnymen classics such as "Rescue," "The Cutter," and "The Killing Moon," were dusted off, and "Rocket Ship,"

After a noticeably hesitant start, this return to live action ultimately proved an unqualified success for Ian McCulloch, perhaps the most enduring of all of Liverpool's favourite sons ... the new songs shone hardest overall, demonstrating both a new maturity in McCulloch's writing abilities and a greater range and authority in his voice. Thoroughly captivating stuff. File under continued longevity, please.   —*Sounds*, 1989

Here he is! Mac the Mouth, Mac the lip, Mac back in a sea of dry ice with his rock star ego! Mac in his leather trousers! [He] plays a fine set tonight. Really, it's hard to differentiate between his Bunnymen and solo material. He always was the band anyway, and now we get his clever, quasi-mystical words buried in ice and brooding chords, moments of high drama and tension, tapped with teasing and distance. McCulloch's always had a tight grip on the rock idiom, on rises and falls, but now he's so professional it's untrue. He's still a prime rock messiah ...   —*Melody Maker*, 1989

"Damnation," "Honeydrip," and "Fear of the Known" indicated in no uncertain terms that Mac's songwriting knife still sliced. These sets also included a devil-may-care take on The Velvet Underground classic "Sweet Jane," and a stunning show-stopper in New Order's "Ceremony." While not quite the Bunnymen at their peak, there was little doubt about the quality of Mac's show.

Well, what did you expect? A new start? The past? Perfection? Mistakes? You could get all of these at the hometown debut solo gig. It's good, but it's not mythical yet. Things are rhythmically melodic (with a touch of Lou Reed) or toying with Doors dynamics. You can pick out the worst or the best, depending on what you expected, but it was the cumulative brilliance of the evening that gave it its power, and the mixture of turbulence, calm, and exuberance that made it so right.   —Journalist Penny Kiley

That tour was pretty much a thrash through the songs, and I quite liked it. After the Bunnymen, people were expecting a finely honed show and we were just busking it, getting bevvied every night. I wanted it to be a bit untidy, ramshackle and stuff. —Ian McCulloch, 1997

Eager to turn McCulloch into an international solo star, WEA released a remix of the radio-friendly "Faith and Healing" on November 6th. The B-sides "Toad," "Fear of the Known," and "Rocket Ship" were all written and recorded with the Prodigal Sons. Despite Mac's fairly successful tours, the single flopped, barely scratching the top 100 in the UK charts. On April 30, 1990, Warner Brothers offshoot East/West tried again, releasing a new Gil Norton-produced version of "Candleland," b/w "Big Days," "The World Is Flat," and "Wassailing In the Night." Although the new version of the song shimmered, it was met with similarly discouraging commercial results. A light, throwaway, almost *vaudevillian* jaunt through Elvis Presley's "Return To Sender" featured on the *NME*'s *Last Temptation of Elvis* tribute LP in the spring of 1990 proved almost as worrisome. Clearly, if Mac was destined to become a solo superstar, it wasn't going to be on the tails of his most recent material.

Turquoise Days |

As Mac was putting the finishing touches on *Candleland*, Pete, Les, Will, and Jake, now an official Bunnyman, had been jamming together on 12 new wordless originals, plus cover versions of The Byrds' chiming "Turn, Turn, Turn" and The Modern Lovers' proto-punk classic "Roadrunner" in a warehouse-cum-studio they'd jointly purchased. Their search for a new singer had been fruitless until April 1989, when Will played a record that had been lying around his flat, unplayed, for months.

The manager of St. Vitus Dance gave me their album a long time ago, but I never got 'round to listening to it because my turntable was broken. When I heard it, I knew [the singer was] our man.
                                                                                    —Will Sergeant, 1990

The defunct St. Vitus Dance had only made one LP, *Love Me, Love My Dogma,* which had been released on Liverpool's Probe Plus Records. After spinning the disc, Will rushed into rehearsal, waving the record and shouting "This is the bloke! This is the bloke!" The band agreed that singer Noel Burke's strong, plummy voice, which bore a passing resemblance to that of 60's crooner Scott Walker, would work well within the context of the Bunnymen sound.

There's no way I would have been interested if long overcoats were involved.
                    —Noel Burke, 1990

But did Burke look the part? Will and Jake began hanging around the bookshop where Noel worked in an attempt to assess his visual viability. After a day or two of ducking behind shelves in the gardening section, surreptitiously sizing up Noel, it was determined that he would do nicely. A meeting was arranged in a local pub.

I was well worried at the start. I thought this could be a bit dodgy, like a cabaret band doing old Bunnymen songs. I had horrible visions. So the first time I met them in the pub, I was really stand-offish and non-committal. Everything was there, though. Did they want somebody to be a Mac clone? Oh no, they said, that ain't good. So I gave it a go.   —Noel Burke, 1990

For the first time in ages, it finally felt like things were going the Bunnymen's way. Their optimism was sharply and cruelly quelled when, just a few short weeks after Noel tentatively agreed to front the band, Pete de Freitas was killed. The blow was excruciating on both a personal and professional level, and, for the first time, Will and Les seriously considered burying the Bunnymen name for good. A Mac-less Bunnymen was a tough enough prospect for many people to consider, but the band without *two* of its definitive members seemed almost insurmountable. Eventually, Will and Les reasoned that if they didn't carry on, Pete's death would have been in vain, as he was killed on his way to meet Noel for the first time.

So after a few weeks of mourning, the band dusted off the old drum machine and began creating music. By the end of October, Noel quit his job at the bookshop and was hired as the band's full-time singer. His vocals were distinct, almost quaint, and he had a deft hand at writing lyrics, something that Jake considered lucky, "because everything we tried sounded like something off a cereal box."

The group recruited drummer Damon Reece, a friend of Jake's who happened by the Bunnymen flat to fix Brockman's motorbike. Although Reece was talented behind the kit, no one could ever really replace Pete, whose picture was permanently affixed in Bunnymen rehearsal rooms, and where, by December 1989, the band had eight brand new songs.

In mid-March 1990, the Bunnymen Mark II played their first live dates, three shows at a fundraiser for the Marsh Lane Community Centre in Bootle, Liverpool. Advertised under the banner "Reverberation," an old 13th Floor Elevators song that the Bunnymen performed each evening, the gigs showcased new Bunnymen material and time-tested classics like "Zimbo," "A Promise," and "Over the Wall." Julian Cope was rumored to be the support act (possibly to indicate that any rift between him and the Bunnymen was entirely Mac's doing), but that never materialized. Instead, amiable popsters Benny Profane and art-funk act Tadzio supported. In the middle of each set, Bill Drummond and his new project, The Kopyright Liberation Front ("The KLF") joined in with a seven-minute version of their "What Time Is Love?". In fact, the Bunnymen Mark II's first appearance on vinyl would be on the KLF's "What Time is Love?" 12-inch, "The Echo & the Bunnymen Mix." Opinions of the Bootle shows varied widely.

And whither the Bunnymen? It's hard to say. Their forte was always the dressing up of essentially simple tunes in mystic drapery; the cultivation of atmospheres. But tonight there was too much that seemed mere bombast, the hollow clang of rhetoric, and a rock band going through its paces.   —*NME*, 1990

Still, the band seemed to have come to terms with Mac's departure.

I knew we were going to be all right when this lad came up to us after the second night at Marsh Lane and said that it was the best that he'd ever seen the Bunnymen, and that we should have got rid of Mac years ago.   —Les Pattinson, 1990

I'm glad Ian left. I didn't want to see us go down a soft path. Leave that stuff to Harry Connick, Jr. Ian wanted to be the ultimate pop star. And he can't take any criticism.
                    —Les Pattinson, 1990

We're very much a team now, and there's no secrets. Mac was a different score, because we never knew what he was thinking or what he wanted.   —Will Sergeant, 1990

Will in particular was enjoying himself, and was looking forward to the new options the Bunnymen Mark II provided.

It's the best time I've had in ages.   —Will Sergeant, 1990

We're not out to prove anything. The only important thing is to know you're not conning yourself, and we never stopped feeling like a group. All I'd say is don't come with any set ideas. Don't come with a dead head on.   —Will Sergeant, 1990

Although Mac didn't attend the Bootle shows, he didn't mince words when it came to "The Bogusmen," as he called them.

Maybe people like records that have a certain name on 'em, rather than what's on 'em.   —Ian McCulloch 1989

It's like The Velvet Underground without Lou Reed doing the record *Squeeze*. It's so sad.   —Ian McCulloch, 1990

In mid-May 1990, the Bunnymen Mark II went to Ridge Farm in Surrey to record with producer Geoff Emerick, who'd engineered The Beatles' *Revolver* and *Sgt. Pepper's Lonely Heart's Club Band*. The band were naturally impressed with those credentials, as well as with Emerick's habit of sitting on the stairs outside the studio to "listen to the mix properly." The provisional title of the resulting album, "Bedazzled," was eventually changed to *Reverberation*—again in reference to the 13th Floor Elevators song.

The first single from these sessions was released on Warner Brothers in early November, 1990. "Enlighten Me" b/w "Lady Don't Fall Backwards" (the title taken from a classic 60's Hitchcock episode) received fairly indifferent reviews, and barely scratched the UK top 100. Critics responded warmly to the full-length album.

Reverberation definitely gets better with increased listening—Sergeant and Pattinson are still quite remarkable musicians and arrangers—and, God knows, there's more power in this record than any Bunnymen record for years.   —*NME*, 1990

Dripping trippily with sitars, tabla, and backwards guitar loops,

We used to do loads of weird things, and then over the last few tours we were just a rock & roll band again. But now we can get away with anything…
—Will Sergeant, 1990

[Noel Burke] has come through under pressure, and done good. On 'King of Your Castle' the whole shooting match comes alive. He turns as good a meaningful/meaningless couplet as Mac ever did. He's got an impossible act to follow, but I reckon he belongs here.
—*Melody Maker*, 1990

Reverberation allowed Will to explore his passion for retro psychedelia more than ever before. It was undoubtedly Will who decided to market the Bunnymen as "The Most Psychedelic Band in the Cosmos."

Immediately after the release of *Reverberation*, the Bunnymen embarked on a 17-date tour. Forgoing the vast majority of the Cosmos, they instead focused on Ireland and the UK.

Tonight the Bunnymen are an object lesson in experience in how to survive and prosper. And 'Silver,' 'Enlighten Me,' and 'Gone Gone Gone'— all were so vital, I wish I'd bootlegged them, for Chrissakes. Top gear. Now I'll buy it: Ian who? —*Melody Maker*, 1990

But as any band will tell you, good live reviews don't necessarily translate into album sales, and such was the case with *Reverberation*, which, these days, is a staple in record shop bargain bins. At the start of 1991, the Bunnymen were unceremoniously dropped from Warner Brothers, their home for 11 years.

Undaunted and feeling freed from the confines of major label dictates, the Bunnymen toured France and did a one-off stopover in Spain, then played one near sold-out gig at the University of London. By this time, the band had dropped all old material in their live set, claiming they'd only included it previously because of a shortage of new songs. The live reviews were stronger than ever.

The way the Bunnymen sound now belongs neither to a particular past or a particular present, but simply to themselves. The Bunnymen still have an aura of mystique. It's not really psychedelia, unless taking liberties with pop songs comes under that category. The music has a built-in drama without any imposed histrionics. It's a mighty mixture of energy and ... melody, of rhythm, humor, and exploding pop songs.

—Journalist Penny Kiley, 1991

Echo's tidal wave guitars still sound awash in luxuriant, rarefied air, as if played at altitude. 'Gone Gone Gone' is mighty tonight, 'King of your Castle' even dreamier. Backs against the wall, yet defiant, Echo & the Bunnymen remain deep and vast as the ocean Mac loved as a lyrical fallback. Amazingly, it's still Heaven up here. —*Melody Maker*, 1991

Early in February 1991, Imaginary Records released a Velvet Underground Tribute LP, *Heaven and Hell Volume 2*, which featured the Bunnymen's five-minute version of "Foggy Notion." Perhaps in an attempt to keep up with the remix-happy vibe of the times, the band engineered two extra versions of the song, the "Ya Ta Ta Ta" mix and "The Sunshine Mix."

Without the push of a major label behind them, the Bunnymen found themselves playing to only smatterings of UK fans. Far Eastern audiences weren't so particular. In April, along with China Crisis and a handful of other bands, the Bunnymen toured the USSR to aid the orphanages of Chernobyl. They played football stadiums to crowds as large as 30,000, and ended each gig with a thrashed-out, joyous version of "Twist and Shout."

Invigorated by the response they received in the Far East, the band returned home in May and began developing ideas for their own label, Euphoric Records. With Euphoric, the Bunnymen conceptualized a Warhol Factory-style multimedia venture, based around 'Euphoria House,' Will and Les's warehouse in Liverpool. Jake Brockman described the Bunnymen's new approach in a fan newsletter: "What price artistic freedom? We feel we can do it with our own label, Euphoric, without all that corporate stuff. And by going independent we can get 'round that side of things which I find morally repulsive ..."

Work began on a new single. Provisional titles of some of the songs were humorously named after characters from the "Dad's Army" television show. Other songs, unveiled on a short England and Wales Tour in June, included "Jonesy," and "Your Eyes" (eventually retitled "Snakebelt Serenade"), plus cover versions of the Velvets' "Foggy Notion" and The Rolling Stones' "2000 Light Years From Home." Aware that they couldn't afford to put out an album on Euphoric's almost nonexistent capital, the Bunnymen intended on releasing a limited-edition single every month.

Sunday, October 12th, marked the official launch of Euphoria Records/Euphoric House. The Bunnymen headlined the event, dubbed Euphoria 1, supported by local bands The Lucid Dream, The Twiggs, and Timeshard. The happening lasted from 10p.m. until dawn. Fans were invited to sleep on the floor after the show. At least for that evening, it seemed that Euphoric might emerge as a hotly tipped independent label.

The Bunnymen followed up Euphoria 1 on October 20th, by releasing the self-produced "Prove Me Wrong" b/w "Fine Thing" and "Reverberation," which they marketed as "an absolute belter, 500 miles an hour and heading for the buffers, no room for a remix whatsoever" and promised that the next single would be "Red hot—better than drugs."

The press didn't agree, apparently—despite being arguably the strongest Bunnymen Mark II song—and chose to virtually ignore the single altogether. The follow-up "Inside Me/Inside You" b/w "Wigged Out World," released on March 2, 1992, was far weaker than the its predecessor, and was again ignored by the UK press and fans alike.

Although the group pressed on for awhile, touring the United States extensively, it was becoming all too obvious that they were never going to set the world on fire. It came as a shock to no one when the Bunnymen name was quietly laid to rest in early 1993. Will looks back on the experience with some embarrassment, although he's proud of the music that the Bunnymen Mark II created.

I enjoyed it at the time and I think what we did was good, but I did it to prove that singer wasn't the end-all or be-all of the band. It's a point that wasn't really worth bothering to prove. A lot of people turned their back on it straight away. The whole thing was a bit mad really. We were never going to convince people, and that's what we were trying to do.   —Will Sergeant, 1995

Marrow and friend, 1995 (courtesy Ochre
Records)

Mac and Jake, 1988 (photo: Jim Kutler)

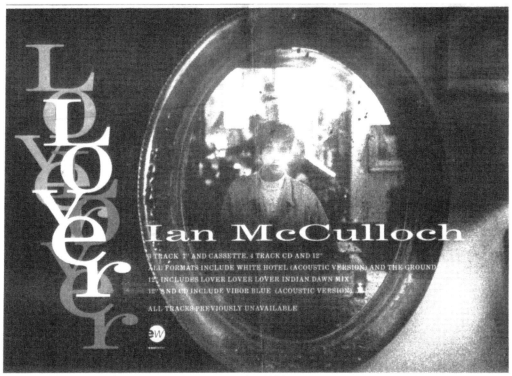

Ian McCulloch East/West Records promo ad, 1992

Les and Mac, Marrakech, 1997 (photo: Voodoo Billy)

Bunnymen Mark II promo photo, 1990 (photo: Mark McNulty)

Will, 1985 (photo: Steve Doughty)

Will, Marrakech, 1997 (photo: Voodoo Billy)

Pete, 1988 (photo: Jim Kutler)

ELECTRAFIXION   **wea**

Electrafixion WEA promo photo, 1994 (photo: Derek Ridgers)

Electrafixion Bubblegirl (courtesy Dave Bats)

Mac, Bionic Records in-store, 1996 (photo: Leticia Duprez)

Mac in America, 1999 (photo: K.T. Rauch)

In 1991 and early 1992, as Will was plugging away with the Bunnymen Mark II, Mac was working on his follow-up to *Candleland*. By this time, he was more eager than ever to shed his association with the past. In an effort to alter his public persona, he stopped teasing his hair into its famous tangled "rooster coif," and also began draping himself nattily in an off-white suit—presenting himself in a manner directly at odds with his image as a dark, sang-froid sage.

I think it was a psychological step forward. For years I've freaked out at the idea of wearing anything other than black or dark-colored clothes. Me wife was always saying, 'Look, ditch the sticking-up hair.' And I'd defend it and say, "Well, that's what I am, and that's what I look like.' [But] it doesn't matter ... I much prefer it now, because I can have a shower and wash me hair, and I'm ready. It's all down to confidence. Now I'm the white angel.   —Ian McCulloch, 1992

I used to be more Mick Jagger, holding me willy on stage and wearing no undies. Now I'm Cary Grant.   —Ian McCulloch, 1992

The spikey hair—I overdid it. I carried it on too long ... [now] I like going for the short fluff, rather than the spike. It's only hair. I became so obsessed with it, especially because it was written about so much … after a while, you get frightened to go out without it looking like people expect it to.   —Ian McCulloch, 1992

Interviews around this time found an earthier Mac, demonstrably less precious about his past with the Bunnymen.

I [have] tried to slip away off the posture that maybe in the early Bunnymen days I was guilty of. Which I didn't know at the time. I thought I was singing it totally true and honestly. I listen to certain things now and think, 'Oough! Who the soddin' hell is that singin'?' —Ian McCulloch, 1992

I've written some crap lyrics over the years, but I put that down to being a pretentious turd. The songs on *Porcupine*—I'd never write stuff like that now, and there's loads of people who actually like 'The Puppet,' which I think is the biggest bag of shite—apart from some of the stuff on the fifth album. When I listen to the way I used to sing, some of it is so po-faced, no wonder they thought it was shite—or poetic and meaningful. I want to discard al that 'c-c-c-cucumber' phrasing. It's like football. Some Argentinean rolls over ten times in front of 150,000 people and it probably looks like a foul, but in front of 100 people or on television, you know he's faking it. That's why I'm doing what I'm doing now, 'cos I was faking it for awhile.
—Ian McCulloch, 1992

Eager to exhibit his approachability, Mac embarked on a short tour of the States with his band (by this time, the "Prodigal Sons" tag had been dropped) under the banner "Ian McCulloch's Mysterio show." These few dates at small venues were low-key, no-pressure warm-ups of the new material he'd written since *Candleland*. But public interest in Mac had waned over the previous two years, and he found himself playing to crowds of as few as 200 fans. Mac tried to convince himself that this was what he wanted.

It was partly done to see if we could play, not softer, but more controlled and intimate, and let me come out more. If people have come to see me and bought tickets, I should maybe speak to them a little bit. 'Cos with the Bunnymen, I used to not really say anything. I mean, I don't think I have to give away me life secrets, but I can make them enjoy their night out a little more. —Ian McCulloch, 1992

These shows found a generally drunken McCulloch at his loosest and most light-hearted—all vestments of the serious rock *artiste* put aside. His inebriated performance at Maxwell's in Hoboken, New Jersey left both fans and critics a little confused.

... the most thawing voice in pop giggled, babbled, told jokes and blagged fags off the front row, like a tuxedo troubadour in a Vegas nightclub. It was Dean Martin meets Jim Morrison with a birra Ken Dodd thrown in, and it was hilarious. But weird. —*NME*, 1991

Mac eventually admitted that alcohol had become an excessive influence in his life.

When you're in a band, you don't just get off it to chill out, but you go to a place where you can get totally out of your mind. It's a part of the game. If Hendrix had drunk tea, he wouldn't have been the same. —Ian McCulloch, 1999

I didn't go barmy but I had definitely lost the plot. I was out of my head and I don't remember entire periods of time. But I could hold it together. I could drink 'til the cows came home, but it was never fun. I was slurring words, turning into a right bastard, but I didn't know it. Lorraine would say 'You're acting bizarre and I'm frightened.' She was frightened of me and I was like *worrayertaawkinabaat?* It's funny. I was drinking whiskey 'til it was coming out of me socks. I was getting out of me mind 'cos I wasn't enjoying myself anymore.
—Ian McCulloch, 1995

Stadiums are like a blockbuster film—crap actors and a crap script, and it still does well. I'd rather play a 100-seater for three years, though they tell me there's no money in it.
—Ian McCulloch, 1992

I drank in the bar Frank Sinatra used to drink in. I didn't wanna leave. I was well bladdered, then someone told me I had a gig to do. In my mind I became Dean Martin, and I thought they were all very privileged to see me doing Dean. The gig was great, in a way, because I was doing something no one'd ever seen before. It was total public suicide. —Ian McCulloch, 1999

Being able to drink a lot makes you feel you've qualified as a proper bloke. The sensitive side to me was getting lost. Instead of being proud of myself, which was how I'd always felt, there was self-pity. So there was a lot of bev going down ... it just became a spiral of sadness. I got scared and used drink to enable me to say, 'I'm still right, I'm still great.'
—Ian McCulloch, 1997

It seemed that Mac's disconcerting taste for alcohol and flagging confidence had not affected his singing and songwriting skills, as reviews the early 1992 UK versions of "The Mysterio Show" indicated—even if they weren't too sure of the quality of his band.

Frankly, Mac's band just don't cut the mustard. Commitment is pointedly lacking from their workmanlike interpretations, and McCulloch himself makes no attempt to dispel the impression that these boys are there merely to make up the numbers. Ultimately, what made this all so infuriating was the fact that not only is Ian McCulloch's songwriting as healthy as it's been for years, but the man's voice is currently a thing of wonder ... right now Ian McCulloch can't help but seem a prodigious talent still searching for a home.

—*NME,* 1992

… delivered with enough confident panache to suggest that he's reasonably sure that she'll turn around and come back the second she hears this coming over the car radio. And if she doesn't, her loss.

—*Melody Maker,* 1992

McCulloch has been honing his art. And his master skill, the trick he's been perfecting since the very first Bunnymen LP, is a superbly aloof and classical rock wiped clear, as one critic once said, of all R&B grime and sweat. Bunnymen rock always was immaculate, and Mac's solo work maintains the great tradition. The ease is all. If the point needs explaining, it's easily done. Ask yourself only this: what did any Bunnymen song ever mean? Ever? McCulloch's muse has always been a willfully oblique one. New songs still take one moody, resonant phrase, often a paradox, and sprinkle them imperiously onto a majestically glacial rock ... Every song is a self-contained, perfectly-polished gem, a triumph of form, a MacNugget. He's also maintained the skill of writing songs which sound instantly familiar. The consummate craftsman is still weaving elaborate, evocative fantasies, still spinning slender song webs, still crafting flawless artifacts and pretending that he's busking 'em. Yep, Mac's back. Again.

—*Melody Maker,* 1992

On February 3rd, as a follow up to the Mysterio shows, East/West released Mac's version of Leonard Cohen's "Lover Lover Lover" b/w acoustic versions of "Proud To Fall," "Vibor Blue," and "The Ground Below."

'Lover Lover Lover' is a coup of the spine-tingling variety, the likes of which the man used to pull off with startling regularity. With a contemporaryish electro-pulse underpinning the busy Spanish guitar vibe—a sorta Bunnyman meets the Gipsy Kings in Vegas scenario—McCulloch casually knocks out what could be his most beautifully measured vocal performance ever. If this treasure gets around he'll have croon deities from Sinatra to Smokey Robinson bugging him with duet proposals. The Voice lives.   —*NME,* Single of the Week, 1992

A beefed-up mid-70's period forgotten Leonard Cohen song, which is quite a lot better than the original, if McCulloch says so himself, which he does. The swirling, dance-friendly groove and McCulloch's secret smile of a voice and Bunnymen-style guitars renders this Cohen whinge into something almost joyful.   —*Select,* 1992

Mac was pleased with his take on the Cohen classic.

I feel that Leonard, my last hero, wrote it for me. It's a privilege to sing it.   —Ian McCulloch, 1992

I can sing Leonard Cohen songs and he always makes me feel like I've written them. When I'm singing the chorus 'lover come back to me ... ' I'm singing about 1982-1984. It's like wanting that same spirit but without all the soddin' hassle.   —Ian McCulloch, 1992

Six weeks after the release of "Lover Lover Lover," WEA issued Mac's 2nd solo LP, *Mysterio*. Um, why Mysterio, the name of a Spiderman archenemy?

I was struggling for a name for the album and then I just thought of 'Mysterio,' and then I thought, 'Yeah, that'll do.' The lettering on the album looks great, it looks dead French.   —Ian McCulloch, 1992

Ian McCulloch can still write a fair song or two. And, as for the guitar playing, this LP will come of something as a revelation to those of us who thought he was merely the best rhythm guitarist since Lou Reed.   —Journalist Mick Houghton, 1992

... a mature LP ... Mac clearly feels he still has plenty to croon about. He's one of a dying breed. Buy this, and help save the species.
                                                —*Select*, 1992

The great man's second solo album is riddled with devil-may-care savior-faire and reckless romance, and is actually rather glorious. *Mysterio* is very much a singer/songwriter's album (verses, choruses, words, tunes) and, as such, revolves entirely around the traditional subject matter of the singer/songwriter: to wit, the singer/songwriter ... a fine and frequently moving offering from a man looking likely all the more heroic and heartfelt the more his cheekbones subside.
                                          —*Melody Maker*, 1992

Mac informed the music press of the new-found *joie de vivre* that *Mysterio* reflected.

I am having a good time now. I just enjoy doing what I do a lot more, and I'm enjoying life—not wincing, maybe, as much as I used to.
                                          —Ian McCulloch 1992

Mysterio sounds a lot more outward-looking because that's how I felt.

He's back and in finer voice than ever. Mac's signature vocal smothers the whole album with passion, style, and arresting arrogance ... he knows what makes great pop music, and the value of genuine talent and class. There are no musical innovations on *Mysterio*, just nearly a dozen fervent, beautiful, driven pop songs. In a world dominated by the graceless and faceless, his elegance is needed more than ever.
                      —*Lime Lizard*, 1992

Mysterio is driven by an rock & roll maverick ... taking us on a journey through tunnels and caves made of clouds. There is a lot of imagery of holes—digging them, falling in them, and being filled up with them. Playing on the harsh contradictions of life with a delicate twist of lemon has always been Ian's specialty as a songwriter.
                      —*New Route*, 1992

It's the most accessible thing I've done. It's a toe-tapper ...   —Ian McCulloch, 1992

It's the sound that I always wanted. I like it when you hear things that are not in the background, but happening in it, so you might have to play it on headphones, or hear it a few time before you get any ideas of what the notes are actually doing. I like that thick sound, without it being a pomp stadium sound.
            —Ian McCulloch, 1992

What I tried to do is clear me voice of all histrionics and go for the throat every time.
            —Ian McCulloch, 1992

Once you've fallen for the instant choruses of 'Magical World,' it's probably safe to assume that the lyrical question 'Is it really such a magical world?' is, at least as Mac sees it, entirely rhetorical. Even when he's filled full of holes, they at least have the grace to be silver shining ones.   —Melody Maker, 1992

The lyrics, the tune, the whole flow of it is fantastic.
            —Ian McCulloch, 1992

My life changed. People stopped dying. [But] ... there's songs on there that aren't really optimistic at all. There's a lot of things that just sound more tongue-in-cheek, more realistic. I like messing about with words and with themes that concern doubt, more then pessimism, and thinking, more than positivism.   —Ian McCulloch, 1992

Despite the air of positivity, in truth *Mysterio* was a fairly patchy affair. Some of the lyrics were glib to the point of throwaway, and a few songs sounded like unfinished B-sides at best. The album itself sank without a trace, both in the UK and the U.S. Mac has since admitted that the album wasn't quite up to his usual standard.

I had a contract to deliver another album, and I completely lost the plot. To call it a solo career is a mistake, because I've never thought of anything I do as a career, 'cos the implication was that I was gonna go off and be this mega solo star, but that was never, ever the intention. I rebelled against that implication, but I should have just stopped making records. Instead I made a second album which was pretty bad, although a few things, I think are really good. But by and large I was just making do with things far too readily. —Ian McCulloch, 1997

MAGICAL WORLD

Raining down on me and it's no
    wonder why
I feel so low
'Cos it's down to you
You sucked away the faith I used
    to have in me
And it's fallen through
Yeah it's fallen through
You pump me full of holes
You pump me full of holes

And all I want to know is
Is it really such a
    magical world?
Is it really such a
    magical world?
Magical world ...

Swept out in the wind it's me
    as castaway
There's no ship to sail
Washed me up on shore
You pointed to my star and then
    it blew away
And you said to me
That's what stars are for
They fill you full of holes
Silver shining holes

And all I want to know is
Is it really such a
    magical world?
Is it really such a
    magical world? ...
Magical world ...

CLOSE YOUR EYES

Nip it in the bud
I'd do it if I could
Do it if I could
Always knew I should and
Never understood
Never understood

I will go where I must
Taking in what I can
I will go if I must
Making up what I can

Close your eyes
(Yeah yeah yeah) ...
Look inside
Look inside

Another idle pain and
Vision down the drain
Going down the drain
And all my yester know days
Will never be the same
Never be the same

I will go if I must
Taking in what I can
I will go 'cos I must
Making up what I can

Close your eyes
(I'm trying to)
Close your eyes
(I'm going to) ...
Look inside ...

My destiny
I know it will be
Deterred this time
Or ever can be

There's no use lying
I'm just as scared of dying
    as everyone
Someone in the know said
You're a long time dead
He's never wrong

Close your eyes
(I'm trying to)
Close your eyes
(I'm going to) ...
Look inside ...

Is there something in your mind?
Are you slipping on a stone?
If there's nothing in your mind
Won't you leave my world alone?
Leave my world
Leave my world
Alone

... an artful, sprightly mishmash of familiar chiming guitars, female backing singers,
and muted horns topped with an
effortless, breezy vocal.
—*Melody Maker*, 1992

... an infectious slice of McCulloch cool, tempered by a whiff of electro-funk and an unhealthy dose of Julian Cope.
—*Select*, 1992

I'm happy with the female vocals. I used to be fairly reluctant to use other people singing with me. I remember the bosses at the record company years ago with the Bunnymen, saying 'You could do with some girl backing singers' and I thought 'Oh no.' I took it as a personal insult, y'know? I'm not as precious about things like that now.
—Ian McCulloch, 1992

DUG FOR LOVE

Lost horizons and tomorrows
Disappeared along the way
Led me on and on
I followed up
Got sent to yesterday
Leaves are falling down
    from Heaven
Autumn in the auburn skies
One and one and five is seven
One and one and three is five

All my love
Buried it deep and you dug it up
All my love
Buried it deep and you dug it up

Destination: life and living
Use the privilege of birth
All you need is all you know is
All you'll get is all
    you're worth
Dot-to-dot I'll take what's given
Golden apples of the sun
Forbid
For bitten
Ending that just begun
Just begun ...

All my love
Buried it deep and you dug it up
All my love
Buried it deep and you dug it up
All your love
Buried it deep and you dug it up

All my love
All your love...

Looking for the piece to put
    me together
Link the link, link the chain
Time for the priest, for the man
    for all weather
Never ever ever gonna think
    it again
Leave me all the scrapings from
    the dregs of Heaven
Just don't leave me waiting at
    the gates of hell
Only wanna go where the great
    are heading
Between the falling and the
    fully felled

All my love
Buried it deep and you dug it up...
All my love
All your love ...

Now this could have been the single to put Mr. McCulloch back where he belongs (i.e. kicking sand in the faces of all other comers in the Golden Tonsil pop sector), but something is wrong. Perhaps it is that Mac's vocals are mixed far too low, or perhaps it has to do with the strangely dithering nature of the actual tune. Never mind. It will come. It has to. Somebody has to foil The Farm's plan to drown the Mersey Sound in a sea of cheesy trainers.
—*NME*, 1992

HONEYDRIP

It's in my mind
In my body and soul
Stuck in the I can't understand
They're selling me views
Wave my flagpole
Don't need my eyes
Tie my hands

Drip honeydrip, drip your innocence
Drip, honey, drip through the night
Drip honeydrip, drip your inner sense
'Cos I'm feeling guilty tonight

Madness comes and then madness goes
Another warship in the night
Know your god, hope Heaven knows
Your wrong from his right

And drip honeydrip, drip your
    innocence
Drip over me through the night
Drip, honey, drip, drip your
    inner sense
'Cos I'm feeling guilty tonight

It's Guy Fawlkes night, pistols
    at dawn
Let's walk upon the misty moors
If luck runs out I'll go and buy
    some more
Chance for the chancers
Fate for the poor

It's in my mind, in my body and soul
It's in my mind, body and soul
...

You can't always get what you want
You can't always get what you want
No you can't always get what you want
But if you try sometimes
You just might find
That it's in your mind
Body and soul
It's in my mind
Body and soul ...
Body and soul

... a sexy song for all sexy people, and for people who want to be sexy.

—Ian McCulloch, 1990

A very simple and easy song to write. The lyrics were written in about five minutes in the snowy hills of northern Wales. Nobody knows you like yourself.

—Ian McCulloch, 1992

DAMNATION

Got my suit of armor on
Trynna find some kind of meaning
A peg to hang a hope upon
Something real to stop me dreaming
I'm thinking
I'm thinking
And thinking starts me feeling

Damn damnation
Damn damn nation
Damn damnation
Damn damn nation

Snowflakes on the oven top
Drumbeats in the wild blue yonder
Didn't hear the penny drop
Shenandoah I'm doomed to wonder
I'm hoping
I'm hoping
No more no longer

Damn damnation
Damn damn nation
Damn damnation
Damn damn nation

Got my ticket to the game
Bullets in a darkened chamber
Every one a different frame
Each an old familiar danger
I'm changing
I'm changing
No more the stranger

Damn damnation
Damn damn nation
Damn damnation
Damn damn nation
Damn damn
Nation

... the best thing he's written in donkey's years: McCulloch reasserting himself as the bête noire of barbed pop to a crazy fractious vortex of foaming guitar. This is the kind of thing to lay the Bunnyghost. —*Select,* 1992

... quite startlingly rocking Neil Diamond-sings-The Replacements rumble ...
—*Melody Maker*, 1992

... a hell for leather attack
—*NME*, 1992

'Damnation' revels is in the sort of flashy guitar raunch that hasn't been rehabilitated until the last couple of years.
—*Sounds*, 1992

... a raging track that cuts the pretty paper kites that some think McCulloch's about into itty-bitty bits.
—*New Route*, 1992

WEBBED

Up above me
And inside me
All around me and you
Are no victims
And no victories
Just the guilty few

Hey
Here comes my world
And hey
Here comes my real world

Stalking dreams
Through wind and rain
I've sold my heart and soul again

In the window
There's a shadow
Someone borrowed from me
There's a sunset
Low and lonely
On an island
At sea

Hey
Is this my world?
And hey
Is this my real world?

Stalking dreams
Through wind and rain
I've sold my heart and soul again

Up above me
And inside me
All around me
Something aching
Something breaking
Something shaking
In me

Hey
Here comes our world
And hey
There goes my real
Real world

POMEGRANATE

On one
Stretching dimensions
My brain so full of tension
And things I cannot mention
That got me on my knees

Far forgone
Along with my conclusions
That came with much confusion
And led to my delusion
But got me on my way
Got me on my way ...

Yes
And the world fell down
When the moon was blue
And you wore a crown
And the word was true

Stop it
Don't live in the gutter
Spread your bread with butter
Enunciate don't stutter
And think before you say

Drop it
String it up and eat it
Be so glad to meet it
Turn around and greet it
Make sure you get your way...

Yes
And the world fell down
When the moon was blue
And you wore a crown
And the word was true
True

VIBOR BLUE

Jigsaw man where have you gone?
Melted into morning
Don't believe in don't belong
Death-defying dawnings

Vibor blue
The have-nots and the have-to's
The frozen chosen few
Destined to see it through
Born to vibor blue

Estoy candalabarar
Obligoing brightly
Voy e vamos a las stars
Twice nightly never lightly

Vibor blue
The have-nots and the have, too
The frozen chosen few
Are here to take us through
Gateway vibor blue

Limitless forsoothiay
Yo tengo muchos nada
Vaya con Dias all the way
Your madness made me sadder
Estoy candelabarar
Obligoing brightly
Voy e vamos a Tas stars
Twice nightly never lightly

Vibor blue
The have-nots and the have-to's
The frozen chosen few
Are here to take us, too
So is vibor blue
Destined to see it through
Born to vibor blue

What sounded live like an epic of surging tunesmithery to treasure alongside 'Bring On the Dancing Horses,' struggles here as a fiddly, over-worked squiggle with vocals that sound like they were sung from the room next door into a glass held against the wall. Shame.
—*Melody Maker*, 1992

HEAVEN'S GATE

All the holes in my head are
    the holes I made
Deep and deeper
Holding me holding me hold
Afraid
Weak and weaker will
You deliver me?
And turn me into someone
That I want to be?

'Cos all I want to do
All I want to do
All I want to do is be a part of you

Take love as you find it
You lose your love breaking
    underneath the weight
Give love like you take it
You'll find your love hanging
    'round Heaven's gate
Heaven's gate

I'm taking what's rightfully mine
By birth
Not giving to you my skin and
    what's left of my mind
Less worth
Are going with me, too
Going with me, too
They're going with me, too
Going with me, too

Take love as you find it
You lose your love breaking
    underneath the waves
Give love as you take it
You'll find your love hanging
    'round Heaven's gate

Hanging 'round Heaven's gate
Hanging 'round Heaven's gate

Is it true what I heard you say
There's nothing going right in
    your world today?
The glitter and the gold never
    come your way
Your starbound ride is
    still delayed

Coming out
Spinning round
Let you in and
Let you down

Take love as you find it
You lose your love breaking
    underneath the weight
Give love as you take it
You'll find your love hanging
    'round Heaven's gate

Hanging 'round Heaven's gate
Hanging 'round Heaven's gate

... if you want to hear Mac down on one knee, that can be arranged—the album's gorgeous high water mark ropes in Liz Fraser, Robin Guthrie, and Roddy Frame, and finds Mac asking to be loved in a voice which swaggers and/or swoons throughout as never before.
        —*Melody Maker*, 1992

A kind of positive 'Rescue.' I love the flow of this song. 'I'm taking what's rightfully mine'—which builds throughout around the theme of affirmation. I'm grabbing back all my virtues and faults and 'going with them to.'
        —Ian McCulloch, 1992

Only one track [on *Mysterio*], the swirling 'In My Head,' with a guitar line that recalls Will Sergeant's pretend-sitar trips, really tries to invoke the Bunnymen's patented psych-out. 'In My Head' is also *Mysterio*'s only real outbreak of McCulloch moodiness.   —*Sounds*, 1992

'In My Head' is electric, a rocket-fueled, panther-lithe lope which could be a sleek, sexy update on 'The Cutter.' Possibly.   —*Melody Maker*, 1992

    ... a revved-up Velvet Underground outtake.
        —*The Independent*, 1992

IN MY HEAD

Round and round
(Deliver)
All the things in my head
(Me from good)
Round and round
(Deliver)
Did the things you said
(Me from good)

On and on and on and on
(A to Z)
On and on and on
(Good as dead)

In my head
Things went 'round
In my head
I fell down

Come and gone
All the things we did
Nights so long
Those things well hid

On and on and on and on
On and on and on ...

In my head
Things went 'round
In my head
I fell down
Down ...

In my in my in my head
In my in my in my head

THE GROUND BELOW

It was you not me who said it
I'll spend my life trying to
    forget it
A numbers game
All that matters
Is count on nothing
Grab what you're after

Let me into your dreams
Where all the darkest jewels glow
You'll be the sky I've never seen
I'll be the ground below

If your memory won't remind you
Nine parts lost to the one inside you
And unfamiliar worlds can't find you
Lead the way I'll stand beside you
Behind you

Just let me into your dreams
Where all the brightest jewels glow
You'll be the sky I've never seen
I'll be your ground below

RIBBONS AND CHAINS

Up above or down below
Deep red brick the valleys know
The streets are wet and rainy
All unveil a veil of tears
When it comes it comes in low
Warns you late to block the blows
All I know is I suppose
It's what I always feared
Something right keeps going wrong

Jesus lived here underground
He's lying low and can't be found
Grew his hair and let it down
And hoped for something new
Everything that made him cling
Tied up with a ball of string
When he held it in the wind
It sprouted wings and flew
And went to find a better view

I can feel the stars shooting in
    my heart like rain
The ribbons give me stars
Turning all the pleasure into
    pain
Point me in the light of the
    bright and shining right
    direction
And then take me back home again

I can feel the stars shooting in
    my heart like rain
The ribbons give me stars
Turning all the pleasure into
    pain
Point me in the light of the
    bright and the shining right
    direction
And then take me back home again.

Into another downward trend
On a slippery slope
Spinning 'round a dangerous bend
On my highway of hope

It's always next time
Always next time
Always last time

Just get me out of this jam
That's stuck to me like glue
I'm forgetting who I am
To be the mirror in front of you

I had things inside my head
They put me behind them
I thought they'd be safe in my head
Now I just can't find them

Waiting for the perfect life
To make me almost feel alive
All churned up inside
The future open wide

There's always next time
Always next time
Always last time

Just get me out of this jam
That's stuck to me like glue
I'm forgetting who I am
To be the mirror put in front of
    you
I had things inside my head
They put me behind them
Thought they'd be safe in my head
Now I just can't find them

It's always next time
Always next time
Always last time

In late 1992, after the commercial failure of *Mysterio*, Mac reunited with Bill Drummond, and although the duo wrote and recorded several demos together, nothing concrete came from these sessions. Shortly thereafter, Mac contributed lyrics and a vocal track to Mancunian techno outfit 808 State. "Moses" appeared as the second song on *Gorgeous*, the group's 1993 album. Although the song itself contained fairly run-of-the-mill Mac-isms, the band's appearance with the singer on the BBC proved to be somewhat eye opening—or eyebrow-raising—for long-time Bunnymen fans. Perhaps still experimenting with his public image, Mac had grown out his hair into a shoulder-length mop, which made him resemble a more delicate-featured Joey Ramone, draped in a massive furry coat and leather trousers. Obviously grasping for some new direction, this was the last public appearance Mac would make in some time.

I'm inside out
Up and over-run with doubt
The price of pain
And self-inflicted wounds again
The need to feel this low
    and lonely
The need to be this low

Feels like I'm going down again
Trynna keep my head in the clouds
Seems like there's something
    up again
So high up it's getting me down

I don't want nobody but you
Don't want nobody body body but you
Don't want nobody but you
I don't want nobody body body but you

I'm torn between
What you know and what I've seen
The parallel
My Heaven right inside your hell
The need to be this high and holy
The need to be this high
Up where I'm gonna fly again
My feet'll be so far off
    the ground
Out there, spinning high again
Never ever gonna come down

I don't want nobody but you
I don't want nobody body body but you
Don't want nobody but you
I don't want nobody body body but you
Nobody but you

MAC AND MARR

Shortly after his TV appearance with 808 State, Mac became reacquainted with former Smiths guitarist Johnny Marr, whom he'd encountered a few times in the mid-80's.

Apparently I'd met him once at "Top of the Pops," though I don't remember The Smiths being on the same show. I didn't notice anyone other
than the Bunnymen. Apparently he came up to me in the corridor and said
'fantastic record!' And I just said, 'Nice choice of words,' and walked
off. I probably didn't know who he was. Plus, I'm blind as a bat. I
met him again just after our last gig, and he'd not long left The
Smiths. I asked him, 'What happened, then?' I wanted to glean some info
about why he'd leave his band. And he said, 'I just thought we'd turned
into a bunch of cunts.' I thought, 'Yeah, that sounds familiar ... '
                                        —Ian McCulloch, 1997

I was never a big Smiths fan, but Johnny Marr was obviously a talented bloke, and I know from various friends that he was impressed by my singing. So after watching some football and hanging out, we started working on some songs together, and just connected almost instantly. He came up with some weird chords that I would bend vocal lines around ... stuff I never would have used with the Bunnymen. Working with Johnny taught me how to stretch myself melodically and helped me to regain my confidence.

           —Ian McCulloch, 1995

Johnny Marr gave me a lot of confidence in me voice, he restored me faith in meself. I need to feel like I've got the greatest voice on the planet and Johnny showed me the way back. He helped me a lot in that respect.

           —Ian McCulloch, 1997

... we met again in '93 in Manchester, through mates. Played him some demos and he had these instant riffs. 'Play that again, Johnny!' It just gelled. He was brilliant. He said, 'You know why no one sings like you, Macca? 'Cos they can't.' It was dead special.

           —Ian McCulloch, 1999

The duo eventually wrote and recorded an entire album, tentatively titled "Touch Down," in Lincolnshire. A lead-off single, "Destiny," or possibly "Nowhere to Nowhere," was slated for an early 1994 release. Other titles from the Marr sessions were: "A Boy's Best Friend," "Blue," "Come on Home," "Dark Age," "Down By the River," "Harry Don't Marry," "Heal My Soul," "Hieroglyphic City," "Me and My Mates," "Overnight Ride," "Rebel," "Three Little Girls," "Time Enough for Love," "What on Earth are Beatles?," and "Where's My Baby Gone?"

The music press seemed genuinely excited about the proposition of the most revered singer and guitarist of the 80's collaborating on a project—and possibly a full-time band—and Marr himself thought that the match-up was classic. Although Mac was happy with the results, which he reckoned were "dead commercial—but it wasn't like what Phil Collins would do"—Rob Dickens didn't think it was "kicking enough," and suggested that Mac bring Will Sergeant in to do some guitar work. Mac hadn't had any communication with Will since Pete de Freitas's funeral, and at first greeted the suggestion by "howling with laughter." Later on, however, he reflected on his experience with Marr, and gave Dickens's advice some serious thought.

Johnny's ... chordal, the thinks chords and arrangements. He's very careful and very precise. He's always trying to invent a new multi-layered chord ... he throws different chords on top of each other. It's very hard to copy. If he's got three chords all doing three different things, try to pick out the exact chord—you can't. He does have a kind of passion when he plays. Johnny came out of the 80's with this reputation for being the guitar player, and amongst people like Lloyd Cole, he was. But they understood that three chords playing at once made this other chord that you can't play. [But] for people who wanted a guitar to kind of emote something, Will was the one. He was for me. He's a freak! He's my favourite. He has no grasp of the workings of guitar technique. It's just pure instinct every time. I was there in this room and he discovered that it went alphabetically, the way the chords move up the fretboard—and this was eight years after we started! He went, 'Wow, A, B, C, D,' even though it starts in E, and that was a revelation! That's what I like about him, that's the difference.

           —Ian McCulloch, 1994

ELECTRAFIXION

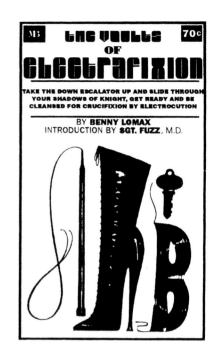

After the Bunnymen Mark II had fizzled out, Will had been dabbling with B*O*M, a techno side project he'd started with Jake Brockman and Damon Reece, and he was also captaining his own "ambient trip-scape" project called Glide. There were also rumors that Will was planning to do some recording with ex-Mercury Rev frontman David Baker. As with Mac, it was fairly evident that Will was adrift without a rudder.

Just as the singer was considering contacting Will to ask for his contributions to the Marr project, a mutual friend, Paul Toogood, exhorted the former bandmates to meet for a drink on a purely social level.

[Paul] realized that it was really stupid and petty that we hadn't
spoken for five years, and it seemed a shame, not only that we weren't
writing together, but more importantly we weren't speaking, y'know?
And that was how we met up, to kind of bury the hatchet and to say to
each other, 'Look, we spent a lot of time with each other growing up
and let's get on with it as friends.'   —Ian McCulloch, 1995

I dunno why, but over the years we just drifted further and further
apart. We became very wary of one another. There was one night in a
club in Milan—I was out of my cake on booze—and Will asked, 'Why do
you do it?' I said, 'I dunno, I don't even like it.' He then said
something that kinda stayed with me, he said, 'You're like me brother, you are.' I ended up in tears. I always remembered that, all
through the period when we didn't speak. He actually cared; not like
'You're fucking the group up,' but 'You've got a really good life,
don't waste it.'   —Ian McCulloch, 1994

Ian McCulloch: "Will and I didn't speak for 5 years. Well, we did
speak, but not to each other."
Will Sergeant: "I didn't speak at all. Except just then, when I said
I didn't speak at all. I've just done it again. Am I speaking too
much? I think I'll shut up."   —MTV Online interview, 1995

As Mac and Will were becoming reacquainted, the tapes of the Marr sessions mysteriously vanished, supposedly in a courier van hold-up. It's been suggested that this highway robbery was a fabrication to cover up a falling-out with Mac and Marr; that Marr was so livid when Mac informed him of Will's potential involvement, he simply refused to turn the tapes over to Mac. Although Mac's manager, Darren Michaelson, issued a plea for the wayward tapes in *Melody Maker*, the singer didn't seem particularly upset by the loss,

I was a little reluctant, but
deep down I wanted to see Will
again. I regarded him as a
brother, so I found it upsetting that we'd become so isolated from each other.
         —Ian McCulloch, 1995

After four or five years of not
speaking, we just buried the
hatchet, and it wasn't that
difficult, really. All the reasons that we didn't speak to
each other were really not that
important.
         —Will Sergeant, 1994

I quite like the near mythical aspect of [the lost tapes] ... those songs will be heard, but it'll be more electric."
—Ian McCulloch, 1994

Will and I had to get back together, because together we can create some of the best stuff on the planet. I like his guitar playing better than anyone's. He's a lyrical guitarist, and there's not a lot of them out there. His lines are like words, phrases. His playing is so intuitive.
—Ian McCulloch, 1995

Ian McCulloch: "When we sat down and started writing, we made an agreement: if either one of us thought that something wasn't special enough, we'd just bin it. Whereas in the past if I really liked something, and it was a bit too pretty for Will's liking, I'd just push it through."
Will Sergeant: "There's enough middle ground to get things done. I'm happy." —Groove, 1994

as he and Will had already started working together on material with a new band they'd assembled, called Electrafixion. Two songs from the Marr sessions, "Too Far Gone" and "Lowdown," would be resurrected.

I'd like to get back with Johnny, but at the moment the band is the main thing. I was thinking about getting back in a band when the thing with Johnny came up. But then Will came along and we decided to get together.
—Ian McCulloch, 1994

Working with Johnny Marr was fantastic, but I've always dreamed of being in a band again. And Will has so much vitriol when he plays guitar, I thought 'this is what I've been missing.'
—Ian McCulloch, 1994

… we're going to make the best debut LP since *The Stone Roses*
—Ian McCulloch, 1994

And what of the legendary tension between Mac and Will?

We agreed right away to say what we soddin' meant. We sat down, and I said, 'Right, you're gonna cheer up,' and he said, 'You're gonna be less of a prima donna.' We met halfway. I'm donna and he's cheeky chappy.
—Ian McCulloch, 1994

It's like Liz Taylor and Richard Burton. They got back together again. You know, it was never properly finished, this whole thing.
—Ian McCulloch, 1995

Electrafixion was not Mac and Will's first choice of a name. They'd considered "Helter Skelter," "The Throne of Feedback," "The Venus Flytraps," and even toyed with (and, sadly, discarded) "Penile Dementia." In fact, on Valentine's Day, 1994, Mac and Will's first public appearance together since Mac had left the Bunnymen, the duo (with bassist Leon da Silva and drummer Tony McQuigan) played a party for French Radio station France Inter under the temporary title "Space Face." How did Mac and Will settle on "Electrafixion"?

It was a dream I had. [Mac] on a cross, except all wired up. Judas pulling the switch. It's like when you're onstage and getting electric shocks, and when you're in a band you're setting yourself up as a sort of messiah. All sorts of pretentious crap like that.   —Will Sergeant, 1994

"Electric." "Shock." The France Inter gig was both for those who expected a thinly-veiled Bunnymen reunion. Electrafixion/Space Face played four songs, titled "Timebomb," "Honey," "Feel My Pulse," and "Bed of Nails," which, although sporting some innate Bunnymen signatures, were much heavier, angrier, and more aggressive than anyone would have imagined. And they blew the roof off the joint.

... nothing short of revelatory. Imagine the best bits of the Bunnymen mixed with The Stooges' Raw Power ... comes at you like a runaway train ... this band rock with incendiary fire.
                                                        —The Duchess, 1994

There's life after the Bunnymen. We used to be the Yardbirds, now we're Zeppelin.   —Will Sergeant, 1995

The heavier sound was partially due to McCulloch's admiration of and influence by American grunge-era groups such as Nirvana and Smashing Pumpkins, which he considered "the only band worth aspiring to." Abandoning his persona as a latter-day Leonard Cohen, Mac opened up his vocals to a husky, throaty, *venomous* roar he'd never previously attempted.

That was Will saying, 'Give it more! Sing with that gruff thing!' I had played him some Nirvana, Smashing Pumpkins—just to show him what had gone on in the years that he was growing potatoes or whatever in the back garden. And he took that as me thinking that's what we ought to sound like.   —Ian McCulloch, 1997

Nirvana were the best out-and-out rock band since ... The Velvet Underground, probably. They just stripped it all away, and it wasn't like the Pistols, with Malcolm McLaren and that very English fake hardboy thing. Nirvana was just about Kurt and what was going on in his head. They dug a lot deeper than all the current rock & roll laddishness. 'All Apologies' is worth entire catalogues of even good bands. There's no fakery. It's the last great honest song.
                                                        —Ian McCulloch, 1994

[Kurt Cobain] affected me just to listen to and to look at. He looked beautiful; he looked like Jesus. And I just loved that kind of grit, and the way he meant it and you couldn't argue with him—he wasn't faking it. 'Cos there are so many fakes around. He was dead fragile and just had one of the best rock voices ever, dead like Lennon. And his words are great, dead simple things that really suck you in. 'All

When I played there it was the best feeling I had in 8 or 9 years. It just proved to me that me and Will weren't just blowing our own trumpet. I felt like I owned the building.
                      —Ian McCulloch, 1995

A lot of people wanted us to reunite as the Bunnymen—but that would be cabaret-ville.
                    —Will Sergeant, 1995

People have expected it to be introspective, ambient and stuff, but it's not. We rock.
                    —Ian McCulloch, 1995

We called Electrafixion a 'gringe' band at first, because it's sort of grunge with a grin on its face.
                    —Ian McCulloch, 1994

[Electrafixion is] like CBGB's in 1976, a sort of hybrid of Television and some future grunge band.
                    —Ian McCulloch, 1994

I can't deny that [grunge] really influenced me. More Nirvana and Smashing Pumpkins than anything else. Some of the Pumpkins stuff reminded me of a sort of Bunnymen-esque musical thing. It's great to be able to use chords again. That whole 80's production thing seemed to do away with rhythm guitar altogether; you'd never hear one.   —Ian McCulloch, 1994

Apologies' ... it's just like ... mega. That, to me, is what bands should be trying to do. —Ian McCulloch, 1994

As Will had always concealed a taste for hard, heavy guitar rock, he was eager to put these previously untested influences—and his effects pedals—to full use.

I'm doing more different guitar sounds than I've ever done before, a lot of forceful stuff. In the early Bunnymen I tried to play as trebly and spindly as I could, but now I like to 'force out' ... This is the groovy thing about the new band: I don't feel like some kind of old rocker. It's more aggressive and wilder than the Bunnymen were.

—Will Sergeant, 1995

If anything, it goes back to when I was a kid listening to Zeppelin and Sabbath, and I saw AC/DC at Monsters of Rock. But when punk came along, you couldn't admit to [liking those bands].

—Will Sergeant, 1995

I always liked heavy rock bands, especially Hendrix and Zeppelin. I just wanted a different guitar sound than I had with the Bunnymen. Back then I would just use the Telecaster. It was just so thin and weak, and everyone used to think it was great. There's still traces in there of Bunnymen stuff, but I wanted to get away from the twiddly bits. I wanted to do more riffs and heavier rock-style things. The sounds send you down different roads. —Will Sergeant, 1995

Electrafixion are about blasting out riffs of Neanderthal simplicity and taking them to the moon, courtesy of the ... effects-drenched guitar fired out by Will Sergeant.

—Select, 1994

With so much water under the bloody bridge, both Mac and Will felt they'd finally shed the shackles of their past with the Bunnymen, and that now, "Electrafixion" was the word.

It's got groove, it's got mood, it's got feeling. —Will Sergeant, 1994

[We're] foxy. Rockier. Grittier. More attitude. More real, less surreal.

—Ian McCulloch, 1994

Maybe we'll do [some Bunnymen material] in a year or two, when people know the songs and the band. Of the Bunnymen songs, 'Killing Moon' is my favourite. 'My Kingdom' stands a chance, and probably 'All that Jazz' and 'Villiers Terrace.' 'Heaven Up Here' would be alright, 'Do It Clean' as well. —Ian McCulloch, 1994

In the 80's, it was more style and image-conscious. Now you can just go out and people either like it or not. We can be ourselves a bit more. We're not so self-conscious.

—Ian McCulloch, 1994

In early July, 1994, Electrafixion embarked on a string of 11 sold-out UK club dates, starting at Liverpool's new Lomax club. Mac opened the set with the simple command—"Don't bother shouting out for the old songs, 'cos we're not playing any," and the band proceeded to slaughter the tiny club.

Electrafixion are nothing less than a revelation. McCulloch's songwriting is as good, if not better, than any of his work with the Bunnymen. Electrafixion are setting an agenda for the rest of the decade. —Melody Maker, 1994

... what's happened, in essence, is that Mac has got halfway to redis-covering what he was once great at. The sterilised pop that was so clean it made much of his solo stuff squeak has been replaced with chest-beating riffola and concrete rhythms that tumble out of the PA at ear-tearing levels ... You briefly entertain the idea that most of [the Bunnymen's] majesty could be recaptured. At which point Bono would surely become an inconsequential slob, grey overcoats would return to thrift shops, and everything would be OK. Probably.

—*NME*, 1994

Electric fiction: Mac's back with Will Sergeant, but nostalgia does-n't come into it. Instead, there's this great, consuming fire, crack-ling out of the guitars and souls of the four men onstage. Sergeant stands head down; his playing is as psychedelic as ever but there's less space, more claustrophobia ... it's now more of a baaad trip, all molten metal, rage, and predatory instincts. Even Mac's voice, that once unmistakably frail and trembling instrument, is scarcely recog-nisable. There's a swagger and threat in his voice I could never have imagined ... If [the band] had have showed anything other than desire, relevance, or adventure, I would've attacked. But Electrafixion are a genuinely exciting proposition. I came armed with a poison pen and left thrilled, my head spinning with imagery and dripping with sweat.

—*Melody Maker*, 1994

Ian McCulloch and Will Sergeant's new group, Electrafixion, is more vibrant than most of today's young bands.   —Pete Wylie, 1994

In late September, as Electrafixion entered the studio to record their debut single, the *NME* issued a free cassette featuring various Warner Brothers artists. Included on this tape was the first, however unofficial, Electrafixion release, a demo titled "Zephyr: The Basement Tape," a nod to Dylan and The Band's legendary *Basement Tapes*.

On November 7th, the official version of "Zephyr," b/w "Burned," "Mirrorball," and "Rain on Me" was issued on Electrafixion's own Spacejunk Records, licensed and distributed via Warner Brothers.

What can you say except 'majestic'? McCulloch/Sergeant, Lennon/McCartney, Jagger/Richard. 'Nuff said.   —*Wig Out*, 1994

... Within seconds Sergeant's guitar sets the song ablaze, and we're reminded of the glory of days of old. It's certainly a confidence boost for McCulloch, who hasn't sounded so assured in ages, whooping

Electrafixion are, well, elec-tric. Sergeant pummels his gui-tar through a gamut of effects pedals while new, youthful bassist Leon da Silva and tem-porary drummer Tony McGuigan provide a solid backing for Mac's voice, a croon that's somewhere between Bowie, Morrison, and Sinatra. Hell, together, they rock ... After Hüsker Dü fell apart, Bob Mould seemed like spent force, making passable but not brilliant solo albums for a diminishing mar-ket. Then he formed Sugar and the world was gobsmacked. Electrafixion is similar.

—*NME*, 1994

If there's any comparison, it's certainly [ex-Hüsker Dü lead singer Bob Mould's band] Sugar. Except we're better! We're cer-tainly better looking.

—Ian McCulloch, 1994

If this performance had been delivered by a set of unknown 24-year-olds, every label in the land would rightly have been queuing to sign them.

—*Select*, 1994

... a seethingly cocky crescendo of Killing-Joke-style intensity ... —*SW*, 1994

and hollering like he used to do during extended encores of 'Do It Clean' ... it suggests more promising stuff to come. Can't wait to hear the album.   —*NME*, 1994

McCulloch gets down to some .throaty roaring, which isn't at all what the Bunnymen were about. Will Sergeant's guitar sound has exploded into a wide gamut of feedback bleeps and blops, crunchy chords and the more familiar twangy bits.   —*The Citizen*, 1994

It's a bit heavier than the Bunnymen. We did 'Zephyr' in Mac's basement on a 12-track, and we did the other three songs in just a couple of days, just basically treating them like a garage band thing. They're a bit 'rough and ready.'   —Will Sergeant, 1994

[With] a single spin of 'Zephyr' ... the noise blaring out of the speakers proves that [Electrafixion] are now giving the Cult a run for their money in the debauched mayhem stakes.
—Reading Festival Program, 1995

ZEPHYR

Can you be the one
To help me understand myself?
The one and only one
Is it you and no-one else?
Can you shoot for things
That others only dream about?
Can you light the fire
When all my flames are dying out?

Can you be the one ...
To tell me about my life
Tell me about my world
Tell me about your life
Tell me about your world

Don't look to the crowd
Aim above and out beyond
Leave the common ground
You never wanted to belong
The sky is open wide
Light the fuse and take a ride
Leave it all behind
Dig in deep and push aside

You know you're the one ...
Tell me about my life
Tell me about my world
Tell me about your life
Tell me about your world

Shoot them down
They wanna drag you down
Got to see
They're your enemies ...

Listen you can't even see
What this world has done to me
Done to me ...

As a first single, this was dead simple. It's got all the elements: a simple groove, and that guitar riff's great. It sounded like a single from a young band, which is what ... we are. It sounded like a fresh thing ... I like the atmosphere; it's dark. —Ian McCulloch, 1994

BURNED

Looking for a taste of the honey
I'm wondering if it ever comes
You said when it comes to the honey
You gotta give it 'til you get some

You look like you got the answers
All I got's a handful of clues
It's too late for choice and reason
Let's do it like the chosen few

All you gotta do for me
Is open up and turn it on
All you gotta do for me
Is open up and turn it on

Closing all the doors of deception
I'm out in the dirty air
I know there's only one direction
I'm gonna live it 'til I get there

You look like you got the answers
All I got's a handful of clues
It's too late for choice and reason
Let's do it like the chosen few

All you gotta do for me
Is open up and turn me on
All you gotta do for me
Is open up and turn it on

Turn turn turn it on

'Burned' has multi-meanings for us. I see a burned generation out there, a real sort of disaffected—not even youth anymore—from teenagers to forty-some-odd year olds. I think people feel ripped off and let down. We want our revenge. —Ian McCulloch, 1995

MIRRORBALL

All the world is sleeping
I can't close my eyes
Watch the darkness deepen
One more time to die
I wanna be redeemed
I need a new surprise

Feeling good-for-nothing
Tastes like salt and rain
Feel the same as you
Say you feel the same

I got it, I got it good
On my white-knuckle ride
Oh yeah, if only I could
Get out the other side

Feels like a nightmare in my head
Feels like there's something
    going down
Feels like an earthquake in my mind
Feels like an earthquake ...

Helter skelter shelter
The freak show's inside
I'm a mirrorball
You're the guiding light

I got it, I got it good
On my white-knuckle ride
If only, if I could
Find somewhere else to hide

Rain on me
I need you for my guide
Heading for the darkness
Death's eating me alive
Down on me
Sink me with that stuff
You can call it anything
But never call it love

Time I held this soul of mine
  together, together
Just don't stand there laughing
  when I call
Fly my heart and soul and mind
  together, forever
I don't want to be here when
  I fall

One last thing
Before we hit it off
Don't you leave me stranded out
  there
Washed up on the rocks
Tied to things

You know I can't undo
Bound and bruised
I'm bending out of shape because
  of you

Tie my heart and soul and mind
  together, together
Just don't stand there laughing
  when I crawl
Fly my heart and soul and mind
  forever, forever
I don't want to be here when
  I fall

Rain on me

'Lowdown' curls around the acrid sort of guitar work Echo fans grew accustomed to,. and then comes crashing down in a screechy, watery haze.
—Warner Brothers, 1995

'Lowdown' is delicately grinding, groovy, and moody all at once ...
—Journalist Sandy Masuo

After a late autumn UK tour, in which the band concluded each set with a lascivious take on the Stooges' "Loose," Electrafixion began recording their debut LP at Olympic studios, where the Rolling Stones had recorded "Sympathy for the Devil."

On August 29th, 1995, the first fruits of these labors were released: "Lowdown," b/w "Razor's Edge," "Land of Dying Sun," and "Holy Grail" on Elektra records. To accompany the single, Bill Butt created a video that cast Electrafixion as various characters from *The Wizard of Oz*, with Will as the Wizard (before morphing into a lava lamp!), and Mac once again in drag as both the Wicked Witch and Dorothy. Although there might be no place like home, the record did not fare well in the UK charts. Reviewers expressed platitudes nonetheless.

It's the twists and the turns of
    the cigarette burns
The holes in the mind of the
    nebulous mass
You'll get no returns if
    you don't learn
The dip between mine and the hole
    in your past
Every city we've been in
Built on the dust of someone's ash
When I die I'm gonna die 'cos
    of living
See you in hell with the rest
    of the trash

I need a love a love without question
A clean mind and a pocket of space
I want a map and a sense
    of direction
Looking for love and the thrill
    of a world
Just spinning 'round
Trynna burn
But you're melting down
You wanna be up there
But you're underground

Do you feel it lowdown?

Too many thoughts put a twist in
    my thinking
I just can't think straight anymore
I've got the bends I can feel
    myself sinking
Just can't keep on keep on coming
    back for more
Hey love, there's no need to worry
I've got nails, so hold on hold on
Think back before you started
    thinking about
The things you were sold on sold on

Can you spin it 'round?
Trynna hold on
But you nail it down
You wanna be up there
But you're underground

Do you feel it lowdown?
Lowdown ...

And the world keeps spinning 'round
Trynna burn
But you melt it down
You wanna be out there
But you're underground

Do you feel it lowdown?

Spinning 'round ...
Ghost riders in the sky
Lowdown ...

It's one of the first things we wrote, actually. We just dug it up and redid it, and it seemed to work, and then we played it live and it really came to life. We did it to go on the album and I thought, 'It's not right,' and then we started playing it live and I thought, 'This is how it should be.' It's a bit more dynamic ... It has really evolved.

—Ian McCulloch, 1995

HOLY GRAIL

There's a broken-down castle
With blood on the battlements
You know how it's gonna end
With a forgotten angel
Who'll never be able
To soar with the gods again

You never know
N-n-no ...

There's a plague in the wind
That's sweeping us in
With a sadness that comes to us all
At the edge of a cliff
Is a bottomless pit
Where all of us have to fall

All the kings and queens
And knights in shining armor
All the holy ghosts
And all our holy fathers

Take what's yours and take
   it boldly
And boldly go where you tread
   so coldly
The drop is sheer and never holy
Just you and you alone
Ride the wave when it
   comes crashing
Be the knight in a shining costume
Slay the dragons if they're asking
For what you've always known

All the kings and queens
And knights in shining armor
All the holy ghosts
And all our holy fathers

Gotta get me in ...

There's a broken-down castle
With blood on the battlements
You know how it's gonna end
With a forgotten angel
Who'll never be able
To soar with the gods again
There's a plague in the wind
That's sweeping us in
With a sadness that comes to us all
At the edge of a cliff
Is a bottomless pit
Where all of us have to fall

And someone above
Is handing down love
Putting a twist in the tale
And left it too late
For someone who hates
To get to the holy grail

Come inside ...

LAND OF THE DYING SUN

Shadows falling on our world
Can't tell the dusk from dawn
Headlights shine on the dark road
As one more fear is born
In the land of the setting sun
In the land of the setting sun

No more light and innocence
When all our beauty's gone
Hit and running left for us
To take it on and on and on

Sleep on through all of
    your nightmares
Too scared, no chance to dream
Alone, it's you and your lost soul
Nothing else feels the way it feels
In the land of the dying sun
In the land of the dying sun

Here it comes the trick of night
That knows your heart too well
Too beaten and too body-bruised
To break out of its spell

Each eye can't see the horizon
It's the blind leading the
    dead and dumb
As we fall, the day keeps on rising
Don't think the light is
    ever gonna come
To the land of the dying sun
In the land of the dying sun
Dying sun

... a twilight Martian landscape that shudders into a sinister chorus, guitars screeching and groaning to get out from under it. —Crossfire, 1995

RAZOR'S EDGE

Cut my teeth on the razor's edge
Passed on the blindfold
I had to be there
Would you meet me in the window ledge?
Just trying to keep a hold
You really had to be there

Will you be around
To pump me up again
Just when I'm going down for the
    last time?

These are the days I have seen
These are the things that are gone
These are the dreams that can
    still be mine
These are the nights that remain
These are the nights I dreamed upon
Seeking that sun going down
    on the fire

Lost my way at the water's edge
Up to my neck in it
Caught in the mudslide
One of these days I'm gonna wake
    up dead
Tied to the sleeping bed
Looking for the downside

These are the days I have seen
These are the things that are gone
These are the dreams that can
    still be mine
These are the nights that remain
These are the nights I dreamed upon
Seeking that sun going down on
    the fire

Electrafixion's full length LP, *Burned,* followed 'Lowdown' on September 25, 1995. Both Mac and Will were vociferously proud of their album.

It just feels great to say we've got a killer record coming out again.
—Ian McCulloch, 1994

It's the best thing we've ever done.   —Will Sergeant 1995

This record is hard-hitting. It's me and Will fighting back and stak-ing our claim. A lot of this current stuff is ours, and we want to claim it back.   —Ian McCulloch, 1995

There's plenty of drama and atmospherics on the album, but I think it's a bit less moun-tainous and stratospheric. It's the atmosphere of darker places.   —Ian McCulloch, 1995

It's the album of the decade.   —Ian McCulloch, 1995

While critics didn't quite rate *Burned* as "the album of the decade," they certainly thought that the record was an outstanding—and unexpected—achievement.

Lock up your grandmothers—Will's coming to town… A friend who's heard it said it was the 'lost Bunnymen album,' but I said it was the lost Bunnymen album of the year 2000, 'cos we were always five years ahead of our time. But with the Bunnymen we were always getting compared to The Doors, so it's nice to end up getting compared to our-selves.   —Ian McCulloch, 1995

If you want adolescent rock thrills blessed with the moody ferocity of the Stones' *Gimme Shelter* and prime Seeds and Stooges, then *Burned* will blow you away. [They] have returned sounding all teenage and shameless about their dramatic power-chord thrust. Even lyrically, McCulloch eschews the poet gibberish of old for your primal, elemen-tal rock & roll angst. High on going down, fire and rain, black nights and white knuckle rides into some unknown danger, low on *Crocodiles* and *The Duchess of Malfi*. Mac and Will have been through their dodgy period and want their Premier League title back. If they don't win it, they're going to thrill a lot of fans trying.   —*Select,* 1995

… a blatant throwback to the prime Satanic majesty of the Bunnymen, mixed up with a very contemporary metallic rage   —*Vox,* 1995

McCulloch brings an intensity and ego-crazed demonism lacking from the Mac-less Bunnymen, while Sergeant adds great elephant guitars and the rock frazzle that was missing on McCulloch's solo records.   —*Q,*1995

… the kind of groove-driven, metal-edged noise that might appeal to the NIN crowd, though post-industrial Echo fans will probably not be disappointed … all the songs are full-blooded guitar feasts, served up on a bed of grinding bass lines and smashing drums, glazed with McCulloch's otherworldly vocals. The new recipe is convincing ...

—Seattle Stranger, 1995

As with most of his work, McCulloch's words were a source of curiosity. In interviews from this period, Mac was frank and remarkably specific about his increasingly simplified and direct approach to writing, and the personal struggles behind his lyrics.

I think some of [these lyrics] are quite cryptic. But it's better being cryptic while being simple. With the Bunnymen it got to be conundrums, some of them even I didn't understand. That was about being clever, when, basically, I know I'm clever ... These lyrics ... I think people will understand. —Ian McCulloch, 1995

A lot of them are lyrics about recent periods. About trying to shake off some of the things that have been around me in recent history. But as much as I want to shake my past, of lot of them are, essentially, about it. —Ian McCulloch, 1995

FEEL MY PULSE

What goes up must come down
What's been lost can't be found
So feel my pulse
Is something there?
Yeah, feel my pulse
I'm sick with it, sick with it,
    sick with it
Yeah yeah yeah ...
Anyway I'm really somewhere
Yeah yeah yeah
And any day I'm really nowhere
Yeah yeah yeah

Push it up, fenced right in
Worlds apart my world within
So feel my love
Is something there?
Yeah, feel my love
I'm hip with it, hip with it, hip
    with it

Yeah yeah yeah ...
Anyway I'm really somewhere
Yeah yeah yeah
And any day I'm really nowhere
Yeah yeah yeah

Feel that I can be real
Feel that I can be real
Start to feel ...

I want you to free my mind
Yeah, I want you one last time
To feel my pulse
Is something there?
Yeah, feel my pulse
I'm sick with it, sick with it,
    sick with it

Start to feel ...

'Feel my Pulse' is like, 'Am I still alive?' —Ian McCulloch, 1995

I was bevvying better than Brendan Behan and anyone who knew me then, it was fucking dreadful. It was just like, you forget the reason why you were doing anything, so you lose touch with—I know it's a cliché but it's true—people. Like my wife Lorraine was saying, 'Stop this,' and I said, 'I can't, it's part of the job.' And then by stopping all that … you gradually sort of piece it all back together again and regain the edge you'd lost. Sometimes you think by doing all that heavy drinking it gives you more of that rock & roll edge, but that's what makes you lose it, I think.

—Ian McCulloch, 1994

Both McCulloch and Sergeant agree that the album's opener achieves their idea of 'blast-furnace rock.' 'What goes up must come down' Mac bellows, like a rocker who's charted both places. The weight he throws behind those words, as well as the muscle Sergeant crams into his frenzied guitar work, speaks volumes about the roads these two have traveled, together and apart.

—WEA press release, 1995

It's the heaviest thing on the album and the first thing we came up with when we started working together.

—Will Sergeant, 1995

'Sister Pain' is a real favourite of mine. It came from a low ebb of realising that all the people who told me that I'd been drinking too much ... were right. But I didn't want to go all Cliff Richard about it, so I kept the ending ambiguous.

—Ian McCulloch, 1995

'Sister Pain' is a post-Nirvana *Marquee Moon:* mind-boggling dynamics, thunderous tension, and all manner of explosions. Fire, brimstone, fury, and pyrotechnics—all the qualities we didn't associate with Echo & the Bunnymen.   *—Melody Maker,* 1994

... old-school strop-outs such as 'Timebomb' reveal The Voice that can transform any witless sixth-form scribblings into stratospheric-stroking poetry.

—Journalist Simon Williams, 1995

SISTER PAIN

Hey little sister pain
Scarred with the taste of angels
My little keeper pain
Hanging over my dark cradle

Shoot
Can I be forgiven?
Shoot
Can I be forgiven?

Stay with me
Stay with me, yeah
Stay with me
Stay with me, yeah

Out in the last remains
Stung by a passing danger
Moth's looking for the flame
I'm looking for a stranger

To shoot
Can I be forgiven?
Shoot
Can I be forgiven?

Stay with me
Stay with me, yeah
Stay with me
Stay with me, yeah

TIMEBOMB

Easy it comes and easy it goes
Over my head and down below
Message received loud and clear
Voices are calling through my fear

In search of the mine
Got nothing to lose
Just after what's mine
How can you refuse?
All sugar and blood
Bad blood in my veins
I wish that I could
Go back where I came

In the goldmine lie the
    buried treasures
Get a piece of what's going down
I'll get mine and you'll
    wait forever
If you don't take it when it
    comes around
It comes around

I wanna see, I wanna know
Who's got the blueprint for my soul?
When did it change, when did I go
Out of my head, too out of control?

Ice station's ahead
Too frozen to move
Too easily lead
Too easy confused
There's no turning back
It's over and gone
Instinct on attack
It's time to move on

In the goldmine lie the
    buried treasures
Get a piece of what's going down
I'll get mine and you'll
    wait forever
If you don't take it when it
    comes around
Around

NEVER

Feeling sick, can I be fixed
Through one more death-defying
    trick?
The lights are on in Heaven
No one's home

I need to tell of how I fell
Into a one-way no-holds spell
I thought I had the answers
Now I don't know
No

Na-na-na-na-now ...
A miss for me, a miss for you
All the things we'll never do
Never

Winter's here, here comes
    the freeze
My heart is dying on its knees
The blizzard's on
No way home
The heat's gone down and out
    the thrill
I'm left to shiver in the chill
Everything is gone
And I'm alone

So mister you
And mister me
Both are people
We'll never be
No ...

Na-na-na-na-now ...
A miss for me
A miss for you
All the things we'll never do

God's on high and so am I
My truth just goes to prove the lie
So open up the gate and let me in
I'm not gonna feel the same again
It's memories in the pouring rain
I feel like going straight, but
    then again
No

Na-na-na-na-now ...
Never

... best defines the state of things between Sergeant and Mac in 1995. The song chugs and splits into a sideways post-psychedelic guitar riff with the ever-guileful Mac snarling his best. Explosive and raw right down to the calluses of Sergeant's nimble fingers, it's the 'screw-you, we're back' song that the duo's fans were waiting for.
—Warner Brothers Publicity, 1994

Girl backing vocals have never been something I've wanted on records, but it was good on that. You always expect the worst but it was done a bit tastefully, and it was just that one thing. We were trynna get a bit of a Rolling Stones vibe on it, y'know?
        —Will Sergeant, 1995

... the original 'Never' [demo] was just fantastic—it's my favourite version. It's like 'Imagine' or something—very Lennon.
                    —Ian McCulloch, 1995

'Too Far Gone' is about literally being too far gone. I suppose that it's also about the
shite being made of the 'edge'
thing ... you don't want to
turn into a boring soddin' get.
But getting out of your head
can be as boring as anything as
well.   —Ian McCulloch, 1995

'Too Far Gone' is about kind of
feeling locked out, but because
of the power of the music and
the way I sing it, and the way
I phrase certain lines, it's
got a defiance to it. It's sort
of about guilt and sin, but
it's got a defiance. That's
what I like about it. It's good
to be too far gone sometimes.
            —Ian McCulloch, 1994

   ... a classic, entwining
Sergeant riff builds into an
epic   Electric   Prunes/
Television-y drama of regret
and revenge
            —Melody Maker, 1994

TOO FAR GONE

Help me, come on
Don't try to catch me when I fall
I don't belong
You won't even hear me when I call

Touch down, there's no warning
Just my spirit falling, falling

Something's wrong
You don't wanna hear the things I know
Too far gone
Gone so far there's nowhere left to go

Touch down, there's no warning
Just my spirit falling

Something's wrong
You don't wanna hear the things I know
Too far gone
Gone so far there's nowhere left to go

Get me out of the here and now
I wanna be another year another
Set me up 'cos I know how
It's easy
To suffer suffer suffer

Shooting stars
Love the way they burn inside your eyes
From here to the end
Burning up the cold and lonely sky

Touch down, there's no warning
Just my spirit falling
Help me, come on…

Been down so goddamn long
That it looks like it's up to me
It looks like it's up to me, now
Looks like it's up to me

WHO'S BEEN SLEEPING IN MY HEAD?

Who's been sleeping in my head?
I know for sure it was not me
All those things I second-handed
    said and
All those things I couldn't see

Empty now I'm a memory
Another you and another me

Sick, sucked, sacked
I want my reason back and
Tell me how'd you fall so low?
Beaten off the ever beaten track and
Where did all those hours go?

Empty now I'm-a-coming soon
Another me and another you
And it's my time ...
Now yeah ...

Underneath another god
I could've believed in you
Underneath another sky
Could've believed in me

Underneath another god…

'Who's Been Sleeping In My Head?' is obvious—[it's] about being out of my head and who-ever was in there wasn't me.
—Ian McCulloch, 1995

HIT BY SOMETHING

Try to ride it, try to hide it
Deep inside, it will not heal
Try to love and try to hate it
Try to touch it, but you can't feel

Hit by something ...
And the weight it just won't heal

Try to shake it, try to make it
Always break it when it gets too real
Try to love and try to hate it
Try to touch it but you can't feel

Hit by something ...
And the weight it just won't heal

Hey, when you dream tonight
Under the stars above
Will you dream tonight
About love ...

Hit by something ...
You've forgotten how it feels
Hit by something ...
I've forgotten how to feel
Feel ...

'It's about me, about rediscov-ering. It's also me telling the public, 'You're about to be hit by this, by us.' Not in the old egotistical way. I think in everybody's life you get to a point where you just get numbed out—you forget what it's all about. And there comes a point where something happens and it just hits you straight in the face.   —Ian McCulloch, 1995

'Bed of Nails' is the 'Do It
Clean' of Electrafixion ...
          —Ian McCulloch, 1995

BED OF NAILS

On this burning burning bed of nails
Torched and needled, got the need
Tables turning turning under me
Open up and let it bleed

Out of the black empty night
Into the dark and hollow rain ...

One more chance to make some
    sense of it
One more push to make the fall
Split in two, I'm getting used to it
Push the button and make the call

Out of the black empty night
Into the dark and hollow rain ...

On this tangled tangled web I weave
I'm the spider and the fly
Split two things I know I'll
    never leave
Burning bed of nails

And I'm out of the black empty night
Into the dark and hollow rain ...

WORK IT ON OUT

Are you gonna cut me in?
Divvy it up 'cos I got it coming
Are you gonna let me win?
Are you gonna do what you know
    you shouldn't?
I know there's only one way in
But I'm still looking for ways
    out, ways out
This tunnel's going nowhere at all
Seizing me up with fear rising

I know there's only one way in
I know there's only one way in
Work it on out
Work it on in ...

Are you gonna break my fall?
Am I gonna crack when I hit
    the limit?
Are we gonna get some more?
'Cos I wanna see what lies within it
That's always the problem with pain
It doesn't hurt nothing, it hits
    you hard

It sends its signals to the brain
Searching around in the black and
    darkness

Are you gonna break my fall?
Are you gonna break my fall?
Work it on out
Work in on in…

Fill no part, feel unsure
Feel like I'm down with something
    I can't cure
It's sad I know, it's sad but true
Face-to-face with nothing left to do
But work it on out
It's coming to you

SUBWAY TRAIN

I looked in the eye of a hurricane
I was blown away
Another storm and another rain
On another day
I was ignorance's rings of fire
As I hit the ground
Meltdown city when I got too high
I'm never coming 'round

In my veins, in my veins
You're the subway and I'm the train

Choo-choo

NOT OF THIS WORLD

God, look at you
Shining through
You could be somebody
Good, almost new
Someone who
Could be anybody

Not of this world
Of this town
Of this house you call home
Born out of time
Out of place
Out there on your own

In the beginning
And then out at the death
I'll be walking behind you
And be your prayer

★★★

As Electrafixion, Ian McCulloch and Will Sergeant couldn't get arrested. A shame, because you could've fried eggs on their taut, psychedelic rock
...
                                                              —*Uncut,* 1999

Despite the acclaim it received, sales of *Burned* proved disappointing. Audiences worldwide, caught up in the 'Britpop' fashion built around bands like Oasis and Blur, had little time for what some perceived as Mac and Will's belated attempt to hop on the long-departed grunge bandwagon.

Not yet licked, Electrafixion followed up the release of *Burned* with a U.S. tour and a new single, "Never" b/w "Not of This World," "Subway Train," "Work It On Out," and "Lowdown (Rest of the Trash Mix)" on October 23rd, 1995. Sales were equally disappointing, as were the numbers of the next release, a three-CD singles box, "Sister Pain," which included a full Electrafixion live set, plus psych/acoustic studio versions of "Who's Been Sleeping In My Head" and "Sister Pain."

No one, least of all the band, seemed surprised when word came down, in mid-summer '96, just before a six-week U.S. tour, that Elektra records were in the process of dropping the band from their roster. Electrafixion were relieved— they felt they hadn't received the support they deserved from the label.

We're [going] to bring 500 to 1000 copies of a new song, 'Baseball Bill' [on the tour]. It'll be a limited-edition purely for this American tour. It's just a demo but it sounds fantastic, and we wanted something that would point to the future and be our souvenir for America. —Ian McCulloch, 1996

'Baseball Bill' starts great, all pseudo-dance bass and a shuffly beat, and it goes swimmingly the first couple of times that Will Sergeant's guitar interacts with Ian McCulloch's cries—not quite like the good old days when they were young Bunnymen, but pretty fine all the same. Still, everything eventually just keeps repeating itself and the song lacks an epiphany.
                    —*Magnet*, 1996

It's just that you get persuaded and you start doubting what it's about. They'll say, 'If you do it this way it will get played on the radio,' even though you don't want the track to go that way. It's a load of crap. If a song's good it will get played on the radio; it doesn't matter if you've got trumpets on it or something. It's a weird little system. You're just soap powder. They just think, 'You're not our brand of soap powder,' and they didn't know how to sell that. It's been difficult getting over that whole Bunnymen thing.   —Will Sergeant, 1996

Electrafixion were eager to press on. They were still amassing rave live reviews—especially in the states—and Geffen records had expressed genuine interest in them. There was also talk of Butch Vig (Nirvana, Garbage) or Noel Gallagher of Oasis producing their next record.

The lack of a contract also allowed the band to put out their own independent release. At the kickoff of the U.S. tour, Electrafixion pressed a new limited-edition single entitled "Baseball Bill," b/w "Baseball Bill (You Talkin' To Me? Mix)" on their own Phree label (distributed by Ochre and Spiffing Records).

BASEBALL BILL

Here I go, it must be four in a row
I've gotta get my head
    down tonight
But you know I know
When the streets are aglow
I'll be headed for the
    city of lights

You talkin' to me?
'Cos I don't want to know, no, no, no
You can't even see
What's already on show

I'm hitting my prime and you're
    wasting my time
Your denominator commonest low
My head's burning up and I'm down
    on my luck
See you in the 48th row
With a matchbox full and a
    sulfurous skull

I'm trynna set my mind to rights
I'm gonna burn, burn, burn as the
    universe turns
Out of mind and out of sight

You talkin' to me?
'Cos I don't want to know, no, no, no
You can't even see
What's already on show

Baseball Bill went in for the kill
He blew it when he found his soul
Lost his will to live when he saw
    someone give
'Cos giving always takes its toll

You talkin' to me?
'Cos I don't want to know, no, no, no
You can't even see
What's already on show

Ooh, Baseball Bill ...

... combines the straight-ahead rock of Electrafixion's first album with the ambient soundscapes created by Will in his side project, Glide. As they have done with each new release throughout their careers, they have created something entirely new from their seemingly endless bag of tricks. Catchy as hell, with enough detail to keep you interested after repeated listenings.   —Hmmm... 1996

'Baseball Bill' balances Roxy Music—old trash-pop phrasing and hard riffs—with the kind of effortless cool that yer Marions are still groping for.
—Melody Maker, 1997

★★★

Despite Electrafixion's optimism, "getting over the Bunnymen thing" proved to be insurmountable over the course of that summer tour. The band found itself in the throes of an identity crisis. Although they had introduced some fine new songs into the set—"Live Forever" and "Baseball Bill —plus a gorgeous take on The Velvet Underground's "Pale Blue Eyes," audiences were still clamoring for Bunnymen material, and the group acquiesced by performing versions of "The Killing Moon," "Villiers Terrace," "Bedbugs and Ballyhoo," "Rescue," and "Do It Clean." Mac in particular was confused. Having screamed the Iggy out of his system, he found that the new Electrafixion songs he was writing sounded a lot like ... well ... like the Bunnymen.

It's ... more poetic songs. The stuff we're working on now is like David Lynch meets Sergio Leone. More mellifluous. —Ian McCulloch, 1996

Adding to the confusion, the band's constantly revolving rhythm section was becoming tiresome. (Over the course of just two years, Electrafixion went through 2 bassists and three drummers.) To top it all off, Mac admitted that he had never really been comfortable with the group's name.

We had to get a press release into the NME. Me and Will were crowded into this phone box, about to make the call, and we still didn't have the name. So Will goes, 'How about Electrafixion?' 'Yeah, that'll do.' When I tell the wife, she says 'Electrafixion? What??? That's a shit name. You're going nowhere with a name like that.' And, of course, she was right on both counts. I remember telling it to a cab driver. He points at this sign which read 'Huddleston's Fishmongers' and said, 'See that? Huddleston's Fishmongers. That's a better name than Electrafixion.' I thought, 'Fuck, he's right.'   —Ian McCulloch, 1997

I hate the name, but we got stuck with it. We had 200 alternatives, but the record company wanted to announce us quickly, so we picked this one.
—Ian McCulloch, 1996

I just thought, 'Oh, who am I kidding?'   —Ian McCulloch, 1997

Will was kind of unhappy, and he kept saying to me 'just think about [changing the name back to Echo & the Bunnymen.'] And then, rather than just saying 'nah,' I sat down one day and thought about it, and it made me feel excited, and kind of like me again ... but I was slightly concerned. I was worried that Will just thought that if we called ourselves Echo & the Bunnymen everything would be great. I knew that if we did it, the songs would have to be written with much more care, more melody, and more instigated by me. I had ideas for songs that I always seemed to be shelving, because they were too good, almost, for a group called Electrafixion.
                        —Ian McCulloch, 1998

As for Will, while he thought Electrafixion was initially a good idea, it ended up feeling like a hollow pretense. On several occasions, he had presented Mac with the idea of exhuming the Bunnymen name.

I was getting a bit cheesed off the Electrafixion thing, because when you're playing, I prefer people to be there because of what you're doing. There were loads of people at the gigs who were just there for the Bunnymen connection, and we were doing like 5 Bunnymen songs in the set. There's only 13 songs—what's the point? Might as well just be the Bunnymen. I never wanted the Bunnymen to pack it in anyway. That whole Electrafixion thing to me was kind of like when Bowie did Tin Machine; I didn't even check it out because I thought 'Oh, it's gonna be crap.'
                        —Will Sergeant, 1997

Having finished the American tour in Boston on July 26, 1996, Mac and Will returned to Liverpool to reasses their situation. By the end of August, Electrafixion had been laid to rest.

THE REVENGE OF VOODOO BILLY

I'm off to New York next week, and that's where I got my definitive Bunnymen coat for $20.00.   —Ian McCulloch, 1996

With these words, Ian McCulloch announced the reformation of Echo & the Bunnymen in a late summer interview with Granada Television. Immediately after he and Will had officially disbanded Electrafixion, they contacted Les, who was initially pretty dubious about the idea.

I'd gone through a divorce, got custody of the kids, and was making life plans. Maybe build furniture in my garage, something like that. I wanted to hear the music first. I was looking at it dead casually, thinking it might be great, but wanting to know what exactly we were going to do.   —Les Pattinson, 1996

After some serious thinking and soul-searching, Les agreed that now was the time to resurrect the Bunnyghost. The trio drafted in Jimmy Page and Robert Plant's powerhouse drummer Michael Lee, and by October were recording at Doghouse studios in Henley-On-Thames. Page and Plant are both big Bunnymen fans. After hearing the Bunnymen's comeback LP, Page sent the band's co-manager, Heinz, a fax that stated that "Echo & the Bunnymen are the greatest band in the world." The new songs in progress were tentatively titled "Crystal Chip," "Don't Let It Get You Down," "Burt," "Evergreen," and "Ribbons and Chains," plus new versions of "Live Forever" and "Baseball Bill." The band was writing and recording prolifically; by late October, they'd completed these tracks, plus four more, entitled "Detroit," "Polly," "The Maraca Woman," and "The Three Stooges." Mac in particular was pleased with the results of these sessions.

We've done two batches of demos—16 or 17 songs—and we've got tons more. It's probably more melodious [than the old stuff]. It's just stronger somehow—maybe slightly less pretentious. —Ian McCulloch 1997

What's more, despite his initial trepidation, he was ecstatic at the prospect of being in Echo & the Bunnymen again, as was Will.

From the second I said 'yeah' I refound my lost soul. There was a part of me I'd tried to pretend wasn't missing, but suddenly I was confident about everything—[even] making a cup of tea in the kitchen. It's a bit like Ian Rush going to Juventus for awhile and coming back to Liverpool. —Ian McCulloch, 1997

Once we started playing together it was obvious. It was like the songs were just dead Bunnymen straight away. As soon as Les turned up, it was just instant Bunnymen. —Will Sergeant, 1997

Les was really the missing link between me and Will. There had been some tension, and Les just knows how to diffuse the blow. He understands things about Will that I don't, and for some reason, with Les in the picture, the three of us just work. —Ian McCulloch, 1997

They know what it is they want to do. They don't want to come back, reform, play the old songs. They are going into this with their eyes open. They know if they are going to come back, they are going to have to make a great record. They don't want to just trade on the past—they have to, to a certain extent—but that's not all they want to do. Everyone is looking forward to making an album. I think everybody knows that reunions don't work unless you make a great record. The Bunnymen want to make a record and tour behind it, and not just their

I like being in Echo & the Bunnymen. It's like being re-Christened. —Ian McCulloch, 1997

We got Les back in last October and it all fell into place. From the first demo we realised that we'd still got that chemistry. I know what I lacked not having the name of Echo & the Bunnymen—I spent 10 years of knowing. I lacked a lot of confidence without Will and Les, and it feels fantastic to have that confidence back. 'Cos I'm great. It would be even better if we had Pete as well, but we can't. For obvious reasons. —Ian McCulloch, 1997

history. One of the things that always made the Bunnymen special was an air of mystery. There's definitely some of that old magic there.

—Brassneck Publicity, 1996

Some questioned why Mac and Will had bothered with Electrafixion at all. Why hadn't they just pulled the Bunnymen back together two years before?

When I agreed with Will that we should do the Bunnymen thing again, the first thing I said was, 'We've got to attempt to make the best record we have ever made.' We didn't want to come back and make it some sort of a revival thing—it had to have heart and soul.

—Ian McCulloch, 1997

I just wasn't ready. I don't think we would have [worked] in '93 and '94. I think it took time through me and Will working together. I was into Nirvana and stuff, and I felt that I wanted to get a bit more of that raw rock element out. I just thought at that point, straight into the Bunnymen, it might have gone all wrong. —Ian McCulloch, 1997

At the beginning of 1997, after turning down an insufficient offer from the soon-to-be-defunct Geffen Records, the Bunnymen reentered Doghouse Studios and began working on their debut LP, with Mac and the band's new manager, Paul Toogood, producing. By March, most of the album was recorded. Adam Peters, who had arranged the strings for *Ocean Rain*, was called in to add similar flourishes to seven of the new songs, which he did in Abbey Road Studios.

As chance would have it, Oasis were in the adjoining studio, finishing work on their third LP. The band's singer, Liam, contributed some backing vocals to the Bunnymen's "Nothing Lasts Forever."

... you had the coolest singer of the eighties in the studio, and the coolest singer of the nineties ... it was perfect.

—Ian McCulloch, 1997

I walked into reception one day and [Liam's] like 'Ian, want to do some tunes?' And I'm like, 'Yeah!' And it was funny, he says, 'Really good haircut. It's fantastic. It used to be a skyscraper—now its a bungalow.' We just hit it off right away, and after a few beers he ended up singing on the record. He's great. He's a rock god. I came away thinking he reminded me of me: he was handsome, a great singer, and he's funny. —Ian McCulloch, 1997

We're a classic band, man, what can I tell you? We always were. Someone asked me the other day why I reunited the Bunnymen. Well, I haven't. I've reignited the Bunnymen. Having said that, they never stopped glowing somewhere in my heart.

—Ian McCulloch, 1997

By the end of March, the album was recorded and mixed—by Clif Norrell, who'd previously produced R.E.M.'s *Automatic For the People*, one of Mac's favorite recent albums. From there, the Bunnymen signed to London Records (home of the Rolling Stones' back catalog), and started planning ways to promote their reunion—no matter what you called it.

Several ideas for the kick-off gig were tossed around. At first, the band planned on playing a show at Litherland Town Hall in Liverpool, (famous for its early Beatles performances), or possibly at the legendary Liver Building on the Albert Docks. For advertising, they considered placing the simple legend "Bunnymen Are Back" on the biggest billboards in Liverpool and London. In the end, they opted for a stark, to-the-point full-page ad in the *NME*, announcing details for their first gig, in the Courtyard of Liverpool's Cream club on Wednesday, May 14, 1997.

In early May, the Bunnymen flew to Marrakech with photographer/videographer Norman Watson to shoot the LP sleeve and the video for the first single, "Nothing Lasts Forever." Just a few days later, the band played its debut at Cream, with Adam Peters on synthesizers, and Owen Vyce, formerly of Starclub, on rhythm guitar/backing vocals. Reviews were ecstatic.

... the epitome of a classic, studiously angst-ridden, psychedelic rock group. Will Sergeant's incendiary guitar work frequently took the breath away, whilst at the heart of the music lay McCulloch's extraordinary voice, if anything improved over the years to a gorgeous transatlantic croon. The acid-rock Sinatra? ... The most startling aspect of this rejuvenation is just how amazing those new songs are. The exquisite ... ballads and ferocious burnouts ... easily held their own with the kaleidoscopic, edgy old material that inspired Radiohead and Suede.
                                                                —*The Guardian,* 1997

The intro tape is a statement of where they always felt they stood. First came the Velvets, The Doors, Bowie and Bolan, then the Bunnymen. It's followed by an amplified loop of monastic chanting and blasts of freezing dry ice. This is to remind you who they actually are; a band who dominated the 1980's with music of poetic splendour and epic aspirations, and who intend to conduct their comeback along similar lines … And at its heart is signer Ian McCulloch, wrapped in a fur-trimmed overcoat, his voice full of rasping-self-confidence and hopeless emotions, still as cool now as he was at any point in the 80's.
                                                                —*NME,* 1997

Immediately after the gig at Cream, the Bunnymen flew to New York to play two hush-hush sold-out dates at The Mercury Lounge on the Lower East Side. These gigs, and the U.S., UK, and European tours that would follow, earned reviews that echoed those of the Cream date.

This was not some embarrassingly half-arsed trip down memory lane by a shower of has-beens attempting to flog glories past to death ... despite their mid-80's split, the musical plot has not yet been lost. Both musically and physically, the crucial trio of McCulloch, Will Sergeant, and Les Pattinson have withstood the ravages of time;

It's not really nostalgia, cos-here's the punch line—the new songs are as good as the old songs, and probably better than almost anything you'll hear this year. [The Bunnymen are] a rock group whose music is still like listening to a kaleidoscope. 'Champagne Supernova' started here. Without the Bunnies' 'Over the Wall' there'd have been no 'I Wanna Be Adored.' Afterwards, nobody can believe just how great they are. This summer, everyone from Gene to The Chemical Brothers will have the daunting task of following them at festivals. The fainthearted should split up now. —*Melody Maker,* 1997

... there are moments tonight when [the Bunnymen] hit heights of numb-toothed, eye-gouging, heady, bloody emotion ... but would the kids ever believe that Echo & the Bunnymen were better than The Verve tonight? Snow-capped peaks were thoroughly kissed.

—*Melody Maker,* 1997

they're as slick, tight, and brimful of attitude as ever. 'Back of Love' had grown men weeping as, in frustration, they pawed the horrid foreheads which, sadly, no longer facilitate the unruly follicular explosions that you just know they sported in their heydays. [The Bunnymen set was] timeless Merseybeat delivered with a smirk, a swagger, and punctuated with the occasional unintelligible pontification from you-know-who.

—*Hot Press,* 1997

★★★

On June 20, 1997, as the Bunnymen were touring festivals throughout the United States, their first two-disk single was unveiled. "Nothing Lasts Forever," b/w "Watchtower," "Polly," "Antelope," "Jonny," "Looking for a Hurricane," and "Colour Me In," rose to #8 in the UK single charts—the Bunnymen's highest placing since "The Killing Moon."

First line: 'I want it now.' Perfect. —Ian McCulloch, 1999

I'd had that song, or at least the beginnings of it, for a good five, six years before. It was a song I'd played to Johnny Marr, and we'd worked on it slightly, but it wasn't what it became ... a different verse, lyric ... too many bits ... I made it musically and lyrically more succinct. It's a kind of love song, I suppose. It's so set in the present ... the whole line 'I want it now'— nothing to do with my past or dreams. It's, 'I want that ice cream, with the Flake in, now ... '—like you say when you're a kid—' ... and I want the raspberry sauce on it.'

—Ian McCulloch, 1998

NOTHING LASTS FOREVER

I want it now, I want it now
Not the promises of what
    tomorrow brings
I need to live in dreams today
I'm tired of the song that
    sorrow sings

And I want more than I can get
Just trying to, trying to, trying to
Forget

I'd walk to you through rings
    of fire
But never let you know the way
    I feel
Under skin is where I hide
A love that always gets me on
    my knees

And I want more than I can get
Just trying to, trying to, trying to
Forget

Nothing ever lasts forever ...

I want it now, I want it now
Don't tell me that my ship
    is coming in
Nothing comes to those who wait
Time's running out the door
    you're running in

And I want more than I can get
Just trying to, trying to, trying to
Forget

Nothing ever lasts forever ...

All the shadows and the pain
Are coming to you ...

Yeah yeah yeah ...

It was much harder to write, in a way, than 'The Killing Moon' … or much more unexpectedly a great song. 'The Killing Moon' was part of a succession of things. The fact that I'd had 'Nothing Lasts Forever' kicking around for a few years helped. I have found that the longer I spend on a song, the better. —Ian McCulloch, 1998

Their majestic comeback single ... possibly the finest Bunnymen song ever. —NME, 2001

People come up and say that I'm singing 'Nothing Lasts Forever' directly to them. Y'know what? They're fucking right. —Ian McCulloch, 1999

'Nothing Lasts Forever' is the best song Frank Sinatra never sung. —Melody Maker, 1997

WATCHTOWER

Skin deep and sinking
Your fingerprints will stay with me
Always I'm thinking
Of how you left your dirt on me
On me

What was I thinking of
To give you a part of me?
I can't get the stuff off
Forever inside me

Say the word and I will come
Burning like the golden sun
Say your will will be done
Your star is shining out in
    everyone
Everyone

Can't stop believing
Life's great untouchables
Can't keep from dreaming
Dreams turn to doubles

How did it get to this?
I never saw it come
How do I get to miss
What I've never done?

Say the word and I will come
Burning like the golden sun
Say your will will be done
Your star is shining out in
    everyone
Everyone

POLLY

Sally-Anne got Summer Sam
And Polly put the kettle on
I met a man in Amsterdam
He told me that the pound was strong
And London Bridge was falling down
So Jimmy put the gas-masks on
We swear we swear we wouldn't dare
Then everybody came along

Don't think you can take it
One more time to make it wrong
Don't think I can risk it
Another heavy biscuit, no

Can I beat the count of ten?
I'm lying just to stay alive
Damning my soul again
Taking a dive
Trynna survive

Where's it going to take you
And how's it going to make you feel?
You can't even spell it
So how you gonna tell if it's real?
A bomb blew up my shelter
I never even felt a thing
I brushed away the dust and
Gave ol' Jimmy Custer a ring

Don't think you can take it
One more time to make it wrong
Don't think I can risk it
Another heavy biscuit, no

Can I beat the count of ten?
I'm lying just to stay alive
Damning my soul again
Taking a dive
Trynna survive

COLOUR ME IN

Crash! Here it comes
Is it nearly over?
Flames, up in smoke
That's the way it burns
Every mother's son
Knows he's going nowhere
Brave and then broken
That's the way it turns

Lost in the tide
Into the ocean
Dust turns to dust
And surf to surf
Trying to slip my life
Into slower motion
Me to earth

Colour me in
Red alert
For all of that sin
And all of that hurt

Hey, who am I?
Yeah, who am I?
Lost in the mirror
Is that really me?
Can't bear to look
Look into my own eyes
I don't see the man
That I want to be

Colour me in
Red alert
For all of that sin
And all of that hurt

ANTELOPE

She's got everything on her mind
He'll take anything he can find
Small horizons fill her eyes
Got his eyes on her in the sky

That's the sound going down
Underground, on the ground
Charlie clown wore a crown
In my town
In my town

She's an antelope in her mind
He's a waste of hope and her time

That's the sound going down
Underground, on the ground
Charlie clown wore a crown
In my town
In my town

LOOKING FOR A HURRICANE

Heading for the midnight sun
We'll meet on top of the world above
Looking down on everyone
Hate in our hearts and talking love
Talking love ...

Driving through the moonlit rain
Two souls lost in a downpour, we are
Looking for a hurricane
Hoping for a shot at a shooting star

Everybody wants to
Everybody wants to now
Everybody wants you
Everybody wants you now …

Are we gonna chase the storm
A silver blaze to Parthenon
Spirit's looking for a home
Trynna keep the lights shining on

Everybody wants to
Everybody wants to now
Everybody wants you
Everybody wants you now ...

JONNY

Smell the smell of victory
Clicking the clocks to give us time
Ringing the bells of history
And making them chime

I don't know where you're coming from
I just know that I've been here
    too long
Trynna get the message through
You'll never be me and I'll never
    be you

Somebody got theirs after me
Wants me deep beneath the ground
He's either gonna save or bury me
Six feet down

I don't know where you're coming from
I just know that I've been here
    too long
Trynna get the message through
You'll never be me and I'll never
    be you

Such was Mac's pride with "Nothing Lasts Forever" that he was only slight-ly disappointed it didn't take the #1 spot in the charts. More important to him was the artistic development and sophistication it showcased.

I think 'Nothing Lasts Forever' connected with people. It was bought by people who didn't have any particular reason to buy it. And I think that makes the difference between what might happen in the future and what happened in the past. I think that might be where I start to feel more like I know my place. I can sing songs like 'Nothing Lasts

Forever' for the rest of my life. I think a breakthrough has been made. —Ian McCulloch, 1998

Even Will Sergeant had to admit things were going pretty well.

I remember not enjoying it as much before. I was always going around with a cob on, like some miserable fucker. Now there's a slightly better class of misery going on. —Will Sergeant, 1998

EVERGREEN

On July 14, the Bunnymen's comeback LP, *Evergreen*, was released, and entered the UK charts at #8. Reviews were unanimously positive.

Compared with even the most optimistic expectations, it's impossibly good. The first comeback in history not to be dogged by a nauseous sense of distress; the first one to actually sound important. —*NME*, 1997

... this is the best Bunnymen album ever. It should be encased in a formaldehyde-filled tank and submitted for next year's Turner Art Prize. *Evergreen* isn't a matter of life and death—more important than that. —Journalist Gunnar Barnes

... a distinguished effort. *Evergreen* is the sound of lost classicists rediscovering the chemistry and stateliness which made them great, and exudes a timeless and, indeed, evergreen magnificence right up to the closing and definitively auto-biographical 'Forgiven.' —*Uncut*, 1999

Evergreen is a collection of classic Bunnymen songs, liberally strewn with all the flourishes that made them great first time around: their off-kilter melodies, Mac's come-to-bed croon, Sergeant's multi-textured guitar sounds, and the underlying sense of faded glamour ... If you were expecting the Bunnymen to have undergone some radical change, then you're in for a disappointing 50 minutes. Wisely, they've stuck to what they know best, and this batch of new songs will stand up alongside the best of the Roses or Oasis. If it ain't broke, why fix it? —*Uncut*, 1997

Maybe the Bunnymen just weren't made for this world, but the planet is eager for an earful of this new music, and rightly so, because most of it is terrific. If they start giving away medals for swimming against the pop tide, *Evergreen* deserves a Victoria Cross. —Journalist Adam Sweeting, 1997

... a near-perfect encapsulation of the ill-starred string-led roman-ticism that made the Bunnymen so great first time around. It's the sound of a band refusing to go gently into middle age, a band who believe they are the best in the world again. It's not difficult to see why.   —Select, 1997

It's all in the winter wear. No sooner did Ian McCulloch don once more his Amazing Monocolour Big Coat and the magic came back. The fury had been tempered, but *Evergreen* was still a great return, ooz-ing lush orchestration and sleazy rock rampages.   —*NME*, 1997

The Bunnymen themselves were extremely proud of *Evergreen*. Mac in particular thought it perfectly demonstrated his continuing advancements as a lyricist, song-crafter, singer, and guitarist.

... I've started writing less cryptically, and that is what I think is the best about this record … Nine out of twelve of these songs were written on acoustic guitars, written on a settee in my living room, while the telly was on, and I just kept working at them. I'm still very primitive when it comes to playing ... I'm a good rhythm guitar player, but there's things I refused to learn when we were doing our thing early on. I'd think, 'Oh, sod it, Lou wouldn't bother'—but Lou *did* bother. So this time, I just thought, 'these are my songs, I wanna make them differently.' It's more care for the songs, instead of just thinking 'I'll make do with this.'   —Ian McCulloch, 1997

My voice is indestructible, and it can do so many things. Now ... it's the best it's ever been. It's just soaring up there with the gods.
                    —Ian McCulloch, 1997

… the sort of chirpy strumalong typical of every generation of Liverpool band *except* the Bunnymen's; dopey, ropey power-age positivity replacing the air of oblique doom that once characterised them …
                    —*NME*, 1997

… a statement of intent, a breezy anthem that could almost be a soccer chant.
                    —*Raygun*, 1997

Containing much of the pop sensibilities and search for glory that made 'Nothing Lasts Forever' such a surprise, it's a peach of a track, with luscious hooks, glorious acoustics, and classic Mac mumbo about moons, stars, and God. Believe … —*NME*, 1997

DON'T LET IT GET YOU DOWN

You were really something else
Made me forget myself
My lights came on
When I got to you
You were almost through
Yeah, almost gone

Don't let it get you down
Don't let it get you down
When the moon and the stars go
    crashing 'round
Don't let it get you down

An angel walked among us
Tried but couldn't love us
Something's wrong
Since you've gone
You know there's nothing, no one
To hang love on

So tell me how it feels
Tell me how it feels

To touch the flame
Tell me who I am
Tell me who I really am
What's my name?

Don't let it get you down
Don't let it get you down
When the moon and the stars go
    crashing 'round
Don't let it get you down

God's above us
And Jesus loves us
Yeah, God's above us
And Jesus loves us

If you want it, you can get it
If you want it, you can get it
If you want it, come and get it
Right now

IN MY TIME

On your wings you'll carry me down
Highways to the shore
And at your wheel you'll steer me
Then steer me no more
Me no more

All my leaves are turning
With the changing of the seasons
And all my dreams are burning up
And looking for a reason

In my time of living I just
    wanted to be true
But I just took your giving and I
    stole the truth from you
And in the line of duty
I turned upon my heels
Peeled the skin off beauty
And too much was revealed
Much too real

All my pages empty
Like a book I never read
And all my words are words I wish

Wish I could have said

All my leaves are turning
With the changing of the seasons
And all my dreams are burning up
And running out of reasons
All my pages empty like a book
    I never read
And all my words are words I wish
Wish I never said

Hitching a ride
Down your highway …

… the kind of cute pop song The Cure have forgotten how to write
—Journalist Adam Sweeting, 1997

'In My Time' begins in a lightweight fashion before being redeemed by a gently euphoric chorus that recalls 'Silver.'   —*NME*, 1997

I WANT TO BE THERE WHEN YOU COME

I wanna be like you
I wanna fly, fly, fly
Want you to take me to
All of your sky

Why don't you wear me down
Why don't you try, try, try
'Cos when you come around
That's when I fly

'Cos I don't wanna go under
It's only just begun
I wanna be there when you come
I wanna be there when you come

I wanna be like you
I wanna laugh and cry
About the things we do
And never ask why

'Cos I don't wanna go under
It's only just begun
I wanna be there when you come
I wanna be there when you come

I wanna be like you
I wanna fly, fly, fly
Want you to take me to
All of your sky

I wanna paint the town
And drink it dry, dry, dry
And when the lights go down
I'll say goodbye

To all the rain and the thunder
I'm headed into the sun
I wanna be there when you come
I wanna be there when you come

EVERGREEN

There's no more wishes in the well
No more dreams to sell
No time in the hourglass
There's no more lies for you to tell
Your Heaven is your hell
Your future dying in the past

Evergreen
Ever, ever, evergreen
Evergreen

I know I'm never gonna learn
Fingers fit to burn
You can't let the fire die
Keep the flames of your desire
Always rising higher
Aim for stars and hit the sky

Evergreen
Ever, ever, evergreen
Evergreen

... like The Velvet Underground produced by Phil Spector.
—Journalist Adam Sweeting, 1997

I think when I wrote it I meant 'when you arrive, I wanna be there.' And then somebody pointed out it was cheeky, a double-entrendre.
—Ian McCulloch, 1997

It's no worse than 'she'll be coming 'round the mountain.'
—Will Sergeant, 1997

Even the name 'Evergreen' has an element of tongue-in-cheek. But that's also what [the Bunnymen] are—evergreen. In our best songs of the past, some may have been heavy on the pretentiousness and melodrama, but others—whether they came out in the 70's, 80's, or in 2010—they fit in. A song like 'The Killing Moon' still sounds relevant to me ... we always set out to do timeless stuff.
—Ian McCulloch, 1997

… a polite rewrite of the Stones' 'Midnight Rambler.'
—*NME*, 1997

In 'I'll Fly Tonight' there's a lyric that's directed mainly at Lorraine, 'cos she's had to go through soddin' nightmares. She saw [my demons] more often than anyone. I was worse at home, sometimes. I'd go out and drink, and Oliver Reed would've had to have got outta there. The lyric is, 'I'm going to mess you up/I'm going to let you down/I'm going to cut you to the bone/You're going to lose your nerve/You're going to learn to hate/You'll have a love you've never known.' And that is kind of how I feel, that through all of that I'll love her in a way that only I can, and it's a strong love. It's not even just with her, it's the way I approach life. I've got to do it me own way. And a lot of people love me despite everything. Because I give a lot. —Ian McCulloch, 1998

... it's a word like Armageddon or whatever ... it's one of them words you can use. It's about self-destructiveness ... kind of puttin' your hand in the fire. Not that I'm glad about it. It's part of being human, but I think I'm more that way inclined than others. And I've got a short attention span—get bored easily.

—Ian McCulloch, 1997

I'LL FLY TONIGHT

I'm gonna lift you up
I'm gonna lie you down
I'm gonna be the king of kings
You're gonna rise above
All of the other stuff
You'll be the queen of everything

Nothing's gonna be the same
Nothing's gonna be the same

I'll fly tonight
I'll fly tonight
Into your light

I'm gonna mess you up
I'm gonna let you down
I'm gonna cut you to the bone
You're gonna lose your nerve
You're gonna learn to hate
You'll have a love you've
    never known

Nothing's ever gonna change
Nothing's ever gonna change

I'll fly tonight
I'll fly tonight
Into your light ...

If I should fall from some
    great height
Will I be caught mid-flight?
If I should steer us far and long
Will you be near when I go wrong?

I'm gonna lift you up
I'm gonna lie you down
I'm gonna be the king of kings

Nothing's gonna be the same
Nothing's ever gonna change

ALTAMONT

Hey now love, I'm right in
    the middle of
A hurricane that's blown my way
God's above and all he's really
    thinking of is
How much pain you've gotta pay

Why do you do it?
'Cos it does for you
Why do I do it?
'Cos it does me, too
Don't mind if I do
No I don't mind if I do
Yeah, yeah ...

Hey now, love what are you so
    scared of?
The light that breaks your
    darkest days

I've done stuff and things you've
    never heard of
Souls lost along the way

Why do you do it?
'Cos it does for you
Why do I do it?
'Cos it does me, too
Don't mind if I do
No I don't mind if I do
Yeah, yeah ... .

Hey now, love, what are you made of?
From the clay up to the dust
It isn't love you're afraid of
It's losing faith in all you trust

It's now, my Altamont
It's now, my Altamont
My Altamont ...

JUST A TOUCH A TOUCH AWAY

You said you could make it disappear
Make my pathway clean and clear
You said I was just a touch away
But I'm not even close
No, I'm nowhere near

You said you could make it disappear
And make my pathway clean
And my pathway clear

How d'you wanna go?
Should we go together?
I don't wanna go
I'm gonna live forever
Live forever

Shadows and the fog are moving in
From the world outside to my
    world within
I'm sucking on the dust that
    moves the air
The pieces move but I'm
    still there
Shadows and the fog are moving in
From the world outside to my
    world within

How d'you want to go
Calm or stormy weather?
If we've gotta go
Let's go together
Together ...

Live forever ...

The real vindication. That's just one of the coolest songs ever written. Out of the current crop of bands, no one could attempt to do a song like that; they just haven't got the imagination.
            —Ian McCulloch, 1997

The real legacy of the Bunnymen is apparent. There's a kind of lopsided grace, a rare spooked stealth ... so that the song's oddly personal, circumspect air is endowed with a beautiful spectral riff and McCulloch's still-terrific voice: an exquisitely matured croon that captures both world-weariness and sublime arrogance perfectly.   —*NME*, 1997

… has all the forlorn grace of 'The Killing Moon'   —*Uncut*, 1997

… will send shivers tingling down your spine.   —*Melody Maker*, 1997

I had it before *Burned*. That was kind of a key song. I played an old demo of it to Will, and he went, 'I don't get it really, I don't think it's that good.' Now it's his favourite on the album.
                        —Ian McCulloch, 1998

There's one bit on 'Just a Touch Away,' the guitar bit in the middle is just soddin' from Jupiter or somewhere. But it's less outer space these days—I wanted it to connect with *people*.   —Ian McCulloch, 1997

... shot through with distinctive Mac one-liners—'Above the Empire State/I saw the angels fly/Heaven above in 10 below' being a personal favorite. It may mean nothing, but it's a great lyric—as striking, cool, and romantic an image as 'Your lips a magic world/Your sky all hung with jewels' from 'The Killing Moon'—[as] guitars peal like churchbells.

—*Uncut*, 1997

It's about me having to go to Sunday School when I was five. And it's about me being 38 now and still being too young to kneel. I refuse to kneel. I used to call it my 'Neil Jung' song.   —Ian McCulloch, 1997

... one for the Sergeant side, its expressively anthemic guitar a reminder that those chords were always the band's real eloquence, paired with that ever-rich voice that still sounds better than the words read.   —*NME*, 1997

EMPIRE STATE HALO

Gazed in the crystal ball
Looks like I'm lost again
Where do I find the tunnel's end?
Followed the rise and fall
Of all the better men
From here to Bethlehem

All free souls beware
The moon is in my hair

Around the Empire State
I saw the angels fly
Heaven above in ten below
We don't have long to wait
Ran out of alibis
Ran out of things I'll ever know

The streets were paved with gold
And I saw your halo glow

And this love is just for you
And your love will learn to
   love me, too
Love me, too

All free souls beware
The moon is in my hair

And this love is just for you
And your love will learn to
   love me, too
Love me, too

The moon is in my hair

TOO YOUNG TO KNEEL

Who's gonna hold you when you're
   too scared to feel?
Who's gonna cure you when the
   pain won't heal?
Who's gonna be there when your
   world goes wrong?
Who's gonna tell you you're the
   only one?

In my blood, in my soul
In this mind of mine
Can your touch turn me gold
Make my glitter shine

Who's gonna reach you when you
   can't be caught?
Who's gonna teach you what you
   can't be taught?

Who's gonna beat you when you
   won't be fought?
Who's gonna buy you when you
   can't be bought?

In my blood, in my soul
In this mind of mine
Can your touch turn me gold
Make my glitter shine

Who's gonna pray for you when
   you're too young to kneel?
Who's gonna fake it when it
   gets too real?
One more question answered in
   the falling stars
I heard they found
Death on Mars

The whole song is probably the one I'm least happy with lyrically … Whenever I hear it, I think they're really good lyrics, but there's not enough twists in them. But I like the purity of it. The last bit's fantastic—'One more question answered in the falling stars/I heard they found death on Mars.' 'Death On Mars'—that was nearly the album title. There was this big news, and all the scientists were getting really pleased with themselves 'cos they'd found that rock that proved there had been life on Mars, and I thought, 'All they found is death on Mars.' A lot of this album is about the transience of everything. I don't want a fossil to prove that I walked here, or that soddin' apemen walked here. I'm against the whole nostalgia thing. 'Death on Mars' was just a kind of tongue-in-cheek—but deep—observation.

—Ian McCulloch, 1997

FORGIVEN

I am just one of many
Who gave a love in vain
Sold it out for pennies
And saved up all my rain

What d'you want from me?
The ocean or the sea?
The salt inside the rising tide
Of tears you got from me
Got from me
Got from me, yeah ...

One day I'll be ready
To take what could be mine
And everything I've buried
I'll lay out on the line

What d'you want to see?
The truth or mystery?
A blinding light, the blackest night
They're both inside of me
Inside me
Inside me, yeah ...

I am just one of many
Who took a love in vain
Sold it out for pennies
Saved up all my rain

What d'you want from me
The truth or mystery?
The salt inside the rising tide
Of tears you got from me
Got from me
Got from me, yeah

I don't want to be forgiven
All I want is to be free
I know I'll never be forgiven
I know I'll never be free

... the weepiest ending in rock. —*Record Collector*, 2001

Penitence is good for the soul, you know? Not in a Catholic confessional way, but I've always had that kind of penitent vibe in my lyrics—[although] there's some sort of glimmer of hope. But I think we're all corrupted from birth; we all do something wrong pretty early on.

—Ian McCulloch, 1999

It's sung to Lorraine. I know I'm not an easy person to live with. But this is what I'm like, and I didn't make me. So it's kind of an apology. It's really a cracked way of asking her to just let me get away with it for a little while longer.   —Ian McCulloch, 1997

The momentous final track on *Evergreen* is as moving a testimony to the power of love as you're ever likely to hear.   —*The Observer*, 1997

In the almost-lullaby that closes *Evergreen*, you're immersed in the poignant child's fantasy world of Brain Wilson. One of the best songs [the Bunnymen have] ever recorded.

—Journalist Adam Sweeting, 1997

At the beginning of 1997, how could anyone have guessed that the Bunnies would rediscover the best form of their lives? Nothing Lasts Forever? By the sound of Evergreen, it looks like the Bunnymen are going to give it a damn good go.

—Melody Maker, 1997

The Bunnymen came ... and conquered the 90's without once breaking sweat. And the buzz in your stomach? That, friends, is the Echo reverberating to the millennium and way, way beyond.

—NME, 1997

'Forgiven' works the kind of sentimental magic that only old liars can feign this unfeignedly. Anyone over the age of reflection will spot it as a have-it-both-ways deal, trading off that ol' devil charm against tender self-pity. But hey babe, that's rock & roll.

—Melody Maker, 1997

The remainder of 1997 saw the release of two more singles: "I Want to Be There When You Come" along with and "Don't Let It Get You Down," a set at The Glastonbury Festival, and full tours of the UK and United States. At the end of the year, stateside critics raised their voices about the Bunnymen reunion: *The L.A. Times* cited *Evergreen* as the best record of the year, and *Magnet* magazine granted the Bunnymen with their "Comeback of the Year" award. The UK rock press was equally enchanted.

... the most stylish [comeback] ever in rock. The reformation of a 'seminal' band is usually greeted by a hail of 'old gits in it for the money' accusations, but the Bunnymen stepped up, looked great, gigged brilliantly, and released an album that surpassed all expectations. Amid the new tribes of vain yobs—the Mansuns, Suedes, and Verves—they looked completely at home.   *—Vox,* 1998

The greatest comeback in the world—ever!   *—Melody Maker,* 1997

Mac closed the year by recording a version of the Sinatra Classic "Summer Wind" with his good friends The Fun Lovin' Criminals.

I met them in America about two-and-a-half years ago when their first album came out. I played that album to death and thought they were the coolest thing since the Bunnymen. We're like the new Rat Pack, doing Sinatra's 'Summer Wind' in an Elvis-in-Hawaii stylee. We're going to record an album with them ... possibly in a studio in Acapulco. At the very least, drinking cocktails over the bay.

—Ian McCulloch, 1999

"Summer Wind" was eventually released as a B-side on The Fun Lovin' Criminals "Big Night Out" single. The FLC later contributed backing tracks to two Bunnymen songs, and, in March 2000, recorded two tracks with Mac.

1998

1998 was a fairly quiet year for the band. Apart from a European tour, the loudest sound emanating from the Bunnymen camp was Mac's verbal broadsides, which were as distinctive as ever.

I say I'm evolving again. I'm growing suction cups on me fingers. No ostrich.
                                        —Ian McCulloch, 1998

Just remember that 99 percent of the shit you hear out there *is* shit.
                                        —Ian McCulloch, 1998

The group only released one exclusively Bunnymen track that year. The epic, gorgeous yearn of "Fools Like Us" was featured on the soundtrack of a film called *Martha Meets Daniel, Frank, and Laurence.*

Let's go and get drunk. Tell you what, the best thing I ever did was giving up not drinking.
                                        —Ian McCulloch, 1998

Do you know any typically Danish restaurants? So we can avoid them? A lot of people kill themselves in this country, don't they?
                                        —Ian McCulloch, 1998

I don't 'do promo'—I make a speech.   —Ian McCulloch, 1998

FOOLS LIKE US

It's fools like us
Always fooled
By the bright side of life
Then life on the cool
How does it turn
How does it turn
Into dying embers
From a love that burned?

On its way to your heart somehow ...

They're falling again
My shining stars
From out of your Heaven

And into my heart
Ribbons and chains
Ribbons and chains
Tie us together
And keep us apart

Got to get to your heart somehow ...

If I could be someone
Someone better than me
I would be that someone
Who's still waiting
Waiting to be free

It's fools like us
Always burned
On the dying embers
Of a love that turned

On its way to your heart somehow ...

Gotta get to your heart somehow
Gotta get to your heart somehow
Gotta get to your heart somehow

Time is on our side ...

... starts out with a playful swing in its hips before giving itself over to this great dazzling explosion. It's Mac's Vegas ballad, and he's never sounded better. Like reading old love letters, it's strangely uplifting, with Mac finding resilience in the midst of melancholy. And isn't it good and right and our only hope, to be 'foolish?'
                                        —*Melody Maker*, 1999

I first wrote ['Fools Like Us'] the year I left the Bunnymen. The verse was just a joke for me to remember the melody—'Je suis, je suis/Je m'appelle, je m'appelle/Le champs d'eleysee/Le tower Eiffel' in a kind of Jacques Brel-ian stylee. And that was how I remembered the tune all through the years. I think in '91 I finally wrote the lyric, and Bill Drummond heard it, and thought it was the best thing I'd ever written. He actually helped me do a demo of it, and he said, 'This is soddin' massive, this song.' And I didn't use it 'cos I thought 'this doesn't fit anywhere.' It's almost as if the return of the Bunnymen legitimized what I wanted to say in this song. It was reflective and had a sense of loss, y'know? I'd always written about that, but it may as well have been, 'I've lost me soddin' train ticket.'

—Ian McCulloch, 1998

The biggest event of 1998 for the Bunnymen was undoubtedly the World Cup. Early in the year, the band was approached to write a theme song for a six-week BBC football series, called "The Golden Boot." Mac dug out a song he'd written during his sessions with Johnny Marr.

The actual lyric for the original song was 'Flying through the falling debris/Burning like a newborn sun/I need someone to help me/Just to feel like anyone.' And the chorus went: 'How does it feel to be on top of the world?/How does it feel/Feeling anything real?' I had no intentions of it being a rallying call, but somebody wanted it to be the World Cup song, because it has the word 'world' in it, I suppose. —Ian McCulloch, 1998

It probably would have been called 'Debris,' because the opening line was 'Flying through the falling debris.' There's a line in it, 'How does it feel to be on top of the world?' that's meant to be full of irony. I haven't got a clue how it feels, 'cos every time I get halfway up the North Face I decide to jump off, taking a few things with me. And that's what the song was about. —Ian McCulloch, 1998

After changing the lyrics to create a suitably football-oriented theme, Mac forwarded the song to the BBC. Colin Bell, London Records' Managing Director, heard it, and suggested the Bunnymen submit it to the Football Association for consideration as the official anthem of England's World Cup Team. Eventually the song, retitled "(How Does It Feel To Be) On Top of the World?" emerged victorious over efforts by Blur's Damon Albarn, Pulp, and The Boo Radleys, and was selected as the song to support England's team.

The FA originally intended to record the song as a "Band Aid" style collaboration sung by a cast of 1998's flavors of the month, including All Saints and Robbie Williams. This didn't sit well with Mac, who thought the intentions behind the song would be dissipated by a cast of thousands. But Bunnymen manager Paul Toogood had a stroke of genius when he suggested that the massively successful—and devastatingly unhip—phenomenon that was The Spice Girls be brought in. Critics—and many Bunnymen fans—cried foul. Mac disagreed.

People said doing that record wasn't cool, but that's rubbish—cool is birthright stuff.   —Ian McCulloch, 1999

What is cool is what you really love. And if you can abide by your own tenets of life and be true to them, you become cool because you believe in it, and no one can sway you from who you are.
                                                —Ian McCulloch, 1998

It certainly wasn't as embarrassing as Pete de Freitas's soddin' beard on that last Bunnymen tour in 1987. That was wrong—singing with Sporty Spice wasn't. It just meant I got to go to the World Cup matches and sing 'Three Lions on a Shirt' along with the rest of the chippie and piehead dudes.   —Ian McCulloch, 1999

Apart from the Spice Girls, the song featured Simon from Ocean Colour Scene and Tommy from Space. It was released on May 25th, under the banner of England United. Mac was proud of the song, especially the populist message of the lyrics.

I suppose it is a feel-good thing. I hate that phrase but [the song] is meant to make people think 'Yes, we do have ties that bind us.' It's not so much patriotic. For me it's about where I and most people who are into footie come from—and that's working-class streets, where you play football with goals painted on walls, or coats down on the grass.   —Ian McCulloch, 1998

It had to be more universal lyrically, and avoid jingoism—we didn't want to put anyone down or have a go at the Germans. I was at Hillsborough, and maybe that opened my mind. Football is about more than 'Us vs. Them.' It brings people together.   —Ian McCulloch, 1998

Mac also had personal motives for writing the song.

I think with a lot of people, like your pie-eating blokes at the match, when I turn up they're like: 'What's he soddin' doing here? He doesn't look like he's a soddin' footie fan.' So I think, more than anything, I want to go to Anfield in a big chair and be taken out onto the centre circle and go: 'There ya go! ... ' (waves regally to imaginary terraces), ' ... and there's me seat up there, row 27.'
                                                —Ian McCulloch, 1998

It was totally 'Bunnymen.' The criticisms came from people who never understood the Bunnymen in the first place. It was like 'Who goes and plays the Isle of Skye, or why have a cow in a video for ' ... Dancing Horses?' I just though it was great.   —Ian McCulloch, 1998

I didn't want to be too precious about this song, so I thought 'why not?' Sporty Spice is a proper football fan, unlike a lot of people who purport to like football. I just though it was brilliant—Echo & the Bunnymen playing this song with the Spice Girls on.
                      —Ian McCulloch, 1998

What critics don't realize is Spice Girls are a lot hipper than the Unbelievable Truth or any angst-ridden shite. Spice Girls stand out, you can tell them a mile off. 'Wannabe' was a great first single, and '2 Become 1' is a great song. If only some alternative band could come out with that ... but instead they come out with even more trite shite.
                      —Ian McCulloch, 1998

You don't expect The Velvet Underground to produce a footie song with Burt Bacharach doing the arrangement, and Herb Alpert in there as well, do you? Originally the song had all this unrequited love, semi-sixth form metaphysical shit going on, which we had to change. There was a point when I was trying to rhyme 'Millichip' with 'chili dip.' Then you start thinking it's unnatural. After that, it was just a case of remembering playing under the streetlights as a kid—that feeling when you never wanted to stop. There's a bit at the end, 'England forever,' which is tailor-made for those Chelsea merchants—which I thought of when I was having a piss. But the song is a beaut. I'm seeing fellas with a pint in each had, Union Jack T-shirts with egg and bacon down their fronts, not realising we've been knocked out, but still singing it.

—Ian McCulloch, 1998

(HOW DOES IT FEEL TO BE)
ON TOP OF THE WORLD?

Looking like it's gonna happen
Knowing that the time is right
With pride on our side and
    the passion
We've got glory in our sights
In streets all over the nation
Are goals we painted on the walls
All our hopes and expectations
Are the world inside a ball
Inside a ball

How does it feel
To be on top of the world?
Now it's for real
We're on top of the world
We're on top of the world

These are the ties that bind us
Everyone part of the team
Leaving our worries behind us
'Cos we're sharing the same dream
It's time to dream

Goals are flying in
We've made the news
'Cos we were born to win
We can't lose
We can't lose

How does it feel
To be on top of the world?
Now it's for real
You're the top of the world
You're the top of the world

Looking like it's going to happen
Knowing that the time is right
The pride's on our side and
    the passion
We've got glory in our sights
In streets all over the nation
Are goals we painted on the walls
And all our hopes and expectations
Are the world inside a ball
Life's a ball

England
England forever
England
Love you forever

[It's] a foot-stomper, and very catchy. It's a very uplifting song—especially for me. It sounds like Echo & the Bunnymen playing someone else's song, which I thought was a good challenge to have. It was done with a certain purpose in mind, almost like a commission—and that didn't harm Michelangelo or Da Vinci!   —Ian McCulloch, 1998

Admittedly less hateful than 'Three Lions,' this attempt to recapture the excitement of being a nipper watching football with our dads is only partially successful.   —*Select,* 1998

In mid-1998, the Bunnymen entered the studio to begin recording their next LP. They were immediately confronted with difficulty, when Les Pattison announced his departure from the band.

He got a call in the morning saying that his mum had cancer. He went back and he just wanted to stay with her. He does the right thing, Les, y'know. We tried to help him, moving the recording to Liverpool and everything, but to no avail, and then when she died ... at the end of the day, the man's personal life has dealt him a terrible hand. But the door will always be open.   —Ian McCulloch, 1999

I think it just dawned on him when he was at home: he felt like he'd done his time in music, and needed to ground himself. It was for one of the most honorable reasons.
                         —Ian McCulloch, 1999

Saddened by the loss of Les but determined to press on regardless, Mac and Will drafted in some session players and continued recording the follow-up to *Evergreen*.

The first results of these sessions were made available on the Ides of March: "Rust" b/w "The Fish Hook Girl," "See the Horizon," "Beyond the Green," and "Sense of a Life."

... its title subliminally suggests Neil Young comparisons which are actually not that misplaced ...
                         —*Birmingham Post*, 1999

'Rust' is magnificent. Beneath its surface there's a strain of heavy-lidded soul, way beyond anything upon which this band has placed its name since *Ocean Rain* some 15 years ago. It's one continuous, effortless swoon … it barely breaks sweat, from the opening harmonium wheeze through spiraling guitars and on to a chorus that's pure Bunny metaphysics.   —*NME*, Single of the Week, 1999

Neil Young never sounded like this... Velvet Underground sometimes sounded like this ...
                         —Ian McCulloch, 1979

Five minutes of sweeping orchestral melodrama, underpinned by McCulloch's heartfelt pleas for forgiveness ... undoubtedly the greatest 45 the band have released since 'The Killing Moon.' It's also the sound of a man coming to terms with himself and his history.
                         —*Melody Maker*

Goddamn it if you're not a fully fledged, born-again fan by the time 'Rust' swoops to a close. How do they do it? Don't question them. Just worship.   —*Melody Maker*, 1999

... me singing to myself, 'Where the fuck have you gone?' When I'm 'down amongst the dust' these days, it's just sadness. —Ian McCulloch, 1999

I always thought I was kinda singing deeply, poetically ... whether I was conning meself or whoever. Now the lyrics are more important, because they're about things that happen, like the simplest thing in life: falling in love with someone. Or, even simpler, falling out of love. And then falling back in love. And I think that's the only miracle worth knowing about—to fall back in love with something. And that's what 'Rust' is about—something gets rusted up, you fix it. You don't go and buy a new Mercedes, you stick with the Ford Pop—that was the first car you ever sat in.

—Ian McCulloch, 1999

Seeing Cohen [live] made me think that it doesn't matter how old you are. You can be 50. I think you only age in music if you've always dealt with rock & roll clichés. And I never have.

—Ian McCulloch, 1990

RUST

I wish that you were here
Down amongst the dust
I need someone to help me
Yeah I need someone to trust
There's something in these tears
Turning me to rust
I need someone to help me
Yeah I need someone to touch

Give me one more try
And I'll come flaking back to you
I wish that you were here
I wish that it was true

I can feel the stars shooting
    through my heart like rain
Leaving all the scars where the
    pleasure turns to pain
Point me in the light of a bright
    and shining right direction
And then take me home again

Just when you think it's over
Just when you think it's done
Out of every nowhere
You never see it come

I know the lines are showing
I can't keep them in
Like everybody's story
It's written on the skin

Give me one last try
And I'll make it up to you
Wish that you were here
Wish that I was true

I can feel the stars shooting
    through my heart like rain
Leaving all the scars where the
    pleasure turns to pain
Point me in the light of a bright
    and shining right direction
And then take me home again

Everything's gonna be alright
Everything's gonna be alright,
    now ...

Wish that you were here ...

For me to actually sing about my aging process—which no-one ever likes to admit to—on 'Rust' is, I think, a lot more cutting-edge or left-field than me singing about 'Killing Moons' or going 'Over the Wall' at this point, to be honest. Because, well, it hurts me more than it hurts you.   —Ian McCulloch 1999

[My hair is] bound to fall out. Me dad had a Fred MacMurray recede-o. But by then I'll be well into the suits and Madison Square Garden. I'm not going to do Vegas. I've decided against it. I wanna do Carnegie and the Garden. The old recede-o'll suit the songs. More songs about unrequited life. That's basically what I write about. Always did. And now, I just know more about it.   —Ian McCulloch, 1998

THE FISH-HOOK GIRL

See the girl with the fish-hooks
    in her
See the boy in another prayer
See the cross slipping through
    his fingers
Going, going, gone nowhere
See the man, a necrophilian
Got boxes full of hair
The streets are God dead willing
Someone dying in the dead air ...

Hey now ...
What am I doing here?

Pick your god and pray he's out there
And hope he hears your voice
Our knees are at the altar
Be sure you make the right choice
See the man with his necrophilian
Got boxes full of hair
The streets are made for killing
Someone dying in the dead air …

Hey now ...
What are we doing here?

SEE THE HORIZON

One of these days I'm gonna
    make up my mind
To crawl or take flight
Yeah, one of these days I'm gonna
    take what I find
And look for the rest in the next life
We all start kneeling before
    we can run
We all come in dreaming and
    we all die young

Everybody wants you now
Now your wings are open
Everybody asks you how
You were never broken

You thought you could keep
    your eyes on
Spinning the world on its heels
You said you could see the horizon
As you fell asleep at the wheel
Some want it aching and some
    want it numb
All of us waiting for someone
    to come

Everybody wants you now
Now your wings are open
Everybody asks you how
You were never broken

One of these days I'm gonna
    make up my mind
To crawl or take flight
Yeah, one of these days I'm gonna
    take what I find
And look for the rest in the next life
We all start kneeling before
    we can run
We all come in screaming and
    we all die young

Everybody wants you now
Now your wings are open
Everybody asks you how
You were never broken

SENSE OF LIFE

Tried to see the future
Had to lose some memory
Tried to do my duty
Had to lose some dignity

Trying to make some sense of life
Trying to get straight tonight
Tonight

Let's walk into the light
The past out of mind and out of sight
Let's make our every wrong
Turn out all right

Looking for tomorrow
Trying hard to not belong
Don't know how to follow
Don't know how to go along

Trying to make some sense of life
Trying to go straight tonight
Tonight

Let's walk into the light
The past out of mind and out of sight
Let's make our every wrong
Turn out all right

Tried to see the future
Had to lose some memory
Tried to find the beauty
Had to lose some dignity

Trying to make some sense of life
Trying to go straight tonight
Tonight

Let's walk into the light
The past out of mind and out of sight
Let's make our every wrong
Turn out all right

BEYOND THE GREEN

I'm still standing in the queue
Trynna get a better view
Of my life whereas it's bending
New days, new ways ever true
But not for me and not for you
Where the stories have no ending

Tell me why
I be the way I be
Six feet high
Ain't high enough for me

Dark clouds hanging overhead
You keep drowning in your bed
We're still waiting for the sun
    to shine
Burning underneath the waves
You'll be coming from the haze
Someday somehow sometime

Tell me why
I be the way I be
Six feet high
Ain't high enough for me
High enough for me

WHAT ARE YOU GOING TO DO WITH YOUR LIFE?

The Bunnymen's 8th studio album (if you count *Reverberation*), *What Are You Going To Do With Your Life?* was released in early spring to possibly the most rapturous reviews of their twenty-plus-year existence.

A record of breathtaking emotional scope and vulnerability, it lays bare those last ten years with unprecedented candor and honesty. After a career of riddles and metaphors, this is a close as you're ever going to get to confession. Even its magnificent title speaks volumes about the reflective and dignified nature of what's contained within ... a magnificent achievement. It's so overpoweringly beautiful, so full of noble sentiment and musical invention. —*NME*, 1999

How apt that 1999 should be The Year of The Rabbit. But could even the most astute Chinese astrologer have foreseen that *What Are You Going To Do With Your Life?* is worthier of the name Echo & the Bunnymen and all its mythic properties than anything since *Ocean Rain*, the self-styled 'Greatest Album Ever Made'? ... At no point does [this album] rock. It glides with a beautiful, uninhibited momentum ... above all it swoons to the tune of its master's voice, an instrument honed by years of life, love, and all the shitty bits in between to a ravished state of molten cashmere. For every flawless second of its defiantly brief 38-and-a-half minutes, Ian McCulloch sings it like he has to: like a man and from the heart ... it's a heart-to-heart between Mac, his questing soul, and nine tunes fit for God's Walkman. In that Great Saloon Bar in the Sky, Frank Sinatra lights another ciggie and smiles. Ian McCulloch is singing songs for young lovers of all ages. A pure, timeless Echo. —*Melody Maker*

Two little Bunnies went to market; all the other little Bunnies stayed home. But just because it walks like Electrafixion and talks like Electrafixion, that doesn't mean it *is* Electrafixion. [McCulloch and Sergeant] have created an album that's at least as satisfying as their last, *Evergreen*, which means, once again, that it's as great as anything they did the first time around. Melody and melancholy are the key words ... with McCulloch's newly gruffed vocals draping a husky, smoked-too-much nocturnalism [sic] over even the album's brighter moments. Sergeant's guitar had never sounded better, either ... What are they going to do with their lives? Let's just hope they'll keep making albums like this. —*AP*, 1999

... this is the record that should have followed *Ocean Rain*, a passionate set of lushly orchestrated songs supposedly intended as McCulloch's tender apology to his wife for having strayed. McCulloch's voice sounds marvelous, and he hasn't written such revealing, intimate songs since his solo debut, *Candleland*. Sergeant's invigorating guitar shimmers as ever, but it's the orchestrations that bring a sense of timelessness and grandeur to the dreamy 'When It All Blows Over' and the gentle epic 'Fools Like Us.' They're delivered on the promise of a decade ago with an album of such maturity and spine-tingling emotional sweep that here's hoping the Bunnymen have found exactly what they're going to do with their life. —*CMJ*, 1999

Mac's view of the album is that it contains the most honest and heartfelt songs that he has ever written.

It's an album I needed to write and sing. It's our most melodic. It's for anyone who has a heart. It's totally our best, by light years. I guarantee this album has hidden depths. It's the Turin Shroud—without the Beard. —Ian McCulloch, 1999

It was just the record to make at this time. It's the truest reflection of what I was feeling. To write for another reason—to try to knock off top 5 singles for the rest of my life—is not what I'm here for; it's to write it all down and sing about it—whatever *it* is, y'know? —Ian McCulloch, 1999

If you want to know what this album's about, it's about dreams of love and life. It's unashamedly romantic, much more than *Ocean Rain* was ... I'm seeing a lot of dudes with muzzies buying this. And a lot of girls, obviously. There are some great photos of me inside, so it'll be like a double whammy. —Ian McCulloch, 1999

Not everyone agreed with Mac. Some argued that not only was the record too short, but, with the absence of Les, and Will's guitar more understated in the mix than ever before, the collection of ballads was, in essence, little more than a too-mellow McCulloch solo album—*Candleland* part II.

It was probably the worst time in my whole life, doing that LP—I hated it ... and I said I was going to leave ... I'm on all the tracks here and there, but generally I just stayed in the tent! It was a horrible experience. If it ever gets like that again, I'm definitely going. —Will Sergeant, 2001

Some of the best records ever are short. Bowie's *Station To Station* has just six tracks, and this album is only just longer than [*Ziggy Stardust*], the one which changed my life. —Ian McCulloch, 1999

Although Will's guitar certainly was marginalized on this particular album, there was no mistaking the power of Mac's vocals. The man agreed, if he did say so himself.

Allegedly, [my voice is] the best it's ever been. But it's because I'm singing proper songs that lend themselves to my voice. There's none of that operatic stuff, particularly. That's something I can do live. I just think I write differently now. If I listen to some of that old stuff on record, I think, 'bloody hell ... I should've just sung it straight.' I think it's more intimate that way. It's really well-sung, but it's not overdone or unctuous. —Ian McCulloch, 1998

More than anything else, the album was the sound of Mac revealing himself, completely and candidly, for perhaps the first time; the sound of Ian McCulloch, the man, finally confronting and successfully overthrowing a public image he had long outgrown. No longer Mac the Mouth, the metaphysical mystery kid, or angst-ridden admiral of the overcoat army, he was now presenting himself as all he ever really had been, or needed to be: Ian Stephen McCulloch.

The thing is, you see—and this is what no-one really understands—I'm having a whale of a time. I've never been so happy. This is like how I was before I joined up with the rest of those miserable bastards. I'm not miserable. I never have been. I only went off with the whole soddin' overcoat business because I had a funny walk and wanted to disguise it. I want to go out, have a pint, crack a few jokes, and see how it goes from there. It's not much to ask, is it?
—Ian McCulloch, 1999

Public soul-baring has never been Ian McCulloch's thing. Until now, that is ... Mac has ditched the opaque ... surreal imagery and is shooting from the hip. And more importantly, the heart. The album's title says it all. This is The Coolest Man In Rock ... taking stock and revealing himself to be as vulnerable, big-hearted, and hopelessly flawed as you always knew, or at least prayed, he would be.
—*Melody Maker*, 1999

WHAT ARE YOU GOING TO DO
WITH YOUR LIFE?

If I knew now what I knew then
I'd wonder how not wonder when
There's something going wrong again
With me and mine
It's only ever what it seems
Memories and might have beens
Heaven's scent: the smell of dreams
We'll never find

Tell me, tell me, tell me

What are you going to do
    with your life?
What are you going to do
    with your life?
What are you going to do?
What are you going to be?
What am I going to do?
I'm going to be me, be me, be me

If I could see what you can see
The sun's still shining out of me
I'd be the boy I used to be
When love was blind
I'd let the light back in again
Walk you to the tunnel's end
I'd be yours and maybe then
You'd be mine

So tell me, tell me, tell me
What are you going to do
    with your life? ...

I will, if you will
Follow me down ...

A fantastic title. It's the question I've asked myself, the question everyone needs to ask themselves—just what the fuck are you going to do?
—Ian McCulloch, 1999

What am I going to do with my life? Keep singing, keep dancing, and keep laughing my head off, hopefully. Laughing's still the best thing.
—Ian McCulloch, 1999

After 39 years spinning 'round this planet, it actually struck me last year, that's all you've gotta be—yourself. All I've done is get a grip on me own life, and thought, 'This is me being as eloquent and articulate as I can be about one simple thing in life.' I'm gonna decide what underpants I wear, when I change me socks, when I have a bath, how I do me hair—all of that shit—and on the next album I'm gonna throw it all up in the air and see what happens. —Ian McCulloch, 1999

There does seem to be a longing for a more innocent time in the song. I think I was directing some of the lyrics toward a version of me when I was 15, when I was just totally absorbed in the music. Bowie, the Velvets, Iggy, Leonard Cohen—that used to be my world. I was a melancholy kid. I couldn't wait for the nighttime, so I could play music and feel weird.
                    —Ian McCulloch, 1999

'Get in The Car' ... is all lazy bongos, warm Mediterranean nights, and cozy, muted brass. It's a worthy inheritor of Bacharach's mantle.
                    —*Melody Maker*, 1999

GET IN THE CAR

Let's go and take a starlit drive
To where the shaping of our lives
Had just begun
When we were young
When everything was coming right
In all our dreams of love and
     life
And we would run
Into the sun

Get in the car
We're taking a ride
We're looking for stars
Looking for satellites
Of love
Of love

Changes coming changes gone
We just want to be someone
Behind the tears
Behind the tears
Nights and days go on and on
And things are coming out all
     wrong
And no one hears
No one hears

Get in the car
We're taking a ride
We're looking for stars
We're looking for satellites
Get in the car
We're taking a ride
You'll be the star
I'll be your satellite
Of love
Of love

Let's go and take a ride
To all those starry nights
We used to fly upon
When we were young
When everything was coming right
In all our dreams of love and
     life
And we would run
Into the sun

Nothing's gonna get me down ...

BABY RAIN

Lost again
Still waiting for the voices
That don't call my name
Had too many choices
And I missed my aim
No pearls inside the oysters

Just a world
With no answers
We all get life
And take our chances

In the rain
Baby rain
In the rain
Baby rain

Glad to be
Alive and still believing
What you said to me
Your love was never leaving
And it comes for free
So what's the use of stealing

From your girl
When she's the answer
And your world
And your chances

In the rain
Baby rain
In the rain
Baby rain

I've got what you want
When're you going to get me?

Home again
I can hear the voices
Singing out my name
Life is where the choice is
And I've found my aim
Don't need pearls or oysters

Just a world
With all the answers
I've got life
I'll take my chances

In the rain
Baby rain
In the rain
Baby Rain

It's as in 'virgin rain,' and it's about the first time you get pissed on—physically and metaphorically. That's when you learn about yourself.
—Ian McCulloch, 1999

When I wrote 'Killing Moon,' I believed that whatever choice you made was predestined. But now I believe we make our own choices. Instead of just wallowing in the wilderness, I've come through. And it's because I do love life. I mean, some days I think, 'What's the soddin' point?' but generally I get excited about every day. I know there was a time when I didn't think anything stacked up. It didn't matter whether you were a rocket scientist or a gravedigger; they were both the same, and they were both a load of crap. But now I think you've gotta bury dead people, and man has to go to the moon. And now I try to make the right choices.   —Ian McCulloch, 1999

'History Chimes' I've had since about 1989. I tried it in loads of different ways with the solo band I had then, but I was never happy with it having drums on. But I know it was an important song for this record, and so I asked our keyboard player Mark Taylor to play it on piano with a few Lennon-esque flourishes, and I know it was totally the right way for it to be done.

—Ian McCulloch, 1999

HISTORY CHIMES

Bells high on a hill
History chimes
And you want a new beginning
Tell me in biro or quill
Your purpose and mine
Prove that our world is spinning
So here goes nothing better
And here's to something else

Until tomorrow
But that's another time
It's just another time
It's just some other troubled
    time

The seed grew up a boy
Turned to a man
Is this the world you wanted?
It seems under the soil
Over the sand
Not quite the seed I planted

I've seen you
And now I know better
I've been you
Now I'm someone else

Until tomorrow
But that's another time
It's just another time
It's just some other troubled
    time

Until tomorrow
Until ...

LOST ON YOU

It's just a dangerous bend
On a slippery slope
Another rainbow's end
On the highway of hope
It's always next time
Always next time
Always last time

Just get me out of this jam
It's stuck to me like glue
And I can't remember who I am
My memory got lost on you

I had things inside my head
And they put me behind them
Thought they'd be safe in my head
And now I just can't find them

MORNING SUN

Show me the hole I can fall in
To the ground to the ground
   to the ground
Speak to me, speak
And give me my calling
'Cos I'm going down, going down,
   going down

It's only lies and alibis
Alibis and lies
We know something dies every day

I've lost or I've forgotten
More than I'll ever know
Born just a someone with
   some kind of nothing
I let it go, let it go, let it go

It's just a trick of light
And some sleight of hand
Another kiss goodnight
Along the rise of man
And it's the last time
It's the last time
'Til the next time

So get me out of this jam
It's stuck to me like glue
And I can't remember who I am
My memory got lost on you

I had things inside my head
And they put me behind them
Thought they'd be safe in my head
And now I just can't find them

It's gone and that's too bad
The best thing that I ever had
Had the whole world in my mouth
Ate it up and spat it out ...

It's only lies and alibis
Alibis and lies
We know something dies every day
Here it comes the morning sun
Another hit and run
And we're just the ones in the way

Coming down with you ...

Give me a hope I can lean on
'Cos I'll bend in the calmest of winds
Give me more than dreams for me
   to dream on
My jury's in, coming in, coming in

It's the story of the Bunnymen's life. We have always been lost on and gone over the heads of the vast majority of the general public. But it's supposed to be a good time: laughing in the face of failure and self-destruction.
—Ian McCulloch, 1999

… something I've had chordally for five or six years, but it never seemed right. On this album, it's the one bit of semi-light relief. It was the song where I could get in a bit of the Frankie Vaughan/Tony Christie thing. It's an homage to the 'Sunday Night at the London Palladium' crowd.
—Ian McCulloch, 1999

It's not about suicide. It's a spiral ... I don't know ... it rhymes ... I haven't a soddin' clue! It's about getting on with life; not worrying. 'Life is for dying, baby, so get on with it.' It's not a down kind of thing. It's just 'get on with it and I'll do the whingeing for you in the song.'
—Ian McCulloch, 1999

... it's about Lorraine. She'd prefer I said it in layman's language, but I don't. She knows most of the album's about her.   —Ian McCulloch, 1999

A marriage song ... as if Paul McCartney's 'When I'm 64' has been brought up to date and stripped of its sentimentality.
     —The Mail On Sunday, 1999

WHEN IT ALL BLOWS OVER

When it all blows over
Can we start again?
When we've both grown older
Will you love me then?
Say you'll love me then

You never had to tell me
I already knew
The first time you held me
It was only you
It was only ever you

Through every change
As I turned with the tide
Through all of my games
You were there by my side

When it all blows over
Can we start again?
When we've both grown older
Will you love me then?
Say you'll love me then

Will you love me then?
Say you'll love me then
Did you love me then?

We've been together 20 years, and you don't get through all that without loving each other. We were on our way home from a funeral recently, and I asked Lorraine 'Do you think I'm funny?' She said 'Of course I do. You're the funniest bastard I've ever met.' That meant a lot to me, because sometimes she'll say 'that's a terrible joke'—so when she said what she said, 20 years on, it made my day. —Ian McCulloch, 1999

YOUNG AT HEART

Bunnymen fans in the UK must have been surprised when, sitting down for tea in front of the TV early in 1999, a familiar voice could be heard dripping honey over the Sinatra classic "Young at Heart" during an advertisement for Bell's Whiskey.

I wanted to do it for Frank's sake. He would have wanted me to. I was invited to BBC Merseyside because I'd once said that Frank meant more to me than The Velvet Underground, so I got boiled in a studio paying tribute to the great man. Everyone was talking about his phrasing, and the way in which he interpreted a lyric. All I could say was that it went way beyond that. He was a dude and he was connected to the Mafia. That's all I ever wanted: to be able to sing, jump a queue, and have anyone who pissed me off sorted out.   —Ian McCulloch, 1999

Frank was just taking the piss. It's like when Elvis sings about Old Shep you know he meant it, but when Frank sings, you know he's just waiting to get out of the recording studio so he can tap off which another girl. Frank wanted people like me to realise that he was taking the piss. You can't rattle off that many songs without thinking, 'Jesus Christ, I've got to get out of here and into the casino.'
—Ian McCulloch, 2001

I'll be the Sinatra of the 21st Century.   —Ian McCulloch, 1995

The best voice ever ... Frank's just a real role model for people who wanna be cool. I love all those bad connections he has ... and great suits.
—Ian McCulloch, 1994

   One wonders, given his obvious admiration of Ol' Blue Eyes, how did Mac first hear of Sinatra's death?

From the telly. Unfortunately, he didn't ring me up beforehand to warn me.   —Ian McCulloch, 1999

NEW MILLENNIUM BUNNYMEN

In the late spring of 1999, the *NME* website announced that the Bunnymen were planning to record a cover of Thunderclap Newman's 1969 hippie anthem "Something In the Air" as a surprise one-off summer single, to compete with the likes of Oasis. Sadly, the song was never recorded, due to leaks to the press.
   Echo & the Bunnymen finished 1999 by playing a free show on New

Year's Eve at the St. George's Plateau, just a few feet from the hall where they'd played their 'Crystal Day' show some fifteen years earlier. As with 'Crystal Day,' Mac saw the show as a way of rewarding both Liverpool and Bunnymen fans old and new for their support and loyalty.

Not everybody has got the money to spend, so we were delighted to be asked to do the St. George's Plateau event. I know it sounds corny, but it's good to be giving something back to the city. It should be a great feeling, looking out at 12,000 faces, in that really beautiful part of the city. It's probably the most beautiful part of the city—apart from Anfield, obviously. We'll be playing a set before midnight, and then after that, coming back on to do some more. We want everyone to have a great time, and for it to be a rocking event, not a maudlin one—so we won't be taking any chances with the songs we play! We wouldn't want to get booed off—it wouldn't be that good a way to start a new Millennium, would it? I can't imaging a better way to spend my millennium. Music has been the focus of my whole life, along with my family, and I can't imagine seeing in the New Year doing anything else.   —Ian McCulloch, 1999

After the countdown to the New Year, the band kicked off the millennium with one of pop's most timeless and transcendent messages—The Beatles' "All You Need Is Love." In an effort to clear away the lively crowd as quickly as possible, a Phil Collins recording was aired immediately afterwards.

★★★

In early 2000, the Bunnymen parted ways with London Records. Was this due to the relatively poor sales of *What Are You Going To Do With Your Life?*

What they said is, 'We'll keep you on if you don't take as much money as in the contract,' and we had no intention of staying anyway, so it was kind of 'were we pushed or did we fall?' I think that was their way of saying, 'We're going to let you go.' If we'd said we'd take the ten bob they wanted to offer us, we'd probably still have been on there, but it just changed so much as a company. The MD there on the first record was great but he went on to manage none other than Elton John by our second album, so we were left in a bit of a hole along with other bands.   —Ian McCulloch, 2001

Manager Paul Toogood amicably departed the Bunnymen camp to form his own record label, and the session journeymen who comprised the 1999 Bunnymen moved on to new gigs. Undaunted, Mac and Will found new management in Pete Byrne and former road manager Peasey—collectively, "Porcupine Management"—and, by word of mouth alone, drafted a new Liverpool-based group. Auditions were, apparently, non-existent.

If we started auditions, me and Will would have to sack *ourselves*.
—Ian McCulloch, 2001

In late 2000, this new incarnation of the Bunnymen released *Avalanche*, an EP available only by the Internet on the Gimmemusic label.

The Internet has interested us for awhile, and it would be wrong not to give it a try. It gives us a chance to control things ourselves and to do what we want. Record companies are really worried about the Internet, but it's their own fault; they don't care about bands, they're just interested in keeping their own jobs. People don't realize that when they buy a CD for 15, bands hardly see a penny. When I was buying a Bowie album in the 70's for 2.50, I used to think [it] would go to him, because it was his songs and his face was on the cover. But of course my money went straight to the record companies. The Internet gives people more of a choice, and gives bands more control.
—Ian McCulloch, 2000

The EP featured the recently written title track, (originally titled "Roxy/Wire" to indicate its influences), brand-new takes on "Silver," "Zimbo," and "Angels and Devils," (rerecorded by fans' request), plus a couple of cover songs. Although the band originally intended to record versions of The Doors' "Moonlight Drive" and, oddly, America's "Horse With No Name," they eventually settled on a spooked chamber-pop interpretation of Tim Hardin's "Hang On To a Dream," and a sublime version of Dylan's "It's All Over Now, Baby Blue," by way of The Chocolate Watchband.

The spark's still there, as is the majestic songwriting on the solitary new track, 'Avalanche.' Today the world wide web, tomorrow the world.
—*Uncut*, 2000

... realigns the critical musical balance between Ian McCulloch, the crooner, and Will Sergeant, the psychedelist ... Given that McCulloch has downplayed the experimental side of the band exemplified by 'Zimbo''s haunting Burundi beat, the song's inclusion here surely represents a welcome volte face. But the final tune, Dylan's 'It's All Over Now, Baby Blue,' justifies the admission. Battling it out with Van Morrison for the definitive reading of this song, Sergeant and keyboardist Ceri James's melodic conjuring is breathtaking, while McCulloch—sounding sadder than ever—journeys into the heart of the song's melancholy and distress. As with the choice and delivery of 'Hang On To a Dream' and old B-side 'Angels and Devils,' both songs of personal crisis, you wonder whether Mac is somehow intimately involved with these words. Is he hiding some enormous personal/career trauma ... or merely exhibiting the hallmarks of one of rock singing's true masters?
—*The Guardian*, 2000

Snowblind
I can't see and I can't breathe
So tired
Turn the lights off when you
      leave

Do-do-do-do-do-do-do-do-do ...

Inside
And I'll never take you there
Would my soul die
When my head came up for air?

Do-do-do-do-do-do-do-do-do ...

So pure
You've been driven like the snow
No cure
Can I take it when you go?

Do-do-do-do-do-do-do-do-do ...

Yeah, mind your head ...

Throughout 2000, in addition to working on new Bunnymen material, Will continued with his Glide side-project, releasing the live LP, *Performance*, on Ochre Records, while Mac worked on solo material. Eventually, his crushed-velvet croon could be heard on two songs for the soundtrack to a British film, *There's Only One Jimmy Grimble and No Substitute for Life*. Combining his talents with Simon Boswell and Alex James from Blur, he recorded a virtually a capella take on the classic "Blue Moon," plus a new ballad, "Do You Believe?"

DO YOU BELIEVE?

Do you believe
Do you believe the world turns
      'round?
Do you believe
Are your feet still on solid
      ground?
Do you believe
Do you think that you were
      told the truth?
Do you believe
Or would you ask to see the
      proof?

I don't know
I can't see
And I can't wait
For you and me

If I look to the sky
If I look to the sky
Will I see a new sunrise
Or set in your eyes?

Am I the one
The one that you've been
      waiting for?

When I'm gone
Will you still be wanting more?

I don't know
I can't see
And I can't wait
For you and me

If I look to the sky
If I look to the sky
Will I see a new sunrise
Or set in your eyes?

As 2000 drew to a close, the Bunnymen signed a deal with Cooking Vinyl Records. Mac and Will were more enthusiastic to record together than they had been in years.

Not being on a major is the best thing we've ever done. We're on an indie now and my feet have hardly touched the ground ... It feels exciting again. Cooking Vinyl heard about us through a mutual friend, and they kept phoning us over the year, and it seemed they were the keenest. It's a small, tight-knit company, with four or five people who know what they're doing, whereas at majors there are 95 people there who don't have a clue. It's good to be somewhere where people care about the music first, and all the other bits later.

—Ian McCulloch, 2000

Mac and I have a plan to make the new record very interesting indeed; as I type, wheels are being set in motion, sounds are starting to form in our skulls, and chemical reactions fizz and pop. Yes, that old black magic has got us in its spell. I am not at liberty to tell you the full story yet, but if all goes to plan the next record will be a stonker, baby.

—Will Sergeant, 2000

Rumor had it that Mac and Will wrote all the material for the new record in under ten hours. In January 2001, they entered Elevator Studios in Liverpool and The Dairy Studios in South London, to begin recording. Within the tiny space of a month, the new album, *Flowers*, was recorded and mixed. Why and how so fast?

We kind of half-discussed it before we started writing: next time we go in the studio, let's not waste time. Let's enjoy it, you know? Sometimes in the studio, I can get sidetracked and bored. Everything seems to take too long. It is the quickest album we've ever written, and one of the quickest to record. I think that shows. I think we just decided 'let's get on with it, not think of orchestras or too many guitar parts. Let's just do it the way we did *Crocodiles*.' We don't want particularly to hearken back to that, but I think that's the way we set out to do it, with as much spontaneity and as much verve. We wanted to do the album with as much vim and vigor as we could muster. It does feel like a debut album. I think, after 22 years, that says a lot about our raging against the dying of the light.

—Ian McCulloch, 2001

It isn't rocket science. Will would come 'round to my house for a couple of hours one day ,and we'd come up with, like, four different things. We'd have the next day off, and he'd come 'round the following day for another couple of hours. One day we just talked on the phone for an hour and got a song out of that.

—Ian McCulloch, 2001

On March 14, 2001, the Bunnymen played their first gig in over a year, a one-off show at the University of London. It was, in Mac's mind, a "curl-your-toes success." Critics agreed.

Strutting like Ali, slithering like a cobra, roaring like a Walker Brother, eyes shaded like the bastard son of Lou Reed, footie-ing the

... although only Ian McCulloch and Will Sergeant still carry the original torch, it doesn't seem to have diluted the live Echo experience much. Mac is as ever the epitome of the scally with the aching voice. He spends much of the gig chain-smoking, swaggering, and muttering unintelligible comments between songs … Still valid and vibrant, the Bunnymen march on.
                    —*Dotmusic,* 2001

dying embers of each cigarette into the audience, Ian McCulloch defies belief. If he wasn't real, you couldn't invent him for the simple reason nobody—not Liam, not even Elvis circa '56—could be this cool. Or so I'm thinking, and it's only the first song, 'Supermellow Man,' the first of several tantalizing previews from the forthcoming [album], all of which hold their own amid Bunnymen heavyweights. As an impression of the greatest band on the planet, this is utterly convincing, leaving us little choice other than to surrender to their genius. Little the Bunnymen do or say this evening seems less than godlike. *Heaven Up Here.*
                    —*Uncut,* 2001

Cooking Vinyl released their first Bunnymen single "It's Alright," b/w "Marble Towers," "Rescue (The Mindwinder's Remix)," "Scratch the Past," and "A Promise (Lo Fi Lullabye #1)" on April 23. The two-disk set also featured the "It's Alright" video.

It's cheeky, it feels cocky and about something. I've described it as 'Nirvana meets Sylvester,' but it's got a weird kinda slant to it ... it's not like a conventional single. It's straight ahead with a twist, it bends and undulates ... I think it's the standout track on the album, in terms of what I'm into.
                    —Ian McCulloch, 2001

It's not alright, it's fandab-bydozee! It's our first UK single release—'Bunnymen back on form' is all I seem to hear lately.   —Will Sergeant, 2001

IT'S ALRIGHT

Somebody wants you
Someone out there
Somebody needs you
Somebody cares
Somebody loves you
Someone somewhere
But if nobody's there

Here they come again
Whispers in my head
Same old sad refrain
Wished I'd never said
What I said ... yeah
Take me to the top
I need more not less
And don't ever tell me when to stop

Here comes tomorrow
And yesterday's news
Empty and hollow
Broken and bruised
No one to follow, nothing to lose
And only you can choose

Somebody wants you
Someone out there
Somebody needs you
Somebody cares
Somebody loves you
Someone somewhere
But if nobody's there ...

A dead-on pastiche of the swirling Doors-y acid rock which so intoxicated them in their youth. It's not a great song, and hackneyed homilies about how the mighty have fallen are hard to resist. The Bunnymen never quite achieved true greatness, but they always acted like they had, which counted for something. They deserve a kinder fate than becoming a Stranglers-type self-tribute band.   —*NME,* 2001

MARBLE TOWERS

Spent the night in marble towers
A million stories high
Saw the lights of meteor showers
Dropping in the sky
Made a wish and wished I'd made it
Home before the sun
Running for the rooftops
Rooftop's on the run

Left the life the life you left me
Crying out for more
Guess you knew you knew I guessed it
What those clues were for
Maps for dreams, hiding places
Underneath the stairs
Hiding in the rooftops
Rooftop's running scared

Don't think twice and roll the dice
Stake your life on a perfect seven
Paradise at any price
Take your slice for a piece of
    Heaven

Don't look twice and roll the dice
Stake your life on a perfect seven
Paradise at any price
Take another slice get a piece of
    Heaven
Heaven ...

SCRATCH THE PAST

If you want somebody you
    can understand
You know that I could be your man
But if it's anybody who can
    hold your hand
When any old nobody can
Rising from the ashes with
    my head in flames
It's good to feel the fire again
Striking all the matches in
    our special game
Burning through old skin to play

Looking for the pieces to my
    jigsaw man
Trynna keep the demons in
Looking for a planet I can
    understand
Just trynna get my world to spin

Just don't try to catch me 'cos
I'm moving too fast
Only trynna scratch the past
C'mon ...

Just don't try to catch me 'cos
I'm moving too fast
Only trynna scratch the past
C'mon ...

FLOWERS

On May 14, Cooking Vinyl followed up "It's Alright" with the release of *Flowers*. As opposed to the previous album, *both* Mac and Will loved this one.

It's a very guitar-based record—it rocks—with odd bits of trippy keyboards and Mac's chiming, timeless vocals ... the mix features radical stereo sounds as used by The Beatles, etc—lots of hard panning and clarity—and it sounds fantastic. The tunes are pure Bunnymen, ranging from the darkest nightmares to a jangly guitar pop ... the overall thing is way cool and every one in the Bunnymen camp (including me and Mac) and record label think its the best stuff we have come up with in years ...   —Will Sergeant, 2001

It's a great Bunnymen fans album ... it's got more of the first three ... than any other. Every song seems like a cornerstone ... It sounds just like a real vintage Bunnymen album. I think that whatever we do is great, but there's definitely a vibe on this record. There's loads of energy ... and we love it. I've always thought whatever we did was brilliant but ... this is probably the most complete [record] we've done since *Ocean Rain*. I think that Will and I have got this bond back that was last evident around the time we recorded *Ocean Rain*. We loved making that ... and hopefully, someday we'll look back at this moment in time the same way. Things in the Bunny camp are probably the best they've been since the eighties, in terms of everyone gelling and feeling like a band, and everyone getting on and feeling confident and positive. Right now, I feel in the right place at the right time. Being in ... Bunnyland.   —Ian McCulloch, 2001

Most critics agreed that the vintage *Flowers* in Bunnyland had a fine bouquet.

Flowers may be the best album of their career. In large part, it's due to the sustained excellence of the guitarist, Will Sergeant, whose instrument credits read like a classic-guitar wish-list, from Fender Jaguar through Gibson, Vox, and Martin, to the ubiquitous Ricky 12-string, all manipulated with precise awareness of their place in rock history. Lyrically, too, it's their best in some while, Ian McCulloch grasping the nettle of his midlife crisis with greater alacrity than you might expect ... acknowledging his burnt bridges and wrong turnings, but taking solace in his attempt to 'get my head back in the clouds.' Which is, of course, exactly where it belongs.

—The Independent, 2001

A classic addition to a celestial guitar pop canon...   *—Uncut,* 2001

KING OF KINGS

Met Jesus up on a hill
He confessed I was dressed to kill
Saw fear eternal in his eyes
He's seen what happens when the
    soul dies

I'm the king of kings
Wearing broken wings
I've lost my crown
The world so far below
And all I really know
Is that you don't look down

Came alive in the dead of night
Sought salvation in the city lights
One more drink then one drink more
Every hour like the one before

I'm the king of kings
Wearing broken wings
I've lost my crown
The world so far below
And all I really know
Is that you don't look down

Don't look down...
It's such a long way to fall

Came alive in the dead of night
Sought salvation in the city
    lights
One more drink then one drink more
Every hour like the one before
You're like me, and I'm like you
Can't see the point in a point
    of view
All time lows we're hitting the
    heights
Two wrongs trying to make it
    alright

I'm the king of kings
Wearing broken wings
I've lost my crown
The world so far below
And all I really know
Is that you don't look down

It's not really about anything, to be honest, other than me and Jesus, kinda hangin'. Me and Jesus and the Rat Pack. It's just a beaut of a song. It's definitely the most Doors-y song we've ever done ... and it's tongue-in-cheek, which is even better.

—Ian McCulloch, 2001

I think it's Doors-esque swagger. [It] will become a part of the furniture of future Bunnymen set lists.

—Will Sergeant, 2001

[The song was] born in my home
studio (The Pod). I planted the
seed of a dubtastic bass line
in the garden of my hard drive
and, with love and a large
amount of tea, we grew us a
trippy surf ride though the
mind—or something like that.
                —Will Sergeant, 2001

It's Will's title ... but it's
not particularly mellow ...
it's more groove/psychedelic,
like the Velvets meets the
Stone Roses with Mani playing
drums and bass ... it's hypnotic. It's about fear the dawn.
                —Ian McCulloch, 2001

SUPERMELLOW MAN

Will you walk through my storm?
Can I be your one and only?
Will you talk me through
      'til dawn?
Never felt so lost and lonely

When night turns into morning
And you don't know how long
      you must wait
As life came without warning
Your destiny will come too late

In the pool of my life
Kissing the ground that made me
Ancient rules, wrong from right
Wish I'd found you when you
      could save me

When night turns into morning
And you don't know how long
      you must wait
As life came without warning
Your destiny will come too late

Can it ever be the same?
Will we ever dream again?
Walk through the sweet,
      sweet pain of love?
No one ever broke the bough
The cradle fell anyhow
There's angels in the thunder
      clouds, above

When night turns into morning
And you don't know how long
      you must wait
As life came without warning
Your destiny will come too late
Kiss the ground ...

I've always wanted to try and write a song about where I came from,
but rather than it being 'Liverpool, Liverpool, Liverpool,' I wanted
to use the phrase by the philosopher Jung, 'The Pool of Life.' I love
that phrase. Liverpool is the center of the universe that Jules Verne
was looking for, and I've been trying to convince people of that for
ages.   —Ian McCulloch, 2001

HIDE AND SEEK

Hide and seek, cloak and find
All the colours in your mind
Tied together, Sunday's clown
Traced and feathered, laced
    and bound

It's you now ... yeah
Everybody's looking for you
    now ... yeah

I know you know we know I'm
    going down
Help me get my feet back off
    the ground

Come with me and I will show
What not to be, where not to go
Chase the shadows through
    black holes
Find the darkness in your soul

It's me now ... yeah
Everybody says it was me
    now ... yeah
Everybody's looking for me now

I know you know we know I'm going down
Help me get my feet back off
    the ground
I know you know we know I'm going down
Help me get my head back in the clouds

Hide and seek, cloak and find
All the colours in your mind
Tied together, Sunday's clown
Traced and feathered, laced
    and bound

I know you know we know I'm going down
Help me get my feet back off
    the ground
I know you know we know I'm going down
Help me get my head back in the clouds

Don't be afraid, it will not harm you. Dark spikey guitars lead you to a baroque world of thunderous chords and lyrical loveliness
—Will Sergeant, 2001

It's basically my recurring Icarus theme, but always knowing that there's someone out there who's gonna help me.
—Ian McCulloch, 2001

Finding new lyrical inspiration after over 20 years can't be easy, but 'Hide and Seek's chorus of 'help me get my feet back off the ground ... help me get my head back in the clouds' is pretty inexcusable.
—Dotmusic, 2001

MAKE ME SHINE

I'll be with you in your Summer
Winter Spring and Fall days
You and me, yeah we've got each other
I'll be there—always

Love it when you say
I'm the gold inside your goldmine
And I love the way
You just make me shine

When our ship hits stormy weather
We'll ride the tidal waves
You and me sailing seas together
In the same boat—always

Love it when you say
I'm the gold inside your goldmine
And I love the way
You just make me shine

It's lovely, it's pretty—it sounds like 'Sunday Morning' Velvets, more than the thrash Velvets. It's more the dreamy, romantic Bunnymen ... the 'Dancing Horses,' 'Seven Seas' lineage. —Ian McCulloch, 2001

'Make me Shine,' with its thread of reversed guitar uncoiling over spangly arpeggios, recalls the best moments of the Bunnymen's own history.
—The Independent, 2001

Comfortably nestling amongst all this neo-psychedelia, we find a beaut of a pop song with a twist—or at least a 'reverse'—like the guitar sound found within.
—Will Sergeant, 2001

It's beautiful, this one. It's very 'Sweet Jane,' but it's nothing like 'Sweet Jane's chords. There's one bit on there that makes me spine tingle when I hear it. Plus a cheeky little reference to 'Sweet Jane,' which I like—and an art reference—references to things I loved as a kid, but just simple lyrics.

—Ian McCulloch, 2001

'Buried Alive' borrows some lines from Dylan Thomas's 'Do Not Go Gentle Into That Good Night' as well as one from Lou Reed's 'Sweet Jane.' McCulloch jokes that 'I must have read all of that Dylan Thomas poem once, and half of another one of his. I always liked dropping literary references when I haven't got a clue what [the writers] did. I'm not a great reader. I always thought those short things were much better than long ones. Novels always bored me. —Ian McCulloch, 2001

BURIED ALIVE

Buried alive
Person unknown
Dying inside
Half the way home

Somewhere under a Delvaux moon
Childhood's end came too soon
Came too soon

Don't want to know when
Don't wanna know why
Don't wanna believe that life
    is just to die

You were the one who sang lullabies
I'm still hanging out to dry,
    out to cry

Hey now, hey now
Don't you cry
It's just the dying of the light
Time to say our goodbyes
I'll look for you in that goodnight

Is anybody here?

I wanna go out
The way I came in
My flame blowing out
In the Summer wind

Somewhere under a Delvaux moon
Childhood's end came too soon
Came too soon

Hey now, hey now
Don't you cry
It's just the dying of the light
Time to say our goodbyes
I'll look for you in that goodnight

Goodnight

Not as dark as the title suggests. It's time to get your blue jeans on and boogie! This is one of me and Mac's favorites, and why not? It's got it all—including a Wurlitzer electric piano, rescued from a skip!   —Will Sergeant, 2001

FLOWERS

I've been laying down the flowers
I've been waiting in the sun
I've been counting down the hours
One by one
One by one

I've been catching my reflection
I'm still looking at someone
Still perfecting imperfection
Like everyone
Every no one

I even saw it come
Knew the hit would run and run
And I, as it came undone
Knew that I'd lost everything
Everything I'd won

Here's to all the things we'll never
Here's to all we could have done
Here's to what became whatever
Whatever web we spun, web we spun

I even saw it come
Knew the hit would run and run
And I, as it came undone
Knew that I'd lost everything
Everything I'd won

I've been laying down the flowers
I've been waiting in the sun
I've been counting down the hours
One by one
One by one

I even saw it come
Knew the hit would run and run
And I, as it came undone
Knew that I'd lost everything
Everything I'd won

… it's about life, and also the inevitability of death—or at least dormant life. The flower I think of regarding the album is a daffodil. Sefton Park in Liverpool has a field where they planted a million daffodils for Marie Curie Cancer Research, and once a year for a couple of weeks you see this field of yellow. Then one day it's all gone—but you know that it will be back. I suppose it's about rebirth and things like that.
                        —Ian McCulloch, 2001

I really dig the blues guitar, soulful croon, and theramin cocktail of this track. Great to play live, as I can really let rip with the junkyard-dog biting tone of my beautiful red fender Jaguar.   —Will Sergeant, 2001

EVERYBODY KNOWS

Everybody knows how your garden grows
Everybody knows how your garden grows
Everyone can see, I'm blind as I can be
The woods look just like trees
Look like trees to me

And I don't even get it
I don't know what you're trying to say
You're never gonna let me forget it
It's always gonna get in the way

It's moving much too fast
You know it ain't gonna last
I think we're heading for a crash
Heading for a crash

It's coming to a natural end
I'm going round my last bend
There's some things you
    just can't mend
Things you just can't mend

I can't even remember
I don't know what the day is today
You're putting the no in November
And taking all the be's out of May

Everybody knows how your garden grows
Everybody knows how your garden grows
Everyone can see, I'm blind as I can be
The woods look just like trees
Look like trees to me

And I don't even get it
I don't know what you're trying to say
You're never gonna let me forget it
It's always gonna get in the way

Yet more wild guitar and a steam train backing track. This will be perfect live. We loved to turn this one up to 11 in the studio and freak out the Cooking Vinyl commanders; they took it like men.
                        —Will Sergeant, 2001

Mac went to make a cup of tea—
when he came back I had some
new riffs to play with. We soon
kicked them into shape and had
us a brand new Bunnymen tune.
So cute and jangly it almost
makes me wanna cry with joy.

    —Will Sergeant, 2001

LIFE GOES ON

How do you stop yourself from
Falling apart and going under?
Lost in a world that's got your
Name tag, nametagged and
  your number

One by one they will find you
Life goes on behind you
Behind you

When does it start to fade and
When do the roads start
  leading nowhere?
When all your prayers have
  been prayed
That's when you know your
  dream is over

One by one they will find you
Life goes on behind you
Behind you

One of these days I'm gonna
Do as I say and do it my way
I'm gonna grow those wings
And learn to fly and hit the skyway

One by one they will find you
Life goes on behind you
Behind you …

AN ETERNITY TURNS

Look ma it's me
No hands on the wheel
Nothing can touch you
When you can't even feel
No one you can trust
'Cos no one's for real
No one's for real

Father forget us
Or father forgive us
Giving us faith
And then calling us sinners
Mixing up the losers
With all of the winners
Tonight … yeah yeah yeah

Kneeling at the crossroads
All my bridges burning
Down the river my life flows
Took another wrong turning

And it turned, and it turned,
  and it turned
And it turned, an eternity turned

Knows what she feels
But he's never felt her
Wanted a home
But he needed a shelter
Never gonna win
With the hand he dealt her
Aces low … tonight
Yeah yeah yeah

Kneeling at the crossroads
All my bridges burning
Down the river my life flows
Took another wrong turning

I will find you …

I know you only want to share my pain
But I've got something weird
Pumping through my veins
Got the type of blood
That can't be changed
Can't be changed

Kneeling at the crossroads
All my bridges burning
Down the river my life flows
Took another wrong turning

When I started with this riff I was thinking, 'Sounds a bit like "Lucifer Sam" by Pink Floyd.' ('No bad thing!' I hear you discerning cats yell.) It soon turned its back on the devil and was born again—hal-lelujah!!! More tea, Vicar?

    —Will Sergeant, 2001

BURN FOR ME

I'm water … swim to me
Be my fire … burn with me

One day, you'll see
After the Fall has fallen
One day, I'll be
The one your heart's still calling

I'm air … breathe with me
Be my prayer … believe in me

One night, you'll see
The moon and stars in motion
One night, your sea
Will melt into my ocean

I'm water … swim to me
Be my fire … burn for me
I'm going out …

One day, you'll see
After the Fall has fallen
One day, I'll be
The one your heart's still calling
One night, you'll see
The moon and stars in motion
One night, your sea
Will melt into my ocean

… basically a kind of slow, 'Zimbo'-esque number, but I think it's better than 'Zimbo.' For any Arthur Miller fans out there, it was gonna be called 'After the Fall Has Fallen.'
—Ian McCulloch, 2001

A great way to close the album, somber and reflective. Sparse guitar and mellotron sounds feather a bed for Mac's poetic and ethereal vocals. Goodnight … sweet dreams.
—Will Sergeant, 2001

★ ★ ★

What next for the Bunnymen? Rhino Records celebrated the band with *Crystal Days*, a 72-song box set that spans 1979-1999. It features 17 previously unreleased songs, including BBC sessions, alternate takes, and rare B-sides. Much of the set comprises live material, including a vast selection of cover songs from the 1985 Scandinavian tour. Plus, there's a month-long world tour to take care of, which will end, fittingly enough, with two shows in Liverpool, where our story began. The shows, at Paul McCartney's LIPA auditorium, will be filmed and recorded for a live album and Digital Video Disc.

Cooking Vinyl also planned a limited-edition single, "Make Me Shine" b/w a version of The Beatles' "Ticket To Ride" and an acoustic version of "Nothing Lasts Forever." From there, Mac will finish working on a "modern-sounding" solo album for Jeepster Records, with producer Ian Broudie and some special guest artists. Mac reckons the LP will be "his version of Lou Reed's *Transformer*." Will plans to continue working on Glide, and possibly even reprise Industrial Domestic with Paul Simpson. Do all these side projects, plus encroaching middle age and seemingly permanent cult status spell an end for the Bunnymen? Don't count on it.

We're going to carry on the way we're doing it ... it doesn't matter how [old] we are. For bands that are still culty and just grooving along, doing their thing ... [age is] not really an issue. Fuck it. It's what I do. I do it quite good.
—Will Sergeant, 2001

Mac: "Do you feel that much different to when your were 19? 'Cos I don't."
Will: "It's other people who put that ageism crap on you anyway."
Mac: "We're like flippin' Red Rum. If Red Rum was still running, it wouldn't necessarily win the Grand National—but it'd still be the best horse."
—*Uncut*, 2001

Just being in the Bunnymen makes you feel like one of the coolest bastards on the planet. It gives me confidence. It's not what we do for
a living—it's what we do in *life*. Heartbreak songs are always for
individuals—it's not for a mass audience. I know, and Will knows, and
quite a few of our fans know. It's a very hard thing to do—to be that
special; I wouldn't have been in any other group. We'll probably get
inducted into the rock & roll hall of fame in 200 years, but we'll
turn it down. We never had any goals, particularly, other than to be
seen as the coolest and the best, and the group that never sold out.
                                                    —Ian McCulloch, 2001

We're still the best band in the world.   —Ian McCulloch, 2001

(photo: *bigcheese* UK)

ABOUT THE AUTHOR

Chris Adams has been a freelance writer for twelve years. His work has appeared in such publications as *The Big Takeover*, *Lollipop*, and *The Fine Print*, where Adams was the music section editor. Adams currently lives in Fort Point Channel, Boston, where he is completing a narrative titled *Chasing Neon Halos* and attempting (in vain, according to his neighbors) to produce something approaching music from his vintage Vox Phantom. He can be contacted via Soft Skull Press.

SOURCES

Acknowledgements are due to the following sources, which were essential in providing illustration to the author's statements, and critical context to the subject matter.

Blitz, *Bluer Skies*, Brassneck Publicity, *CMJ New Music Report*, *Creem*, *Dotmusic*, *From the Shores of Lake Placid and Other Stories* by Bill Drummond, *Goldmine*, *GQ*, *Head-On* by Julian Cope, *History of Rock*, *Hot Press*, *Jamming*, *Lime Lizard*, *Liverpool Explodes* by Mark Cooper, Liverpool Hoopla, *Magnet*, *Melody Maker*, *Mojo*, MTV Online, *Musicians Only*, *Never Stop* by Tony Fletcher, *New Route*, *NME*, *Offbeat*, *Q*, Radio Merseyside, *Raygun*, *Record Collector*, *Record Hunter*, *Record Mirror*, *Rolling Stone*, *Select*, *Smash Hits*, *Soundcheck*, *Sounds*, *Stylus*, *SW*, *TheBig Takeover*, *The Bristol Recorder*, *The Buzz*, *The Citizen*, *The Duchess*, *The Face*, *The Guardian*, *The Independent*, *The Observer*, *The Right to Imagination and Madness* by Martin Roach, *The Vibe*, *Uncut*, *Vox*, *Wig Out*.

RECOMMENDED

45 by Bill Drummond
Head-On by Julian Cope
Never Stop by Tony Fletcher
The King of Cool by Mick Middles
Liverpool Explodes by Mark Cooper

ONLINE

www.bunnymen.com
www.echoingthebunnymen.co.uk
www.cookingvinyl.com
www.bunnygod.com